MW01252940

Managing Business in the Twenty-first Century

Managing Business in the Twenty-first Century

edited by

Anindya Sen • P.K. Sett

OXFORD
UNIVERSITY PRESS

OXFORD
UNIVERSITY PRESS

YMCA Library Building, Jai Singh Road, New Delhi 110001

Oxford University Press is a department of the University of Oxford. It furthers the University's objective of excellence in research, scholarship, and education by publishing worldwide in

Oxford New York
Auckland Cape Town Dar es Salaam Hong Kong Karachi
Kuala Lumpur Madrid Melbourne Mexico City Nairobi
New Delhi Shanghai Taipei Toronto

With offices in
Argentina Austria Brazil Chile Czech Republic France Greece
Guatemala Hungary Italy Japan Poland Portugal Singapore
South Korea Switzerland Thailand Turkey Ukraine Vietnam

Oxford is a registered trade mark of Oxford University Press in the UK and in certain other countries

Published in India
by Oxford University Press, New Delhi

First published 2005
Second impression 2006

ISBN-13: 978-0-19-566525-3
ISBN-10: 0-19-566525-2

Printed at Roopak Printers, Delhi 110 032
Published by Manzar Khan, Oxford University Press
YMCA Library Building, Jai Singh Road, New Delhi 110 001

Contents

Abbreviations

ABB	Activity Based Budgeting
ABC	Activity Based Costing
ACD	Activity Cost Drivers
ABM	Activity Based Management
ANPR	Automatic Number Plate Recognition
ATM	Automatic Teller Machine
B2B	Business to Business
B2C	Business to Consumer
BoK	Body of Knowledge
BPO	Business Process Outsourcing
BPR	Business Process Re-engineering
BSC	Balanced Score Card
CAPM	Capital Asset Pricing Model
CD	Compact disc
CoP	Communities of Practices
CRM	Customer Relationship Management
CVP	Customer Value Proposition
DC	Developing Countries
DD	Duration Drivers
DNA	Deoxyribo-nucleic acid
EDI	Electronic Order Quality
EPS	Earnings Per Share
E&R	Education and Research
ERP	Enterprise Resource Planning
ESOP	Employees Stock Options
EVA	Economic Value Added
FASB	Financial Accounting Standard Board
FMCG	Fast Moving Consumer Goods
FRA	Forward Rate Agreements
FRS	Financial Accounting Standard Board
FTL	Full Truck Load
GAAP	Generally Accepted Accounting Principles
GATT	General Agreement on Trade and Tariffs
GDP	Gross Domestic Product
GM	General Motors

GRI	Global Reporting Initiative
HLL	Hindustan Lever Limited
HM	Hindustan Motors
HR	Human Resources
IASB	International Accounting Standards Board
IBP	Internal Business Process
ICAI	Institute of Chartered Accountants of India
ICI	Imperial Chemical Industries
ICT	Information and Communication Technology
ID	Intensity drives
IFRs	International Financial Reporting Standard
IPRS	Intellectual Property Rights
IS	Information Systems
IT	Information Technology
JIT	Just in time
KCU	Knowledge Currency Unit
KDD	Knowledge Discovery in Databases
Kg	kilogram
FMM	Knowledge Management Maturity
KMS	Knowledge Management Systems
L&G	Learning and Growth
LIBOR	London Inter Bank Offered Rate
LIFO	Last in, first out
LT	Lead Time
MIS	Management Information Systems
MNC	Multinational Company
MVA	Market Value Added
NGO	Non-government Organization
NOPAT	Net Operating Profit After Tax
NRV	Net Realizable Value
NSE	National Stock Exchange
OCS	Operational Control System
OECD	Organization for Economic Cooperation and Development
OLAP	On Line Analytical Processing
OTC	Over the Center
OTD	On Time Delivery
PC	Personal Computer
PV	Present Value
R&D	Research and Development
RIL	Reliance Industries Limited
ROCE	Return on Capital Employed
ROI	Return on Investment
SBU	Strategic Business Unit
SCM	Supply Chain Management
SEBI	Securities Exchange Board of India
SFL	Sundaram Fasteners Limited

SFO	Strategy Focussed Organization
SKU	Stock Keeping Unit
SPE	Special Purpose Entities
TCS	Traditional Cost-accounting System
TD	Transaction Drivers
TE	Transition Economies
TISCO	Tata Iron and Steel Company
TPL	Third Party Logistics
TPM	Total Productive Maintenance
TQM	Total Quality Management
TV	Television
UK	United Kingdom
USA	United States of America
USSR	Union of Soviet Socialist Republics
VAT	Value Added Tax
VHS	Video Home System
WACC	Weighted Average Cost of Capital
WTO	World Trade Organization

Tables, Figures, and Boxes

Tables

Figures

Boxes

Contributors

Amitava Dutta, School of Management, George Mason University, Fairfax, USA.

Anindya Sen, Economics Group, Indian Institute of Management Calcutta.

Anup Sinha, Economics Group, Indian Institute of Management Calcutta.

Asish K. Bhattacharyya, Finance and Control Group, Indian Institute of Management Calcutta.

Balram Avittathur, Operations Management Group, Indian Institute of Management Calcutta.

B.B. Chakrabarti, Finance and Control Group, Indian Institute of Management Calcutta.

D.N. Sengupta, Visiting Faculty, Indian Institute of Management Calcutta. Formerly Director, A.F. Ferguson & Co., Mumbai.

Haritha Saranga, Visiting Faculty, Operations Management Group, Indian Institute of Management Calcutta.

Leena Chatterjee, Behavioural Sciences Group, Indian Institute of Management Calcutta.

P.K. Sett, Human Resource Management Group, Indian Institute of Management Calcutta.

Rahul Roy, Management Information Systems Group, Indian Institute of Management Calcutta.

Sougata Ray, Strategic Management Group, Indian Institute of Management Calcutta.

Sudas Roy, Marketing Management Group, Indian Institute of Management Calcutta.

Vidyanand Jha, Behavioural Sciences Group, Indian Institute of Management Calcutta.

1

Introduction

Anindya Sen • P.K. Sett

In India, till a few years ago, there was no widespread interest in management theories. This was reflected by the fact that even major newspapers would spend very little space on business matters and there were no business magazines to speak of.

The situation has changed radically in recent years. Getting a Master degree in Business Studies is the first preference for many students. Newspapers have started to devote an inordinate amount of space to business matters. Sometimes the movement of share prices of particular business organizations grabs headlines from the political events of the day. Interest in management issues has spread beyond students of management. Anybody and everybody has come to feel that it is imperative to take an educated and informed interest in the problems and practices of management. In short, management is now on everyone's mind.

Unfortunately, this spread in interest has not been accompanied by any serious attempt to educate the public about management theory and practice. Many concepts that have critical applications in the business arena are used loosely in regular discourse and, sometimes, even incorrectly. The resultant confusion often invests many of these concepts with an air of mystery for the general reader.

The present volume is an effort on the part of various faculty members at the Indian Institute of Management Calcutta to communicate some important management concepts in a clear, uncluttered, and elegantly simple way to a wider audience. Managing business in the twenty-first century is a difficult and challenging task. The present volume aims to provide the reader with a fare that is rich enough to convey some idea of what managers today have to learn and practise for the survival and growth of their firms in an increasingly competitive marketplace. India is no longer a country where tariff and non-tariff barriers make life easy and uncomplicated for anybody fortunate enough to get a licence to produce. Almost every industry has to benchmark itself against global standards. The rewards from this benchmarking are incomparably larger than anything firms experienced earlier. However, the price of failure is equally great. An entire industry can be wiped out without much ado if it clings to its traditional ways and refuses to learn.

We feel that it is no longer enough for only a select circle of managers heading various organizations to be trained in the latest theories and concepts of management. There has to be a paradigm shift in the general understanding of business management. Just as in a political democracy, it is incumbent upon voters to be able to distinguish between different parties and their agenda, and to be able to foresee what certain voting patterns would lead to, we feel that for economic democracy, too, everyone should be familiar with management theories and practices. For example, if equity markets are to grow and play the needed role in channellizing the savings of the nation to investors, and share prices are to be freed from the manipulations of a few players, then Laxman's Common Man must understand why and how stock options are used, whether a company has gained sustainable competitive advantage, and so on. Our book is the first step towards this goal.

Fundamentally Different

The way firms are managed today is fundamentally different from the way they used to be managed even 20 or 30 years ago. Much of this change is attributable to two important developments.

First, during the latter half of the twentieth century, business management evolved from a purely practice-oriented, pre-academic state to a theory-grounded, research-based, cross-functional discipline that drew directly from, and often contributed to, the basic academic disciplines like economics, sociology, psychology, mathematics, and statistics. Gone are the days when marketing used to be taught—even in the leading business schools—by retired or practising marketing executives, and marketing classes focused on the anecdotal experiences of these managers. Today, the subject is handled by academics with relevant research background who expose the students to the underlying theoretical constructs and provide the students with the opportunity to apply the theory to the socially complex context of live organizations through case analyses, business games, and exercises. Similar is the story in other functional disciplines of management. For example, operations management has not only become an arena where sophisticated mathematical and statistical models are applied but it also incorporates learning from psychology and sociology in managing operations like, say, quality assurance of products and processes. Jay B. Barney (1997) says in his book, *Gaining and Sustaining Competitive Advantage*, that 'there really isn't anything quite as practical as a good theory'. Advancements in the discipline of management over the last half a century or so have firmly established the truth of this adage that is particularly relevant for a predominantly applied discipline like business management.

The second major development is the emergence of a new wave of globalization, which has information technology as its cornerstone. In this new information age global economy, the rules of business for almost every business have undergone some fundamental changes.

Managing business in the twenty-first century would, therefore, require knowledge and application of a set of new concepts, theories, and business models that match the sophistication and complexity of the contemporary business environment. Issues that have become central to academic discourse and business deliberations alike include the following:

- What are the distinguishing features of the global economy in terms of macroeconomic trends, financial systems, industry structure, and microeconomics at firm level?
- How different are the rules of the New Economy from those of the old economy?
- How do firms navigate in turbulent environments and continue to create future value for all stakeholders—shareholders, customers, employees, and the community?
- How do firms meet the customer needs better by customizing their offerings and yet remain profitable?
- How do firms maximize the wealth they create and respond faster to the environmental changes by managing their value chain—right from their supplier-end to the end-consumer—better?
- How can firms negotiate a new psychological contract with their employees, which is so very necessary for creating and sustaining the competitive advantage of the firms in the new marketplace?
- How can firms facilitate learning and knowledge accumulation by both the individual and the organization?
- How can firms discover the underlying structure and dynamics of the firm–environment relationship so that they can predict reasonably accurately the consequences of their decisions and actions?
- How do the managers meet the social obligations of business by providing ethical, transparent, and good governance of the enterprises?

In many ways, these are not new questions. Managers and business academics have had to face similar challenges at each major turning point in the history of modern business. However, what is important is that each epoch calls for a different approach to answering them.

About the Book

The purpose of this book is to address the major issues confronting the business enterprises in the beginning of a new century and the approaches they should adopt in meeting those challenges. To do that, we have invited and obtained articles from a distinguished panel of academics, each with a proven expertise in the field they have covered. Our objective was to position this book as something more than a typical textbook. This book is targeted not only at the students and the teachers in the business schools, but also at working managers who want to update themselves on topical issues, and members of the general public who may have an interest in the affairs of business organizations and want to know more.

Keeping in mind the composite nature of the targeted readership, the style and content of the chapters have been so chosen that any reader should be able to get an accurate understanding of the subjects covered without losing interest because of the rigour normally associated with a typical piece of academic writing. Each chapter carries numerous case examples to help the reader establish links with the happenings of a live organization. This balance has been carefully crafted to ensure that even an uninitiated reader gets a theoretically sound understanding of the subjects and does not have to unlearn anything in case he/she wants to pursue the topic in greater depth. In short, we aim to present an enjoyable read without in any way sacrificing the academic rigour of the topics handled.

There are fifteen chapters in the book. Each chapter is a self-contained essay on a subject of present day relevance. The chapters have been arranged in a logical sequence that guides the reader through a broad understanding of the business environment and firm-level strategy formulation and implementation, to issues which need to be addressed for creating and sustaining the competitive advantage of a firm. However, because of their self-contained nature each chapter may also be read as an independent piece of writing.

Chapter 2 introduces the reader to the features of globalization and their implications for the world economy, nation-states, industries, firms, and common citizens. Chapter 3 argues that the unprecedented upsurge in creation, analysis, and distribution of information on a global scale is creating structural changes which have important ramifications for the macro- and micro-environment of the business firms as also for the public policy issues. The next two chapters build on this background. The sources of sustainable competitive advantage in the information age are discussed in Chapter 4. Chapter 5 presents the essence of corporate and firm level strategies. As a cohort, Chapters 2 to 5 outline the context and the content of the strategy-making process in the business organizations in the twenty-first century.

Chapter 6 introduces the concept and methodology of the balanced scorecard (BSC) that is used by world-class organizations to translate business strategy into the desired daily activities of employees. It is a navigational tool that aids firms to see how their current activities are helping them to create future value—essential for their continued survival and growth. Chapter 7 supplements this discussion by introducing the concept of activity-based management (ABM). While the BSC is about mapping the strategy, ABM is about mapping the activities to create an economic map of the enterprise. Together, they help the firm to choose products, processes, and customers that can be the basis for a sustainable firm profitability. In Chapter 8 this discussion is logically extended to explain the concepts of economic value added (EVA) and market value added (MVA). These are metrics for measuring a firm's performance in terms of its capability for creation of shareholders' wealth. Chapter 9 deals with the modern financial market instruments like options, futures, and derivatives which are used by the modern corporations as sophisticated ways of managing the financial risks arising out of market volatility. These four chapters form the second cohort that deals with the important issue of sustainability of firm profitability and growth through effective implementation of a viable business strategy.

Chapters 10 and 11 look at both ends of a firm's value chain. Chapter 10 introduces the reader to the modern paradigm of relationship marketing that transcends the limitations of essentially transaction-based classical marketing mix instruments. Different approaches to relationship marketing along with their associated operational issues are discussed. Chapter 11 addresses the critical issue of the management of a firm's supply chain that involves coordination of material, information, and financial flows between the suppliers, producers, distributors, and consumers. Demand and supply side uncertainties associated with the turbulent business environment of the twenty-first century makes efficient management of the supply chain a core capability for every firm in order to avoid costs of idle capacity, excess inventory or stockouts, and lost sales.

As we all recognize, the ultimate source of a firm's competitive advantage is its human capital base. Human capital impacts the firm's performance in two important ways: one, by generating employee behaviour that is congruent with the strategic objectives, and another, by accumulating the individual and the organizational learning as a knowledge pool residing within the organization.

As the rules of competition undergo qualitative changes in the New Economy, there should be a corresponding shift in the terms of exchange between a firm and its employees. In the present environment, firms need to earn the commitment of their employees to use their judgement, discretion, and entrepreneurial initiatives, more than ever before. The old order based only on compliant employee behaviour as per the formal contract of employment is no longer sufficient to meet the demands of continuously evolving competitive environment. A new psychological contract with the employees as required in the New Economy, with its contours and essential features, is discussed in Chapter 12. The next chapter discusses the other building block of organizational human capital, the knowledge management system that empowers the employees through storage, transfer, creation, and application of knowledge obtained in work by each employee. It provides a platform for meaningful interactions and exchange of daily experience, as well as being a process through which data gets processed into information and then into knowledge that the organization can leverage to create wealth for all its stakeholders. It also plays a critical role in explicating 'implicit' knowledge of individual employees into organizational knowledge.

Chapter 14 introduces the topic of system dynamics. Based on systems thinking, the concepts and the tools of system dynamics enable managers to develop mental models that conceptualize organizations holistically as an interdependent part of a larger network of processes. They help the managers to express their mental model, share it, question its underlying assumptions, test hypotheses and generate alternate models and assess the consequences of alternate action plans. Ability to conceptualize organizations in systemic terms is considered as an essential skill for managers in the twenty-first century.

The last chapter, Chapter 15, deals with the challenges of corporate governance in the twenty-first century. The evolution of modern corporations as public limited companies is regarded as one of the greatest human innovations of the nineteenth century. With increasing pace of globalization, the big corporations are managing enormous amounts of societal wealth. Therefore, the society has a significant stake in ensuring that these corporations are governed well so as to address the concerns of all stakeholders, including the common citizens.

In developing the ideas in this book we have interacted with many of our colleagues in the Indian Institute of Management Calcutta and elsewhere. We have learned from each of them. Rather than list them individually, we wish to thank them collectively for allowing us to enhance the contents of this book. They have collaborated in our efforts to string together a series of articles on a common lingering theme. They have been receptive to our suggestions and have been extraordinarily accommodating by agreeing to modify their drafts whenever we approached them. But for their patience and understanding we would not have been successful in our endeavour.

2

Globalization: Features and Possibilities

Anup Sinha

Globalization is all about the changes taking place in the way we work and play. New technologies offer new gadgets and appliances that make living more comfortable and easy. New technologies also alter the ways by which we produce familiar things of everyday living. They change the way we transact business and organize production. They provide opportunities to meet our requirements as buyers and customers in a more precise and detailed fashion. Such changes, in turn, affect the growth of firms, affect markets across countries, increase economic interdependence, and alter the economic policy environment in which business organizations operate.

Protagonists of globalization believe that such changes are inevitable and contribute towards economic and social prosperity and progress. Those who are wary about the consequences of changes in the world economy, view globalization as a process that facilitates the rich and powerful nations to increase their domination of the world in terms of greater profits and power. Since globalization is about a process of quite rapid and often dramatic change it is bound to generate differences of opinion. Put somewhat starkly, the crux of the debate about globalization is about its implications for the reduction of poverty and enhancement of access to new economic opportunities. Around this central question there are other important political and cultural issues that are frequently debated. In this chapter we will discuss only some aspects of the contentious changes taking place in the environment in which twenty-first century business will have to operate.

The most common mental image of globalization is the internationalization of the economic system, more specifically about the integration of markets for goods and services—an integration that transcends geographical and political borders. In other words, the image is one of an increasingly homogeneous economic system the world over. It may be tempting to argue that market integration through trade and exchange has been known to human society for a very long time. Indeed, the discovery of the world and the extension of exchange have always gone hand in hand.

The great industrial revolution in western Europe that took place roughly four centuries ago ushered in an era of modern industrial growth. The advent of capitalism had spread-effects on the rest of the world, in Europe itself, in

America, Asia, Africa, and Australia. Capitalism, as an economic system, is based on private property and voluntary exchange in markets. Profits are not guaranteed, though private property is. The essential driving force is to use one's property (including the ability to work) to its most efficient level and earn the highest possible return. The system works on its incentive to grow and expand in seeking more value. It also seeks more productive property (capital) not merely in terms of volume, but also in terms of greater efficiency. The greater efficiency is built into capital by new technologies and innovations that reduce costs of production. The fundamental dynamic is to grow relentlessly, by seeking new markets for resources, new technologies, and new destinations for final products for sale. This dynamic of economic growth is universal, based on the internal logic of how capitalism functions. It, quite obviously, is independent of geography or politics. It is in this sense that capitalism is, and has always been, a global system.

What then is new about contemporary globalization? Some argue that there is nothing new at all. Some, at the other extreme, declare the current pattern of market integration as the end of history. Most, however, tend to agree that while globalization is not something entirely new, there are several distinguishing features of change that are new and worth some reflection in terms of the ways they affect the economy, global power politics, and the patterns of daily living.

Distinguishing Features of the Global Economy

The second half of the twentieth century has witnessed an impressive growth in international trade in goods and services. This has been accompanied by a tremendous growth in international flow of financial funds, especially since the decade of the 1970s. There has been a revolution in communications and information technologies, along with some remarkable developments in biological sciences. Many of these changes have dramatically altered our sense of space and time. Manufacturing technologies have changed modern production processes at a quite phenomenal pace. Some of these have had deep influences on the workplace and its structure. In general, the markets for manufactured products covering a wide range of goods are characterized by growing concentrations. In these oligopolistic markets, six or seven giant multinational firms often control well over 50 per cent of global market shares. The economic power of many of the giant conglomerations, measured in terms of sales figures or the size of the annual budget, exceeds the national product for most low-income countries of the world.

International Trade

The impressive growth of international trade in the past few decades has been characterized by some stylized facts that may be worth the while to keep in mind. First of all, the growth in international trade has been the most significant between the developed industrial countries. This is in contrast to the growth in trade between the relatively poor developing nations, or in the growth of trade between the developed and developing countries. The growth in trade has taken place under the aegis of national governments pursuing their own economic strategies, often very protective ones in terms of restrictive trade policies like tariffs, quotas, and prohibitions.

The second stylized fact is that over the last two decades or so the share of developing nations in global trade has been increasing along with their share in global manufacturing. Third, there has been a sharper rise in the trade in intermediate products and components, as compared to the trade in finished products, indicating an internationalization of production processes. For instance, a car is no longer entirely manufactured in Germany, but has been manufactured in many countries if one traces the points of manufacture of the car's component parts. Finally, there appears to be a major shift in thinking about trade policies pursued by national governments. This is reflected in the creation of the World Trade Organization (WTO) that emerged after a number of rounds of trade negotiations called the General Agreement on Trade and Tariffs (GATT). Nations have sought fewer restrictions on trade, and more rule-based global policies for accessing each other's markets. The debate about WTO and the whole issue of whether the rules are fair or not, stem from the fact that in bargaining situations the economically powerful nations have far greater strength in pushing their national interests with least sacrifices made to attain their aims. The well-known argument about the mutually beneficial gains from free trade does not reveal anything about the distribution of the gains from trade. Thus, with the advent of WTO and a global regime of freer trade, global incomes are supposed to rise. All estimates, however, indicate that the gains for the developed economies of Europe and North America would be substantially larger than the gains estimated to accrue to a much larger number of developing countries.

Table 2.1 shows the growth in global trade between 1965 and 1990. The figures are for imports measured in US dollars. Transition economies (TE) imply the erstwhile Union of Soviet Socialist Republics (USSR) and other East European countries, while the category 'developing' countries (DC)

Table 2.1: Global Trade 1990 as Compared to 1965

(Total Imports in US$ Million)

1990	OECD	DC	TE	Total
OECD	1,925,909	451,122	53,304	2,430,335
DC	527,610	219,333	18,825	765,768
TE	58,182	17,090	44,813	120,569
Total	2,511,701	688,029	116,942	3,316,672
1965	**OECD**	**DC**	**TE**	**Total**
OECD	100,719	26,222	4,750	131,691
DC	27,393	7690	3439	38,522
TE	4565	3285	14,083	21,933
Total	132,677	37,197	22,272	192,146

Source: World Resources (1995)

include all countries of the world barring the transition economies and the Organization for Economic Cooperation and Development (OECD) nations.

Table 2.1 clearly indicates the overwhelming magnitude of developed-to-developed economies trade (OECD to OECD) in total trade in the world economy. In 1998 the regional shares in trade were similar as revealed by Table 2.2.

Table 2.2: Share of Regions in World Trade in 1998 (%)

Regions	Shares
Industrial Countries	72.0
(Of which intra EU plus intra North America)	(50)
East Asia	12.2
South Asia	1.1
Europe and Central Asia	5.2
Middle East	2.5
Sub-Saharan Africa	1.3
Latin America	5.7

Source: Hoekman and Kostecki (2001)

A trend in contemporary trade patterns, especially in the developed-to-developed country trade, is the growing importance of intra-industry trade, fuelled largely by the increased flow of foreign direct investments. This is the exchange of similar but differentiated products such as components and semi-finished goods that are processed further after importation and then re-exported subsequently. Of total global trade, around 40 per cent is intra-firm, involving exchange between affiliated firms. An estimated 30 per cent of global trade in manufactures comprises of components. These trends are striking illustrations of the globalization of production.

Despite the overwhelming weight of trade between developed industrial countries, many developing economies have exhibited greater openness in trade. Their exports have grown either through conscious strategies to access global markets for economic development or through the compulsions exerted by the GATT accord resulting in the formation of the WTO. Indeed, WTO will ensure far greater global integration in the markets for goods and services after 2005 when all aspects of the accord will be implemented. Table 2.3 shows the increase in the rate of growth of exports in the past two decades.

Table 2.3: Average Annual % Growth in Exports of Goods and Services

Region	1980–90	1990–8
World	5.2	6.4
High Income Countries	5.1	6.1
East Asia and Pacific	9.6	14.0
Latin America and Caribbean	5.4	9.3
South Asia	6.6	10.5
Sub-Saharan Africa	2.4	4.6

Source: World Bank (2000)

Table 2.4 shows the growing importance of trade relative to gross domestic product (GDP) and the growing importance of trade amongst a number of developing nations. Every region of the world barring sub-Saharan Africa experienced a rise in export to GDP ratio during the past two decades. A possible reason why sub-Saharan Africa, despite being so dependent on exports, became an exception to the trend is that its exports are almost entirely commodity exports.

Table 2.4: Exports of Goods and Services as % of GDP

Region	1980	1998
World	20	25
High Income Countries	20	24
East Asia and Pacific	21	34
Latin America and Caribbean	12	14
South Asia	8	13
Sub-Saharan Africa	33	30

Source: World Bank (2000)

Not only have many developing countries begun to open up and pursue policies of integrating with the global economy, the factor intensity of exports are changing too. East Asia and Latin America have utilized their advantage in technology and human capital intensive activities in international markets. South Asia has availed of its advantage in cheap unskilled labour to make exports competitive. Table 2.5 shows the changing factor intensity of exports during a 10-year period between 1988 and 1998.

Table 2.5: Factor Intensity of Exports 1988 and 1998

	Natural Resource		Unskilled Labour		Technology		Human Capital	
	1988	1998	1988	1998	1988	1998	1988	1998
Industrial Countries	22.5	17.9	9.8	9.7	39.4	45.2	28.3	27.1
Developing Countries								
East Asia	27.2	16.8	30.5	24.0	23.8	42.6	18.5	16.6
South Asia	50.2	15.9	35.9	81.2	7.9	2.2	6.1	0.6
Latin America	67.0	42.4	5.8	9.3	13.4	25.4	13.8	22.9
Sub-Saharan Africa	78.3	79.0	6.0	5.9	6.6	7.7	9.1	7.4
East Europe and C. Asia	38.0	37.6	23.9	18.4	20.2	21.3	17.8	22.7
Middle East and N. Africa	80.3	65.6	3.7	8.0	13.1	22.0	2.9	4.3

Source: Hoekman and Kostecki (2001)

International Finance

Over the last three decades or so, there has been an astonishing growth in the volume of daily international financial transactions along with a volatile mobility across international borders. Once again, like trade, international capital flows are not something new. What is new is the rapidity of its growth, especially for purely speculative and arbitrage purposes. The movements of international capital are largely unregulated. Some of the big players who dominate the global market for financial capital are very big, and collectively they are far stronger in terms of financial muscle than most central banks of the world. According to one estimate (Nayyar 1995) the average daily international financial transactions in 1973 was US$15 billion. This increased to US$900 billion in 1992 when the combined reserves of the world's central banks stood at US$693 billion. A later estimate (Frankel 2000) puts the figure at US$1.5 trillion per day. What is interesting to note is that this growth far outstrips the growth in international trade in goods and services. According to Korten (2001) in the decade of the 1970s, roughly 80 per cent of the transactions could be traced back to the settlement in goods and services trade, the residual 20 per cent being attributed to speculation and currency arbitrage. Now the ratio is reversed, with about 80 per cent of the daily transactions attributable to trade in forward markets, currency arbitrage, and derivatives.

These developments in financial capital markets have far reaching consequences that are likely to shape and influence the course of global integration. First of all, the overwhelming bulk of global financial capital aims to maximize short-term returns for its owners, by availing of market fluctuations and taking the risks associated with those fluctuations. To be able to take a great deal of risk and earn quick, substantial profits imply that portfolios are typically large and diverse. This trend is likely to be more pronounced where long-term funds requirements may, perforce, be met by short-term borrowings. As risk increases, there will be an inherent propensity for financial consolidation and concentration. Players must be large enough to have a reasonable probability of systematically making profits.

The second implication is that because of the nature of the funds that thrive on uncertainties and fluctuations, they are very short term in aims. When such finances find their way into corporate finances, the same thing happens. Corporations are under constant pressure to create ever-increasing short-term profits. This may be one possible explanation of why many well-known global corporations in the twenty-first century were found 'manufacturing profits and shareholder value' by creative accounting methods.

The third implication is that volatile movements in short-term funds often triggered by a sudden change in market sentiment can lead to instability and financial crisis. This has been the case in many of the crises witnessed in the decade of the 1990s in South East Asia and in Latin America. Short-term funds exhibit a herd behaviour that can have devastating effects. In most cases the institutional investors are much stronger than Central Banks. For instance, if a fund manager decides to pull out of a small economy (even for erroneous reasons) he is likely to be followed by others. Other similar funds may think that the fund manager pulling out knows something that they do not. It may well be that the small economy loses 20 per cent of its reserves in a matter of days in trying to defend its currency. The whole episode can have devastating effects on the economy. It is unlikely to have a major effect on the institutional investor's profits since, in all likelihood, the funds employed in the small economy would be a tiny fraction of the global resources available with the organization. The big institutional investors are capable of precipitating or preventing major financial crises in economies both large and small. The bigger ones are called hedge funds, and nobody really knows exactly how big they are. They have been referred to as the 'Masters of the Universe' (Krugman 2000) as a reflection of their influence and power.

The Revolution in Technologies

The remarkable developments in information and communication technologies (ICT) revolving round innovations in microelectronics, computing (both hardware and software), and telecommunications have led to the age of personal computers (PCs), the Internet, mobile phones, and satellite television. The products of the new technologies have not only changed the ways in which business is transacted by firms, but have also brought new appliances into the workplace and at home. Extremely complex tasks including very large computations can now be done astonishingly fast, with phenomenal accuracy, and shared around the networked world in a matter of seconds. In a similar vein, enormous quantities of information can be stored and mined, efficiently accessible on a computer screen at the press of a few buttons on a keyboard.

Parallel to this, there has been a quantum jump in our knowledge of nature and life processes. Biology has emerged as the new frontier of science. Modern biotechnology, that is, recombinant deoxyribo-nucleic acid (DNA) technology has transformed our understanding of and our ability to control genes and genetic patterns. Science is capable of influencing life attributes like diseases and rates of physical growth. This has a number of fundamental implications for developments in medicine and agriculture. In fact, the list is much longer. Developments in material science, transportation, satellite imagery, aerospace engineering, and military hardware have been substantial.

These technologies have developed fast in converting laboratory evidence and theoretical results into actual saleable goods or services with vast commercial potentials. There is reason to believe that we have merely seen the tip of the iceberg in terms of commercial applications of emerging technologies. There is much more to come. Every aspect of daily living is being radically transformed by technology.

Any revolutionary change in technologies and scientific understanding is bound to create social tensions and anxieties. While nobody really doubts the enormous potential benefits, the dangers inevitably associated with new technologies take a while to be fully understood and made safe. There is also an adjustment cost involved in socially adapting to the changes. Do new wonder drugs also have unknown side effects? How do we adjust to a computer-controlled shop floor in a factory? What are the social costs of watching too much cable TV? When technologies are relatively new the potential benefits and the possible costs both appear somewhat hazy, especially to the end user who is usually not a person of science.

Technology comes at an economic cost too. The cost of accessing a new technology may be prohibitive for many people. Usually new technologies are expensive, especially to begin with. Yet technology has a strange liberating role. Those who cannot access it for economic reasons, yet see the potential benefits, feel deprived and left out. This itself can create social instability and conflict between the technology-haves and the technology-have-nots.

In the age of globalization, new technologies drive market change, but it is also true that markets (reflecting purchasing power) drive the pattern of technological and product innovations by largely determining the priorities of applied research and development (R&D). For instance, slow ripening tomatoes or cosmetic creams that reduce the signs of ageing may command far more resources in R&D than a drug for malaria. Yet the potential power of the new technology to solve and alleviate social problems such as those pertaining to health, education, the quality of governance, and the reduction of poverty is awesome. As a result of this market-driven technological change, the reach of the new products is limited to those who can afford them, and they are often quite small in number. Little wonder that even as late as in 1999, in the age of the great computer revolution, the proportion of the global population who had ever accessed the Internet was only 6 per cent. We are still a long way from realizing the full social potential of the technological revolution. Private corporations are supposed to earn profits, and indeed that is their primary objective. Left to themselves they are unlikely to ensure an adequate social reach. The government is expected to step in where markets are inadequate. However, in many developing countries, myopic political preferences as reflected in the patterns of public spending, biased social policies, and inadequate resource allocation constitute major stumbling blocks in this respect.

The importance of technology in production processes is reflected in the fact that technology-based manufactures have grown very rapidly compared with primary products and resource-based manufactures. This is to be expected. What is very revealing is the fast rate of growth of high-tech manufactures as shown in Table 2.6.

Table 2.6: Technology and Export Growth

(average annual percentage growth in exports, 1985–98)

Area	High-tech manufacture	Medium-tech manufacture	Low-tech manufacture	Resource-based manufactures	Primary products
World	13.1	9.3	9.7	7.0	3.4
Developing Countries	21.4	14.3	11.7	6.0	1.3
High-income OECD	11.3	8.5	8.5	7.0	4.4

Source: UNDP 2001

Globalization propels rapid technological change with competition and incentives provided by the world's marketplace along with global financial and scientific resources. Global markets are technology based, and competition is driven by new technologies. Production processes have rapidly become significantly more efficient, costs of production and transmission of knowledge have dropped dramatically, and speed and accuracy of manufacturing have increased to degrees never witnessed before. Production networks can be controlled and coordinated from a central point. UNDP (2001) sums up the production effects of the new technologies:

> Structures of production and other activities have been reorganized into networks that span the world. In the industrial age—with its high cost of information access, communications, and transportation—business and organizations were vertically integrated. In the network age, with the costs of communications and information down to almost zero, horizontal network makes sense. Production is increasingly organized among separate players—subcontractors, suppliers, laboratories, management consultants, education and research institutes, marketing research firms, distributors. Their complex interactions, with each playing a niche role, create the value chains that drive the technology-based global economy.

The wonders of new technologies, however, have gone hand in hand with the concentration of market power. Horizontal networks do increase competition down the value chain, but when it comes to control in selling the final product, the trend has been one of less, and not more, competition. For instance, when a Philip Morris acquired a Kraft and a General Foods (as happened in the United States of America (USA) in the 1980s), it created the world's largest food company, with obvious monopoly power on a global scale. A few giant corporations in almost every major industry of the world economy are increasingly dominating markets.

Economists often define a global market to be monopolistic when five firms control more than 50 per cent of sales. *The Economist* (27 March 1993) estimated five-firm concentration ratios for 12 industries in global markets. In consumer durables the top five's share was 70 per cent. In automotive, airlines, aerospace, electronic components, electricals and electronics, and steel, the top five account for more than 50 per cent of the global market. In oil, PCs, and media the top five account for more than 40 per cent. There is more competition at the bottom than at the top. If we track the history of the largest corporations in any market we may see some that have lost their power, but most have held on to their markets for decades on end. For instance, General Motors (GM), Ford, and Toyota are still amongst the biggest in the car business. They have been so for a very long time. What is interesting to note is that their products have changed, their product mix has also changed. The life cycle of a business conglomerate is much larger than the life cycle of a product.

There is also a new phenomenon that is emerging in global production strategies, and that is the relationship enterprise. The relationship enterprise (Dunning and Boyd 2003) is a network of strategic alliances among firms spanning different industries and different nations to act as if they constituted a single entity. The alliance is usually for a particular project. This phenomenon may have emerged due to the multi-disciplinary nature of complex products requiring core competencies in different aspects of technology. However, the economic power (and potential political influence) that goes with it is awesome.

Korten (2001) mentions a news report in *The Economist* (6 February 1993).

> ... Discussions among Boeing, members of the Airbus consortium, McDonnell Douglas, Mitsubishi, Kawasaki, and Fuji about cooperating on the joint development of a new super-jumbo jet and to the group formed by the world's major telecommunication firms to provide a worldwide network of fiber-optics, underwater cables....these corporate juggernauts will dwarf existing global corporate giants, with individual relationship enterprises reaching combined revenues approaching $1 trillion by early next century, making them larger than all but the six largest national economies.

The really big firms have strategic alliances that help keep competition within manageable limits. The intensity of competition in the rest of the value chain is intense.

Jobs and International Migration

Workers around the world are living increasingly interdependent lives. As production processes become more integrated so do the fortunes of networked workers. Most of the world's population now lives in countries that are rapidly becoming integrated into world markets for goods and services, as well as capital. Unlike the growth in trade and, to a lesser extent, the growth in capital flows, labour flows have not been significant. In fact, they have fallen in the last 30 years or so. According to an estimate of Streeten (2001) about 60 million people migrated from Europe to the Americas during the period 1870–1913. Migration is no faster now than what it was in the early 1970s. The migration that does take place is heavily biased in favour of skilled workers for knowledge-intensive industries. The overall effect of international migration is much smaller than trade or capital flows; only around 2 per cent of people born in low or middle income countries do not live in their country of birth.

In fact, capital also moves in search of cheap labour across regions and across nations. There are two ways in which this occurs. The first is the typical, more commonly observed phenomenon of foreign direct investment whereby a firm brings technology and capital to a host country and creates some employment opportunities locally. There would be risks associated with the possible adverse effects of local economic policies such as taxes, labour regulations, and industrial relations problems. In more recent years, with globally integrated production processes, the phenomenon of business process outsourcing (BPO) has enabled firms to shift certain jobs and tasks to locations where labour is cheap, yet has the requisite skills. The jobs are usually information technology (IT)-enabled services such as call centres, data entry, or software related tasks. Moving jobs without physically moving people does reveal some equivalence to international migration of workers, though real wages and the quality of life that a person would enjoy are likely to be quite different in the two cases.

In terms of globalization's effect on wages and the real income of workers, there does not seem to be any set pattern. Growth through international trade would be expected to drive up demand in the export sector, which we had seen is dominated by skill and knowledge intensive workers. In most nations their wages have increased (World Bank 1995), but the wages of unskilled workers, especially those in the informal sector, have fallen or, at best, remained more or less stagnant. This need not necessarily be so. There are many nations, such as Hungary, China, and Malaysia, which have used global opportunities to move into new and sophisticated manufacturing. Governments have been able to strategically use the inflows of foreign investment and new technologies to improve the conditions of workers with better careers, training, and benefits. This is also contingent on good macroeconomic management that induces foreign investors to come in. Success in improving the conditions of workers in general, also depend crucially on good public education and a society where prosperity is widely shared. *Business Week* (6 November 2000) describes the strategy:

> But it takes more than geography and low wages to move up the economic ladder. It requires a track record of business-friendly policies to lure multinationals and domestic tycoons alike to invest for the long term—training workers, investing in modern technology, and nurturing local suppliers and managers.

What is happening to global inequalities in incomes and wealth? How potent are internal policies that not only create a business-friendly macroeconomic environment, but also ensure that prosperity from growth and development are widely shared? Some of these issues are addressed in the next section 'Globalization and Inequality'.

Before moving on, however, it is worth mentioning a growing feature of modern sector skilled jobs. New technologies are increasingly labour displacing in nature. As a result of which the rate of growth of employment opportunities has been far less than the rate of growth of capital and output. Organizations, in waves of adopting the latest technologies, invariably 'downsize' or 'rightsize' the organization, implying a significant shift in the security of a job, even when one is educated, creative, and efficient. *Fortune* magazine (1994), in a cover story, aptly sums up the insecurity (as the flip side of new challenging and creative jobs that have emerged in the past three decades):

> ... managers who were trained to build are now being paid to tear down. They don't hire; they fire. They don't like the new mandate, but most have come to understand that it's not going to change. That realization makes the daily routine different: Work no longer energizes, it drains. Under the circumstances it seems almost immoral to take much joy in work. So they become morose and cautious, worrying that they will be washed away in the next stage of discharges. Meanwhile they work longer and harder to make up for the toil of those who left. Fatigue and resentment begin to build.

Jobs in the modern new economy associated with new technologies are insecure adding to workplace stress and anxieties. Technological development demands lower numbers, newer skills. The overall effect of this, in terms of total jobs need not be negative as the expansion of economic activities and growing opportunities create new investments and new jobs. However, the full adjustment in labour markets may take much longer than the two or three decades of rapid change. While firms are compelled to be flexible and nimble enough to adjust to changing markets and forces of competition, workers too need to have multiple skills and quick adjustment abilities to change jobs and to change skills. Till such adjustments in the labour market occur, the rapid obsolescence of skills and large redundancies of workers will continue to cause concern.

Figures 2.1 and 2.2 depict a broad trend of international labour migration, and capital flows in developed and less developed countries during the last 30 years. It is quite clear that capital flows have been far more substantial than labour flows.

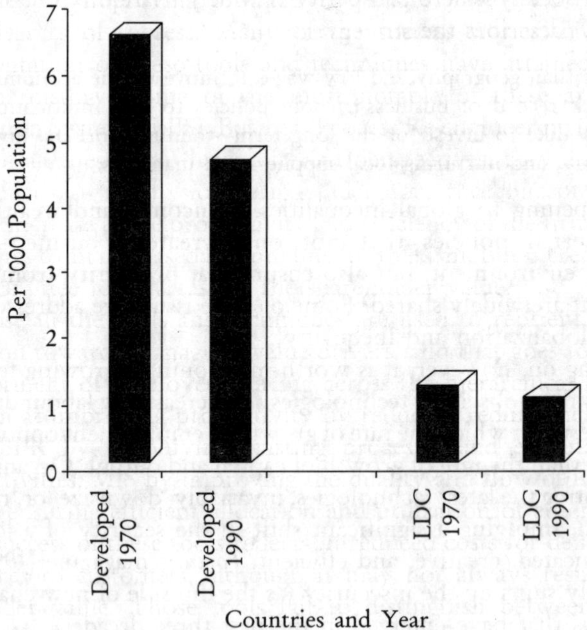

Fig. 2.1: International Migration

Source: World Bank (1995).

Globalization and Inequality

Few people would seriously doubt the fact that there are substantial inequalities in income and wealth in the world. Why is it important to understand the trends in inequalities from the perspective of managing or running a business? It is certainly a matter of human concern in itself, especially to the extent it may imply that the level and magnitude of

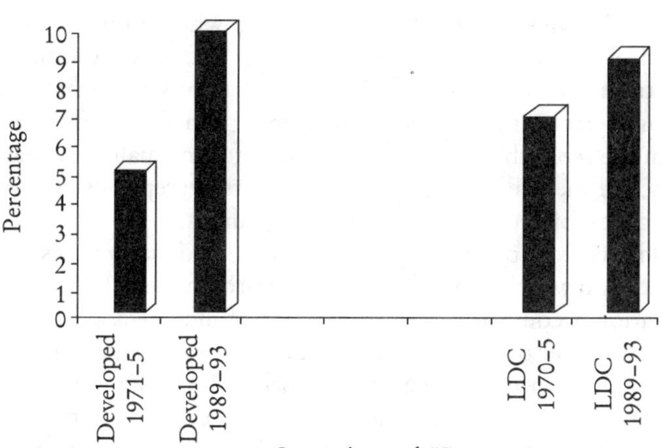

Fig. 2.2: Capital Flows as Share of GDP

Source: World Bank (1995).

economic deprivation are unacceptable. The trends are also important, to the extent that a declining inequality would imply a better quality of life, at least for some people who are very poor. Inequality is also important for instrumental reasons since a rise or fall in inequality affects other economic outcomes. For instance, think about a national or regional economy that is extremely poor with only a few people having income and purchasing power comparable to the global average. Compare this with a nation or region where inequalities are lower and the average income is slightly higher. Where would we perceive greater opportunities for growth and expansion and like to set up business? Economic growth along with reductions in income and wealth inequalities generally creates more business opportunities than economic growth with rising inequalities. That is why there is so much concern about reducing poverty and increasing the capabilities of poor people to avail of market opportunities.

Inequalities can adversely affect the business environment in a number of different ways. First of all, they can exacerbate the effects of market and policy failures in the sense that the poor in society are more vulnerable to economic fluctuations. Thus imperfect markets and institutional frailties appear more threatening in poor countries of the world, as are the anxieties of recovering from market downturns. There is also the fact that, more the poverty, more the efforts and resources that will be required to eradicate, or at least significantly reduce, the problem of deprivation. Inequality and the concentration of income can undermine the agenda of public policies. They could either be more geared to the needs and requirements of the rich whose access to markets is more and where collective voice is politically louder. On the other hand, public policies, in the presence of acute poverty, could be driven by a concern for support that violates economic logic for the sake of political populism. Consider, for example, the range of subsidies in a variety of infrastructure services in many poor countries, which inhibit efficiency in the allocation of scarce resources. Inequality can also erode social capital in the form of trust and responsibility. Public institutions perform poorly and corruption and crime increase with inequality. Finally, inequality breeds callousness in the sense that a society's tolerance for inequality increases with the persistence of inequality. That, in turn, affects perceptions and priorities about the urgency of reducing economic inequalities.

The world's consumption of goods, services, and natural resources are highly skewed. A few rich countries housing approximately 20 per cent of the global population account for over 80 per cent of income and consumption. A much larger number of countries with over 80 per cent of global population house some of the poorest people of the world. More than a billion people live at less than one dollar a day. Not only is the inequality in income and wealth marked across countries, there is much inequality *within* countries too. An obvious question that may be raised pertains to the link between inequalities and globalization. Has economic inequality been increasing or decreasing globally? A second question, distinct, yet related to the first, pertains to the issue of globalization and the reduction of poverty and deprivation. The answer to the first question has not only to demonstrate the trends of global inequality, but also provide a logical link to the process of globalization of markets. In other words, we need to establish a causal relationship between rising or declining inequality with the pace and depth of globalization. The second question pertains to something more fundamental. Even if economic inequality is found to be rising, what is happening to absolute poverty and deprivation worldwide? Are the poorest of the poor reaping any benefits at all from global economic changes?

Table 2.7 indicates some recent levels of inequality.

Table 2.7: Global Inequality

(Figures represent global control in % in 1993)

	GNP	World Trade	Savings
Richest 20% people	84.7	84.2	65.5
Poorest 20% people	1.4	0.9	0.7

Source: UNDP 1996

The growth in global GDP during the last 50 years of the twentieth century has been quite remarkable, increasing from US$3 trillion to US$22 trillion. Global population has grown from 2.5 billion to 5.5 billion during the same period. This means that per capita income has risen approximately three-fold. Despite this growth there continue to be substantial inequalities. The richest 20 per cent of the world's population consume 70 per cent of global energy, 75 per cent of metals, 85 per cent of wood, and 60 per cent of food (UNDP 1996). On the other hand, there are 1.3 billion people living below the poverty line, while 800 million are undernourished. Hundreds of millions are without basic education and health facilities and proper shelter or sanitation.

Has world economic inequality increased or decreased over the past 20 years or so? There does not seem to be a single answer to this basic question. The answer depends on how some technical difficulties in measurement are resolved, such as taking countries or individuals as the unit of measurement, or how income in dollars is converted into income in rupees. However, almost all the alternative indices and measures that can be constructed reveal the result that there is no reason to conclude that inequalities are on the decline (Wade 2001). In fact, most of the indices reveal the opposite—that income inequalities have been increasing over time. The real difficulty is, however, establishing the causality of the poor remaining at least as poor as before, while the rich get richer, with the issue of rising market integration. For a review of what trade theory, both classical and modern versions, predicts about inequality and international trade, see O'Rourke (2002).

The dominant trend of the economic history of the twentieth century has been the feature of increasing inequality, both within countries as well as across countries. The ratio of the richest per capita income to the poorest per capita income (across nations) increased quite dramatically from 11 in 1870, to 38 in 1960, to 52 in 1985. Table 2.8 shows the trends in divergence over the past couple of centuries measured in terms of the Theil Index where a larger number indicates greater inequality.

Table 2.8: Trends in Global Inequality

(Theil Index)

	1820	1900	1960	2000
Total inequality	0.525	0.775	0.775	0.900
Between country inequality	0.050	0.275	0.475	0.525
Within country inequality	0.475	0.500	0.300	0.375

Source: O'Rourke (2002)

The dominant pattern of divergence is based on the relationship observed between growth performance and initial per capita income. This relationship is statistically very stable and has been tested across more than a hundred countries. However, some recent cross- country studies have revealed that if one takes initial investment rates and stock of human capital, over and above the initial level of per capita income, then countries with lower initial levels tend to grow faster. The major implication of this is the fact that if all nations had the same investment rate and stock of human capital, then the incomes of the countries of the world would converge, rather than diverge. This finding is referred to as 'conditional convergence'.

There is an intuitive appeal in the concept of conditional convergence. It highlights the urgent need for resource and technology transfers from the rich to the poorer countries. Despite this optimistic theoretical prediction, world inequality refuses to go away because poor nations find it difficult to augment their investment rates and improve the quality of the labour force in terms of health and educational capabilities. Relatively speaking, the economies of

Europe and the USA have converged more with integration, since their initial conditions were not too different.

All the reasons behind the rising (or, at least, not falling) inequality between countries and within nations cannot be attributed to globalization. Some plausible reasons are certainly international in nature, such as falling non-oil commodity prices, problems associated with international debt and recessionary financial crisis. The phenomenon could also be related to the trend in labour demand and the importance of specific skills and knowledge that are emerging in trade patterns and organizational structures, affecting labour markets across the world (World Bank 1995). But there are local national issues as well. The increasing population growth-rate differential between poor and rich nations, the low ability and political will to invest in poverty eradication programmes, and the inadequacy of public policy strategies in education and health are government failures. Nations that have failed to build human capabilities and create enabling institutional structures of good governance have remained poor. Poverty and inequality, in a major way, represents the failure of many post-colonial governments in their agenda of building strong and prosperous nations that can help their own economies to avail of emerging global opportunities.

Globalization and National Policy Autonomy

This brings us to the important issue of national economic policy and the power of the nation to create the conditions for rapid growth and economic development. This is of paramount importance to business and private investments. The business implications of fiscal policies, monetary policies, and policies affecting international trade and exchange rates are well known. No business organization or decision-maker can afford ignorance on these subjects.

The spread of modern economic growth brought with it the historical development of the nation-state, as we know it today. Specific goals for national development and the agenda for nation building were the basis of independent national economic policies that marked the decades following the Second World War. Newly independent nations, free from the shackles of colonial domination asserted their autonomy through a vigorous pursuit of inward looking strategies for self-determination. The nation-state was fashioned within the 'people-nation-state-government' boundary. In theory the four elements coincided. However, as the economic forces of integration grew with new technologies and new market structures, the relative autonomy of the nation-state has been reduced. This is one aspect of globalization that is debated with a good deal of vigour. Hobsbawm (1992) aptly describes the changes taking place:

> ... it will inevitably have to be written as the history of a world which can no longer be contained within the limits of 'nations' and 'nation-states' as these used to be defined, either politically or economically, or culturally, or even linguistically. It will

be largely supranational and infranational, but even infranationality, whether or not it dresses itself up in the costume of some mini-nationalism, will reflect the decline of the old nation-state as an operational entity. It will see 'nation-states' and 'nations' or ethnic/linguistic groups primarily as retreating before, resisting, adapting to, being absorbed or dislocated by the new supranational restructuring of the globe.

What does it really have to do with globalization? Globalization, in terms of an ideal benchmark, means a perfect integration of goods, services and factors-of-production markets throughout the world. Compared to this ideal situation, the current state of the process of globalization is highly incomplete and fragmented. Despite the growth of trade and factor mobility, and a significant decline in protective trade barriers, the law of one price and perfect arbitrage does not hold. Real interest rates are not driven to equality even in well-integrated financial markets of the developed economies. Restrictions on labour movement and large inter-country wage differentials are the rule rather than the exception. Price arbitrage occurs very slowly. There is a lot of home bias in financial investment portfolios in the developed economies, in the sense that investors hold more domestic assets than warranted by principles of portfolio diversification. What could be the reasons for this?

One plausible explanation is the distinction made by some economists between 'shallow' and 'deep' integration. Trade rules that are commonly shared by different countries certainly facilitate the movement of goods and services, but there are constraints imposed by national regulations within an economy. Rodrik (2000) mentions that even political borders like the US–Canadian one (which demarcates two societies that are quite similar in many respects of economy, polity, and culture) have a significantly depressing effect on commerce and trade. The constraint acts in terms of transaction costs that emerge from discontinuities in political and legal systems, especially when it comes to cross-border enforcement of contracts. Rodrik describes the situation as:

> When one of the parties reneges on a written contract, local courts may be unwilling—and international courts unable—to enforce a contract signed by residents of two different countries. Thus, national sovereignty interferes with contract enforcement, leaving international contracts hostage to an increased risk of opportunistic behaviour. This problem is the most severe in the case of capital flows, and has the implication that national borrowing opportunities are limited by the *willingness* of countries to service their obligations rather than their *ability* to do so. But the problem exists generically for any commercial contract signed by entities belonging to two different jurisdictions.

Contracts, whether explicit or implicit, are usually incomplete in terms of all the possible contingencies that may arise in enforcing it. This problem, as economists are well aware, is taken care of, to some extent, by laws, social customs, and practices. Unless internal rules, regulations, and norms converge, there will be difficulty in moving the process of globalization from the shallow to the deeper variety of perfect arbitrage. While economic forces of technologies and markets become increasingly international in character, will politics continue to be national?

The possibilities of politics and policies continuing to be national in character are low, certainly in the longer haul of the next two or three decades of the twenty-first century. The last two decades of the twentieth century have witnessed the erosion of national autonomy in economic policy-making of most nations. This has occurred in three important areas of policy-making. The first important effect has been a result of the GATT negotiations resulting in the formation of the WTO. The large majority of nations have agreed to have common rules and regulations governing trade in goods and services, common rules governing laws on investments, and common laws on intellectual property rights. This is a big step in enabling impotent national governments to frame their own rules of playing the international commercial game.

The second important area where there has been a perceptible loss of autonomy of national governments to formulate policy is in the area of controlling money supply and interest rates. The compulsions of allowing freer mobility of international finance, while maintaining reasonable stability in exchange rates, render the money supply of the economy (the net foreign exchange assets part) beyond the control of the monetary authority or the central bank of the nation (Krugman 2000). Thus the conventional role of using monetary policy to stimulate investment demand and spending to fight recession and unemployment becomes significantly restricted. The stability of exchange rates, allowing capital mobility, and having an independent monetary policy is referred to as the impossible trinity or open-economy trilemma. One can have any two of them. A flexible exchange rate system can allow for independent monetary policy with mobility of capital. However, the volatility of exchange rates can play havoc with the growth of international trade, especially in developing nations.

The third area where national policies can be influenced by international compulsions is in terms of fiscal policy. A government's ability to borrow and spend on essential social and physical infrastructure is largely determined by the management of the national fisc. Taxation is an important ingredient in the making of fiscal policy. From a government's point of view taxes represent non-borrowed resources. However, if foreign fund flows, whether in terms of direct investments or portfolio capital, are allowed and are sought to augment the nation's internal savings, then no country can afford to have tax rates and interest rates that are out of tune with those prevailing in other countries. Thus fiscal policy, like monetary and trade policy, has begun to feel the compulsions of market integration. This is not restricted to the developing countries alone. Many developed nations too have felt the pains of recessionary stagnation where standard fiscal or monetary policies have not worked (Krugman 2000). In short, when a nation is competing with other nations for goods and services, financial capital, skilled labour, and technology, it cannot afford to be 'different' from its competitors in any persistent and significant way.

With geographical boundaries becoming porous both in terms of political control and conceptual exclusivity, what is the likely fate of the nation-state? The nation-state is bound to change in significant ways as the twenty-first century unfolds. We have already mentioned the declining importance of national autonomy with a growing convergence in economic policies. Business in the twenty-first century will increasingly have to track global events and trends that are likely to have effects on government spending, taxes, interest rates, exchange rates, and regulations that govern business such as competition laws or environmental rules. Unlike in the past the typical business leader will now have less influence on these parameters since their determination will become more complex. It is also quite likely that the global political force behind new forms of economic governance that will shape international economic policy will become more accessible only to really big and powerful business corporations.

Human Consequences

Globalization brings with it increasing freedom and reach, but it also increases uncertainties for the individual, for a business organization, and for a nation. The prospects for greater efficiency in the economic allocation of resources and the awesome technological changes that are emerging have also led to a remarkably rapid rate of change. That, in turn, has created fluid inconstancies that have contributed to rising insecurities in many different aspects of living (UNDP 1999, Sinha 2002).

The first, and arguably the most important uncertainty and insecurity arises from the way in which market forces can bring about financial volatility and economic contraction. The decade of the 1990s have repeatedly demonstrated that bad things may happen (and quite suddenly too) to good economies. Profligacy or a lack of prudence in economic affairs does not always precede crisis and recessionary downturns. Collapses occur suddenly and can have quite disastrous effects on the profits of business organizations and the livelihoods of people. Good companies can go bankrupt, efficient workers can lose their jobs. It has happened from Mexico to South Korea, from Japan to the USA. The contractionary trend, like a contagion, can spread with astonishing speed. In times of crisis, the state recedes further with forced budgetary conservatism making deep inroads into the resources available for education, health, and social infrastructure. The lesson is clear. Every economy (and, hence, every business) is vulnerable to the vagaries of market fluctuations. The ones with the higher initial stock of wealth, both material and social, can bear the brunt of a crisis through better staying power and the ability to recover fast. Smaller and poorer economies are not only vulnerable, but also their ability to weather market-storms may be quite limited. In the latter cases the human costs of market downturns are bound to be high.

A related, though distinct, aspect of rising human insecurity pertains to the job market. The arrival of new technologies in rapid streams forces firms and business organizations to upgrade their own operations and organizations.

Thus, not merely during recessions, but also during market booms, downsizing and rightsizing continue to perturb labour markets. Technological progress has been essentially labour saving in nature, leading to an informalization of the workforce, with more short-term contracts being the order of the day, rather than the earlier long-term security of organized sector jobs. Skills become obsolete faster, jobs become scarce suddenly and people become redundant.

Insecurities are not merely perceived in terms of livelihoods and incomes. Opening up of economies bring with it, inevitably, new goods, new services, and new ways of living and of enjoying leisure. New aspirations and lifestyles threaten to crowd out older traditions of culture—the entire gamut of local practices, preferences, and prejudices. Hollywood (or even Bollywood for that matter) with the magic of special effects and dreams of the good life, or the big corporations playing out their advertisement wars, are increasingly reaching the remote corners of the world. No culture is completely insulated from the influences of the great market-driven popular parade of images of material success and unending celebration of consumption.

To cope with the strong lure of unlimited consumption, stepping up of economic growth must be of the essence. However, planet Earth is a closed spaceship, and natural resources are exhaustible. The distribution of, and access to, natural resources are highly uneven. In a world where 20 per cent of the people have been able to corner 80 per cent of the pie, economic growth at current rates may not be sustainable after five or six decades. This is despite the impressive range of new technologies that are becoming available. The lifestyle of the affluent and the compulsions of survival of the acutely deprived, both play havoc with environmental fragility and the stability of ecological systems. Technological change, along with the underlying research and development (R&D) programmes of business organizations, will feel the pressure to address environmental sustainability. Social and political pressures will mount. Firms and business organizations that adopt a short-term 'business as usual' attitude will lose out on a host of opportunities.

Whereas globalization, with its openness and connectivity, gives rise to enormous potential benefits for human living, it also brings about new personal insecurities such as new types of crimes, terror, and violence. In a gender-divided world many of these personal insecurities take a greater toll on women. Patterns of terror and the war against terror have changed dramatically too, especially after 11 September 2001. The leaders of the most powerful armies of the world have announced that in the fight against terror there are only floating coalitions that will evolve and change. There are no fixed rules, but it is obvious that the geographical territory of the enemy is less important than its communication networks. In the twenty-first century there will be fewer fortresses stormed and more opportunities and lifelines cut off. Threats to doing business will change too. Hackers located far away may well be of greater concern than the local mob demanding protection money.

In the globalized world of fluid uncertainties, there are no permanent friends or foes. There are only temporary relationships. Change and flexibility are the key words. Strategic coalitions and alliances seem to be the most reasonable alternative to a long-term partnership. The turbulence in which day-to-day living takes place makes friendship and a helping hand scarce and very precious. Extreme individualization can create deep-rooted anxieties about uncertainties and insecurities that elude clear demarcations or measures. None of us are entirely free from these stresses—either as individual consumers, or as workers. In a similar vein, larger organizations such as business firms and communities are also vulnerable to the turbulence of global change. Globalization has contributed to greater managerial stress, and with it, new ways and means of coping with the pressure.

The Inherent Tensions

We have argued that new technologies and knowledge, along with trade, travel, migration, and cultural exchanges have shaped the world for many centuries in terms of economic and social progress. The real problems of contemporary globalization discussed earlier can be reduced to some basic issues of inequalities in wealth and power within nations as well as across countries. The resolution of these basic issues does not imply shutting out the rest of the world. Dreze and Sen (2002) describe the crucial contributions international exchange make:

> The economic predicament of the poor across the world cannot be reversed by withholding from them the great advantages of contemporary technology, the economic advantages associated with international trade and exchange, and the social as well as economic merits of living in open rather than closed societies. Rather, the main issue is how to make good use of the remarkable potential of economic intercourse and technological progress in a way that pays adequate attention to the interests of the deprived and the underdog.

We are living in an era of rapid changes that can arguably go down in history as a revolution. Historical changes are often described as inevitable and inexorable. Perhaps in certain aspects they are, especially if one takes a long view of historical trends in technology and knowledge that have remarkably shaped our ways of living and modes of thinking. However, human beings are also capable of making their own histories in exercising choices, forming social institutions, and framing the rules and norms that govern the dynamics of daily life.

We are unique as a species to the extent that we constantly apply conscious intelligence to increase our stock of knowledge about nature and the world. In the process we acquire knowledge about ourselves too, since human beings are an integral part of nature. The continuous propensity of this stock of knowledge to gain in depth and scope is fundamental to human history. In this sense technology and science is the prime mover of history. However, social choice and the balance of political power determine what we do with technology. We may, for instance, have books but choose to remain ignorant or, worse still, keep others from learning. This is how the inexorability of history is moulded by human agency. Thus, what we do today to resolve the major tensions arising out of the process of globalization will influence the future of this century.

The first tension, and undoubtedly the most important one, pertains to the sway of markets with enormous concentrations of power and wealth on the one hand and the rise of democratic movements across the world. Efficient markets, based on voluntary exchange and private property do guarantee equality of opportunities for all, but they do not guarantee equality of outcomes in terms of incomes. In fact, more often than not, markets aggravate inequalities in economic power. Democracy, on the other hand, demands a more egalitarian outcome in terms of incomes and wealth, in terms of the voices in determining socio-political outcomes, and in terms of ensuring basic capabilities like education and health for all. There has been a resurgence of faith in markets as witnessed in the last two decades of the twentieth century. This has been accompanied by a significant move towards political democracy in a large number of countries. This tension between the inequities of market outcomes and the growing demands of egalitarianism will be shaped by the power of public action, from direct protests to more subtle reforms in policies and procedures governing markets.

The second important tension that will shape the eventual pattern of economy and society in the current century is an issue of culture and identity. It is the tension between the homogenizing forces of centralization of power—cultural uniformity in terms of language and lifestyle on the one hand, and the constant anxiety to preserve ethnic and more local, particularistic identities on the other. As the power of the large business organizations grow and the autonomy of the nation-state gets eroded, sub-national, communitarian identities become important in the face of the powerful cauldron of market-driven popular culture. To be able to become global without losing one's distinctive identities is a big challenge of our times. The choice of an identity that lies between exclusive separatism and relentless autarky on the one hand, and becoming buried under the uninteresting sameness of the mass produced popular culture on the other, will be shaped by what we decide to do and how we decide to act.

The third important tension lies in striking a balance between the new needs for global governance and the imperative of empowering economically and politically deprived individuals at the local, village, and community level. These represent the two extremes of governance and self-determination. There is an urgent need for global rules and global coordination, especially in the face of eroding powers of the nation-state. Equally important are the concerns of the underprivileged and the poor in having their voices heard and the plurality of their different identities respected. This calls for a whole new set of institutions and procedures of governance where individual advantage is married to a concern for all.

No manager or business strategist can afford to ignore the trends in these tensions as they get manifested in political demands and debates. What stance should we take for the welfare of not only those who work for an organization, but also those who are stakeholders in a wider sense? What attitude do we adopt towards autarchic demands like *swadeshi* when we are in the business of selling a multinational brand? Do we decide on the fairness of the WTO rules exclusively in terms of whether they raise or reduce profits for our business? Do we comprehend the voices raised? Are we prepared for political changes that may shape the markets we deal in?

The most important driver of change in the twenty-first century global economy is likely to be technology. The power of global finance, along with the institutional arrangements that create access to resources and market opportunities, will be important too. Together, these forces have tremendous potential to improve the quality of life around the world for everybody. However, there are several complex problems that will have to be resolved before that can actually happen. It depends on how the important issues of economic inequality, instability, and environmental sustainability are tackled on a global scale. A more equitable and secure sharing of the fruits of change, not only between people living today, but also between the present generation and that of the future, is certainly possible. New institutions and initiatives are needed. In this context the nation-states are likely to undergo substantial alterations in their political and social fabric. The power to manage rapid change requires a forward-looking, inclusive vision. The architecture of that power is determined by human choice. There is nothing inevitable about it.

REFERENCES

Business Week (2000) 'Global Capitalism: Can it be made to work better?', cover story, 6 November.

Dreze, J. and Amartya Sen (2002) *India: Development and Participation*, Oxford University Press, New Delhi.

Dunning, J. and G. Boyd (eds) (2003) *Alliance Capitalism and Corporate Management*, Edgar Elgar, UK.

Fortune (1994) 'Burned-Out Bosses', cover story, July.

Frankel, J. (2000) 'Globalization of the Economy', NBER Working Paper.

Hobsbawm, Eric (1992) *Nations and Nationalism Since 1780: Progress, Myth, Reality*, second edition, Cambridge University Press, Cambridge.

Hockman, B.M. and M.M. Kosecki (2001) *The Political Economy of the World Trading System*, Oxford University Press, Oxford.

Korten, D. (2001) *When Corporations Rule The World*, second edition, Kumarian Press and Berrett-Koehler Publishers, San Francisco.

Krugman, P. (2000) *The Return of Depression Economics*, Penguin Books, Hammondsworth.

Nayyar, D. (1995) 'Globalization: The Past in Our Present', Presidential address at the seventy-eighth annual conference of the Indian Economic Association, Chandigarh, mimeo.

O'Rourke, K. (2002) 'Global Inequality: Historical Trends' in B. Pleskovic and N.Stern (eds) *Annual World Bank Conference on Development Economics 2001/2002*, World Bank, Washington D.C..

Rodrik, D. (2000) 'How Far Will Economic Integration Go?', *Journal of Economic Perspectives*, Vol.14, No.1.

Sinha, A. (2002) 'Consuming to Live: Living to Consume—Globalization and Some Human Consequences', paper presented at the conference on Business–Social Partnerships: Beyond Philanthropy, Indian Institute of Management Calcutta, December 4, 7, mimeo.

Streeten, P. (2001) 'Integration, Interdependence and Globalization', *Finance and Development* IMF, Washington D.C..

UNDP (2001) *Human Development Report*, Oxford University Press, New York.

— (1999) *Human Development Report*, Oxford University Press, New York.

— (1996) *Human Development Report*, Oxford University Press, New York.

Wade, R. (2001) The Rising Inequality of World Income Distribution', *Finance and Development*, IMF, Washington D.C..

World Bank (2000) *World Development Report*, Oxford University Press, New York.

— (1995) *World Development Report*, Oxford University Press, New York.

World Resources Institute (1995) *World Resources: A Guide to the Global Environment*, Oxford University Press, Delhi.

3

The New Economy

Anindya Sen

Information and communication technologies seem to impinge directly on every aspect of our life. The spread of IT in the recent past has been mind-boggling. By the end of the 1950s, there were probably 2000 installed computers in the world, with average processing power of perhaps 10,000 machine instructions per second. Today, in terms of rough magnitudes, there are perhaps 300 million active computers in the world with processing power averaging several hundred million instructions per second (Delong and Summers 2001). Two thousand computers times 10,000 instructions per second is 20 million instructions per second. Three hundred million computers times, say, 300 million instructions per second is 90 quadrillion instructions per second—a four-billion-fold increase in the world's raw automated computer power in 40 years, at an average annual rate of growth of 56 per cent per year.

In 1965, Gordon Moore, the co-founder of Intel, had predicted that the processing power of a silicon chip would double every 18 months. His theory came to be referred to as the Moore's Law. Moore's Law seems to be in operation even today, leading to enormous increase in computer processing capacity and a sharp decline in costs. Some scientists think that Moore's Law will hold good for another decade.

The increase in computer power has been accompanied by the growth of technologies for disseminating information. The rapid growth of the Internet and telecommunications has made it possible to send vast amounts of information over huge distances at very little cost. Therefore, an important observation about the New Economy relates to the revolution in connectivity and the upsurge in creation, analysis, and distribution of huge amounts of information on an international scale to an extent not seen before the 1990s. This revolution in IT sparked a revolution in information availability.

This growth in IT coincided in the USA with a period characterized by high growth rates, low inflation and unemployment rates, and significant productivity gains, and was commonly attributed to the effects of IT in general, and of the Internet in particular. As a result many people started to talk about the 'New Economy' where the increasing use of IT would make cyclical downturns a thing of the past. The Bureau of Economic Analysis, for instance, describes the New Economy as the expansion of the US economy in the 1990s, characterized by its 'unprecedented length, strong growth in real GDP and per capita GDP, higher rates of investment as well as low inflation and unemployment.' (Fraumeni and Landefeld 2000).

The phenomenon of change is not new to human civilization. In the past four centuries alone we have witnessed one economic revolution after another. The industrial revolution (the first application of steam and mechanism) was followed by the second industrial revolution of steel and chemicals, which in turn was followed by the third industrial revolution of electric motors and internal combustion engines. Now it seems that we are undergoing a digital revolution.

In what sense is the New Economy new? Is it going to change the world, as we know it, more profoundly than the other revolutions? Is the New Economy a strange, unknown creature or can we try to make sense of it with the tools we already possess?

Some of these questions cannot be answered today. We can only peek into the future, as though through a crystal ball, when we try to anticipate what is going to happen to human society 50 years down the line. We can see communication tools developing to the point where our basic privacy is threatened. While I can keep touch with members of my family 24 hours a day with a cellphone from anywhere in the world, I am also flooded with pop-ups and junk mail every time I switch on my computer and try to access email. We search for information online, buy online, and date online. At the same time all kinds of barriers are springing up to prevent free access of information online.

The key to understanding the New Economy is to look at information as a commodity in today's marketplace. So, in this chapter, the question of establishing and maintaining property rights over information and the creation of monopolies is also discussed.

What is the New Economy?

On 10 March 2000, the technology-stock bellweather, Nasdaq, soared to a height it had never reached before—past 5000 to a record 5047.69. It took a mere four months for the Nasdaq to climb from 3000 past 4000 to its new record. But the Nasdaq's rapid rise saw an equally rapid fall. A year after achieving its record high, the Nasdaq was struggling to maintain a level less than half of that high (around 2200). Some tech-related stocks whose shares once went for exorbitant sums were trading at less than 10 per cent of their 2000 highs. The Internet-portal, Yahoo!, for example, fell nearly 90 per cent from the levels of a year to around US$21 a share.

When the dotcom shakeout occurred, the press equated the digital revolution with e-commerce and quickly reached the conclusion that 'the New Economy was a bust'. Combined with the negative economic indicators, it seemed to point to the imperative of getting back to 'old economy' fundamentals and forgetting all this talk about capitalizing on the next 'new new thing'.

However, to define the New Economy as merely an acceleration in the rate of technical advance in the IT industry in the second half of the 1990s is to take too narrow a view. In fact, if account were taken of the effects of IT in other sectors of the economy, then it would become obvious that very few industries have remained untouched by the new technological developments. The distinction between the old economy and New Economy is getting increasingly blurred. There are illustrative (and, of course, anecdotal) examples of farmers who track their cows via wireless transmitters, profile them, and use electronic markets on the Internet for procurement or distribution of their products. In developed countries, in a meaningful sense, there is, with few exceptions, little of the truly 'old economy' left.

While the distinction between the old and the new economy is getting blurred and while it remains true that all technological developments to date have been based on some former invention, there are certain developments which might be characterized as new (although they are also based on earlier inventions, too), because they can only be found in the 1990s. Most importantly, these include the interconnection of computers via the Internet on an international scale which has its roots in the launch of the World Wide Web by the CERN in 1990, the inclusion of commercial traffic on the Net in 1991, and the release of the Mosaic browser in 1993.

Whichever definition we prefer, the New Economy seems to be characterized by three central features:

1. The economy's information sector contributes importantly to the GDP growth rate.
2. In the economy's business sector, there is widespread adoption of the Internet as an infrastructure for economic transactions.
3. A large and growing proportion of all households have a computer and access to the Internet.

One important reason why IT is having such an impact on social and economic organizations is that the nature of the technology has undergone a critical shift. The first computers were seen as good at performing lengthy and complicated sets of arithmetic operations. But as time passed, it became evident that the computer was good for much more than performing repetitive and complicated calculations at high speed. It was also an organizer. For example, American Airlines used computers to create its SABRE automated reservations system and the insurance industry automated its back-office sorting and classifying. The next important step was to use the computer as a 'what-if' machine. The computer can create the model of what would happen if an airplane or, for that matter, even molecules, were to be built in a certain way. 'It, thus, enables an amount and a degree of experimentation in the virtual world that would be prohibitively expensive in resources and time in the real world' (Delong and Summers 2001). In 1985, it cost Ford US$60,000 each time it crashed a car into a wall to simulate an accident. Now a collision can be simulated by a computer for around US$100[1].

[1] *The Economist*, 23 September, 2000.

How then do the new technologies differ from the old ones? As Delong (2000) puts it, IT and the Internet amplify brain power in the same way that the older technologies amplified muscle power. Computers and IT have a number of noteworthy features that distinguish them from some of the older technologies.

1. IT is general purpose technology. It can help to improve efficiency in almost everything that a firm does, and it can be used in almost every sector of the economy. An important consequence of this is that demand for IT can be expected to be steadily growing over time.
2. By increasing access to information, it can enable markets to work more efficiently. In theory, it seems to make markets move closer to the ideal form of perfect competition—with abundant information, larger numbers of buyers and sellers, low transaction costs, and low barriers to entry.
3. IT is global. It makes it possible to store huge amounts of knowledge as a string of zeros and ones and send them anywhere in the world at negligible cost. The reduction in the cost of communications helps to globalize production and capital markets.
4. IT speeds up innovation itself, by making it easier to produce, store, and process large amounts of data and reducing the time needed to produce new products. The mapping of the human genome would have taken much more time if computers had not steadily become more powerful.
5. The rate of decline of the cost of the new technology seems to be far greater than anything experienced earlier. Over the last three decades the real price of computer processing power has fallen by almost 1000 per cent, an average decline of 35 per cent a year. Compare this with some of the older technologies. By 1850, the real cost of steam power had fallen by only 50 per cent from its level in 1790. Electricity prices fell at an average of 6 per cent a year in real terms between 1890 and 1920.
6. The first and the last point taken together mean that computers and the Internet are being adopted more quickly than previous general purpose technologies, such as steam and electricity, at least in the developed countries.

The New Economy and Change

The New Economy is really about a set of structural changes taking place in the economy with IT as the driver. This point is emphasized further by those who choose to use the term 'network economy' rather than 'New Economy' to describe the changes taking place. Thus the focus is not on technology, but on the fundamental changes taking place in social and economic organization due to the spread of IT.

We next present three examples to show how IT can profoundly change the way companies operate. The ensuing discussion is by no means an exhaustive listing of the possible ways of harnessing IT.

Reduction in Transaction Costs

First consider B2B e-commerce (business-to-business electronic commerce). Businesses enter into a whole range of transactions with each other, including financial transactions. B2B e-commerce means that instead of labour services used to carry through these transactions, computer data processing and Internet communications are used (Lucking-Reiley and Spulber 2000). Automating transactions can lead to significant savings in transaction costs, including the costs of searching out buyers and sellers, maintaining records of transactions, information exchange, and so on. Now, as the literature pioneered by Ronald Coase has shown, the 'make or buy' decision—the choice between carrying out activities in-house and outsourcing—hinges crucially on the nature and magnitude of transaction costs. As the transaction costs of using the market fall, we would expect to see a greater reliance on the market rather than in-house transactions. Take a vertically integrated firm that engages in substantial internal sales and procurement activities. The advent of B2B e-commerce might induce it to reorganize to outsource production of goods and services that were previously produced internally, as well as outsource management of these transactions. For example, many car manufacturers have spun off their parts manufacturing units to outsiders. GM, Ford, and Daimler-Chrysler have established a company called Covisint to handle auto parts transactions from suppliers. The significance of this move can be realized once we know that the supply chains of these three companies total almost US$250 billion.

Box 3.1: How Does B2B e-commerce Help a Firm to Cut its Costs?

It can do this in several ways. First, by making it easier to find the cheapest supplier and through efficiency gains, it reduces procurement costs. It is cheaper to place orders online and there are likely to be fewer errors in orders and invoicing. Cisco reported that before it switched to online ordering, a quarter of its orders used to be reworked because of errors in its phone and ordering systems. The switch to online ordering brought down the error rate to 2 per cent, saving the company US$500 million a year. Of course, the savings from procurement are likely to be different in different sectors. A report by Goldman Sachs estimated that online purchasing could save firms anything from 2 per cent in the coal industry to perhaps 40 per cent in electronic components.

Firms can benefit significantly from lower distribution costs of goods and services that can be delivered electronically, such as financial services, software, and music. For a bank, for example, the marginal cost of transaction over the Internet will be much lower compared to transaction via an automated teller machine (ATM) and even lower compared to transaction over the bank counter. Online commerce cuts out layers of middlemen and allows more efficient supply-chain management. Also, better information enables firms to operate with smaller inventories.

B2B exchanges are being set up in various industries. These are expected to provide more efficient marketplaces for buyers and sellers of steel, cars, construction, and other commodities.

Source: 'The New Economy', *The Economist*, 23 September 2000.

Reshaping Processes Within an Organization

One can go further and argue that IT can fundamentally transform the way business is done by relaxing many of the constraints that once defined the way companies had to be run. IT enables companies to question each and every process in the production and distribution chain and re-engineer the corporation.

Hammer and Champy (1993) are at pains to emphasize that '...merely throwing computers at an existing business problem does not cause it to be re-engineered'. They cite the example of IBM Credit Corporation[2]. In the early days, each application for financing went through five steps; at each step a specialist, for example, a credit checker, a pricer, or somebody to modify the loan covenant, vetted the application. Thus the processing of an application took, on an average, six days to be completed, and sometimes even two weeks. To make the process faster, IBM Credit at first installed a control desk to keep tabs on each stage of the process. This did not solve the problem, though it did enable the person at the control desk to provide information about where precisely an application was located at that instant. IBM finally realized that it had to rethink the entire process of clearing an application. What it did was to replace the specialists with generalists. Instead of sending an application form from office to office to get various clearances, one person called a deal structurer, could now deal with the whole process from beginning to end.

Where did IT come into the picture here? IBM Credit realized that most requests for credit were simple and straightforward and fell well within the capability of a single person supported by an easy-to-use computer system providing access to all the data and tools that the specialists would use. The enabling role of IT was crucial in cutting down the six-day turnaround time to four hours.

Reshaping Businesses Between Companies

Even in the recent past, the relationship between a firm and its input suppliers used to be one of arms length trading. The firm would assess its needs at periodic intervals, place orders with its input suppliers, and expect to get the required inputs after some time. This worked fine so long as the firm was dealing with mass-produced, undifferentiated goods in a non-volatile market where demand was predictable. Inventory requirements were predictable and manageable.

But the situation changed when the firm's size of operations grew along with customization. The firm now was required to produce very large numbers of a product like a car, but at the same time attend to the different requirements of different customers. In such a situation, it became necessary to integrate the vendors more closely with the firm's operations.

GM's Saturn plant in Spring Hill, Tennessee, exemplifies this new relationship between a firm and its vendors. GM included an online

[2] This and the next example come from Hammer and Champy (1993).

manufacturing database in its Saturn plant that is accessible by the company's component suppliers. As a result, the suppliers do not have to wait for a purchase order from GM. They simply consult the database to find out the production schedule and then deliver the appropriate components to the assembly plant as required. After the parts are shipped, the vendor sends an electronic message to Saturn stating what they have shipped. When the shipments arrive, the receiving clerk scans the bar code on the box with an electronic wand. The computer tells the clerk to what part of the plant the goods should go and also initiates the payment process.

How has the effect of IT on business practices translated into its effect on the economy as a whole? In other words, in terms of having an effect on the performance of the economy as a whole, how does the new economy compare with the old economy?

Traditional models of growth developed by economists focused on inputs of capital and labour and had nothing to say about technological change. Technological change was viewed as something exogenous, raining down from the heavens at some pre-determined rate. But a new theory, developed in the 1980s by Paul Romer and others, put technological change at the centre of things. In the new growth theory, knowledge creation is endogenous, responding to market incentives like better education or improved profit opportunities. Such endogenous technological change is expected to account for a significant part of the growth of an economy, by increasing productivity growth rates.

However, paradoxically, massive investments in IT seemed to have been a failure in terms of growth in productivity, a fact that came to be known as the productivity paradox. Productivity growth slowed in most countries in the 1970s and 1980s. It is only in the 1990s that the USA experienced a surge in productivity growth.

There are many explanations for this paradox. One is that a technology starts having a significant effect on productivity only after a certain penetration level is reached (50 per cent according to Paul David). The penetration rate for computers is still less than 50 per cent in many countries. However, as we have pointed out above, there is one characteristic of the New Economy that is often missed out. IT often helps to do things better, rather than do new things. The benefit of IT can come in the form of improved product quality, time savings, and convenience which rarely show up in macroeconomic data.

Another point to note about the New Economy is that it has been largely an American phenomenon, with little sign of an increase in productivity in Japan or in larger European economies. By the late 1990s, the USA had outperformed the others and its lead in IT and the Internet can provide it with a huge advantage for many more years to come. But even though the other economies invest less on IT as a share of the GDP, it is open to them to imitate or adopt American technology and catch up with American productivity growth.

What about the developing countries? With IT now set to be the main engine of growth, people worry about a new 'digital divide': The income gap between the rich and poor countries will widen further because poor countries will be unable to access the new technologies. Rich countries account for only 15 per cent of the world's population but 90 per cent of global IT spending and 80 per cent of Internet users. The two billion people living in low income countries (with average incomes below US$800 per head) have only 35 telephone lines and five personal computers for every 1000 people, compared with 650 phone lines and 540 computers in the USA (*The Economist*, 23 September 2000).

However, the New Economy works by breaking down geographical borders and speeding up the diffusion of knowledge. OECD figures show that IT spending in developing countries has been growing more than twice as fast as in developed ones over the past decade (starting from a low base). In developing countries, well thought out low-cost options such as initiatives to provide computers at village centres linked with government departments, can have significant effects on productivity and growth.

The new technologies affect not only the way business is done. Since they deal with the very essence of human society—communication between people—they can be expected to bring about fundamental social changes. These social changes are likely to take place faster and on a more extensive scale than before because of the speed at which the technologies are developing[3]. We will discuss the effects on privacy in particular later in this chapter.

Understanding the New Economy[4]

The New Economy is, therefore, characterized by the creation, analysis, and distribution of huge amounts of information. Shapiro and Varian use the term 'information goods' to focus attention on this critical output of the New Economy. As we have already pointed out, the easy availability of huge amounts of information is enabling companies to do things previously unheard of.

Such information goods have a number of striking features that distinguish them from the old economy products. It is not as if some of these features are not present in the old economies. But what we want to emphasize is that they are simultaneously present in the New Economy in a greater degree than ever before.

The Cost of Producing Information

It costs a very large sum of money to produce the first compact disc (CD) of a music album. The performers have to be paid, recording the album costs money, and so on. However, the cost of producing the second or third or the millionth CD is negligible, because the cost of copying is very low. Similarly,

[3] For a plausible but rather scary picture of a society in the near future, see the *Economist*, 23 September 2000.

[4] The discussion in this section is based largely on Shapiro and Varian (1999) and Varian (1998)

suppose that an e-book is made available on the Internet. The publisher has to pay the author and incur some costs for putting up the book on a website. But after this is done, it does not cost anything to make it available to anybody who has a computer and an Internet connection.

In the language of economics, information goods involve large fixed costs of production but low marginal (additional) costs. This cost structure gives rise to substantial economies of scale—the more you produce, the lower your average or per unit cost of production.

As an example, consider a CD that involves a fixed cost of US$1 million and per unit cost of 10 cents. The total cost of producing q units is then $C = 1,000,000 + 0.1q$, and the average cost of production is $A = C/q = 1,000,000/q + 0.1$. It is easy to see that as q increases, A goes on falling. When 100,000 units are produced, the average cost is US$10.10. When one million units are produced, the per unit cost drops to US$1.1.

Moreover, a substantial part of the fixed costs tend to be sunk costs that are not recoverable if production is halted. If you purchase a building to house your office, then you can sell it off to recover its costs if you decide to dismantle your organization. But if your film flops, the script will not have much of a resale market.

A further feature of information goods is important. The cost of producing an additional CD usually does not change with an increase in the number of CDs produced. There are no natural capacity constraints faced by producers of information goods. But think of airlines seating capacity. So long as some seats are vacant, it does not cost extra to carry additional passengers. But once all the seats are filled up, an aircraft simply cannot accommodate more passengers.

These features are not unique to information goods. It costs a lot to lay optical fibre, buy switches, and make a telecommunication system operational. But once the first signal has been sent, it costs next to nothing to send additional signals, at least not until capacity is reached.

What are the implications of the presence of substantial economies of scale in the digital market? For one thing, such markets cannot look like the textbook-perfect competitive markets. Perfectly competitive markets are characterized by many small sellers offering similar products, each lacking the ability to influence prices. The result is that price comes to be set at the level of marginal cost. But if marginal cost is very low, then marginal cost pricing will not let producers recoup their high fixed costs. So it is of the utmost importance for them to gain some market power, that is the ability to set their own prices.

One strategy left to a producer is to try to become a dominant firm in terms of volume over other firms in the industry. Thereby the firm gets so much of a cost advantage (with very low per unit costs generated from high volumes), that it gains immunity from all but very large competitors.

The success of this strategy sometimes depends on a firm being able to gain a first mover advantage in the market. A leadership position can be secured if the firm has an early presence in the market and an opportunity to build up its volumes before other firms enter the market. Otherwise, in trying to build up volumes, it might get involved in bruising (and sometimes disastrous) price wars with its rivals.

Another way firms can gain market power is by differentiating their products from each other, so that buyers will not readily switch from one product to another. For example, while some cable TV channels are of omnibus nature, and show a little bit of everything, many channels are beginning to focus on niche markets. Thus there can be channels showing only horror movies, or only action movies, or only old classics. It used to be thought that large volumes and product differentiation cannot go together. However, as the Saturn example in the section 'The New Economy and Change' shows, IT can enable producers to both realize the benefits of economies of scale and produce differentiated goods by catering to the idiosyncratic demands of customers.

Information as an Experience Good

An experience good is something that has to be used or experienced before its attributes are known. I can go to a store, take a shirt off the display rack, run my fingers over the material, try it out, and then purchase it. But I can only tell if I want to buy some information once I know what it is. For the seller this poses a problem. She has to let the customer experience her product—listen to a song, read an article—but then it is too late to charge the customer. How can one transact in goods that you have to give away in order to show people what they are?

This problem regarding information goods is overcome in a manner that is similar to the one used for ordinary goods:

Previewing and Browsing

Information producers typically offer opportunities for browsing their products. Many firms producing movies offer previews, the music industry offers radio broadcasts, and the publishing industry offers bookstores. Similarly, on the Net, it is possible to read selected portions of a book before buying the book itself.

Reviews

Another way to overcome the experience good problem is for some economic agents to specialize in reviewing products and providing these evaluations to other potential consumers. Critics review books, films, and music. On the Net, bookstores sometimes allow purchasers to post their own opinions and evaluations where other potential purchasers can easily access them.

Reputation

A third way that producers of information goods overcome the experience good problem is via reputation. Many newspaper houses go to great lengths to ensure that the reputation is carried over from the off-line version to the online version of their newspapers and magazines. So they invest heavily to establish and maintain their brand identity. Examples of investment in brand and reputation are the MGM Lion and the *Time* magazine logo.

Information as a Public Good

A pure public good displays two features. One is that of non-rivalry—one person's consumption does not diminish the amount available to other people. The other is that of non-excludability—one person cannot exclude another person from consuming the good in question. Classic examples of pure public goods are goods like national defence, radio broadcasts, and so on. More generally, a good is said to be a public good if it displays non-rivalry in consumption.

Information goods are inherently non-rival, due to the tiny cost of reproduction. But whether they are excludable or not depends on the legal regime. Most countries recognize intellectual property laws that allow information goods to be excludable. However, as the experience with the implementation of intellectual property rights demonstrates, it may be very expensive to ensure excludability.

Easy excludability allows suppliers of information goods to sell such goods in the market like other goods. Those who not are willing to pay the going price are excluded from the consumption of these goods. On the other hand, there is a tension between excluding customers totally and luring potential customers to purchase an experience good. *The Economist*, for example, allows free access to most, but not all, of the content on its website, *Economist.com*, even though it can potentially make the site available only to paying viewers. It then has to depend more on advertising to offset the loss from subscription. This model works because advertisers are more willing to advertise on sites with higher rate of 'hits' and, by allowing free access to most of the content, *The Economist* is ensuring more hits.

The question of exclusion is intimately tied up with the question of intellectual property rights (IPR).

Intellectual Property Rights and Other Ways of Dealing with Exclusion

Intellectual property rights are created to provide incentive for the production of information goods. I will write a book only if I am assured that the proceeds from the sale of the book benefits me at least to some extent and that pirated copies do not capture the market for my book. Thus IPR tries to secure a monopoly position for me for a limited time, so that the ensuing monopoly profits give me the incentive to engage in the production of information goods in the first place.

The key phrase in the above sentence is 'for a limited time'. Intellectual property rights create incentives by providing rights of excludability. But any monopoly, by restricting output and increasing price above the competitive level creates a so-called deadweight loss to society. The length of time for which IPR is given will depend on the trade-off between the need to provide incentive and the need to restrict deadweight losses.

Length is only one of the parameters of intellectual property protection. The others are 'height', in the sense of the standard required for novelty, and the 'breadth', in the sense of how broadly the IPRs are interpreted. Different forms of intellectual property have different combinations of these characteristics. For example, copyright protects the expression of ideas for quite long periods (up to 75 years), with a low standard for novelty, but a narrow scope.

Other than assigning of property rights, excludability can be ensured by bundling the content with a good that is excludable. Traditional media for transmitting information goods, such as books, records, video tapes, and CDs do not face this problem. Only one person can read a book at a given time. This does not work for purely digital information goods. The same content may be available on many PCs. But recent technologies like cryptographic envelopes play a similar role by bundling the information good with an 'excludable' authentication mechanism.

A third technique for dealing with the exclusion problem is using auditing or statistical tracking. ASCAP[5] and BMI[6] perform this task for the music industry while the Copyright Clearance Center deals with print media by auditing photocopying practices over a period of time and bases a yearly fee on this sample[7].

A fourth technique for dealing with exclusion is to embrace it, and bundle the information good with information that sellers want widely disseminated, such as advertising.

The development of exclusion measures cannot take care of the problem except temporarily, because users try to develop counter code breaking and hacking tools. 'This, in turn, will lead to sophistication of the exclusion tools and to a continuing technological race between the two sorts of devices' (Elkin-Koren and Salzberger 1999). The extent to which information goods are public goods will, therefore, depend on the technological state of the art and who manages to stay a step ahead—the provider or the hacker.

Moreover, creation of IPRs does not automatically solve the problem of enforcement. Illicit copying or piracy has still to be tackled. It seems evident that piracy is much more prevalent in lower-income countries, especially because of inadequate enforcement of IPRs. This is not surprising because such countries have little to lose if they pirate software and have neither the resources nor the inclination to invest in enforcement. However, as a country experiences growth more and more local content is produced and the country begins to feel the need for intellectual property protection. As enforcement of intellectual property laws increases, both domestic and foreign producers

[5] American Society of Composers, Authors and Publishers

[6] Broadcast Music Incorporated

[7] For a less than flattering look at the activities of ASCAP and BMI, see *www.woodpecker.com/writing/essays/royalty-politics.html*

benefit. Taiwan, for example, initially refused to sign the International Copyright Agreement. It became notorious for intellectual property violations. However, once the country became prosperous and developed a large publishing industry, it joined the international copyright agreement in order to assure a market for its own publishing and printing industry.

Box 3.2: Software Patents

There are several policy issues raised by software patents. First, until recently, even the US patent office has not had adequate expertise to evaluate the novelty of submitted patents. Consequently, there are ludicrous examples of the grant of patents. Second, there is the problem of 'submarine patents'—patents that are not publicly available due to the fact that they are under consideration by the Patent Office. In some cases, applicants have allegedly purposely delayed their applications in order to wait for the market to 'mature' so as to maximize the value of their patents, and to let them make improvements before others are apprised of their basic patent. These tactics can distort the returns to patent holders, frustrate the disclosure of patented inventions, which is a basic quid pro quo for patent protection under the patent system, and lead to unnecessary duplication of effort and lawsuits.

Many of these problems are especially severe for software patents. Innovations that are embodied in physical goods can be bought and sold for a listed price in the open market, so there is no uncertainty about the cost of incorporating a new innovation into a product. However, the market for software components is still primitive, so much software is created in-house. Thus, one software developer can easily infringe upon another developer's algorithm, and, after years, find itself in a very vulnerable position if the algorithm ends up being patented.

All these reasons suggest that patents on algorithms should be narrowly interpreted, and subject to high standards of novelty. Davis et al. (1994) also argue that software patents should have a shorter lifespan than other types of patents.

Source: Varian (1998)

Network Effects

In the New Economy, entry costs into an industry tend to be smaller than in the non-virtual world. Consider, for example, the publishing business. Producing books requires substantial investment in printing presses, purchasing paper, and paying distributors for shipping and handling. In cyberspace, anybody can upload a book and with a click of the mouse, distribute text to millions of Internet subscribers.

Moreover, in the real world, markets are sometimes too small to justify more than one producer. But business in information goods through the Internet faces no such limitations. The market operating through the Internet is a global market. It has no defined territorial unit and the use and movement of information goods has no territorial restrictions.

Does the above discussion lead to the conclusion that markets in the New Economy will be more competitive than markets in the old economy? Not necessarily, because the presence of network effects can have opposite effects on market structure. The New Economy is driven by the economies of networks and positive feedbacks. A network, whether in the real or the virtual world displays a fundamental characteristic—the value of the network to any user depends on the number of other people using the network.

Suppose that a new phone company comes into existence and requests you to be their first subscriber. Your immediate reaction would be to refuse them because, by joining this company, you cannot speak to others, which is what having a phone is all about. In general, if you had to choose between rival phone companies, you would always prefer to be connected to the one with a bigger network than a smaller one.

Why do agents want to be part of larger rather than smaller networks? One reason, other than the obvious one from the telecommunications industry given earlier, is that people often 'enjoy' consuming goods that are consumed by other people. When I hear that a lot of my friends have watched a certain movie, I want to watch the movie because I want to be part of the network of people who have seen the movie and can discuss it. But there is another important reason from the production side. An operating system in my computer gains in value as the number of software written for it increases. That is, consumers gain satisfaction from the variety of complementary products, called support services, that are available with a product. But providers of the complementary products will find it more profitable to produce complementary goods for the system with the larger number of users. A larger network will have more supporting services and, therefore, be more valuable to a new user.

By how much does the value of a network increase with an increase in its size? Metcalfe's Law, named after Bob Metcalfe, the inventor of ethernet, provides an answer. The law is more a rule of thumb than a law. Suppose that there are n people in a network and that the value of the network to each of them is proportional to the number of others. Then the total value of the network to all the users is proportional to $n \times (n - 1) = n^2 - n$. If the value of the network to a single user is Re 1 for every other user, then the network with 10 people has a total value of approximately Rs 100. If the size of the network is 100, then the total value is roughly Rs 10,000. A ten-fold increase in the size of the network leads to a hundred-fold increase in its value.

Box 3.3: Xbox and PlayStation 2

Sometime in 2001, Microsoft introduced Xbox, a video game console that is technologically sophisticated and, by many accounts, the best way to play games against competitors over the Internet. However, Xbox is unable to make headway against Sony's PlayStation 2. Microsoft has been able to sell only about nine million Xbox consoles and lost money on each unit it sold.

Part of Microsoft's problem is the ambitious design of Xbox. Its chipsets and other electronic components are more expensive than those of the PlayStation. Microsoft has also been unable to realize certain economies of scale because sales have not been as robust as expected. Microsoft declines to say how much it loses

Contd.

Box 3.3 Contd.

on each console, but industry analysts estimate the figure at close to US$100. Sony, by contrast, does not sell PlayStation 2's below cost.

Larger sales would help Microsoft realize these economies of scale. But sales are not taking off and avid game players like Brian Green, who spends hours each week on both consoles, have a simple explanation for why Microsoft has yet to make the inroads it sought. 'The Xbox is cool,' he says, 'but the PlayStation is where the games are at.'

This means that there are still not enough video games for Xbox to make it attractive over PlayStation 2. The issue is of no small significance. The market for consoles and video games is worth more than US$9 billion a year. Even while losing on selling consoles, Microsoft could still make a lot of money from game makers. They pay the console makers about US$10 for each copy of the games they manufacture—and they made well in excess of 50 million games in the USA last year. Games typically sell at retail for US$50.

Analysts said Microsoft must persuade video game makers to produce versions of their products for the Xbox. According to figures provided by Microsoft but compiled by NPD Funworld, an industry research group, there are 458 games available for the PlayStation 2, versus 207 for the Xbox and 168 for the Nintendo GameCube.

Source: *Richtel* (2003).

The size and value of the network, therefore, depends on interconnectivity. The Internet, for example, is a vast network that connects many smaller groups of linked computer networks, on and through which information is stored and transmitted. The 'interconnected' character of the Internet is one of the qualities that make it so popular and powerful in facilitating communication and e-commerce.

However, 'interconnectivity' has also given rise to increasing legal controversy and turmoil. Various methods of enhancing or exploiting the web-like structure of the Internet have been attacked as violations of others' intellectual property or other proprietary rights. Moreover, in the context of interconnectivity of communication networks like telephone systems, there is the important issue of revenue-sharing. A call originating in India is routed through to an address in the USA. Who gets to keep the revenue generated by the call—the Indian company, the local American company, or the firm which provides the facility for routing the call?

The presence of network effects has some important implications for business strategy:

Positive Feedback Effects and Market Dominance

Positive feedback effects can lead to a winner-take-all situation. With network effects, a product continues to increase in value with an increase in the number of users. As the network grows in size, it becomes even more attractive to a new user. Success feeds on itself. Beyond a certain stage, a network becomes so large that its advantages completely dwarf that of any other and it becomes the sole winner in the marketplace.

Nintendo is an example of a company that grew enormously by harnessing positive feedback. Nintendo entered the US market in 1985, a time when the market for home video games was considered to be saturated, with Atari, the dominant firm in the market showing little interest in rejuvenating the market. By December 1986, the Nintendo Entertainment System transformed the market. 'The very popularity of Nintendo fueled more demand and enticed more game developers to write games to the Nintendo system, making the system yet more attractive' (Shapiro and Varian 1999).

Tipping

After a certain stage, the market tips one way or the other and it is highly unlikely that more than one player can survive. That is, when successful, product penetration can be very fast. Once consumers expect a standard to 'win', fears about getting stuck with the wrong standard diminish, and there is a self-reinforcing rush to adopt new standard.

Box 3.4: VHS and Betamax

An example of tipping is the victory of the video home system (VHS) format over the Betamax format in the video recorder market. When video taping of television programmes went mainstream, these two competing standards were both released into the marketplace. They were incompatible with each other and the consumer was left to determine which standard would ultimately win. Those who guessed Betamax were severely punished when the cheaper VHS standard won the majority of buyers. Betamax purchasers were forced to relegate their machines to the junk pile and buy into the VHS standard. One possible explanation for the tipping that occurred is that Sony, the producer of Betamax, got one simple decision wrong. It chose to make smaller, neater tapes that lasted for an hour, whereas the VHS manufacturers used basically the same technology with a bulkier tape that lasted two hours. The Betamax tape was not long enough to record an entire movie. And although Betamax playing times were extended, they never caught up with VHS.

Source: *www.guardian.co.uk/online/comment/story/0,12449,881780,00.html*

Lock-ins and Switching Costs

An important element in reaping network economies is being able to hang on to customers who are already using a product. If users can freely switch from one product to another, then a firm may never be able to build up a sufficiently large base of customers. To ensure that customers cannot easily move from one product to another, producers try to create switching costs for their customers.

A switching cost is a one-time cost incurred when an agent switches from one product to another. This may be the cost incurred by a buyer when she switches from one supplier's product to another. Porter (1980) mentions the following as examples of switching costs:

- employee retraining costs,
- cost of new ancillary equipment,

- cost and time in testing or qualifying a new source,
- need for technical help as a result of reliance on seller engineering aid, product redesign, or even
- the psychic costs of severing a relationship.

It is obvious that a switching cost reduces the benefits from an alternative course of action and, thereby, can have a lock-in effect. In other words, if a switching cost is present, then an economic agent finds it more difficult to shift from one product to another or from one decision to another. An example of how switching cost is created is the use of frequent-flier programmes by airlines. If I have been flying by British Airways and have accumulated a lot of points in their frequent-flier programme, then I shall hesitate to switch to another airline and, thereby, forego my accumulated points.

Switching costs are the norm, not the exception, in the information economy. We can compare between cars and computers to illustrate this. If you have been driving a Maruti, there is no compelling reason for you to buy another Maruti if you decide to replace your car. The driving skills acquired on the Maruti and the technical knowledge gained can very easily be transferred to a Santro or an Indica. But somebody who has been using a Macintosh computer has also invested significantly in complementary assets like Mac software or Mac printer. The switch to a PC or Unix machine involves a substantial switching cost for this user, since she has to replace all the complementary assets too. Such switching costs will make it more difficult for the user to change to another technology. In other words, the user will face a lock-in effect.

Standardization versus Variety

Suppose that two networks have been established. If they can be linked up, then the size of both would increase and all the users will gain. On the other hand, if it is not possible to link them up, that is, they use different standards, then it seems that everybody is a loser. Establishing common standards and adhering to them requires a great deal of cooperation between firms. In the presence of network effects and positive feedbacks, cooperation emerges as a key element in a firm's strategy. However, such cooperation is tempered by competitive elements of the firm's strategy. Even though you tend to gain from standardization by getting access to a larger market, there always remains the threat that one of the rival firms will elbow out all others and gain control over the entire market. The term 'coopetition' captures the tension between cooperation and competition in network industries.

Having common standards allows for compatibility or interoperability. It is reassuring to know that 3 ½″ diskettes can be used on all PCs. For those who learnt how to work with Lotus spreadsheets, the value of Microsoft Excel is enhanced if it can handle Lotus files. Thus consumers generally welcome standards. They benefit from reduced uncertainty since they do not have to figure out which standard is going to be the winner in the long run. They can enjoy the greatest network externalities possible. They are also less likely to get locked into a single vendor. On the other hand, they pay a price in terms of reduced variety, and this price may be high if an inferior standard is established in the market.

Sellers of complementary products also welcome standards. So long as their products comply with the standards they benefit from expanded markets. Companies developing new technology also collectively welcome new standard, because these lead to an expansion in the sizes of the markets and may even be needed for creating the markets in the first place. Conversely, incumbent firms with older technology fear the establishment of new technologies with new standards. If the new standards increase the network effects and create positive feedbacks, then the older technologies can soon face extinction.

Establishing common standards has two other important implications. First, the focus shifts from competing for the market to competing within the market. That is, instead of 'standards wars' or the struggle to establish dominance for one's own standard, companies turn their attention to gaining larger market shares. Second, standards tend to commoditize products and leave less scope for product differentiation. Inevitably then competition becomes based on costs and pricing. The leeway left to producers to differentiate their products, of course, depends on how specific the standard is.

Box 3.5: The QWERTY Story: Efficiency or Lock-in to an Inferior Product?

Once a product is established in the market, demand for similar products might collapse in the presence of strong network effects. Consumers can get locked in to an inferior product. Is the adoption of the QWERTY keyboard an example of such a lock-in to an inferior product? Opinions on this sharply differ.

The QWERTY keyboard refers to the first five letters on the top left-hand corner of the keyboard. Christopher Latham Sholes patented his typewriter in 1868. Sholes and his collaborators then worked on improving the typewriter. Jamming was one of the major problems and it was addressed by the arrangement of the keyboard. When certain combinations of keys were struck quickly, the type bars often jammed. To avoid this, the QWERTY layout put the keys most likely to be hit in rapid succession on opposite sides. This made the keyboard slow, the story goes, but that was the idea.

A different layout, which had been patented by August Dvorak in 1936, was shown to be much faster. The Dvorak Simplified Keyboard (DSK) is alleged to have been easier to learn and to allow typing at rates that were 20, 40, or perhaps even 80 per cent faster (depending on the source) than QWERTY typing. Yet the Dvorak layout has never been widely adopted, even though (with electric typewriters and then PCs) the anti-jamming rationale for QWERTY has been defunct for years.

The QWERTY story appears to be the perfect illustration of path-dependent market failure. An early start for the QWERTY arrangement led to its adoption as the standard and superior rivals have been unable to dislodge this entrenched incumbent.

But 'The Fable of the Keys', a paper by Stan Liebowitz and Stephen Margolis, argues that the QWERTY story was wrong because the standard layout is not, in

Contd.

Box 3.5 Contd.

fact, demonstrably worse than the alternatives. Lock-in is inefficient (that is, it is a kind of market failure) only if the inferior product survives despite the fact that the benefits of switching would exceed the costs. If the inferior product survives because the costs of switching are high, that is as it should be. In that case it would be inefficient to switch.

Moreover, where lock-in is a factor, on both sides of the transaction, there is an incentive to find ways round the problem:

- On the demand side,
  - › groups of consumers can get together and coordinate their choices.
- On the supply side,
  - › producers can start by selling their superior new product at a loss. If it really is superior, the market will adopt it and move across;
  - › they can spend heavily on advertising; or
  - › they can help newcomers to switch by promising compatibility, as when cable-TV companies offer to convert old TV sets to the new system.

Source: 'The Qwerty Myth', *The Economist*, 3 April 2000.

Public Policy in the New Economy

Traditionally, economists have called for government action to correct for market failures. The term 'market failure' refers to things like (a) significant departures from competitive market structures; (b) presence of public goods, externalities, and network effects; and (c) imperfect and asymmetric information. We have already discussed some of these possibilities in the context of the New Economy.

Market Structures

In the New Economy, we expect competition to be more intense because low entry and transaction costs will tend to attract more entrants, many of which will be small start-ups. At the same time, the presence of network effects might mean that the most fleet-footed and innovative of these small enterprises would quickly develop into larger firms and dominate the industry. It has, therefore, been suggested that competition in the New Economy will resemble not the standard model of perfect competition but the Schumpeterian model. Members of the Austrian school (von Mises, Schumpeter, and Demsetz, to name a few), argue that economists in the mainstream tradition misuse the term 'competition' by applying it to a state of affairs rather than a process. In other words, firms are engaged in a continuing dynamic competitive process, '...constantly creating new products and processes in order to gain a competitive advantage over their rivals' (Audretsch, Baumol, and Burke 2001). Firms may temporarily gain monopoly power that allows them to earn monopoly profits. But this can only happen till rivals replicate their innovation or replace it with one that is superior. In industries where entry and exit is easy, firms will continue to enter till an additional firm can expect to earn only normal profit.

The Austrian school would argue that governments should not intervene to reduce the profits of firms, for (a) such profits are temporary prizes for winners in the competitive environment and (b) reducing the profits will reduce the incentive for existing firms and prospective entrants to engage in competitive innovation. The Austrian approach has, therefore, drawn attention to the need to reward with monopoly profits the product and process innovators who incur costs and take risks. However, once a firm attains a dominant status, it can try to exploit various types of entry barriers to maintain its dominant status and ward off attacks from new, smaller firms that come up with new and innovative improvements over an existing product or process. It is, therefore, not clear whether the Schumpeterian process will be sufficient to prevent the creation of long-term monopolies[8].

Privacy

Consumers are increasingly concerned about the confidentiality of personal information provided to web merchants and other parties, particularly in the context of business-to-consumer (B2C) e-commerce. This mistrust constitutes a significant barrier to the development of Internet commerce. Concerns relate to the misuse of private information provided over the Internet, for example, credit card fraud. Concerns also relate to invasion of privacy. Every website one visits will be trying to plant 'cookies'—small text files that collect information about the browsing habits of the user. If you change the default setting for cookies in your web browser from 'accept' to 'prompt', and then start surfing the web, then you will soon be overwhelmed with notices of cookies trying to plant themselves on your computer.

The monitoring of habits is not confined online. Off-line, too, the use of credit and debit cards or use of phones leaves a trail of electronic data. As monitoring of telephone calls, email, and computer use becomes easier, organizations of different types (governments, companies, non-government organizations (NGOs) are collecting these data and using them to further their own goals. As *The Economist* puts it, '...a society capable of constant and pervasive surveillance is being rapidly built around us, sometimes with our cooperation, more often without our knowledge'.

In the debate over privacy, there are those who take the view that privacy is akin to a human right, while others argue that privacy is an artifact of modern western culture and more primitive societies exhibit very low levels of privacy. Corresponding to these views, there are three approaches to privacy. One is the market-based approach, which says that the market will deliver the right amount of privacy. A company that does not provide the amount of privacy desired by consumers will suffer lost business. A second approach is to rely on industry self-regulation, whereby industry formulates and implements a voluntary code of conduct. The third approach is based on government enforcement of rules defined by law. Most countries have based

[8] For an example of the regulatory dilemmas in the New Economy, you can read an account of the U.S. vs. Microsoft case in Gilbert and Katz (2001).

their privacy and data protection laws on the 1980 OECD Guidelines on the Protection of Privacy and Transborder Flows of Personal Data.

Box 3.6: Privacy in the New Economy

The effects of loss of privacy had been grimly painted by George Orwell in his book, *1984*. In Orwell's London of 1984, two-way televisions are installed in every home and only the most privileged can turn them off. They provide live sound and video feed to the authorities, detecting everything above a very low whisper. 'You had to live—did live, from habit that became instinct—in the assumption that every sound you made was overheard, and except in darkness, every movement scrutinised.'

With the new tools for monitoring behaviour available cheaply and easily, particularly in the advanced economies, both the corporate sector and the government are slowly but surely intruding in every aspect of an individual's life.

The United Kingdom (UK), for example, is thought to be one of the countries with the greatest degree of surveillance in the world. Hundreds of thousands of cameras have been installed both indoors and outdoors. The Environment Agency has even installed disguised cameras (hidden in drinks cans) in rural beauty spots. There are also Home Office proposals to legalize the government's access to more information. Under such proposals, state investigators working on a crime can get permission to get 'communications data', such as the number of times one is online, whom one emails, who emails back, etc.. Similar information can be collected on telephone calls. The widespread use of mobile phones now allows the tracking of the user of a switched-on phone to within a few 100 feet in urban areas. Moreover, automatic number plate recognition (ANPR) cameras are used by several police forces to identify a vehicle's owner.

Source: *Hindustan Times*, 24 June 2003.

Reliability of Information

By making it easy to create and distribute information, the New Economy creates enormous amounts of information. But it imposes a cost on users in terms of the reliability of information. As we have mentioned earlier, the relatively low cost of on line publishing allows literally every user to become an information provider. Everyone can post information and make it accessible to millions of users around the world.

But decentralized sources of information create, in turn, a problem of ascertaining the reliability of such information. The distribution of information in the physical world includes clues that indicate reliability. If one reads an article published by *The Telegraph*, one can assume that writers took standard steps to certify the reported facts. If one reads news in a tabloid, one is less likely to assume that an event really happened.

How can you know whether things you read on the Internet are reliable? To some extent one may use information from the non-virtual world. Thus, if one reads an article on the site of a trusted newspaper, one may rely on it, but not if one takes the article from an unknown source. Identification of the source in the real world is performed by physical assets, geographical locations, identifying actual people and names which are protected by trademarks. Authentication in cyberspace cannot rely on such agencies. It is technically easy to disguise the source to an extent that makes it unidentifiable or misleading. Moreover, information presented digitally is very easy to change. While printed information is fixed, digitalized information may be easily manipulated.

So how should the government address the question of reliability of information? It seems safe to predict that government intervention should assume a different nature in correcting market failures. For instance, rather than impose disclosure duties, it may be necessary to standardize authentication means on the Internet, to facilitate name registries, to document identification means, etc..

Global Aspects of Regulation

The world is organized into separate jurisdictions of nation-states. The digital revolution, by its very nature, is global. It straddles different jurisdictions. It allows business to move at a low cost from an uncongenial jurisdiction to a more congenial jurisdiction. This might lead countries to compete with one another to reduce their regulatory oversight to attract business. Moreover, there might be jurisdictional conflicts. When a country finds that its laws are being violated on the cyberspace, it might be helpless to do anything about it because the source of offence is working from another country. A lot of international cooperation and harmonization of rules will have to take place before these problems are overcome.

Conclusion

The New Economy is fast changing the rules of the game—for consumers, businesses, and governments. The traditional ways of determining purchasing decisions, doing business, or formulating regulation in all probability will no longer work. Understanding the way the New Economy functions is a prerequisite for survival in the New Economy and in this chapter we have sought to provide a roadmap for anyone trying to figure out how to get around in the changed times.

References

Audretsch, D.B., W.J. Baumol, and A.E. Burke (2001) 'Competition Policy in Dynamic Markets', *International Journal of Industrial Organization*.

DeLong, J. Bradford and Laurence H. Summers (2001) 'The 'New Economy': Background, Historical Perspective, Questions and Speculations', *Federal Reserve Bank of Kansas City Economic Review*, fourth quarter.

DeLong, J. Bradford and A. Michael Froomkin (2000) 'Speculative Microeconomics for Tomorrow's Economy', in Brian Kahin and Hal Varian (eds), *Internet Publishing and Beyond: The Economics of Digital Information and Intellectual Property*, MIT Press, Cambridge; pp. 6–44.

Elkin-Koren, Niva and Eli M. Salzberger (1999) 'Law and Economics in Cyberspace', *International Review of Law and Economics*, 19, pp. 553–81.

Fraumeni, Barbara and Steven Landefeld (2000) 'Measuring the New Economy', May, *www.bea.doc.gov/bea/papers/newec.pdf.*

Gilbert, Richard J. and Michael L. Katz (2001), 'An Economist's Guide to U.S. v. Microsoft', *Journal of Economic Perspectives*, 15(2), pp. 25–44.

Hammer, Michael and James Champy (1993) *Reengineering the corporation: A Manifesto for Business Revolution*, Nicholas Brealey Publication, London.

Lee, Boon-Chye (2002) 'Regulation in the New Economy', University of Wollongong, Department of Economics Working Paper Series, WP, pp. 02–18.

Lucking-Reily, David and D. Spulber (2001) 'Business-to-Business Electronic Commerce' *Journal of Economic Perspectives*, 15.

Mathieson, S.A. (2003) 'Keeping 1984 in the Past', *The Guardian*, reproduced in the *Hindustan Times*, 24 June.

Porter, M.E. (1980) *Competitive Strategy*, The Free Press, New York.

Richtel, Matt (2003) 'Who's Blocking the Xbox? Sony and Its Games', *New York Times*, 16 February.

Shapiro, C. and Hal R. Varian (1999) *Information Rules*, Harvard Business School Press, Boston, Mass.

The Economist (2000), 'The New Economy', 23 September.

— (2003) 'Digital Dilemmas', 23 January.

Varian, Hal R. (1998) 'Markets for Information Goods', mimeo.

4

Sustainable Competitive Advantage

D.N. Sengupta

SUSTAINABLE COMPETITIVE ADVANTAGE

Sustainable competitive advantage may be defined as an advantage a firm has over its competitors that enables it to earn a positive economic profit over a long period of time. The economic profit of a firm is its residual revenue after paying for the cost of the material and other inputs, labour, and capital that it uses to generate the revenue. This is different from accounting profit, which is the residual revenue after paying for the cost of inputs, labour, and debt capital only. It therefore includes not only economic profit but also the opportunity cost of risk capital, that is, the return that shareholders would have earned if they had invested their money in an alternative venture with comparable risks. Clearly, it is possible for a firm to earn a positive accounting profit, but a negative economic profit.

Link between Competitive Advantage and Economic Profit

What is the link between competitive advantage and economic profit? To understand this, we have to first understand the concepts of value created, value added, and value appropriated by a firm. This is best done with the help of a numerical example.

Take the case of a firm that buys raw potatoes, edible oil, salt, additives, preservatives, packaging materials, energy, and other inputs, and uses capital and labour to convert these inputs into packaged potato chips. Let us assume that the firm's cost of inputs is Rs 40 per kilogram (kg) of chips. But it is able to sell the chips in the market at Rs 150 per kg, because consumers value the output more than the inputs that go into it. In other words, by transforming the raw potatoes and other inputs into packaged potato chips and marketing the chips to the consumers, the firm creates value.

The market price reflects the value of one unit of output as perceived by the marginal consumer, that is, the consumer who would not buy the chips if they were priced higher than Rs 150 per kg. Other consumers who buy the chips, however, would do so even if the chips were priced higher. Therefore, in their perception, the value of 1 kg of chips is more than Rs 150. The value of the chips, as perceived by the average consumer, is the average of the maximum prices that all consumers would be willing to pay for them. The value created by a firm is the difference between the price that the average consumer would be willing to pay for the output and the cost of inputs. Let us assume that the price that the average consumer would be willing to pay for the chips is Rs 200 per kg. The value created by the potato chip producing firm is, therefore, is Rs 160 per kg. The difference between the price that the average consumer would be willing to pay and the price she actually pays, which in this instance is Rs 50 per kg, accrues to her as a consumer's surplus. The remaining Rs 110, which is the difference between the price actually paid by the consumer and the cost of inputs, is the value added by the firm. The firm pays out a part of this to the providers of labour, debt capital, and risk capital as wages, interest, and the opportunity cost of risk capital respectively. Let us assume that these figures are Rs 50, Rs 10, and Rs 15 respectively. This leaves a residue of Rs 35, which is the value appropriated by the firm as its economic profit. We may note in passing that the firm's accounting profit, which is its revenue minus the cost of inputs, labour, and debt capital is Rs 50. As noted earlier, it includes not only the economic profit of the firm but also the opportunity cost of its risk capital.

Thus, the value created by a firm is shared by the consumer as a consumer's surplus, the provider of labour as wages, the provider of debt capital as interest, the provider of risk capital as the opportunity cost of risk capital, and the firm as an economic profit. If no firm had any advantage over other firms, all of them would compete for consumers, labour, and capital on exactly the same terms. As a result, they would depress selling prices and push up wage and interest rates and the cost of risk capital, until the entire value created by them accrued to consumers, labour, and capital, and the firms were left with no economic profit. In reality, however, some firms do earn an economic profit because they have some advantages that enable them to create more value with the same input of bought out resources than their competitors. And they are able to maintain this profit because they can sustain their advantages over a period of time. In this chapter, we explain what these advantages are, how they arise, and how they are sustained and exploited.

External and Internal Advantages

The competitive advantage of a firm may be external or internal to the firm. The external advantages enjoyed by a firm are not created by the firm, but acquired by it by virtue of being in the market already. The firm is able to sustain these advantages because, although other firms could replicate these advantages, they are prevented from doing so by economic or legal considerations. On the other hand, the internal advantages of a firm are those created by the firm itself. These advantages are sustained by the fact that they are unique to the firm and cannot be replicated by other firms.

This brings us to the concept of added value. The added value created by a firm is the value that would not be created at all if that particular firm had not existed. Clearly, when a firm earns an economic profit by exploiting an external advantage, its added value is zero because, even if that firm had not existed, some other firm would have acquired and exploited the same advantage, created the same value, and earned the same profit. But when a firm exploits its internal advantages to create more value than its competitors and earn an economic profit, it creates a positive added value because, if that firm had not existed, no other firm would have been able to replicate its internal advantages and create the same value.

External Advantages

External advantages enjoyed by a firm can be many. We discuss below three main categories, namely, strategic assets, economies of scale, and network externalities.

Strategic assets are bought out resources that enable a firm to create more value than its competitors. Examples are valuable patents or trademarks bought or leased from an MNC, a bauxite mine that yields more bauxite than other mines, a shop site so located that it attracts more customers than other sites, or a licence to offer telecom services in a lucrative market. A firm that has an exclusive right to use such superior resources does create more value than other similar firms, but the latter create less value only because they are legally prevented from using these resources.

Economies of scale arise when the fixed costs of production are high in relation to variable costs. As output increases, the fixed costs are spread over an expanding output and the cost per unit of output falls. When the market is limited and firms already in the market have a large share of the market, they can create more value by producing more economically than new firms that want to enter. The former have large production volumes and, therefore, low unit costs, while the latter have high unit costs because their production volumes are low initially. Here again, the existing firms are at an advantage not because new firms cannot acquire the facilities or resources required, but because they cannot build a large enough volume of production.

Network externalities arise when a firm builds a network of buyers or suppliers over time and the benefits that the buyers or suppliers derive by remaining in the network increase, as the size of the network increases. This enables a firm that has a large network of buyers or customers to create more value for its buyers and suppliers than a firm with a smaller network. Such a firm is often able to appropriate a part of this extra value by charging a higher price for its products or paying a lower price for its inputs. Maruti Udyog has, for example, built a large network of customers and suppliers over time. The existence of a large number of Maruti customers and suppliers leads to external economies of scale and allows the customers to get their cars repaired and serviced and the suppliers to access the required skills and inputs cost effectively. This puts Maruti at an advantage over car manufacturers who do not have a large network of customers and suppliers. But this advantage is external to Maruti, because other firms would also have the same advantage if they could establish an equally large network of customers and suppliers.

How Does a Firm Acquire and Exploit External Advantages?

A firm acquires its external advantages by occupying a market and securing the use of strategic assets or building a large volume of production or establishing a large network of customers and suppliers ahead of its competitors. It could do so in a number of ways. It could become the first mover in a new market. Alternatively, it could become a predator, that is, instead of moving in first, it could acquire the external advantages enjoyed by an existing firm by taking it over or driving it out of the market. It could also become a strategic ally of an existing firm that enjoys these advantages. In some situations, it could also be a privileged licensee, who has been allowed by the licensing authorities to enter a market reserved for special categories of firms (for example, indigenous or public sector undertakings).

A firm that acquires these advantages earns an economic profit by charging a price that includes a monopoly rent, or a margin that can be extracted by restricting supply and forcing the consumer to pay a high price. This profit can, however, be sustained only if new firms do not enter the market and bid the price down. To prevent new entry, therefore, the incumbent firm, or the firm that is in the market already, erects entry barriers, or impediments, that make new entry unprofitable.

Limit Pricing

One way of erecting an entry barrier is to charge a limit price, or a price that is unprofitable for the new entrant, but profitable for the incumbent firm. Assume, for example, that because of the external advantages it enjoys, the incumbent firm's cost of production is Rs 100 per unit of output, while that for a new entrant is Rs 110. If the incumbent firm charges a price of Rs 109, it can make an economic profit of Rs 9 per unit. But the new entrant makes a loss at that price and does not enter.

The limit pricing approach requires the incumbent to produce an output that is large enough to maintain the market price at the level of the limit price. In effect, the incumbent pre-empts the market by keeping his own output high and the residual demand available for the new entrant low, so that the latter cannot match the ability of the former to bid for strategic assets or exploit economies of scale or take advantage of network externalities. This, however, has two problems. First, if the incumbency advantages are not very large, the limit price may not allow the incumbent to maximize his profits. To maintain the market price at the level of the limit price, the incumbent may have to keep his price so low and his supply so high that he may have to take up some unprofitable business. Second, even a low price may not deter the new entrant. He may take the view that once he enters the market, the incumbent will be forced to curtail his output and the market price will rise to a level where he can make a profit.

Strategic Entry Barrier

The incumbent can, however, avoid these problems by erecting a strategic entry barrier. He maintains his price and output at profit-maximizing levels, but deters new entry by threatening to expand his output and bring down the market price to the level of the limit price, should a new firm enter the market.

However, this threat will work, only if the potential entrant finds it credible. To make his threat credible, therefore, the incumbent makes some market-specific investments up-front. These investments are in the nature of a sunk cost because they become valueless if the incumbent leaves the market. They, therefore, represent a commitment on the incumbent's part to stay in the market. These investments are made to corner the external advantages that a firm may be able to gain by virtue of its presence in the market. If, for example, the economies of scale are significant, the incumbent would invest in building a large production capacity. If consumers have varying requirements or if they are spatially dispersed, he would invest in establishing a large number of products, brands, or supply points. If network externalities or strategic assets are important, he would enter into contractual obligations with a large number of customers, suppliers or strategic asset owners. Having made these investments, the incumbent sets his price and output at profit-maximizing levels and keeps his investments under-utilized.

The situation changes, however, if another firm enters the market because, in that event, the incumbent has to share the market with another firm and his profit falls. He could respond to this situation in one of two ways. He could reduce his output and make room for the new entrant. In that case, the market price would not fall, but his up-front investments would become further under-utilized and his unit cost of production would rise. Alternatively, he could maintain or expand his output. In that case, his unit cost would not rise, but the market price would fall. The incumbent deters new entry by limiting the options available to him. He so chooses the level of his up-front investments that he minimizes his loss by staying in the market and expanding his output, until the market price falls to the level of the limit price. This, as we know, is the price at which its entry becomes unprofitable for a new firm. If the incumbent's external advantages are large, he may still be able to make a profit at this price. If they are not, he may make a loss himself. But even if he makes a loss, he stays in the market because, if he leaves, his up-front investments become valueless and the loss on that account is such that it is higher than the loss he makes by staying in the market. Faced with this prospect, the potential entrant does not enter the market, allowing the incumbent to maintain his output and price at profit-maximizing levels.

In principle, this strategy is not dissimilar to the limit pricing strategy. But there are two important differences. The incumbent pre-empts the market not by keeping his actual output high, but by making up-front the investments required to corner the external advantages. And he deters new entry not by keeping his actual price low, but by threatening to bring down the price. His threat becomes credible because he makes a commitment in the form of market-specific investments. The price he pays to deter new entry is that he has to keep some of these investments idle.

Internal Advantages

Although many firms do indeed make a handsome profit by exploiting their external advantages, research shows that internal competitive advantages, or the advantages created by a firm itself, are a more important source of profit. To understand what these are and how they lead to profits, we first need to understand the economic role of a firm.

What is a Firm?

If I want to build a house, I could hire an architect, a civil engineer, and a few masons, carpenters, electricians, plumbers, and painters and ask them to build the house by interacting with one another. Alternatively, I could give the entire job to a firm of building contractors. In the former case, I build the house by transacting with the experts and artisans through the market. I go to the market, hire the experts and artisans, and leave them to work on their own. If I find that some of them are not performing satisfactorily, I discipline them by threatening to terminate their contracts or by withholding payments. In the latter case, I build the house by routing all the transactions through a firm. I transact with the firm and the firm transacts with the experts and artisans. Thus, a firm is an institution that organizes production by internalizing the transactions required to produce an output.

Why Do We Need a Firm?

I shall use a firm only if it meets my requirements more efficiently than the market. If I need to get a leaky tap fixed, I shall probably choose to call a plumber directly because, by going through a firm of building contractors, I will have to contribute towards its overheads and may end up by paying much more. But when I want to build a house I am likely to entrust the job to a firm. The reason for this is that when production requires the cooperative effort of a number of owners of productive resources, three types of problems arise and the firm can often deal with them more efficiently than the market.

The first is the problem of mobilizing, coordinating, and motivating resources. By using a firm, I can avoid the hassles of finding suitable experts and artisans, negotiating terms with each of them individually, monitoring their activities, resolving conflicts among them, measuring their work and paying accordingly. The firm deals with these problems by establishing an architecture that brings multiple owners of productive resources into long-term relationships with one another.

The second problem is one of information asymmetry. The experts and artisans I hire know what kind of work they are capable of. But as I do not build a house every day, I am unlikely to have used them before and do not know what kind of work they will deliver in the end. This is not a major problem when I call a plumber to fix a tap because even if he does a bad job the cost of this from my point of view may not be very high. But the problem becomes quite acute when I have to hire a large number of people because it may not be possible for me to check their credentials individually and, if they fail to perform, the resultant loss for me can be very high. Rather than risking these losses, I may even decide not to build a new house at all, and buy or rent an existing house instead. However, if I can find a reputed firm of building contractors to do the job for me I may build a new house, because, although this way I may pay a little more, I have some assurance of the kind of work I can expect from them. In other words, the firm solves the problem of information asymmetry by building a reputation that bridges the information gap between the firm and those who have not dealt with it before, and makes possible transactions that may not have taken place otherwise.

Finally, there is the problem of know-how. Even if the experts and artisans I hire are very good at their own work, none of them can be expected to have complete knowledge of how to build a house. By appointing a firm of building contractors, I can take advantage of its collective knowledge of how a house should be built.

The Proprietary Assets of a Firm: How Do They Create Value?

We may now draw the following general conclusion. When two or more owners of productive resources have to work together to produce an output, the firm often becomes a more efficient alternative to the market because the architecture, reputation, and knowledge—or the so-called proprietary assets—of a firm enable it to utilize these resources more efficiently, and create more value, than the market. These assets are intangible, created by the firm itself, unique in the sense that they are different from similar assets of other firms, and available for the exclusive use of the firm.

The architecture of a firm creates value by reducing transaction costs, or the production losses that arise because of the failure of the owners of productive resources to cooperate effectively. These losses arise because some of them may hide behind team performance to shirk responsibility, or fight with one another for a higher share of the pie, or fail to communicate with one another and work at cross purposes. The firm's architecture minimizes these problems by creating an organization structure that lays down job responsibilities, authority relationships, and communication channels; a performance evaluation system that evaluates individual and team performance; and a compensation system that relates compensation to performance.

While a firm's architecture creates value by reducing transaction costs, its reputation creates value by making possible transactions that would not have taken place otherwise. Many transactions do not take place because of an information asymmetry between buyers and sellers. The seller knows what he will supply. But the buyer does not know what he will get and does not buy for fear of being cheated. The firm breaks this impasse by charging a quality assuring price that builds in a premium for quality and by incurring a cost to build a reputation. The firm builds a reputation by making a promise to its customers through advertising and other means, and living up to its promise consistently. The cost of doing this is a sunk cost because, if the firm fails to live up to its reputation, it loses its reputation and cannot recover the cost it has incurred to build that reputation.

Once these arrangements are in place, the firm does not cheat because, if it cheats, it can no longer get a premium for quality and the loss on that account is more than the one-time profit it can make by cheating. The buyer will buy, in spite of having to pay a premium, because she is now assured of quality. She knows that if the firm cheats it will lose the investment it has made for building a reputation. Not so long ago, there was no market for high quality *atta* (whole wheat flour) in India, because atta was produced only by a large number of faceless producers who could not command a premium for quality. Hindustan Levers and a couple of other reputed firms created a market for high quality atta in India by branding and packaging their atta and charging a premium for quality.

While the architecture and reputation of a firm create value by facilitating transactions, its knowledge creates value by increasing the productive capacity of bought-out resources. This is best explained by using the concept of production function. The production function is a technical relationship that tells us the maximum output that can be produced with each and every set of inputs, given a certain state of knowledge. If the state of knowledge improves, the maximum output that can be produced with the same set of inputs increases, and we move to a higher production function. Assume that 10 software engineers agree among themselves to work together. By working full steam for 100 hours together, they can produce 100 software programmes of a particular type. The knowledge that they have at their command is the total of the knowledge each has individually. Now assume that the same 10 engineers work together as employees of a software firm and produce the same type of software programmes. The firm has worked on similar programmes before and has documented the knowledge it has acquired thereby in the form of an instruction manual. If the engineers work together as employees of the firm their state of knowledge improves because they can now use not only their own knowledge but also the instruction manual that enables them to avoid pitfalls and take shortcuts. Consequently, by working together for 100 hours they can now produce more, say 125 programmes. The extra 25 programmes that they can now produce is the surplus generated by the firm's knowledge.

The defining characteristic of knowledge is that it resides in the minds of individuals. But the collective knowledge of a firm is greater than the sum of the knowledge of individuals that make up the firm. There are two reasons for this. First, the firm creates for itself an organization capital, or knowledge about the capabilities of specific individuals and how well they complement one another. This enables it to put the right person on each job and create cohesive teams. Second, the firm also creates new knowledge by managing knowledge, or managing the process of acquisition, preservation, and propagation of knowledge in a planned and systematic manner.

Asset Superiority and Competitive Advantage

Since the proprietary assets of each firm are unique, their capacity to create value varies from one firm to another. This means that the assets of some firms are superior, in the sense that they enable these firms to create more value with the same input of bought-out resources than the marginal firm, or a firm that just breaks even. If the input markets are competitive, all firms pay the same price for their bought-out resources. Therefore, a firm that has superior assets and creates more value than the marginal firm with the same input of bought-out resources, makes an economic profit. Such a firm makes a profit because it has some internal advantages over its competitors.

However, not all assets of a profit-making firm are equally superior. The superiority of Reliance Industries Limited (RIL) or the Aditya Birla group, for example, lies not so much in their ability to create new knowledge as in their capacity to build an architecture that can exploit the knowledge created by others. On the other hand, the superiority of Infosys, Wipro Technologies, Dr Reddy's Laboratories, or Ranbaxy Laboratories lies primarily in their ability to create knowledge through adaptive R&D, although, to be able to exploit this knowledge, they also have to develop an appropriate architecture and reputation. The most important asset of successful fast moving consumer goods (FMCG) firms like Nestles, Proctor & Gamble, or Britannia Industries is the brand image or the reputation of their products, although, to create, sustain, and exploit this reputation, they also have to develop a good knowledge base and a strong architecture.

Depending on the strength of its assets, a firm may enjoy a cost advantage or a differentiation advantage. The former arises when the firm is enabled by its assets to produce the same product at a lower cost than its competitors. The latter arises when these assets enable the firm to sell something different, something that buyers value more and are prepared to pay a premium for. The difference between cost and differentiation advantages can be illustrated by the competitive advantages of the two major players in the Indian ice cream market—Hindustan Lever Limited (HLL) and Gujarat Milk Marketing Federation. The latter has a cost advantage because its architecture brings together milk producers, processors, distributors, and retailers into an effective partnership with one another. It, therefore, sells a standard range of ice creams under its umbrella brand name—Amul—at very competitive prices. HLL, on the other hand, has a differentiation advantage because it has two very strong brand names—Kwality and Walls—and a range of internationally developed and tested recipes to cater to a variety of tastes and flavours. It, therefore, sells a wide range of premium products at much higher prices.

Asset Scarcity and Quasi-rent

By definition, proprietary assets are scarce, in the sense that they are available only to their owners and their services are available in the market only to the extent their owners choose to supply them. By restricting the supply of the services of its superior assets, a firm can avoid paying out as lower product prices and higher factor prices some of the extra value created by its assets by virtue of their superiority. The value so retained is a rent that accrues to the proprietary assets of the firm and can be shared by the firm and its proprietary assets. Thus, even under conditions of free entry, by making its superior assets scarce, the firm is able to generate a surplus after paying for its bought out resources at their market price.

The rent that accrues to the superior proprietary assets of a firm is in the nature of a scarcity rent, similar to the rent that accrues to a superior piece of land. However, there is an important difference. Land is scarce because its supply is fixed by nature. Proprietary assets are scarce because their supply is quasi-fixed, or fixed only to the extent their owners choose not to supply them. Therefore, the rent that accrues to the proprietary assets of a firm is called a quasi-rent, to distinguish it from the pure rent that accrues to land and other resources the supply of which is fixed naturally.

Imperfect Imitability of Assets and Sustainability of Rent

The rent earned by the proprietary assets of a firm is not sustainable if other firms notice the rent-yielding capacity of these assets and can replicate them. If, for example, a firm earns a profit by using a new process that reduces costs, it cannot sustain this profit if other firms are also able to reduce their costs by copying the new process. The reason for this is that imitability increases the supply of superior assets and erodes their scarcity value.

Firms are able to sustain the rent earned by their superior assets because they are protected by isolating mechanisms, or barriers to imitation. In principle, isolating mechanisms are no different from entry barriers, except that while isolating mechanisms are internal to the firm and protect individual firms, entry barriers are external to the firm and protect all firms in an industry. We consider below three types of isolating mechanisms—causal ambiguity, the asset accumulation process, and social complexity.

Causal ambiguity arises when a profitable firm has several rent-yielding assets and it is difficult to identify the exact contribution made by each asset to the overall profitability of the firm. This discourages other firms from imitating these assets because imitation involves a sunk cost and the pay-off is uncertain. For example, the profitability of HLL is the result of a number of factors like its distribution network, the quality of its marketing staff, the strength of its brand names, its technological and managerial strengths, and a whole host of other assets. One reason why other firms do not try to replicate these assets is that they do not know for sure which of these are most worth replicating.

The process of asset accumulation is difficult to repeat and cannot be imitated because some assets, like a firm's knowledge base or reputation for quality, have to be accumulated incrementally over time. These difficulties are three-fold. First, there are time compression diseconomies. It may be expensive or infeasible to crash the accumulation process. For example, in the automobile market where only a limited number of customers buy a new car every year, a new firm may not be able to match the customer base of an established firm by crashing its marketing programme. Second, there is a problem of asset mass efficiency. A firm that has a large stock of a particular asset may be able to add to it more cost effectively than another firm which has only a small stock of that asset. To go back to our earlier example, an automobile manufacturer who has accumulated a large customer base already may be able to expand it in a more cost effective manner than a new producer who has to promote his product more vigorously. Finally, the imitability of a particular asset may also be limited by the interconnectedness of asset stocks: it may not be possible to accumulate one asset without accumulating another. It may not, for example, be possible to build a large base of customers without building a wide service network. Consequently, a would-be imitator who does not have a large service network cannot replicate the large customer base of another firm.

The social complexity of some assets defies imitation. Such assets are based on complex social relations. Examples are the culture of a firm, the interpersonal relations of its managers, its reputation amongst customers and suppliers, etc. The reason why such assets cannot be imitated with any degree of accuracy is that each firm is a unique social entity and the social relations that characterize one firm cannot be faithfully reproduced in another. The more complex these social relations, the more difficult it is to replicate them.

Imperfect Tradability of Assets and Appropriability of Rent

The rent earned by an asset does not translate into a profit for the firm unless the firm can appropriate a part of this rent. The firm can do so if the asset earns a higher rent within the firm than outside because, in that case, the firm can retain the asset by paying it a little more than what it would earn in its next best use (the opportunity cost) and keep back the rest as profit. The difference between the rent earned by the asset within the firm and the rent it would earn in its next best use is the rent that is appropriable by the firm. It arises because the asset is imperfectly tradable, in the sense that it does not command the same price in all its uses.

We can illustrate this by considering the case of a chemist who works for a pharmaceutical firm and is specially trained to produce the firm's products. Being specially trained to produce the products of his present employers, he can produce more in his present firm than he would in any other firm. The difference between what he produces in his present firm and what he would produce in another firm is the rent that accrues to his employer's proprietary knowledge, embodied in him. His employer can retain his services by paying him a little more than what he would earn in his next best employment and keep back the rest of the rent as profit. The position does not change substantially if the asset is owned and not hired by the firm. Assume, for example, that the rent-yielding asset is a superior process owned by the firm and designed specifically to meet the production requirements of the firm. The appropriable rent is still the difference between the rent earned by the process within the firm and the royalty that can be earned by renting the process to the highest bidder outside the firm. The firm's revenue from using the process internally is the gross revenue earned by the process and the firm's cost of using the process is the royalty it foregoes by not renting it out to the next best user. The difference is the appropriable rent or profit. There is one difference, however. If the firm owns the asset, it can appropriate the entire quasi-rent. If the asset is hired, the quasi-rent may have to be shared with the owner of the asset (for example, the chemist). While the asset owner needs the firm, the firm also needs the asset owner and the firm's share of the quasi-rent depends on its bargaining power vis-à-vis the asset owner.

An asset may be more productive within the firm for three main reasons. First, the asset may be firm-specific, or designed specifically to meet the idiosyncratic requirements of the firm. The scientist in the pharmaceutical firm who has been specially trained to produce the firm's products is an example of a firm-specific asset. Second, the asset may be embedded in the firm and, therefore, be non-transferable, so that its productivity outside the firm is zero. Third, the asset may be co-specific. Even if it can be separated from the firm and transferred to another, it may produce most only when it is used in conjunction with other assets that are embedded in the firm.

Requirements for Long-term Success

We often see firms remaining very profitable for a few years, or even a few decades, but declining and dying over a longer period of time. From mid-1950s to mid-1970s, for example, five British MNCs, namely, HLL, Imperial Tobacco (now called ITC), ICI, Metal Box, and Indian Oxygen (now called BOC), were almost equally profitable. Today, only HLL and ITC continue to do well. ICI and BOC have managed to keep their heads above water by shrinking themselves from time to time, while Metal Box is virtually dead. Why does this happen?

Although many firms are able to sustain their competitive advantages for some time and their position seems very secure, yet, over a longer period, competitive pressures dissipate their profits and they cannot deal with these pressures adequately. In the dynamic context, firms compete with one another by innovating, or introducing new methods of using productive resources that enable them to create more value with the same input of bought-out resources. A part of the increase in productivity accrues to these resources as higher earnings, and the residue accrues to the firm as an increase in its economic profit. If the firm is able to increase the productivity of its bought-out resources faster than its competitors, what it gets out of these resources rises faster than what it pays out to them, and its economic profit keeps rising. But if it falls behind its competitors in the race for productivity increase, it suffers erosion in its profits and is eased out of the market eventually.

What are the requirements for ensuring the long-term success of a firm?

Innovation

The first requirement for long-term success is that a firm must keep innovating or finding new methods of utilizing productive resources. This may involve finding new products, new processes, new markets, or even new ways of organizing production and marketing. Conceptually, this calls for the acquisition of new proprietary assets. This may be done by developing new assets in-house (through R&D, building new brands, etc.), or by buying them from outside (for example, patents and trademarks), or even by replicating the assets of other successful firms (for example, reverse engineering). Whatever the method, the firm has to make an investment to acquire these new assets. Unfortunately, firms that are currently successful often suffer from technological inertia, that is, the unwillingness to adopt new methods of doing things. This happens for two reasons. There is a sunk cost effect. These firms already have a lot of investments in business-specific tangible and intangible assets which become obsolete and irrecoverable if the existing methods are changed. There is also a replacement effect. These firms tend to think that the new investments they have to make to change their existing methods of production will not yield much by way of extra profits because the profits that might result will largely be in replacement of their existing profits. They do not, therefore, consider it worthwhile to invest in new methods of production. However, experience shows that this kind of thinking reflects a lack of foresight, or strategic myopia. In a dynamic environment, any profitable business attracts new firms with better methods of production and existing firms cannot compete and survive if they do not match these better methods.

Growth

The second requirement for long-term success is that a firm should keep growing. This requirement follows from the first. By innovating successfully, the firm acquires new proprietary assets that increase the productive potential of its bought-out resources. Unless it grows in order to exploit this potential it is likely to under-recover the sunk cost of acquiring these assets and suffer an erosion in its profitability.

To understand why this is so, consider the case of a firm that produces computer software. Its proprietary assets consist of its accumulated knowledge. It buys the services of software engineers by paying them a salary. The engineers use the firm's accumulated knowledge to produce software programmes. In period 1, the sunk cost of the firm's accumulated knowledge is Rs 160 lakhs. The firm employs 20 software engineers. Each engineer produces Rs 10 lakh worth of programmes, so that the total output of the firm is Rs 200 lakhs. The firm pays a salary of Rs 6 lakhs to each engineer, so that its total salary bill is Rs 120 lakhs. The residue appropriated by the firm is, therefore, Rs 80 lakhs, which represents a 50 per cent return on the sunk cost of its proprietary knowledge.

In period 1, the firm also invests Rs 40 lakhs to acquire new knowledge, so that in period 2 the sunk cost of its accumulated proprietary knowledge is Rs 200 lakhs. The 25 per cent increase in the firm's stock of knowledge brings about a 25 per cent increase in the productivity of its software engineers, so that in period 2 each engineer produces Rs 12.5 lakh worth of programmes. The 25 per cent increase in productivity also results in a 25 per cent increase in the engineers' salaries, so that in period 2 each engineer has to be paid a salary of Rs 7.5 lakhs. If the firm retains its existing complement of engineers, its total output and salary bill will increase to Rs 250 lakhs and Rs 150 lakhs respectively. The residue accruing to the firm will increase to Rs 100 lakhs and the firm will continue to get a return of 50 per cent on its expanded proprietary knowledge. If, however, the firm decides not to grow and peg its output to Rs 200 lakhs, it will be able reduce its complement of software engineers to 16 and the salary bill to Rs 120 lakhs in period 2. But in that event, the residue accruing to the firm will also remain pegged at Rs 80 lakhs, and the return on its expanded stock of proprietary knowledge will fall to 40 per cent.

A Changing Product Portfolio

The third requirement for long-term success is that a firm has to keep making changes in its portfolio of products. This requirement follows from the second. In a dynamic economy characterized by product and process innovations, rising per capita incomes and changing consumer tastes, the market growth of existing products tend to taper off over time, while new products with high market growth emerge. In this environment, a firm cannot maintain its rate of growth if it sticks to the same products. It must over time shed old, low-growth products and introduce new, high-growth products. This has to be a continuous process because products that are high-growth today will become low-growth after some time and new high-growth products will emerge.

Entrepreneurship

The fourth requirement of long-term success follows from the first three and it is that a firm must be entrepreneural in its approach. To achieve this a firm must be able to spot the profit potential of new methods of production and emerging markets earlier than its competitors; it must back the potential winners by making the investments required to exploit them; and it must be prepared to take the losses if these investments do not yield the expected return. This is necessary for two reasons. First, the outcome of investment in projects involving new technologies and markets is highly uncertain. Empirical studies conducted in the UK and the USA show that only one out of four such projects succeed. Second, even if a project succeeds, the firm may not be able to reap any profits from it. Typically, there is a patent race for a promising project. It is pursued by a number of firms and the firm that completes it first takes away most of the initial profits. What is more, even these profits often get competed away quickly, as the leader is followed by a number of imitators.

Luck

The final requirement of long-term success is that the firm must be lucky in what it does. Since the outcome of investment in projects involving new products, processes and markets is uncertain, a firm cannot succeed unless it enjoys a certain amount of luck. Its R&D projects must yield fruit, its new product introductions must click, its forays into new markets must work, and so on. While business success is not the result of luck alone, it plays an important part.

REFERENCES

Barney, Jay (1991) 'Firm Resources and Sustained Competitive Advantage', *Journal of Management*, 17, pp. 99–120.

Kay, John (1993) *Foundations of Corporate Success*, Oxford University Press, Oxford.

Oster, Sharon M. (1994) *Modern Competitive Analysis*, Oxford University Press, New York.

Peteraf, Margaret A. (1993) 'The Cornerstones of Competitive Advantage: A Resource-based View', *Strategic Management Journal*, 14, pp. 179–191.

Porter, Michael E. (1985), *Competitive Advantage*, The Free Press, New York.

—— 1980, *Competitive Strategy*', The Free Press, New York.

Sengupta D.N. and Anindya Sen (2004) *Economics of Business Policy*, Oxford University Press, New Delhi.

5

The Essence of Strategy

Sougata Ray

The concept of strategy has emerged as one of the broadest and most complex concepts in management. It is also perhaps the most used and abused word in the business lexicon. It is now fashionable to use any business term with a prefix of strategic and a suffix of strategy. Everyday even the casual readers of business dailies cannot miss the many headlines announcing a plethora of strategies adopted by various organizations—branding strategy, pricing strategy, mergers and acquisitions strategy, shareholder value creation strategy, BPO strategy, Enterprise Resource Planning (ERP) strategy, Customers Relationship Management (CRM) strategy, e-commerce strategy, first mover strategy and so on. The list can be endless. The mind-boggling array of strategy pronouncements by organizations as reported in the business press, no doubt, signify the growing importance of the concept. However, many a time, the use of the term 'strategy' is quite misplaced. This indicates the woeful lack of clarity that prevails among the executives and the commentators alike about the concept of strategy, its domain, and applicability. No wonder that Hambrick and Fredrickson (2001) conclude that strategy has become a catch-all term used to mean anything.

The origin of 'strategy' can be traced back to the ancient Greeks. The term is coined from the Greek *strategos* meaning a general's set of moves carried out to overcome an enemy and finds extensive use in military parlance. However, in the parlance of business and non-business organization, the word 'strategy' marked its entry only about five decades ago and shot into prominence in the recent decades. Many thoughtful attempts have been made to define and explain the concept of strategy by a number of scholars over the years. But, due to the multifaceted and eclectic nature of the concept and complexity and dynamism associated with strategic phenomena in organizations, no two authors are in complete agreement about the term. The efforts to define and redefine the concept continue with the addition of new facets as new complexities are faced by organizations and new discoveries are made about how to manage them. This chapter is one of the many such attempts and, therefore, should not be viewed as the be all and end all of the explanation of the concept of strategy!

To understand strategy one needs to be aware of the basic tenets of strategic management, a relatively young field of management. Strategy is the core concept of strategic management—around which the discussions revolve and theories are built. Strategic management deals with the issues, concepts, theories, approaches, and action choices related to an organization's interaction with the external environment. It entails identification of opportunities and threats, exploitation of opportunities through formulation of goals and strategies, that is, the means to achieve goals and implementation of the same by acquiring, nurturing, deploying, leveraging, and stretching different resources and capabilities (Hofer and Schendel 1978, Hamel and Prahalad 1994). It spreads across different levels from corporate headquarters to single businesses to functions and even to specific actions within those functions and provides an integrated, future-oriented and long-term view of organizations.

One of the distinctive characteristics of strategic management field is that it advocates purposive or goal-directed behaviour of organizations. It advocates that every organization should have a vision, mission, and a set of core values and beliefs to survive and succeed for a long period of time. While vision provides the stimuli and mission sets the limit to which an organization attempts to reach, core values and beliefs provide the base or foundation. Strategy acts as the conduit (the means) to take the organization towards the vision standing on the foundation of core values and beliefs. Therefore, any attempt to formulate the strategy of an organization starts with visioning-identification of its purpose/mission and core values and beliefs. Further, the purpose and mission, get translated into a set of specific and measurable objectives that act as the milestones towards reaching the vision.

It is to be noted that like any living entity, the vision and values of an organization are not static and permanent. These change with time and place. As a result, strategy, the conduit between the two, is also dynamic and changes as the organization modifies its vision or values or both. Take the example of the public sector enterprises in India and many other economies in transition. Many of these organizations were founded with a vision to achieve self-reliance for the nation guided by a set of core values very much rooted in socialistic thinking. However, in the last one or two decades, for many of these enterprises, the vision of self-reliance has been replaced by the vision of global leadership or economic success. Similarly, many of the core values, such as financial austerity and equitable distribution of wealth among employees, are given a go-by in favour of consumerism and performance linked distribution of wealth. Therefore, the strategy adopted by these enterprises have to make a dramatic departure from the past.

Pioneering scholars (Andrews 1971, Ansoff 1965; Chandler 1962) conceptualized strategy as a comprehensive and descriptive concept. It was used to subsume purpose or goals and means to achieve the same, that is, the broad approaches, policies, and tactics to be adopted. However, with the development of the field, modern day strategy scholars explicitly separate goals and means for greater clarity and precise evaluation of the efficacy of the means (Venkatraman 1989). Therefore, the boundary of strategy is now more narrowly defined. If the goal is to maximize shareholder wealth, strategy provides the road map as to how the company will maximize shareholder wealth. It indicates the businesses the company will be in, the competitive position that it will hold in each of these businesses, and how it will create and sustain corporate and competitive advantage over other competing firms. Similarly, if the goal of the organization is to spread education, the strategy would provide the road map in terms of whether to target illiterate people, school-going children, unemployed youth, or the working population, what would be the content and delivery model, and how to go about reaching out to the targeted people and deliver value. Accordingly, it is envisaged that the strategy of an organization serves the two primary purposes of defining the segment of environment in which it operates as well as providing guidance for subsequent goal-directed activity within that niche (Hofer and Schendel 1978). In the process strategy provides the basic direction and prepares the company to meet future challenges (Goold and Luchs 1993).

It is also realized that since organizations are collective representations of different business and functional units, each of them must have its own set of goals, which may not necessarily be the same as the goals of the corporate headquarters looking after the interests of the entire organization. Hence, if the goals are different, the means to achieve them, that is, the strategies are likely to be different. This understanding has led to the hierarchical division of strategy into three broad levels—corporate, business, and functional strategy. Since strategic management aims to integrate key functions by adopting a general management perspective, the field is concerned with the corporate and business strategy only, leaving the functional strategy to be dealt with by respective functional areas.

Strategy is a multidimensional concept. It has pieces or elements. Once these elements are identified, orchestrated, and fitted properly, they give rise to a coherent and comprehensive whole, called strategy. While it is now a well accepted belief that without a set of integrated and coherent pieces of strategy, organizations are highly ineffective and hardly ever achieve their purposes, controversies abound regarding what should be considered as the elements of strategy. Taking a cue from Mintzberg (1987) some authors adopt an eclectic view and argue that the strategy of an organization consists of five Ps and their interrelatedness—position (a means of locating an organization in its environment); perspective (the way strategists perceive the world which is often guided by the core values and beliefs and becomes the shared frame of reference in an organization), plan (consciously intended course of action, a guideline to deal with a situation); ploy (a specific manoeuvre intended to outwit an opponent or influence other actors in the market), and pattern (a pattern in a stream of actions that emerge over time). These five Ps may be considered different elements of strategy. However, a critical analysis suggests that neither are these elements exhaustive enough to explicitly include all the critical elements of strategy at corporate and business levels nor do all of these Ps qualify to be the distinctive elements of strategy. Plan and pattern cut across multiple elements of strategy, present these elements and their linkages pre facto and post facto respectively and, hence, cannot be considered the elements of strategy. Recently Hambrick and Fredrickson (2001) have given a quite comprehensive and very lucid description of some of the critical elements of strategy. However, though not explicitly mentioned, they have focused primarily on business level strategy.

In the following section, a set of elements of strategy are identified and explained at two levels, that is, strategy of the whole corporation and strategy of a business within the corporation. The strategy of the whole corporation is called the corporate strategy and the strategy of the individual business unit is called the competitive strategy. In the list of strategy elements mentioned here position, perspective, and ploy figure prominently along with some more important elements unique to corporate and competitive strategy. The scope and ramification of each of these elements vary in nature and application depending on whether the strategy in question is that of a whole corporation or an individual business unit. A comprehensive strategy statement must include all these elements and their linkages.

Essential Elements of Corporate Strategy

Corporate strategy, simply put, is the overall strategy for a diversified firm—a firm having more than one business. The classical definition of corporate strategy, as given by Andrews (1971), by combining all these aspects, states that 'It is a pattern of major objectives, purposes, or goals and essential policies and plans for achieving these goals, stated in such a way as to define what business the company is in or is to be'. Business here signifies the combination of both the product/services (a vehicle to fulfil a certain need of the consumer) and the market (consumers whose need is being fulfilled). According to this definition corporate strategy is concerned about defining the organizational purpose, selection of business, allocation of resources among different businesses (Chandler 1962), and the method of managing the array of businesses.

The scope of corporate strategy was quite broad in Andrews' definition and is far too general to provide meaningful practical guidance to corporate strategists in resolving some of the critical problems facing diversified corporations (Goold and Luchs 1993). In the subsequent years, since the seminal work of Rumelt (1974), corporate strategy became synonymous with diversification strategy, until a spate of corporate restructuring in the 1980s and 1990s restored the balance by directing the focus on enquiry to many other facets of corporate strategy. Diversification is viewed as the entry of a firm into new lines of activities for broadening the base of its businesses by investing in new products, new consumer or geographic markets, or market segments (Ramanujam and Varadarajan 1989). Several action choices are made within the broad rubric of diversification strategy itself. Depending on the variation in the scope of product and/or market, and its relation with the existing businesses of the firm, these choices are termed differently such as vertical and horizontal integration (Ansoff 1965, Harrigan 1985), related diversification (Kazanjijan and Drazin 1987, Porter 1987, Rumelt 1974), conglomerate diversification (Rumelt 1974), and globalization (Dess et al. 1995). Integrating some of these action choices, Porter (1987) argues that strategic management at the corporate level involves mainly one of the following four activities—portfolio management, restructuring, transferring skills, and sharing activities across businesses.

In other words, primary choices in corporate strategy are the choice of businesses and how to manage the interlinkages of different businesses (that is, organization) to better utilize corporate resources (Goold et al. 1996). This conceptualization, however, limits the scope of corporate strategy as outlined by the founding scholars such as Andrews and Ansoff. This narrowing down of the scope of corporate strategy, though it has helped bring in more clarity in the concept, provides an incomplete treatment of the same from a corporate strategist's point of view.

A corporate strategist is concerned not only about choice of business portfolio, but also about portfolio of geographical markets for acquisition of inputs, locating various value chain activities, and selling of outputs. He is concerned about the fundamental choices regarding direction and priority of growth. He is also concerned about modes or vehicles through which such choices are effected. There are concerns about how to sequence and time the different corporate strategic moves for greater effectiveness. A corporate strategist is also concerned about facilitating efficient allocation of corporate resources, linking the businesses and geographically dispersed activities, and transferring resources across businesses and locations to build synergy leading to corporate or parenting advantage. This requires putting the right organization structure, systems, processes, and policies that would bind and guide different business and organizational sub-systems to work in unison towards a common purpose. Finally, he is also concerned about the corporate perspective, fundamental values and beliefs, and the economic logic that would shape managerial assumptions, help take positions in the face of trade-offs, and guide him to make strategic choices. If a corporation has to have a corporate strategy, then it must necessarily have these elements as depicted in Figure 5.1. These elements are developed and the domains of choice illustrated in more detail in the following section, with emphasis on how essential it is that they form a unified whole.

Corporate Positioning or Scoping

Decisions regarding selection of a portfolio of businesses and decisions regarding geographical markets both in terms of factor inputs, transformation processes, and other value chain activities and reaching the customers by selling of outputs determine the position of the corporation in the environment. More specifically, this positioning element of corporate strategy reflects the scope of the corporation by defining the breadth and spread of the range of activities engaged in, namely, product/market scope (line of business), nature and geographical scope of factor inputs (technology, land labour, capital,

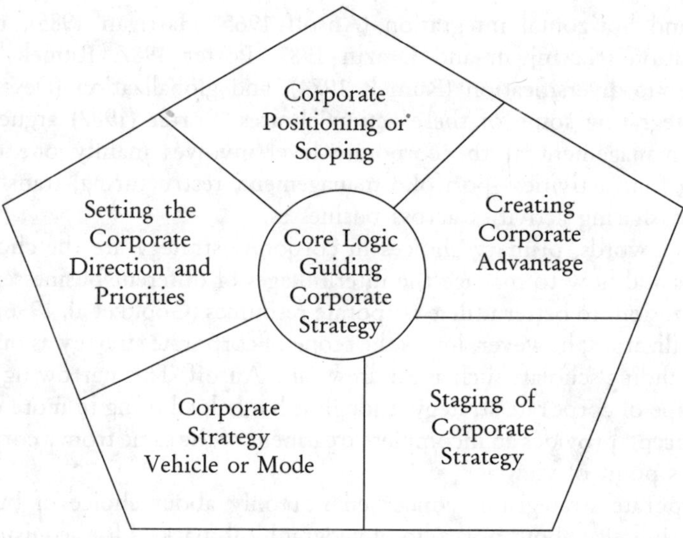

Fig. 5.1: Elements of Corporate Strategy

equipment, information, etc.), composition of capital structure, location of value chain activities, manufacturing and service units, targeted consumers, etc.

> **Box 5.1: Defining the Corporate Position**
>
> Johnson and Johnson defines its corporate position as a global baby care company that fulfils the need of parents around the globe by providing a complete range of baby care products, produced in multiple continents. This position gets redefined from time to time. For example, Asian Paints, that had a corporate position of a focused national paint company by catering to industrial and household customers in the Indian market, has been systematically repositioning itself in the recent years to become a global player by entering into a number of other country markets. Similarly, RIL, a vertically integrated company covering the complete textile value chain has been repositioning itself to be a diversified conglomerate by entering into a range of businesses such as power generation and distribution, insurance, telecommunication, and ICT services.

Strategy literature has identified three dimensions related to the scope of a corporation, that is, vertical scope, product scope, and geographical scope (Barney 1998). Vertical scope and product scope respectively indicate the vertical and horizontal spreads of product market choices and together outline the total domain or scope of business of a firm. In a pioneering study of MNCs, Stopford and Wells (1972) identified the extent of area diversification, that is, geographic scope, as an important growth strategy which captures geographical spread of both factor and product markets. Therefore, it is emphasized that decisions regarding entry into and exit from lines of business, geographical spread of manufacturing, marketing, and other value chain activities for catering to customers, composition and acquisition of resources such as capital, technology, raw material, physical and human assets together determine how the corporation is positioned. This position is characterized by different labels such as focused or conglomerate and regional, national or global.

Setting the Corporate Direction and Priorities

Another important element of corporate strategy is setting the direction for growth and priority in order to heighten the likelihood of success. Most organizations begin as single business corporations serving a limited geographical market. At this stage most of these organizations have various options to grow—by grabbing more share of the local market, moving to other markets, or diversifying into new businesses. They can expand their current business by choosing these options either one at a time or simultaneously. For large diversified global corporations too, the growth options are not limited. They can add new businesses in their portfolio to become more diversified, divest or sell off businesses to downsize or consolidate, enter new country markets or withdraw from some, expand the capacity of all businesses, or rationalize the asset and employee base. However, given limited organizational capacity and resources, most corporations are rarely in a position to pursue all the options simultaneously. Priorities are assigned and trade-off are often made in choosing these options. Moreover, even if the corporate positioning leads to the choice of more than one business and location, the choice has also to be made on how much emphasis will be placed on each of them. Some business, for instance, might be identified as centrally important, while others are deemed secondary. Priorities are assigned with respect to the treatment meted out to different stakeholders. For some companies the shareholders' interest is supreme, for some the customer is the king, while for some their employees' interest is the ultimate priority. Accordingly, depending on the priorities, the strategies adopted by these companies are likely to differ. Therefore, one must remember that an important element of corporate strategy is to provide clear direction of growth and corporate priority in resource allocation.

Box 5.2: Providing Clear Direction on Growth

This is evident in the following examples. One-time opportunities to enter many new industries beckoned most Indian companies after the initiation of economic liberalization in the early 1990s. There were also opportunities to expand capacity and consolidate the competitive position in existing businesses. In response to the emerging situation some companies made a trade-off by going for either capacity expansion and improving global competitiveness or diversifying into new industries. However, there were others which availed of both kinds of opportunities. Asian Paints and Ranbaxy were companies which concentrated on the existing businesses to enhance capacity and improve global competitiveness. However, the former gave more priority to consolidating their position in the domestic market, while the latter vigorously pursued the goal of becoming a global player. On the other hand, companies like Videocon and HLL aggressively expanded their existing businesses and diversified into many new businesses.

Corporate Strategy Vehicles or Modes

Beyond deciding on the corporate positioning and direction of growth, the strategist also needs to decide how to get there. The means for attaining the needed presence in a particular business or geographic area should be the result of deliberate strategic choice. If the decision is to expand the business portfolio, one needs to specify how the company is going to accomplish it—by relying on organic greenfield expansion, or by trying out other vehicles, such as joint ventures or acquisitions, that offer a better means for achieving the broadened scope. If the decision is to go for international operation, what should be the entry mode or vehicle—greenfield ventures, acquisitions of a company already existing in the target market, or some sort of cooperative arrangement either through licensing, joint venture, or strategic alliance? For example, RIL decided to start its telecom business through a greenfield expansion, unlike Tata Sons that entered the telecommunication business through an alliance with AT&T of the USA. Similarly, though its arch rival, Pepsi Cola had entered India through a joint venture, Coca-Cola decided to enter the Indian market with a wholly-owned subsidiary,

Each of the vehicles has its merits and demerits that need to be carefully considered. For example, an acquisition can give access to complementary resources quickly, but problems may arise due to overestimation of synergy and, thereby, overvaluation of the target and sometimes, during post acquisition integration, requiring managers to waste too much time. Similarly, synergistic alliances help diversify risk associated with a single business and create economies of scope across multiple businesses at a much lower capital investment and financial risk. Cross-business and cross-border strategic alliances also give the corporation greater flexibility to switch modes, if required, at a later date. However, gains in alliances need to be shared with the partners and due to lack of complete control by one firm, managing an alliance is more difficult compared to managing other modes.

Staging of Corporate Strategy

Yet another important element of corporate strategy is staging—sequencing, timing, and pacing of major corporate moves of market entry, expansion, divestment, etc. Most organizations face multiple choices to grow—either by entering new businesses or geographical markets. They have options to become leaner and more efficient by selling off businesses or withdrawing from some markets, or rationalizing the asset and employee base. However, as mentioned earlier, given the limited organizational capacity and resources, most corporations are rarely in a position to pursue all the options simultaneously. Sometimes, if more than one option are chosen, sequencing is needed in implementing these. Moreover, corporate strategy has to provide guidance not only in sequencing the corporate moves but also for when to time such moves and how rapidly to progress. These may pertain to decisions regarding when to enter into or exit from a business, when to enter or exit a country, upgrade the technology, resort to financial restructuring and go for initial public offering, etc. For market acceptance and overcoming resource limitations the timing of these moves becomes critically important. The staging is very much unique to a corporation, depending on its own internal and external situation. This is evident from the examples in Box 5.3.

Box 5.3: Sequencing and Timing

Over the last one decade, in response to economic liberalization, some companies in India expanded the scale of existing businesses as well as diversified into many new businesses. There were some companies which had divested some businesses to reduce their size of business portfolio. However, the sequencing and timing of scale expansion, diversification, and divestment moves differed across companies. For instance, Tata Iron & Steel Company (TISCO) had first consolidated its position in the core steel business, then divested some of its non-core businesses, and recently started diversifying into new areas. However, RIL, while consolidating its position in the existing businesses such as textile and petrochemicals, aggressively entered new areas such as IT, insurance, petroleum, power, and telecommunication. Yet, there were companies like Videocon and BPL that had first diversified into new businesses and then, faced with stiff competition, started consolidating.

Creating Corporate Advantage

The role of corporate strategy does not end with the entry into chosen businesses and geographical markets and setting the stage for subsequent development. It has to devise means that facilitate long-term survival and success of the company in those businesses and markets. In other words, the corporate strategy must create corporate or parenting advantage for the corporation on an ongoing basis (Goold et al. 1996). However, before proceeding further one would like to explain what one means by corporate or parenting advantage.

Let us say there are three businesses A, B, and C, A stands for automobile, B for banking, and C for cement. There are a number of single business companies operating in these industries. The shareholders of a company X have the choice to buy shares of these single business companies from A, B, and C industries any time. The company X is justified in entering all the above three businesses only if, by virtue of simultaneous existence in A, B, and C businesses, the company can create more value for the shareholders than what they could have achieved from the return on the investment made in three independent stocks in these industries. In other words, the shareholder value of the diversified company X has to be more than the summation of the shareholder value of A, B, and C independently. This is because shareholders have the choice to invest in independent stocks in A, B, and C industries, thereby diversifying their own portfolio of investment. The company X must be able to create this additional value, called the corporate or parenting advantage, linking these three businesses together to create more value for the shareholder. This is achieved, if multimarket presence leads to the enhancement of competitive advantage in individual businesses rather than to its depletion; and the corporate overhead costs of managing a diversified corporation is less than the advantages obtained by bringing together various skills and resources.

The moot question here is—how is the corporate advantage created and sustained. To achieve corporate advantage a corporation needs to create at least the following:

- better choice of the business to compete in;
- superior acquisition and development of corporate resources;
- effective deployment, monitoring, and controlling of corporate resources; and
- sharing and transferring of resources from one business to the other leading to synergy.

Land or property, capital, information, patents, brand names, goodwill and relationship with the regulators, suppliers, bankers, and investors are the corporate resources of a firm that are useful for all businesses. Typically, the corporate headquarters of a diversified corporation works as the internal market where different business units compete for various corporate resources. Moreover, any diversified corporation needs a set of distinctive resources and competencies or strategic assets that are competitively superior and have the potential to contribute to the benefit of multiple businesses. In fact, these resources lie at the heart of creation of corporate advantage. Core competencies and capabilities are such types of resources, perhaps the most valuable among them. Therefore, in spite of the internal competition among businesses for corporate resources, the corporate headquarters has to ensure that the spirit of collaboration exists and joint use of assets and sharing of core competencies and capabilities happen across businesses.

Ownership structure (relative amounts of stock owned by individual shareholders and institutional investors), composition of the board of directors (individuals responsible for representing the firm's owners by monitoring top-level managers' strategic decisions), executive compensation (use of salary, bonuses, and long-term incentives to align managers' interests with shareholders' interests), complex organization structure (creation of individual business divisions), and management control systems and managerial processes are the major internal governance mechanisms used to perform the above activities effectively.

Core Logic Guiding Corporate Strategy

At the heart of a corporate strategy must be a clear logic of how the corporate objectives, both profit as well as non-profit, will be achieved. Most of the strategic choices of successful corporations have a central economic logic that serves as the fulcrum for profit creation. Some of the major economic rationale for the choice of corporate strategy elements as identified by decades of research are:

(a) exploiting operational economies of scope (shared activities, core competencies);

(b) exploiting financial economies of scope (internal capital allocation, risk reduction, obtaining tax advantages);
(c) exploiting anti-competitive economies of scope (cross-subsidizing multipoint competition, market power advantages);
(d) uncertainty avoidance and efficiency;
(e) possession of general management skills that help create corporate advantage;
(f) overcoming the inefficiency in factor markets; and
(g) long-term profit potential of a business.

These rationale are driven by the fundamental corporate objective of creating greater shareholder value. Some of the non-economic rationale for the choice of corporate strategy elements are:

(a) dominant logic of the top management;
(b) inertia and commitment owing to corporate history;
(c) employee incentives to diversify (maximizing management compensation);
(d) desire for more power and management control;
(e) ethical considerations; and
(f) corporate social responsibility.

Box 5.4: Core Economic Logic

The core economic logic that drives General Electric's choice of business is market power advantage. Therefore, it enters and remains only in those businesses where it can have a dominant market position, by having either the highest or the second highest market share. On the other hand, the core economic logic that drove RIL to undertake a series of vertical integration moves was to overcome the inefficiency in the factor markets. This is evident from the following statement of Dirubhai Ambani, as quoted by Ghoshal and Ramachandran (2001):

'I was a buyer of this product (Polyester Fibre Yarn) all over the world and I was observing what was going on... I went to a major company in the West and saw how inefficient they were...and the cost of all these inefficiencies were loaded on to the product and was being passed on to me. I knew that we could manage the business lot better, make more money than them, and yet supply better and cheaper products to our mills.'

Essential Elements of Competitive Strategy

Competitive strategy of a business is about how to compete in an industry and emerge victorious in it. It is an integrated and coordinated set of commitments and actions designed to provide value to customers and gain a competitive advantage in specific, individual product markets. As competition is at the core of a business-level strategy, it is often termed 'competitive strategy'. Several coherent action choices to create value for customer and gain competitive advantage together constitute the competitive strategy of a business unit. The underlying philosophy guiding the competitive strategy of a company should be that of being distinctively unique, superior and, therefore, different from other competitors. The uniqueness may stem from doing a different set of activities or doing the same set of activities differently. More importantly, this uniqueness should not be just for the sake of being different, but it must lead to some sort of competitive advantage.

Some of the most fundamental choices that are to be made for competitive strategy formulation are: what generic product and product categories to develop; what generic market and market segments to target; which value creation stages in the industry to compete in; which technology to use and what core competence to be developed and exploited; and which geographical markets to operate for acquisition of inputs, locating various value chain activities and selling and servicing products. Together these define the business arena and competitive scope of the business unit.

Then a unique competitive position in the competitive terrain needs to be identified. Appropriate competitive moves have to be planned to grab and sustain the competitive position and create sustainable competitive advantage. This would require effective configuration of the value chain activities, designing of the right organization structure, systems, and processes, and deployment of the assets to create and sustain by erecting entry barriers and guarding against imitation and substitution. Many a time strategic and tactical moves need to be orchestrated that will undermine or destroy the position of competitors. Choices are to be made on the modes or vehicles through which entry and exit from the competitive terrain may be executed. Decisions on the fundamental orientation and approaches towards the target market are also to be taken, which will guide the sequence, speed, and timing of different strategic moves. Finally, the business perspective and logic that consist of fundamental values and beliefs and the economic rationale that shape managerial assumptions, help take positions in the face of trade-off, and provide guidance in making strategic choices, are to be clearly spelt out.

If a business has to have a competitive strategy, then it must necessarily have these elements, as depicted in Figure 5.2. These elements are developed and the domains of choice illustrated in more detail in the following section, emphasizing how essential it is that they form a unified whole.

Defining Business Arena and Competitive Terrain[1]

Given that the broad industry landscape is already defined, one of the most fundamental tasks business-level strategists face is to draw a more precise boundary of the business in terms of consumers' needs, value propositions and product categories, market segments, geographic areas, competitors' profile and core technologies, as well as the value-adding stages (for example, product design, manufacturing, selling, servicing, distribution). We discuss

[1] This section builds on a number of notable treatises on competitive strategy such as Barney (1998), Ghemawat (2000), Hambrick and Fredrickson (2001), Porter (1980, 1985 and 1996), and Thompson and Strickland (2000). I have avoided separate referencing at every point to improve the readability.

Fig. 5.2: Elements of Competitive Strategy

below the task of defining the competitive terrain, which is constituted by the interaction of target consumers, customers, and competitors along with all resource providers such as suppliers, bankers, institutions, channel partners, and complementors.

The task of defining the business arena and competitive terrain starts with a strategic definition of business. To arrive at a strategically revealing business definition three issues need to be considered—what (the needs of the subjects), who (subjects to be served), and how (the core technologies and competencies that can be used to satisfy them). Defining a business in terms of what to satisfy, whom to satisfy, and how to satisfy produces a comprehensive definition that indicates what a business unit does or, in other words, what business it is in. McDonald defines its business as 'serving a limited menu of hot, tasty food quickly to a broad base of fast food customers worldwide in a clean, friendly restaurant for a good value'. This crisp business definition makes the task of identifying the business arena and the competitive terrain that much easier. For instance, a global consumer electronics company may define its business arena and competitive terrain in the following way. It aims to provide middle and high income household consumers and customers in all major countries around the globe with high quality personalized entertainment solutions capitalizing on its core competence of miniaturization of electronic goods. If it does so, all global companies such as Philips, Sony, Thompson, and Panasonic and many local companies in different country markets operating in consumer electronics industry and offering comparable products will be its competitors. Therefore, the middle and high income household consumers and customers, the suppliers, complementors, and the competitors in all major countries around the globe constitute the competitive terrain for this company.

Box 5.5: Defining the Business Arena

Companies competing in the same industry may define the business arena and competitive terrain quite differently. For example, in India, for a number of decades, the business arena and competitive terrain as defined by the detergent division of HLL was quite different from that as defined by Nirma Chemicals. HLL defined its detergent consumers as the fabric quality conscious people needing to wash clothes. Accordingly, its target customers were those people who wanted quality detergent and were willing to pay a price commensurate to quality. Therefore, HLL considered only the quality detergent producers in India as its competitors.

On the other hand Nirma defined its detergent consumers as all those people needing to wash clothes and aspiring to use branded detergent for this purpose. Accordingly, the company defined its target customers as those who wanted to buy branded detergent at a low price. Therefore, Nirma's competitors were all the detergent manufacturers selling both branded and non-branded detergents in India. Though in terms of geography both HLL and Nirma targeted Indian market, the latter had a much broader definition of the business arena and competitive terrain. As a result, HLL took almost two decades to identify Nirma as a competitor in detergent business and, thereby, allowed Nirma to grab a substantial share of the detergent market in India.

Moreover, in articulating business arena and competitive terrain, the strategist needs to indicate not only where the business will be active, but also how much emphasis will be placed on each. Some market segments, for instance, might be identified as centrally important, while others are deemed secondary. A strategy might reasonably be centred on one product category, while others, being of distinctly less importance, may be necessary for defensive purposes or for offering customers a full line. For instance, though HLL had a number of beauty soaps and detergent brands catering to different segments of the market, it historically gave more emphasis on the middle and higher ends of the market and promoted those brands that fetch higher margins.

Competitive Positioning

Once the business arena and competitive terrain is defined, the strategist needs to identify an absolute and relative competitive position vis à vis the incumbents and potential entrants. In a competitive world, winning is the result of distinctiveness, being different, and making a difference in a positive way. This does not happen automatically. Rather, it requires executives to make up-front, conscious choices about which weapons will be assembled, honed, and deployed to beat competitors in the fight for customers, revenues, and profits. For example, Gillette uses its superior razor products developed by proprietary product and process technology and a distinctive brand image as the major differentiating features to win over the customers. Harvard Business School distinguishes itself from all the business schools in North America by adopting case-based pedagogy to teach every management concept, theories, tools, and techniques and, thereby, occupy a unique position in management education.

The competitive position of a firm may be characterized by a vector consisting of five dimensions, namely, non-price value proposition, price, cost structure, volume, and variety. Each of these dimensions can differentiate firms from one another. The combination of these dimensions gives a company a unique identity relative to all other competing firms. For instance, Intel corporation's competitive position in the microprocessor industry can be identified as a vector consisting of technological performance leadership, premium price, low cost, high volume, and wide variety. On the other hand, a vector of innovative application leadership, premium price, high cost, low volume, and moderate variety captures Motorola's competitive position in the microprocessor industry.

Differentiation may be either tangible or intangible, that is, either the physical product or the service may actually carry some convincing difference that the consumer values, or there may be some perceived superiority of the business over its rivals. Achieving a superior competitive position does not necessarily mean that the company has to be at the extreme position of at least one, if not all the differentiating dimensions. Sometimes, having the best combination of differentiating dimensions, even without having the extreme position in any of them, confers a highly valuable competitive position. This is the case with Honda in automobiles (Hambrick and Fredrickson 2001). There are better cars or less expensive cars than Honda's, but many car buyers believe that there is no better value, quality for the price, than a Honda—a unique and highly valuable position the company has worked hard to establish and reinforce.

As there is a high degree of structural heterogeneity within an industry, all positions are not equally attractive. While some competitive positions hold the potential for earning supernormal profits, others may offer the opportunity of only normal or below normal profits. Therefore, mere positioning has a bearing on a firm's profitability potential in an industry. The effort has to be to find a unique, distinct, and valuable position that not only distinguishes the company from its competitors, but also gives the opportunity for earning supernormal profit. Intel's position holds a much higher profit potential than Motorola's in the same microprocessor industry. It is also possible that a new entrant may identify and intend to occupy the same competitive position already occupied by the incumbents. In that case the new entrant has to overcome all the entry barriers created by the incumbents to replicate the position. This is often costlier compared to establishing a unique position. In a highly competitive market, oftentimes several companies, owing to their inability to find a unique position, vie for the same competitive position. However, in the long run only a handful of these competitors can capture and sustain the same position.

It must be realized that once a company decides on a competitive position, it cannot and should not alter that position every now and then. Though continuous improvement, some tinkering and fine tuning of different dimensions within a given competitive position has to be maintained so as to keep pace with the dynamism of the competitive market, there needs to be some degree of stability of the occupied position. A company needs to make a lot of investment to acquire a particular competitive position. In the process, it builds a basket of path-dependent idiosyncratic resources suited to the position. These resources and several other mobility barriers that get developed over time around the chosen competitive position obstruct the easy navigation of the company from one position to other. Therefore, frequent attempts to alter the competitive position are not only prohibitively costly, but often become futile and counterproductive.

One should not, however, be led to the conclusion that competitive positioning is static and a once-in-a-lifetime strategic task for a company. The company faces the demands to alter its competitive position from time to time for a variety of reasons owing to internal or market dynamics. It may find the position difficult to service because of change in its own organization or in market condition. For example, Onida used to command a premium position in the mid price segment of the Indian colour TV market. However, a number of foreign brands, particularly the Korean brands such as Samsung and LG, captured Onida's position in recent years, forcing the company to look for an alternative position. Sometimes, the imitators may acquire the same competitive position leading to a loss of uniqueness and, therefore, the premium associated with the same. For example, Videocon used to hold the value-for-money position in the Indian colour TV industry. Akai entered the Indian TV market by taking Videocon head-on with a superior medium value and low price combination and gained substantial share of the market. Soon after, AIWA also entered the Indian market with similar competitive positioning. The value-for-money position suddenly became cluttered with a number of players fighting for the same slot. As a result, this position no longer remained as profitable for Videocon as it used to be earlier.

The competitive position over time may also yield diminishing return due to a change in consumer preferences. The position may lose its value due to substitution effects. For example, in the early 1980s, with the advent of more modern music cassettes technology, Gramaphone India faced a situation where its high value, premium price, high cost, low volume, and limited variety competitive position became highly unprofitable. For survival the company had to alter its competitive position dramatically by bringing down the cost, producing large volumes of records and cassettes, and offering greater varieties at different price points ranging from medium to high.

Gaining and Sustaining Competitive Advantage

Identification of unique, distinct, and valuable competitive position is not enough for a company. It has to overcome the entry and mobility barriers that exist in the industry and capture this position ahead of any competitors by appropriate value chain configuration, acquisition, development, and marshalling of resources and capabilities. It has to devise strategies to appropriate the share of the industry value commensurate with its competitive position and contribution to industry value creation. Moreover, it has to erect entry barriers and imitation barriers to ensure that no other competitor can capture the same position and, thereby, share the profit generated in that position. It has to maintain the relative supremacy over competition by continuous and incremental innovations on various positioning dimensions and, thereby, guard against the potential threat of imitation and loss of position to competitors. The company also needs to guard against substitution of competitive position, in which the current position loses its profit potential and some other competitive positions occupied by competitors become more profitable. To create entry, imitation, and substitution barriers companies apply a variety of strategic, contractual, and behavioural means to hold up the customers and suppliers. They sometimes create over-capacity to show escalation of commitment and, by sending the necessary signals, persuade potential entrants not to disturb the apple-cart. Some of the ways by which a company can prevent imitation is by making it difficult for competitors to understand the reasons for its success, and also by presenting obstacles in the path to acquisition and imitation of key success factors.

In the long run competitive advantage is also gained by creating geographical monopoly due to multimarket presence and operating in multiple segments with varied and higher profit potential. The localized geographical monopoly and existence in multiple segments provide a company with an opportunity to cross-subsidize and consolidate its position in the more competitive segments. Sometimes companies deliberately try to undermine or destroy the competitive positions of other competitors. This is particularly prevalent in a situation when companies find it difficult to create a distinct position and more than one competitor are trying to capture the same competitive position. Competitive attack and response are more likely when awareness and motivation are present. Awareness of the competitor's ability to attack or respond is facilitated by resource similarity among competitors. Firms with similar resources are more likely to attack and react compared to those firms having less overlap in resources. The tooth and nail fight between Coca-Cola and Pepsi (made famous as 'the Cola War') has become a part of business folklore. The negative advertisement campaigns that are aired on TV by the two cola companies with punchlines such as 'nothing official about it', 'all sprite no *gyan*', 'business *thanda matlab* Coca-Cola', and 'I don't want to Do (Dew)' are testimony to the struggle between the two.

Competitive Strategy Modes or Vehicles

The competitive strategy must also indicate the vehicles to be used for attaining a specific competitive position in a particular product category, market segment, geographic area, or value-creation stage. Is the company going to accomplish the tasks by relying on organic, internal development, or are there other vehicles, such as joint ventures or acquisitions, that will be in vogue? For example, while Pepsi tried to capture the Indian soft drinks market by promoting its global brands, Coca-Cola decided to acquire some of the prominent brands, such as Thums Up and Limca, to achieve the same. Similarly, whereas most steel companies preferred greenfield ventures, LM Mittal's Ispat International acquired a series of sick steel plants around the globe and turned them around to capture a leading position in the world steel industry.

The means by which business arenas are entered and competitive positions captured matter greatly. Whether the company will be able to successfully capture and defend a competitive position depends very much on the mode or vehicle that is chosen. For example, consider the case of Hindustan Motors (HM) which wanted to have a presence in the higher end of the market by introducing a new high value product category. A decision to enter new product categories is always rife with uncertainty. But that uncertainty may vary immensely depending on whether the entry is attempted by licensing other companies' technologies, where perhaps HM has prior experience, or by internal product development, where the company is a novice. HM rightly judged that it lacked the capability to develop a series of suitable products at the higher end, it looked for partners like Mitsubishi and General Motors (GM) and, thereby, expanded its product line successfully. Had HM tried to use the internal product development route, the entry at the higher end could have been delayed, costly, and even, in all probability, might have failed to happen at all.

Each of the vehicles has its merits and demerits that need to be carefully considered. For example, an acquisition can give quick access to complementary resources. But problems may arise due to overestimation of synergy leading to overvaluation of the target, or sometimes, during post acquisition, of integration, forcing managers to waste too much time. Similarly, synergistic alliances help diversify risk associated with a single business and create economies of scope across multiple businesses at a much lower capital investment and financial risk. Cross-business and cross-border strategic alliances also give the corporation greater flexibility to switch modes, if required, at a later date. However, gains in alliances need to be shared with the partners and due to lack of complete control by one firm, managing an alliance is more difficult compared to managing other modes.

Staging of Competitive Strategy

Just as for corporate strategy, the important element of competitive strategy too is staging—sequencing, timing, and pacing of the strategic and tactical moves. Sequencing of moves cannot be ad hoc as most strategies do not call for equal, balanced initiatives on all fronts at all times. Instead, some initiatives must come first, followed by others, and then still others. Consider the case of Sundaram Fasteners Ltd (SFL). It got an opportunity to be the global supplier of radiator caps for GM. For that SFL had to first upgrade the quality of its products to meet the GM standard, then reduce the cost of manufacturing and supply chain to give the most competitive offer as compared to other potential suppliers of GM and, finally, had to invest heavily to create a large capacity to honour large orders and a demanding delivery schedule which is mandatory to continue as a major global supplier of GM.

Similarly, the timing of a strategic move has to be planned keeping the overall strategic objectives in mind. Does the company want to be the first mover, second mover, or a very late entrant? There are advantages and disadvantages associated with both the early mover and late entrant strategy. First movers need to take more risks and often need to incur the cost of educating customers, creating primary demand, and setting regulatory standards. However, they can easily capture a lucrative competitive position and gain customer loyalty. Late entrants may sometimes have competitive advantage because they can imitate first movers, without incurring the market development cost. For instance, as a late entrant Mohan Meakins Ltd incurred a much lower cost to capture a lion's share of the cornflakes market in India that was virtually developed by Kellogg.

Pacing is another important decision managers need to take. For example, though RIL had entered the telecom business in the mid-1990s, it had maintained a low profile presence for a number of years when the regulatory regime had been in a flux and rapidly evolving. It launched the business in a big way only recently with meticulous planning and groundwork and mobilization of massive resources to rapidly acquire a substantial share of the market. On the other hand, Air Tel had entered the telecom industry immediately after deregulation, rode the tide of the deregulated market, and progressed at a steady pace.

Of course, in reality there is no universally superior sequence, timing, and pacing. It depends on the context and, therefore, the strategist's judgement is required. The decision about staging can be driven by a number of factors. One of the most important factors is availability of resources. Funding and staffing of every envisioned initiative at the needed levels is generally not possible at the outset of a new strategic campaign. Urgency is a second factor affecting staging. Some elements of a strategy may face brief windows of opportunity, requiring that they be pursued first and aggressively. A third factor is the achievement of credibility. Attaining certain thresholds or critical mass can be very valuable for attracting resources and support of important stakeholders that are needed for executing other parts of the strategy. A fourth factor is the pursuit of early wins, testing the water and, thereby, gaining confidence. It may be far wiser to successfully tackle a part of the strategy that is relatively easier to achieve before attempting more challenging or unfamiliar initiatives. These are only some of the factors that might be considered while making decisions about the speed and sequence of competitive strategy moves.

Core Logic Guiding Competitive Strategy

As the foundation for all competitive strategy choices there must be a clear and compelling logic that will make the choices a coherent set. Some of the major economic rationale for the choice of competitive strategy elements, as identified by decades of research, are:

(a) need to differentiate on value proposition;
(b) need to improve the cost position;
(c) need to gain greater volume share of the market (dominant position and market power);

(d) need for increasing the per unit profitability;
(e) exploiting the economy of scale and scope;
(f) exploiting the heterogeneity in consumers' augmented need;
(g) appropriating greater share of the industry value;
(h) overcoming resource crunch; and last but not the least
(i) relative bargaining position *vis à vis* other players in the industry.

Some of the non-economic rationale driving the choice of competitive strategy elements are:

(a) dominant logic of the managers;
(b) inertia and commitment owing to past investment decisions;
(c) managerial desire for higher status and financial benefits;
(d) ethical considerations; and
(e) environmental concerns and corporate social responsibility.

These logics not only shape the assumptions behind competitive strategy analysis and choice but help managers take positions in the face of trade-off in strategy choice. There is more often than not a tradeoff involved in making strategy choices. Is the company mandated for high growth, market dominance, long-term or short-term profit objectives? Is the company likely to be driven by cost consideration or value leadership? What should be the orientation—skimming and exploitation or developing and exploration? What should get priority—breadth or depth, volume or variety? Should strategic choices be guided by economic rationale only or should non-economic rationale also be considered?

The above questions are only indicative. Managers face many such questions. The core logic of competitive strategy must provide answers to these questions and, thereby, help managers make the trade-off consistently. The inherent inconsistencies across a set of strategy elements pose extraordinary resource demands and often lead to failure. In selecting differentiating dimensions of competitive position, strategists should give explicit preference to those few forms of superiority that are mutually reinforcing (image, product styling, and channel), consistent with the firm's resources and capabilities. For example, if BMW or Mercedes Benz have showrooms that look like countryside dump yards manned by a set of haggard looking persons, rich men are unlikely to visit those showrooms to buy BMW or Mercedes cars. Befitting to the image and style associated with these companies' products the dealer showrooms have to look more like plush corporate offices with appropriate amenities and ambience.

Strategy formulation at all levels is a reiterative exercise. At every stage the strategist has to move back and forth to ensure the logical consistency across different strategy elements. Once a set of logically consistent elements of strategy is arrived at, commitment of the whole organization is needed to implement the same. Structure, systems and processes and functional strategies, policies and action plans are put in place that fit with, rather than contradict, different elements of strategy. Achieving an internal fit of the organization with strategy, getting all the resources channelled towards a given direction and winning the commitment of the people do not happen instantaneously. They take time and investment. Therefore, though large investments, knee-jerk reactions, and short-term tactical moves can often be camouflaged as strategy, they are not the right ways of devising strategy. The claim of an executive does not make any corporate move a strategy unless it fits into a broader, integrated, and consistent game plan of the company.

Doing a good job of managing an enterprise inherently requires a good dose of strategic thinking and actions. Strategy is a multidimensional concept having an internally consistent set of elements. Surprisingly, most strategists emphasize one or two of the elements without giving any consideration to the others. However, development of a strategy without attention to all these elements leaves critical omissions and caveats. The better conceived a company's strategy and more proficient its execution, the greater are the chances that the company will be a leading performer in its markets. High-achieving enterprises are nearly always the product of astute and proactive management, rather than the result of lucky breaks or a long run of good fortune.

Strategic management in a dynamic environment is fascinating and challenging because it is akin to managing a paradox. On the one hand, effective strategy implementation requires a high degree of commitment of the entire organization towards a set of interrelated strategy elements fitting in with the environment. On the other hand, good strategy making demands flexibility to be in tune with the changing mood of the environment and adjust continuously. The need for managing this duality simultaneously by continuous fine tuning of the strategy elements at the periphery and occasional major changes in the core suggests that strategic management can no longer be a prerogative of a chosen few at the top aided by a group of strategic planners. A larger number of people across the hierarchy primarily responsible for implementation of strategy must be allowed to play an important part in shaping the strategy and fine tuning strategy elements.

REFERENCES

Andrews, Kenneth R. (1971) *The Concept of Corporate Strategy*, Dow-Jones Irwin, Homewood, Illinois.

Ansoff, H.I. (1965) *Corporate Strategy: An Analytical Approach to Business Policy for Growth and Expansion*, McGraw Hill, New York.

Barney, J.B. (1998) *Gaining and Sustaining Competitive Advantage*, Addison-Wesley, New York.

Chandler, Alfred, D. (1962) *Strategy and Structure*: *Chapters in the History of American Industrial Enterprise*, MIT Press, Cambridge, Mass.

Dess, G.G., Anil Gupta, Jean-Francois Hennart, and Charles W.L. Hill (1995) 'Conducting and Integrating Strategy Research at the International, Corporate and Business Levels: Issues and Directions', *Journal of Management*, 21(3), 357–94.

Ghemawat, Pankaj (2000) *Strategy and the Business Landscape*, Addison-Wesley, New York.

Ghoshal, S. and J. Ramachandran (2001) 'Reliance Industries Limited: Growth as a Way of Life' in S. Ghosal, G. Piramal, and S. Budiraja (eds) *World Class in India*, Penguin Books India, New Delhi.

Goold, M. and K. Luchs (1993) 'Why diversify? Four Decades of Management Thinking', *Academy of Management Executive*, 7(3), 7–25.

Goold, M., A. Campbell, and M. Alexander (1996) 'Developing a corporate strategy', in M. Goold and K.S. Luchs (eds) *Managing the Multibusiness Company*, Routledge, New York, 425–52.

Hambrick, D.C. and J.W. Fredickson (2001) 'Are you sure you have a strategy?', *Academy of Management Executive*, 15(4) 48–59.

Hamel, Gary and C.K. Prahalad (1994) *Competing for the Future*, Harvard Business School Press, Cambridge, Mass.

Harrigan, K.R. (1985) 'Vertical integration and corporate strategy', *Academy of Management Journal*, 28(2), 397–425.

Hofer, C.W. and D.E. Schendel (1978) *Strategy Formulation: Analytical Concepts*, West Publishing, St. Paul, Min.

Kazanjian, P.K. and R. Drazin (1987) 'Implementing Internal Diversification: Contingency Factors for Organizational Design Choice', *Academy of Management Review*, 12, 342–54.

Mintzberg, H. (1987) 'The Strategy Concept I: Five Ps for Strategy', *California Management Review*, Fall, 11–24.

Porter, M.E. (1996) 'What is Strategy', *Harvard Business Review*, 74(6), 61–78.

— (1987) 'From Competitive Advantage to Corporate Strategy', *Harvard Business Review*, May–June, 43–59.

— (1985) *Competitive Advantage*, The Free Press, New York.

— (1980) *Competitive Strategy*, The Free Press, New York.

Ramanujam, V. and P. Varadarajan. (1989) 'Research on Corporate Diversification: A Synthesis', *Strategic Management Journal*, 10, 523–551.

Rumelt, R.P. (1974) *Strategy, Structure and Economic Performance*, Harvard University Press, Cambridge, Mass.

Stopford, J.M. and L.T. Wells, Jr (1972) *Managing the Multinational Enterprise: Organization of the Firm and Ownership of the Subsidiaries*, Basic Books, New York.

Thompson, A.A. and A.J. Strickland III (2000) *Strategic Management: Concept and Cases*, McGraw-Hill, New York.

Venkatraman, N. (1989) 'Strategic Orientation of Business Enterprises: The Construct, Dimensionality and Measurement', *Management Science*, 35, 942–62.

6

The Balanced Scorecard

P.K. Sett

The Balanced Scorecard (BSC) is about measuring a firm's strategy in order to manage it. It is said: 'If you can't measure it, you can't manage it.' So, if you want to manage your strategy deployment and implementation, you have got to first measure it. When you compare what you have achieved with the measures of your intended strategy, you would know whether your strategy has worked or not. Variances may arise for a variety of reasons. The implementation of your strategy may have been poor, you might have chosen an incorrect strategy, or your business environment may have changed in significant ways since you framed your strategy. But then, how do you diagnose the cause of failure of your strategy? To do that you need to know the theory of the business of your firm.

The theory of the business, like any theory, is a set of assumptions with hypothesized causal linkages between them. These assumptions are about how the market functions, customers behave, or employees get motivated to produce surplus value for the firm. The causal linkages are the relationships between these external and internal factors as postulated in the firm's strategy.

As we shall see later, BSC articulates the theory of the business of a firm, as it translates the strategy into actions through a set of causally interlinked objectives and measures. It thus helps a firm to manage its strategy better by ensuring strategic control of its implementation as well as by allowing the firm to continuously validate its strategy as it is being deployed.

Why are the Traditional Measures Not Sufficient?

Reading the chapters on globalization and the New Economy you have learnt how the old paradigm of business has changed in the information age. Managing business in the globalized economy of the twenty-first century is like flying an aircraft blind in turbulent weather. The pilot is equipped with only the knowledge of the destination and a set of cockpit meters to help him navigate and stay on course. He has to be aware of and constantly monitor external weather conditions like wind speed and direction, cloud conditions, and gathering storm in the horizon, as well as conditions inside the aircraft like engine performance, cabin pressure, fuel level and so on. He has to monitor not one but a whole set of meter readings—each depicting a critical aspect of the flight. Likewise, in today's turbulent business environment, no single measure of corporate performance alone can provide a clear indication of whether a firm is performing well in terms of its envisioned future. To navigate his firm to its cherished future a manager, like a pilot, needs multi-dimensional information about his external and internal environment and a constant feedback on not just a single, but multiple aspects of his business.

Traditional corporate performance measures, like return on investment (ROI) and earnings per share (EPS), are based on accounting records of past transactions. They tell you the history of your voyage. In the relatively stable business environments of the past decades, they worked reasonably well as predictors of future business success because your future was more or less a continuation of your past. Today, this is no longer true. There are discontinuous changes arising out of rapid technological advancements, much shorter product life cycle, and continuously evolving consumer preferences, to name a few. These changes, in turn, are altering the structures of markets, industry, and competition, driving value to migrate from one industry to another. So a firm cannot rely any longer solely on historical accounting measures to predict its future performance. Higher profits may be the result of under-investment in innovation, technology, market development and human capital—the very assets which are necessary for creating future value. Balance sheets do not capture intangible but critical firm assets like brand equity, a loyal customer base, and employee competencies, or organizational capabilities like a reliable and responsive supply chain that the firm may have developed by investing in its future, foregoing short-term profits.

On the other hand, improved operations do not guarantee financial success. Higher productivity or reduced manufacturing cycle time may not translate into higher revenue or increased margin—if the firm has stopped creating value for its customers. Financial measures would soon reveal this failure.

More importantly, in the globalized economy, the ability of a firm to mobilize and exploit its intangible or invisible assets, like the ones mentioned earlier, are becoming far more important as sources of competitive advantage than investing in and managing tangible assets like capital, technology, and plant and equipment which are becoming increasingly commoditized. Financial accounting measures which have to conform to the strict principles of materiality and verifiability cannot realistically be expected to meet these emerging needs. We, therefore, need a new framework for corporate performance measurement that recognizes this new reality.

To navigate the firm in turbulent environment and manage its future performance, a manager needs, like a pilot, a set of measures or a measurement system that looks at all critical aspects of business and presents an integrated view that tells him how the firm is performing in all these areas. Then only can a manager know how well his firm is creating future value and not just how well they have performed in the past.

What is a Balanced Scorecard?

A Corporate Performance Measurement System

The true metaphor for a BSC should be a flight simulator, not a dashboard of instrument dials. Like a flight simulator, the BSC incorporates the complete set of cause-and-effect relationships among the critical variables that describe the trajectory—the flight plan—of the strategy. It translates a firm's strategy into actions by articulating its theory of the business and mapping the strategy into a set of causally interlinked objectives and measures, covering the four basic perspectives of business: shareholder/financial, customer, internal business process, and human capital. Through these interlinkages it tells the story of the firm's strategy—what it intends to achieve and how. This is done by addressing the four fundamental concerns of any business: how do we create shareholder value; how do our customers view us; what must we excel at; and how do we continue to learn and innovate.

The sequences in which the four fundamental concerns are addressed are extremely important from the point of view of strategy deployment and implementation (Figure 6.1). The sequence defines the direction of causality

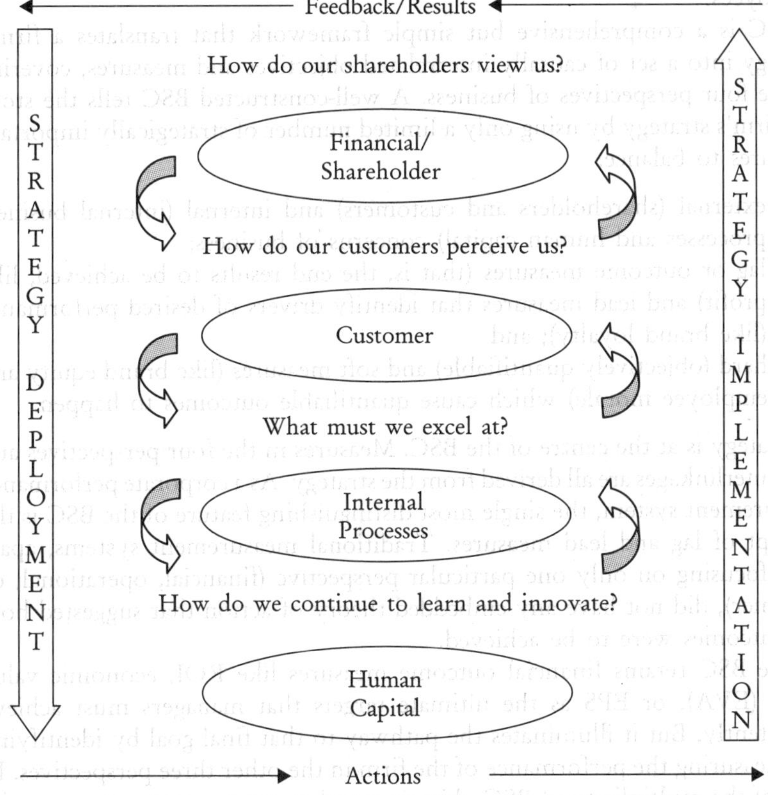

Fig. 6.1: Theory of the Business—BSC Perspectives

of business decisions and their outcomes. The ultimate objective of business as an economic activity is to create sustained shareholder value. The process of strategy-making starts with this final goal in view and successful implementation of a good strategy delivers it. But how do you create shareholder value? To create shareholder value, you need to have a base of satisfied, loyal, and profitable customers. You can have such a customer base if you create value for them through your product and service offerings. To be able to create the desired customer value you must be able to design and operate an internal business process within your firm which develops, makes, and delivers products and services which customers need. This internal business process has to be capable, efficient, and reliable enough to generate a surplus value for the firm which is sufficient to create the shareholder value desired by the firm, after appropriation of the customer value from it. Finally, you must have employees who are capable and willing to create the surplus value you need by running your internal business process effectively and efficiently—from the customer's point of view. For that to happen, your employees must perceive enough value in their employment in your organization. So, ultimately, the surplus value that your business creates must be large enough to meet the expectations of your shareholders, customers, and employees.

BSC is a comprehensive but simple framework that translates a firm's strategy into a set of causally interrelated objectives and measures, covering all the four perspectives of business. A well-constructed BSC tells the story of a firm's strategy by using only a limited number of strategically important measures to balance:

- external (shareholders and customers) and internal (internal business processes and human capital) concerns of business;
- lag or outcome measures (that is, the end results to be achieved, like profit) and lead measures that identify drivers of desired performance (like brand loyalty); and
- hard (objectively quantifiable) and soft measures (like brand equity and employee morale) which cause quantifiable outcomes to happen.

Strategy is at the centre of the BSC. Measures in the four perspectives and their interlinkages are all derived from the strategy. As a corporate performance measurement system, the single most distinguishing feature of the BSC is the concept of lag and lead measures. Traditional measurement systems, apart from focusing on only one particular perspective (financial, operational, or customer), did not have any embedded theory of action that suggested how the outcomes were to be achieved.

The BSC retains financial outcome measures like ROI, economic value added (EVA), or EPS as the ultimate targets that managers must achieve consistently. But it illuminates the pathway to that final goal by identifying and measuring the performance of the firm in the other three perspectives. In spite of the multiplicity of BSC objectives and measures, spanning across the four perspectives, there is a discernible unity of theme and purpose provided by the underlying strategy. An assortment of financial and non-financial measures without a unifying causal link provided by the theory of the business cannot achieve this.

We will examine the four BSC perspectives in some detail later in this chapter. For now, let us reveal the full potential of the BSC as a conceptual framework and see how it transcends from a corporate performance management system into a strategic management system that helps firms to navigate into the unknown future.

A Strategic Management System

Traditional management systems, particularly the management control systems that are based mainly on historical cost-financial accounting models, pose some major barriers to effective strategy implementation. Four specific barriers identified are:

- traditional systems which cannot translate a firm's vision and strategy into terms that can be understood and acted upon by the people in the organization;
- long-term goals which are not linked to current actions to be taken at departmental, team, and individual levels. Current actions focus on how to reduce the variances from the targets set in the quarterly financial budgets which is the primary control mechanism in traditional systems;
- failure to link action programmes and resource allocation process with the long-term strategic priorities. Firms often have separate processes for long-term strategic planning and for short-term (annual) budgeting. The consequence is that discretionary funding and capital allocations are often unrelated to strategic priorities; and
- lack of feedback on how the strategy is being implemented and whether it is working. Traditional systems emphasize control of current operations because they use short-term performance-oriented measures like gross margin (a cost-financial measure) or cycle-time (an operational efficiency measure) as the principal feedback mechanism.

If a company continues to follow these traditional practices, its focus remains not on strategy but on control of current operations. It hardly spends any time to regularly review its strategy and its implementation. As a result, once it has been formulated, its strategy remains hidebound and the firm hardly makes any decision about it. The BSC puts strategy—not control—at the centre. A good BSC is one which should be able to tell the story of the firm's strategy.

By defining the hypothesized cause–effect relationships between the lead and lag measures, the BSC not only helps more effective implementation of strategy but it also provides an opportunity for a review of the strategy itself. It provides for both single- and double-loop feedback. The former helps managers to better control the process of strategy implementation by acting on the reported variance from the target. The latter urges the managers to question their assumptions in the wake of changes in markets, competition, and technology—even if there may be no reported variance in the current performance.

The BSC gives firms much more leverage when it is used as a strategic management system rather than as a performance measurement system. Such use, however, needs a four-stage iterative deployment process (Figure 6.2) that seeks to continuously validate the strategy as it is deployed. The deployment process uses the measurement focus of the BSC to accomplish this. We will learn more about the four-stage process later in this chapter.

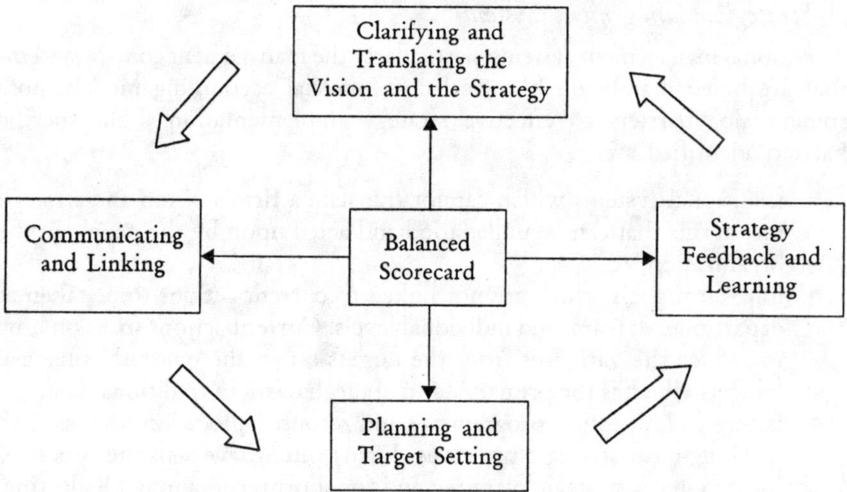

Fig. 6.2: The BSC as a Strategy Management System

Source: Kaplan and Norton (1996)

Measuring Strategy: Four BSC Perspectives

The BSC measures strategy by making the relationships among the objectives and measures in the four perspectives explicit, so that they can be managed and validated. The chain of cause and effect should pervade all four perspectives of a BSC. Let us illustrate this point through a simple example of a firm that wants to increase its shareholder value by pursuing a strategy of repeat and expanded sales from existing customers. The firm's strategy makes explicit what it wants to do and what it does not. It wants to increase its shareholder value by selling more to its existing customers, rather than by trying to expand its customer base. This is the strategic choice the firm has made after considering everything. Our interest here is to see how the firm measures its professed strategy. How would the firm translate its strategy into a set of causally interrelated objectives and measures across the four BSC perspectives?

The beginning is simple. The firm has to put one of the familiar measures of shareholder value like ROI, return on capital employed (ROCE), or EVA as the final outcome or lag measure in the financial perspective of its BSC. Let us suppose that the firm has chosen ROCE for this purpose. Then the real story of strategy has to begin by unravelling the firm's assumptions about its markets, competitors, customers, and employees. This is what the theory of the business of the firm is all about. As indicated earlier, the firm has made the assumption that it could make more money by selling more to its existing customers. This assumption may be entrenched in a number of other assumptions relating to the nature of the market competition, or the belief that customers prefer to have a stable long-term relationship with their suppliers and so on. Underlying the firm's strategy is also the assumption that its existing customers have latent demands for its products which it might exploit more profitably rather than if it tried to create new customers. So it has to convert this latent demand into actual sales by retaining its existing customers and making them buy its products more frequently and in larger quantities. For this to happen, the firm should be able to create loyalty among its existing customers. So measures of customer loyalty—which will ultimately be reflected through repeat and expanded purchases by them—should appear in the customer perspective. But how will the firm achieve customer loyalty?

Analysis of customer preferences may have revealed that given the product quality standards already being offered by the firm and its competitors, customers would highly value reduced lead-time (LT) and on-time-delivery (OTD) of orders. Thus, reduced LT and improved OTD are expected to lead to better financial performance. So these two metrics should appear as outcome or lag measures in the internal business process (IBP) perspective. To achieve LT and OTD standards desired by the customers the firm may need to substantially improve its cycle time, process reliability, and quality. Improvements in these areas of a firm's operations then assume strategic importance as they have a critical impact on customer loyalty. So the firm must bring about desired improvements in these critical process parameters. For that to happen it must measure the rates of improvements against a target set based upon customer requirements. Naturally, therefore, measures of these process parameters should appear as performance drivers or lead measures in IBP, as they help the firm to achieve LT and OTD targets.

Finally, how might a firm improve the quality, reliability, and cycle time of its internal processes? It may do so by training and improving the skills of its workforce and also by raising their morale and motivating them to apply their upgraded skills to improve the performance of the processes they are running. In this particular case, if it is actually diagnosed that the achievement of strategic goals relating to LT and OTD is critically dependent upon improvement in employee skills and motivation, then these objectives and their related measures should appear in the human capital or learning and growth (L&G) perspective of the firm's BSC. This is how the BSC articulates the theory of the business of the firm, as espoused by its strategy , through a logical sequence of cause-and-effect relationships across the four perspectives of business. Figure 6.3 shows the strategy map that depicts the causal relationships underlying the firm's strategy. Table 6.1 shows the related BSC objectives and measures in each of the four perspectives.

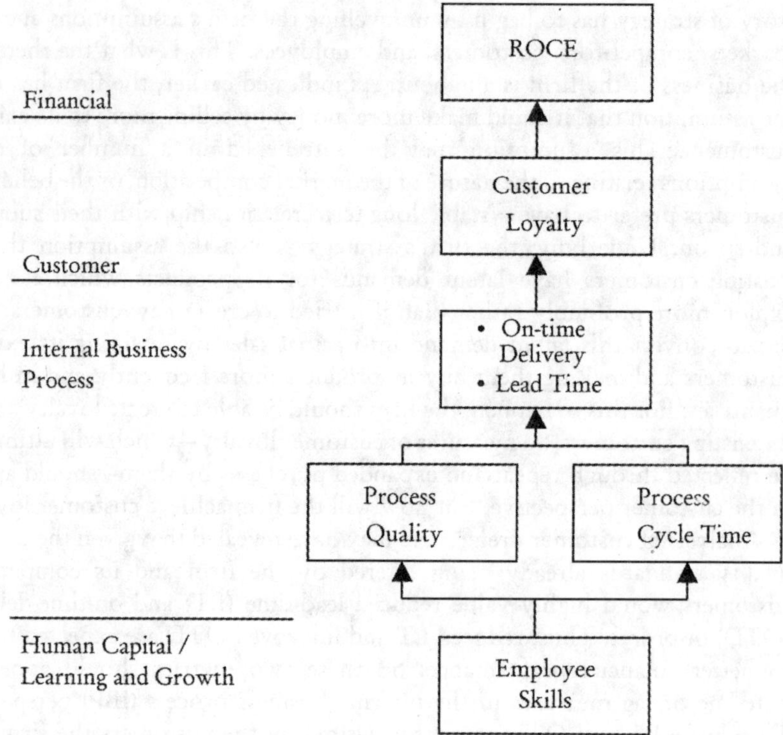

Fig. 6.3: Strategy Map of the Firm

The above example illustrates in a simple way, how a properly constructed BSC should tell the story of the firm's strategy. It identifies and makes explicit the sequence of hypotheses about the cause-and-effect relationships between outcome or lag measures and lead measures or performance drivers of those outcomes. As the example shows, ultimately, causal paths from all the measures on a scorecard should be linked to the financial outcome objective. Every measure selected for a BSC should be an element in a chain of cause-and-effect relationships that communicates the meaning of the firm's strategy to its people. By reverse logic, looking at a properly constructed BSC one should be able to tell what the strategy of the firm is. Thus, a good BSC should transparently show a firm's strategy from both the directions.

Having dealt with a simple but complete case of translating a firm's strategy into BSC measures, let us cover, in brief, the fundamentals for building objectives and measures in each of the four BSC perspectives.

Financial Perspective

The ultimate wish list of any business is to increase revenue, reduce cost, increase productivity, improve asset utilization, and reduce risk. This can be captured in a simple formula:

Table 6.1: Balanced Scorecard of the Firm

Perspective	Objective	Metrics	
		Lag	Lead
Financial	Increase shareholder value	ROCE	Increased sales revenue
Customer	Repeat and expanded sales to existing customers	• Average sales per customer • Repeat sales revenue as a per cent of total sales	• Customer satisfaction index (on critical parameters valued by the customers) • Stability index of existing customer base
Internal Business Process	• On-time delivery • Reduced lead time	• Per cent orders delivered on time • Average lead time	• Rate of improvement in process cycle time • Rate of improvement in process quality • Rate of improvement in process reliability
Human Capital/ Learning and Growth	• Employee skill development • Employee motivation	• Employee morale	• Average employee skill

Source: Author' calculations.

$$\text{Return (R)} = \text{Margin (M)} \times \text{Velocity (V)}$$

Restated in more familiar terms, the equation would be:

$$\text{Return-on-Investment (R)} = \frac{\text{Profit}}{\text{Assets}}$$

This simple equation captures the criterion for the success of any business—ROI has to be greater than the cost of capital (adjusted for risk). Breaking R into two factors M and V add a whole lot of meaning to it in terms of managerial thoughts and decision-making. However, M and V are different kettle of fish. You have to pay separate attention to margins and velocity. Each is its own concept, with its own components and relationships among components. Velocity is the most unappreciated component of ROI.

The final outcome measures in the financial perspective of the BSC of any business firm are traditional measures of shareholder value like ROI and ROCE, or a modern measure like EVA. The skill lies in selection of lead measures that should be customized to fit the strategy. A firm can follow different strategies ranging from aggressive market share growth, consolidation, harvesting of the investments already made, exit from a particular business. The choice of lead financial measures should reflect the particular strategy adopted—growth, sustainance, harvest, or exit. You cannot, for example, put reduction of unit cost through standardization as your performance driving lead measure when you are aiming at building the market by offering the customers a wider variety of products.

For each of the firm-level strategies of growth, sustainance, and harvest there are three financial themes that drive the business strategy:

- revenue growth and mix;
- cost reduction and/or productivity improvement, and
- improved utilization of assets and investments.

The revenue growth and mix theme may involve one or more of the following approaches: new products, new applications (say, for drugs), new customers and markets, expanded sale through cross-selling, shifting product-service mix to add more customer value, or by re-pricing the offerings following activity-based cost information. The objective is common, namely, to increase profitable revenue sources. The particular approach, or a combination of approaches adopted to boost profitable revenue, would dictate selection of a lead measure. If revenue growth is contemplated, say, on the double planks of new product introduction and cross-selling of existing products, then the lead measures to be chosen should be: total revenue growth; percent of revenues earned from new product sales and cross-selling, separately. If, however, the revenue growth strategy relies on consolidating and increasing the market share of existing products in existing markets, then the corresponding lead measure should simply be: growth in market share.

The cost reduction and productivity improvement theme basically aims at reducing the cost of earning a unit of revenue. This can be done in diverse ways. One approach can be to attack the direct and indirect costs in order to bring them down. This itself can be done in a number of ways—by reducing wastage, idle-time, spillage, defects, etc. or by improving productivity of labour, machine, equipment, etc. Activity-based cost analysis can reveal hidden inefficiencies in indirect and support functions. These, however, can be removed. You can even reduce unit cost by spending more, say, by investing in superior process technology. Business units in the growth phase are unlikely to focus on such cost reduction. They may still have a productivity objective like, say, increase in revenue per employee. Such a measure would be consistent with their strategic theme because it would encourage shifts to higher value-added products and services, and leverage the physical and personnel resources already in position for earning more revenue. Still another way to reduce cost of earning revenue is to shift customers and suppliers from, say, high-cost manually processed channels to low-cost electronic channels like the Internet or the electronic data interchange (EDI). Here the reduction in cost is achieved through change in the way the firm transacts with its customers and suppliers. In fact, transaction costs can be greatly reduced simply by bringing about changes in customer or supplier behaviour—even without changing the channel. We will see examples of this in the next chapter, on activity-based management.

The theme based on improved asset utilization applies to both short- and long-term assets. One of the objectives is to reduce the cash-to-cash cycle for both types of assets. For working capital management, it represents the time required for the company to convert cash payments to suppliers into cash receipts from customers. Similarly, for projects involving large capital investments, the objective should be to reduce the lag between actual investments and the time when revenues start flowing out of them. The investments include intellectual and human capital, such as skills and competencies of people as well as creation of shared knowledge base. Companies can increase the leverage from the investments in such 'soft' areas by sharing the knowledge, best-practices, etc. across multiple business units. More importantly, such sharing of intellectual assets has the double benefit of reducing cost and enhancing revenue-earning capability of the organization. Measures like premium margin or per cent of revenues earned from new or patented products can capture the tangible benefits flowing out of such efforts, while a measure like improvement in time to market a new product can be an early lead indicator.

Objectives and measures that manage business risk may or may not appear explicitly in the financial perspective, depending upon the nature of the business, sources of risk, and the firm's perception about those risks. Many businesses include an objective in their financial perspective that addresses the risk dimension of their strategy—for example, diversifying revenue sources away from a narrow set of customers, one or two lines of business, or particular geographical regions. Sometimes, the risk perceptions are factored into other perspectives like wider product portfolio, general-purpose technology (as against a highly specialized one), multi-skilling of workforce and so on. The rule is simple. Include explicit measures when they are strategically important and incorporate them in appropriate perspectives of the BSC.

Customer Perspective

Customer perspective of the BSC should most eloquently express the firm's strategy—its choice about which customer and market segments it wants to compete in and in which it does not. This choice is the essence of strategy. No firm can meet every customer need profitably.

Lag Measures: The customer and market segments chosen represent the sources that will deliver the revenue component of the firm's financial objectives. The core customer outcomes (lag measures) which are generic across all firms are customer satisfaction, loyalty, retention, acquisition, and profitability—measured separately for each targeted segment. See Figure 6.4 to find out how these measures are causally interrelated.

For translating a particular strategy, however, these generic measures should be customized to the targeted groups from which the firm expects its greatest growth and profitability. Market share can be measured in terms of the number of customers, units sold, or rupees of sales—in comparison with the total size of the market segment. It can serve as an important signal for

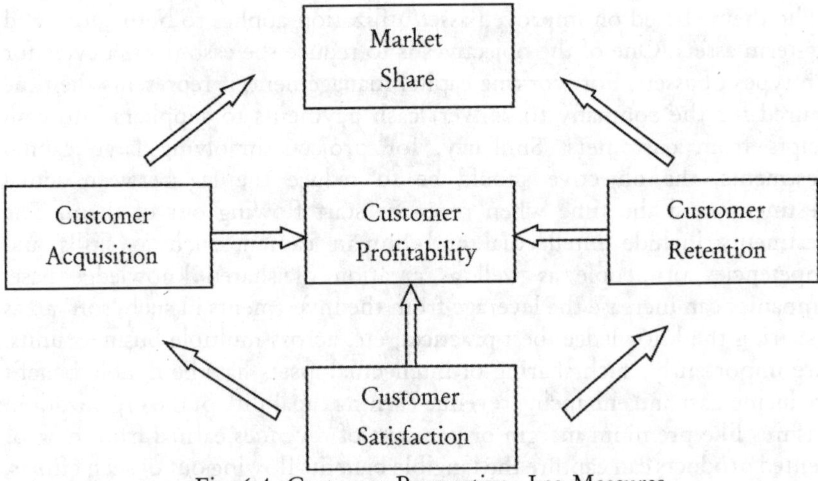

Fig. 6.4: Customer Perspective—Lag Measures

effectiveness of firm strategy. If total sales are increasing but market share is dwindling, obviously segmentation strategy is not working. A firm can use more focused measures to gauge its penetration in the product or service category in which it is competing. For example, a bank can have 'share of wallet' as a measure representing what percentage of targeted customers' investments or transactions it is capturing. Customer acquisition can be measured, in absolute or relative terms, by the rate at which a firm is able to attract new customers or business. It can also have a measure like number of new customers acquired per sales call or per unit of money spent on sales promotion, for measuring the effectiveness of its acquisition process. Examples of customer retention indices are: repeat purchase percentage, proportion of customer accounts that are, say, more than three years old and so on. Customer satisfaction survey is one of the common things every firm does. However, to be meaningful and actionable, the survey instrument must use criteria based on customer value propositions being offered. Profitability of customers, individually or as a group, is an important internal measurement the firm has to make using tools like activity-based costing which traces the total cost to serve a customer or a group. The measurement helps the firm to identify targeted but unprofitable customers. The firm can reconfigure its relationship with such customers in a number of ways to convert them into profitable ones.

Lead Measures: lead measures or customer value propositions (CVP) are the attributes of a firm's product and service offerings that create customer value and drive the core customer outcomes of satisfaction, acquisition, retention, profitability, and market share among targeted customer segments. They should be expected to vary across industries and across different market segments within industries. Nevertheless, they can be classified into three generic categories that are common to almost all industries (Figure 6.5):

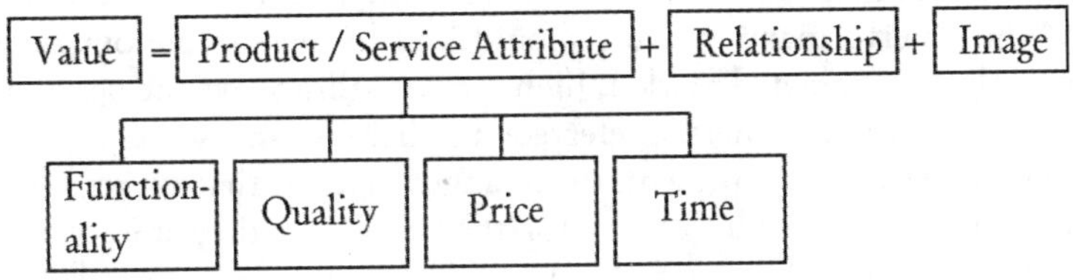

Fig. 6.5: The Customer Value Proposition—Generic Model

- product/service attributes
- customer relationships
- image and reputation

Let us consider each of these factors briefly.

Product and service attributes encompass functionality or features, quality, price, and speed of delivery. Saliency of each of these attributes depends upon the needs of the customers in the segment in which the firm is competing. Typically, there are at least two segments of customers in any industry: the price sensitive customers and the quality, feature, or novelty conscious customers. Price sensitive customers want a standard or basic product with no defects, delivered as promised, and at the lowest possible price. For firms serving such a segment, critical customer lead measures would be: price (relative to competition), defect or field-failure rates, and timeliness (shorter lead-time and OTD rate). For the premium segment, the strategic measures should be: new product or feature introduction rate (relative to competitors), quality of design or technology used, ability to customize design and delivery, etc. For such segments, measures like defect or field failure rate should be treated as diagnostic (as distinct from strategic) measures and monitored at the operational level. They will not find a place in the BSC.

Customer relationship includes everything that contributes to customers' buying experience with the firm. The end objective is to gain customer loyalty. Key elements of a firm's relationship with its customers depend on several factors like the firm's strategy, its nature of operations, and competitive context. For example:

- A retail store can build and strengthen customer relationship by recognition of customer loyalty, friendly service, and prompt and generous replacement of defective products.
- A retail bank, on the other hand, can deepen its relationship with customers by providing a wide product variety, 24-hour access to account information, etc.
- A supplier of industrial products can achieve similar purpose by establishing electronic data interchange link with its customer firms. It can encompass—beyond simple buying/selling relationship—shared design of products, linked production schedules, and electronic ordering, invoicing, and payment.

The challenge is to convert these critical elements into measurable entities. Finally, these performance drivers should lead to measurable outcomes like improved share of targeted market, higher cross-selling revenue per customer, higher position in customers' preferred supplier list and so on.

Image and reputation represents the intangible factors that attract a customer to a company. Buyers will not pay for the value that they do not perceive, no matter how real it may be. So firms need to create signals of value beyond the tangible aspects of the product and service. A firm must strive to proactively define itself for its targeted customers by creating an image and reputation which fits their lifestyle, aspirations, and preferences. This process of brand building takes time and investments before it can contribute to revenue earnings. Companies can use different platforms depending upon their positioning strategy, nature of operations, and market context. For example:

- A company selling premium consumer goods (like fashion garments) can address consumer lifestyles while companies in the same industry selling standard products at competitive prices would pitch on delivering reliable and consistent quality at affordable prices, as their value signals.
- A retail financial investment company needs to create an image of a trusted and knowledgeable financial adviser.
- A company selling sophisticated industrial products needs to create an image of technological superiority of its products, professionalism, and technical competency of its sales engineers. Value signals can be transmitted in multiple ways: packaging, advertising and promotion, the manner in which the company and its employees interface with the customers, and so on.

Finally, however, a precise definition and measure of signalling criteria are important in order to be actionable. Again, there are many ways in which a firm can measure the impact of its value signals on its targeted customers. Standard techniques applied in market research to measure the strength of a brand are one option. Image or reputation can be measured in harder ways also. Premium price earned on branded items, market share in key product categories, measuring customer satisfaction index on key value propositions—audited and benchmarked by an independent audit agency—and measurement of channel acceptance as a preferred brand are such examples. It has been observed that the value propositions of a successful firm reflect one of the following three dominant strategic themes to identify in the marketplace:

- Product Leadership: Corporations like Sony and Intel epitomize such a strategy where the company uses development of new generation products as its key differentiator. On a lesser scale, this would mean thrust on new product or feature development to attract targeted customers.
- Customer Intimacy: Good examples in this category are Singapore Airlines and Ritz-Carlton Hotels. Such companies try to build bonds

with customers by delighting them with personalized service. The physical attributes of their offerings (like the aircrafts Singapore Airlines uses, or the rooms the Ritz-Carlton Hotels have) may be comparable with those of their competitors. But they differentiate themselves with the quality of their customer service.

- Operational Excellence: Operationally excellent companies deliver a combination of quality, price, and ease of purchase that no one else can match. They are the best in their class in the management of their supply chains—for example, fast-food chain of McDonald's Corporation.

Typically, successful companies excel at one of these three dimensions of value while maintaining threshold standards on the other two. This is because of trade-offs existing between the different positions. Different positions require the companies to organize their activities differently, leading to different economies of operations.

Internal Business Process Perspective

A firm's strategy not only specifies the desired outcomes as embodied in the shareholder and customer-perspectives, but it must also describe how they are sought to be achieved. The essence of strategy is in the activities—choosing to perform activities differently or to perform activities different from those of the rivals. Activities are the basic units of competitive advantage. The art of developing a successful and sustainable strategy lies in choosing activities that correctly address the third fundamental question: what should we excel at? In this perspective, the managers identify the critical internal value-chain processes that the firm must excel in:

- to deliver the value propositions that the firm has chosen to offer so as to attract and retain targeted customers, and
- to satisfy shareholder expectations regarding financial returns.

One of the distinguishing features of the BSC methodology is that it forces managers to develop a new vision for the business processes and to discover ab initio strategically important activities and measures that would be necessary to manage those new processes. This sequential, top-down deployment usually reveals entirely new business processes at which an organization must excel. Quite often, the measures appear before complete anatomy of the new processes has emerged. It is a story of the tail wagging the dog! In BSC implementation, you do not slap measures on to your existing processes—however efficiently they may be running. You first look for their continued relevance in the context of the new strategy. The objectives and measures for the IBP perspective are derived from explicit strategies to drive outcomes in the shareholder- and customer-perspectives.

Each business has a unique set of processes for creating value for customers and producing final results. Moreover, the same customer value can be created in a variety of ways. You have to choose keeping both customer value and cost in view. You must know how to integrate your value-chain activities so as to obtain among the activities: consistency, reinforcement (for example, preventive maintenance supporting precision machining with existing machines), and optimization (doing one thing better—like pre-despatch quality check—reduces the need for another activity, for example, field repairs). However, there are some generic elements in the value-chain that are common to all firms (Figure 6.6). This generic value-chain provides a template that companies can customize in preparing their IBP perspective. This generic model encompasses three principal processes:

- innovation
- operations
- customer management

Let us now discuss, in brief, the objectives and measures corresponding to each of these three processes.

Innovation Process: In the innovation process, managers research the needs of customers and then create the products and services that will meet those needs. Market research also identifies the market size, customer preferences, and economic value of the demand.

Measures can be both input- and output-based. Often, a combination of both is more effective. Input-based measures like the number of new product ideas thrown up by market research or the time spent with important customers help encourage initiatives and innovation. Linked output measures such as percentage of sales from new products, new product introduction rate (versus competition) or success rate in competitive bidding signal the effectiveness of innovation efforts in producing business results.

Operations Process: The operations process represents the short wave of value creation that starts with receipt of a customer order and finishes with delivery of the product or service to the customer. This process stresses efficient, consistent, and timely delivery of existing products and services to existing customers.

Traditionally, operating processes have been monitored and controlled by cost accounting measures, such as standard costs, budgets, and variances. In today's customer driven competitive environment, companies are supplementing the traditional cost accounting measures with measurements of: cycle time, quality, and cost of business processes. Intense competitive pressures are forcing the firms to monitor a few more characteristics of their products and processes like flexibility/customization, responsiveness, reliability, and durability. Each firm needs to identify critical elements of its customer-value propositions and select the measures accordingly.

Post-sale Service Process: The final stage in the internal value-chain is post-sale service. It includes warranty and repair activities, treatment of defects and returns or customer complaints, quality of servicing a product like, a credit card or an insurance policy. Quality and reliability of post-sale service may indeed be the critical differentiator in many industries where products are

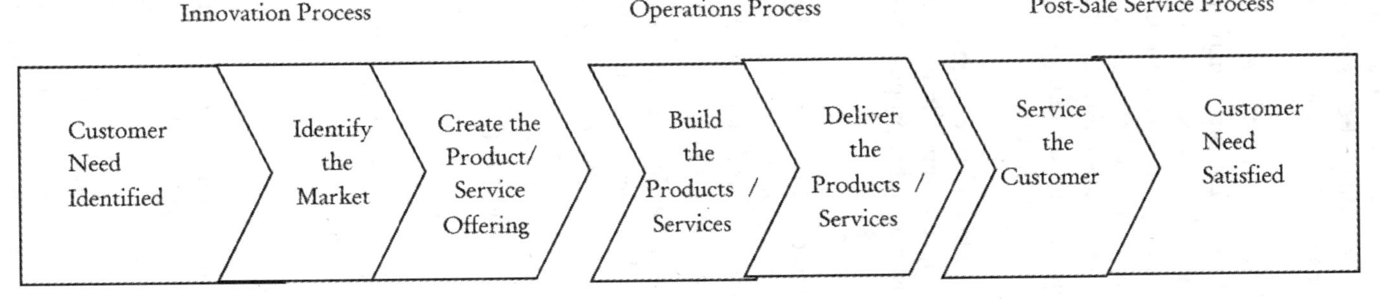

Fig. 6.6: Generic Value-chain Model

getting commoditized—like credit card, insurance products, consumer electronics, and consumer durables. For products like elevators and sophisticated medical equipment responsive service is a key customer purchase consideration.

The measures of post-sale service tend to be generic: time, quality, and cost of post-sale processes. Quality measures may include attributes like responsiveness and friendliness. Quality of a repair service (like auto repair) can be measured by the number of repeat calls for the same defect and so on. Cost of field repairs can be reduced by better inspection before delivery. In service firms, defective service, which imply additional activities and costs, can be avoided by better training in product knowledge or customer handling. So, while the final measures are generic, the drivers tend to be peculiar to the context of the firm.

It is also to be noted that while all three segments of a firm's value-chain are important, successful companies typically try to excel at the one that has maximum impact on its customer-value propositions.

Learning and Growth Perspective

The fourth and final BSC perspective of learning and growth (L&G) identifies the organizational capabilities and infrastructure that a firm must build for continuous learning and improvement that alone can make long-term growth possible in a rapidly evolving environment.

Performance and Learning Model: A firm's ability to create and deliver value to its customers and other stakeholders depends ultimately upon the abilities and willingness of its employees to perform in a manner as desired by the firm's strategy. Figure 6.7 depicts a simple model of performance and learning for building an effective organization.

Possession of required skills and competencies is the starting point. It is necessary but not sufficient for effective performance. For consistently good performance, an employee should be provided with two types of information. One, information required for decision-making, such as knowledge about company strategy, product, or customer profitability, customer segments to be given priority and so on. Two, feedback on performance, such as quality of goods and services delivered, their impact on customers and the company's financials and so on. The feedback on performance provides opportunities for learning and improvement as well as motivation for sustained efforts, particularly when rewards or other types of reinforcements accompany it. To be effective, employees should be given both the types of information at the right time and at the right place in their activity sequence. Availability of information is empowering, but only partially so. For full empowerment, employees must be given sufficient authority and freedom to act, using their skills, discretion and judgements. This completes the 'ability' part of the performance and learning cycle. The second part starts with motivation or willingness to act using ones skills, judgements, discretion, creativity and initiative as required by the firm's strategy. Motivation is a complex issue

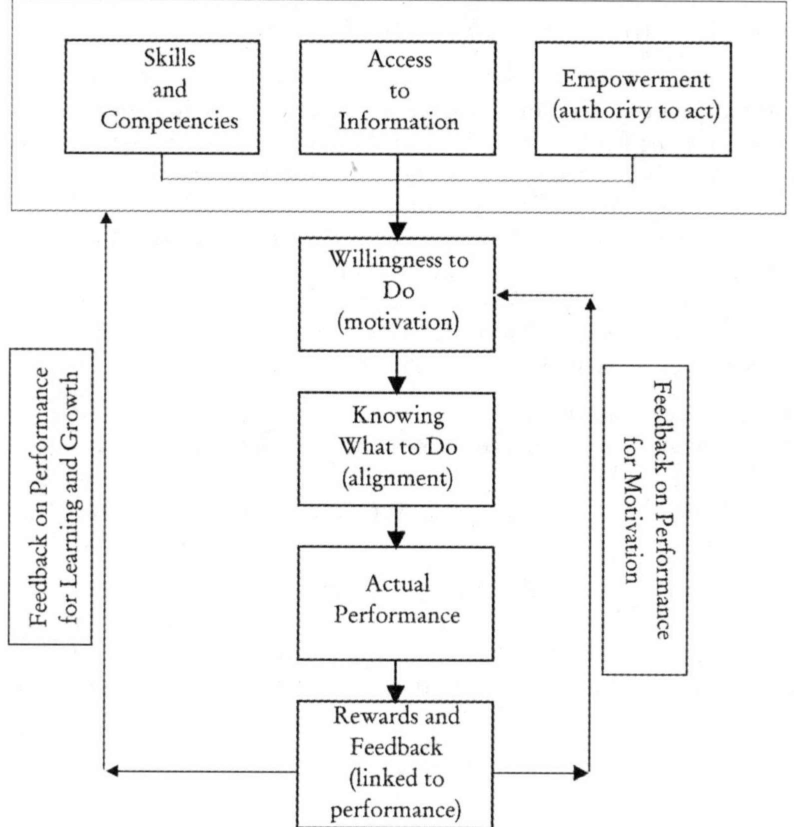

Fig. 6.7: Model of Performance and Learning

because of its multiple causation. So it needs a multi-pronged action strategy—right from inspiring leadership at the top, through skill development for achieving a sense of self-efficacy, to linking rewards to performance. Strategic performance outcomes may still elude us unless the energy and efforts of the employees and deployment of other organizational resources are aligned to the strategic goals. This calls for a careful strategy roll-out plan that aligns the operational goals at individual, group, and departmental levels with the strategy milestones of the strategic business units (SBU). This need for strategic alignment is the third element of the model. Finally, to sustain superior performance, one needs to reinforce desired employee behaviour by linking it to rewards—both financial and non-financial—which they value. This final linkage between performance and rewards completes the circuit between strategy and daily operations. This cycle needs to be repeated through feedback on performance both for learning and improvement as also for encouraging the employees to sustain and attain still better levels of performance. An organization ensures effective implementation of its strategy by translating it into what employees should do well in their daily activities, through the iteractive process as displayed in Figure 6.7.

Lag and Lead Measures: Study across a wide variety of service and manufacturing organizations has revealed a general typology of lag and lead measures for the L&G perspective and their interrelationships as depicted in Figure 6.8. This is consistent with the theory of organizational learning and performance as propounded earlier in this chapter.

The three lag (outcome) measures are: employee satisfaction, employee retention, and employee productivity. Within this core, the employee satisfaction objective is generally considered the driver of the other two measures.

The lead measures or the performance drivers of the outcomes in L&G perspective, as depicted in Figure 6.8, are:

- employee competencies;
- information systems capabilities for organisational performance and learning; and
- organizational capital—empowerment, motivation, and strategic alignment.

New strategy almost always requires new employee competencies. The demand for reskilling employees can be viewed along two dimensions: level of new skills required and percentage of workforce requiring such reskilling. For the organizations needing massive reskilling another measure would be

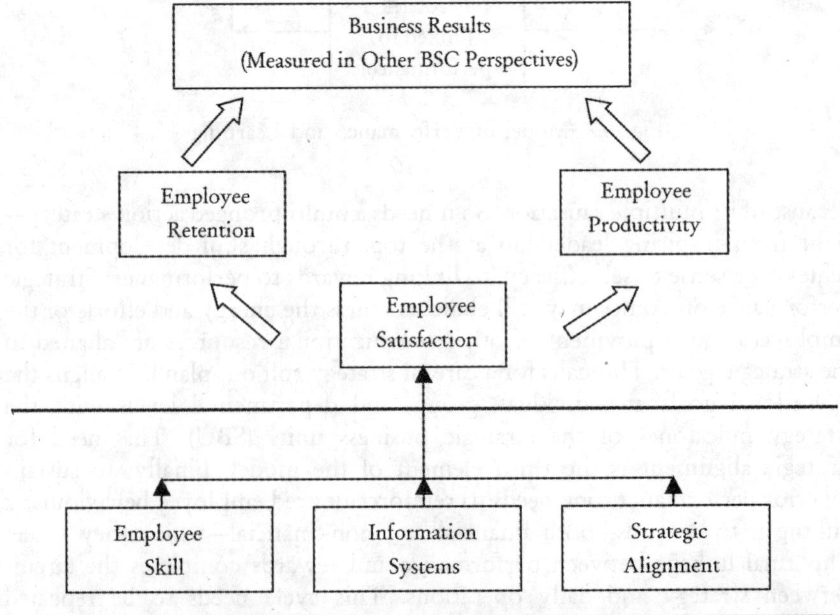

Fig. 6.8: Learning and Growth Perspective—Measurement Framework

the length of time required to take existing employees to the new levels of competency. Ability to reduce the cycle time of reskilling itself may be a source of competitive advantage for the firm.

Information system capabilities represent the infrastructure that is essential for providing the employees with information both as decision inputs and feedback for learning and improvement. Front line employees need accurate and timely information about firm strategy, product and customer profitability, transaction cost drivers and so on. They should also be informed about the firm's customer segmentation strategy so that they can regulate their behaviour and allocate their efforts between existing and potential customers. Employees in the operations need rapid, timely, and accurate feedback on the product just produced or the service just delivered. Only by having such feedback can employees be expected to sustain improvement programmes where they systematically eliminate defects and drive excess cost, time, and waste out of the production system. Finally, information sharing across different parts of the organization—be it functions, processes, or business units or project teams—is an important challenge. The wheel gets invented several times, errors are repeated, redundancies get built in. To prevent these costs, organizations have to integrate the sub-units by coordinating their activities and linking the packets of information and knowledge.

Building organizational capital and strategic alignment is the ultimate objective in the L&G perspective. Individual employee skills and strategic information systems are important enablers. Ultimately, however, a firm's competitive success depends on its ability to exploit the full potential of its resources and capabilities to create competitive advantage.

To be effective, BSC implementation, like any change initiative, must be able to capture the heart and mind of the people. So one can view it as an internal marketing campaign and measure it accordingly. One very effective and rigorous way to measure improvements in core business processes is to use the half-life metric that measures the length of time required for process performance to improve by 50 per cent. The half-life metric can be applied to any process variable such as cost, quality, or time.

Managing Strategy: A Four-step Management Process

As already indicated earlier, firms realize full potential of the BSC when they use it as a strategic management system to manage their strategies over long term. To accomplish this objective they should undertake a four-step iterative process involving: clarifying and translating the vision and the strategy; achieving strategic alignment; planning, resource allocation and target setting; and strategic feedback and learning (Figure 6.2). These four sub-processes are briefly discussed below.

Clarifying and Translating the Vision and the Strategy

Effective implementation of a strategy begins with translation of the firm's vision and strategy into terms that can be understood and acted upon. Despite the best intentions of those at the top, lofty statements about becoming 'the best in class', 'the number one supplier', or 'an empowered organization' do not translate easily into operational terms that provide useful guides to action at the local level.

The very process of building the BSC with its interlinked set of objectives and measures clarifies the vision and the strategy and creates consensus and teamwork among key managers which is vital for effective strategy implementation.

Achieving Strategic Alignment

In today's turbulent environment, no firm can centrally determine or lay down what employees need to do in response to every emerging situation or new developments. Market success depends much upon how the employees act locally using their judgement, initiative, creativity, and an overall sense of purpose in support of the organization's shared vision. The BSC with its cause–effect linkages of objectives and measures across the four perspectives facilitates such a top-to-bottom alignment.

The alignment of an organization to a shared vision and common direction is an extended and complex process. Typically, three distinct mechanisms need to be used:

- communication and education programmes;
- goal-setting programmes; and
- linking rewards to performance.

The strategic alignment gets complete only when strategy drives daily behaviour of the employees.

Aligning Other Resources and Business Initiatives With Strategy

What is true of human resources is also true for other resources. The business must also align its financial and physical resources to the strategy. Here again, strategy must drive daily operations. The BSC, with its causally interlinked lag-lead combinations of objectives and measures, integrates long-range strategic planning with annual operational budgeting process. By operationalizing strategy through lead measures, the BSC converts annual operational budgets into the milestones to be reached in successive years. Thus, it removes a major disconnect between strategy and operations. The actual process involves four steps:

- set stretch targets;
- identifying strategic initiatives;
- identifying cross-business and corporate initiatives; and
- link to annual resource allocation and budgets.

Feedback and Learning

The three steps discussed earlier help effective deployment of strategy. Together they form an important single-loop learning process in which any deviation of the actual results from the plan is viewed as a shortcoming to be corrected. They by themselves, however, do not tell you whether your strategy is still valid or not.

The fourth and final step that must be added to have a complete strategic management system is a process of feedback, analysis, and reflection that tests the hypotheses on which the strategy was based and adapts the strategy to emerging conditions.

The BSC supplies the three ingredients that are essential to strategic learning: the hypothesized links between daily activities and long-term strategic goals; the essential strategic feedback system; and a cross-functional team problem solving process. The identification of strategic issues that require further exploration and clarification closes the loop on the strategic double-loop learning process.

Creating a Strategy-focused Organization

Experiences of a large number of organizations show that the ability to execute strategy is more important than the quality of the strategy itself. In the majority of the cases, the real problem is not bad strategy, but bad execution.

Why do organizations have difficulty implementing well-formulated strategies? The answer is that while economy has changed from old to new, the tools for managing strategy have not kept pace. In an economy that was dominated by tangible assets, financial measurements were adequate measuring devices. Today the book value of tangible assets account for only 10–15 per cent of the market value of companies. Clearly, opportunities for creating value are shifting from managing tangible assets to managing knowledge-based strategies that deploy an organization's intangible assets: customer relationships, innovative products and services, high-quality and responsive operating processes, IT and databases, and employee capabilities, skills, and motivation. Also, the global competition in the new information age is forcing companies to change from a centralized functional structure to decentralized SBUs that are much closer to the customers. These changes call for a new framework for communicating and measuring strategy as well as processes and systems that help them to implement strategy and gain feedback about their strategy. Success comes from translating strategy into daily operations, thereby making it everyone's everyday job. We have seen how the BSC addresses all these issues and shortcomings of traditional management systems by linking the intangible assets with the tangibles and describing through the strategy map how a new age company creates shareholder value (tangible assets) from intangible assets.

The BSC offers a new age management system—one designed to manage strategy—which has three distinct dimensions.

Strategy: The BSC puts strategy—not control—at the centre. By translating strategy into the daily activities of every employee, it makes strategy the central organizing principle of an organization.

Focus: The BSC pervades all the four perspectives of business with cause–effect. It, thereby, creates a very high degree of focus in all that an organization does. Every resource and activity is aligned to the strategy. Thus, the BSC navigates the organization to its cherished future.

Organization: The BSC provides the logic and architectural design to establish new ways of organizing a firm's activities: structure, systems, linkages across SBUs, shared services, and redesigned linkages between departments, teams, and individual employees. It remobilizes the firm and its employees to act in fundamentally different ways which are in tune with new strategy.

The BSC helps to create a strategy-focused organization (SFO) that can make all the difference. Many successful adopters of the BSC framework have amply proven it. They used the BSC to execute strategies that used the same physical and human resources that had previously produced failing performance. The strategies were executed with the same products, the same facilities, the same employees, and the same customers. The difference was a new senior management team using the BSC to focus all organizational resources on a new strategy. They all created a strategy-focused organization.

References

Drucker, Peter F. (1994) The Theory of the Business, *Harvard Business Review*, September–October.

Kaplan, Robert S. and David P. Norton (2001) *The Strategy-focused Organisation*, Harvard Business School Press, Cambridge, Mass.

—— (1996) *Translating Strategy into Action: The Balanced Scorecard*, Harvard Business School Press, Cambridge, Mass.

Simons, Robert (1995) *Levers of Control: How Managers Use Innovative Control Systems to Drive Strategic Renewal*, Harvard Business School Press, Cambridge, Mass.

7

Activity-based Management

P.K. Sett

Think about the difference between two firms; one making 1000 units of a single product sold to a single customer, and another making one unit each of 1000 different products sold to 1000 different customers using diverse delivery channels. Let us assume that the direct material, labour, and machine hours spent for producing one unit of any product is same in both the cases. This means that the direct expenses for producing 1000 units will be identical for both the firms. However, we all agree that the second firm has to perform a much more complex set of activities to design, produce, and deliver 1000 different products and will be requiring much larger amounts of indirect and support resources than the first. Variety and complexity of processes, products, services, customers, and channels make the economics of production of the two firms fundamentally different.

Activity-based Management (ABM) is about unravelling the economic map of an enterprise—that is, knowing how much resources a firm's various processes, products, services, customers, and channels are consuming and why—and taking actions based on that knowledge to enhance the profitability of the firm. You need a map both to tell you where you are with reference to your final destination and how to reach there. Need for an accurate map is particularly critical when you are traversing an unknown territory in turbulent weather—something that the economic environment of the twenty-first century resembles closely. To ensure continued viability, today's firms must know accurately the sources of current profits and costs as well as the drivers of future profits and costs in the context of anticipated market and technological changes.

To build this all important economic map of the enterprise, ABM relies on activity-based costing (ABC) which establishes the causal link between the activities that the firms need to perform in order to develop, produce, deliver, and support goods and services sold to their customers, and the demands those activities make on the firms' resources. Activities represent the basic units of analysis used to determine the economics of operations of any firm. Only by knowing the patterns of the activity–resource linkages can managers get a clear picture of whether a particular product, service, customer, process, or channel is generating—or can generate—enough revenues to recover the cost of the activities performed on it. So one has to view organizational costs from multiple perspectives—products as well as processes. Figure 7.1 provides a visual representation of these ideas.

The ABC system emerged in the mid-1980s to meet the need for accurate information about the cost of resource demands by individual products, services, customers, and channels—which the traditional cost-accounting system (TCS) failed to provide. Firms that produce multiple products and services for diverse customers and markets and use a variety of distribution channels would receive incomplete and highly distorted information from their TCS. As a result, managers using the TCS can often make poor decisions about:

- pricing of individual products and services;
- determining cost to serve individual customers;
- establishing priorities for process improvements;
- designing products and services that are less expensive to manufacture and deliver;
- identifying the most profitable mix of products and customers;
- structuring the most profitable relationships with customers and suppliers; and so on.

Interestingly, however, the TCS does not distort the aggregate financial statements like balance sheet and income statement prepared for investors, creditors, and regulators. Rather, information about the components that comprise the aggregate numbers can be highly distorted, concealing underlying profits and losses of individual products, services, and customers, and economic efficiency of individual processes. But the aggregate income statement, though correct , cannot help managers decide what to do to improve the numbers for the financial statements of the following year. To discover which actions will increase selling margin and reduce operating expenses, managers need to understand patterns of resource consumption by the activities performed by the firm. It is at the activity level that the profits or losses are really made.

The TCS was designed for the more simple and stable business environment prevalent more than a century back. They are founded upon assumptions which are no longer valid. Their limitations arise from their structure which we must understand before we embark on our discussion on ABC and ABM.

Limitations of the TCS

The TCS was developed at a time when firms produced either a single or a narrow range of products employing relatively simple technologies and delivered them to mostly local customers. Absence of variety and complexity made it possible for the firm to trace most of the costs directly to the output, and this also kept indirect and support costs low. This context allowed the cost system designers of the time to develop a simple two-stage cost system (Figure 7.2) which could perform all the three functions required of a cost system, namely, external financial reporting, estimation of the costs of

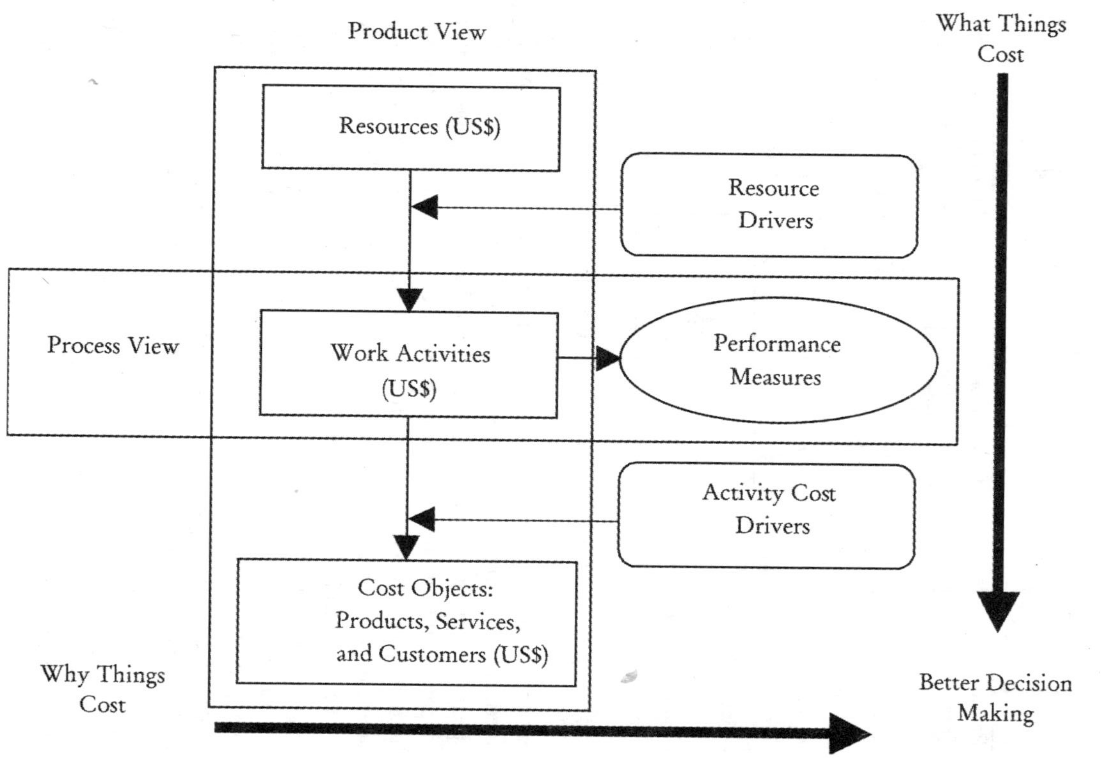

Fig. 7.1: Activity-based View of Cost

Source: Cokins (1996).

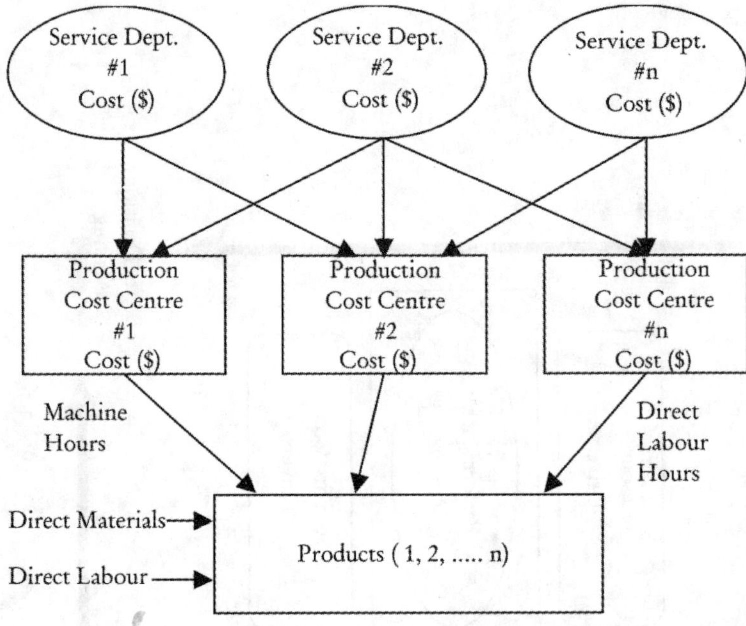

Fig. 7.2: Traditional Two-stage Cost System

products, services, and processes for strategic decision- making, and providing economic feedback on efficiency of operations.

Briefly speaking, the two-stage TCS works as follows. In stage one, service or support department costs are assigned to production/operating departments. Most of these indirect expenses are difficult to be causally related to any particular operating department. Typically, they are accumulated in a common pool called overhead and then allocated to different operating departments based on some arbitrarily chosen bases like head count, direct labour hours, and machine hours worked. Costs directly arising in the respective operating departments are also traced to them. Thus, after the first stage, all organizational expenses—excepting what are regarded in accepted accounting practices as period costs (for example, sales and distribution, advertising, R&D, employee training and development)—are assigned to the operating departments. In stage two, costs of each operating department are assigned to the products processed through it. Again, the assignment is by way of allocation using some arbitrary bases like direct labour hours consumed by a product and so on.

Here, we can draw two important lessons about the TCS. First, in both stages the TCS allocates costs with the help of some arbitrarily chosen allocation bases without establishing any sort of causal link between the costs and their drivers. That is, the allocated costs do not reflect the actual consumption of resources made by the operating department, or the product, concerned. Second, a large amount of the expenses constituting the so-called period costs are left unanalysed. These expenses appear only as a line item in the income statement of the firm. The limitations of the TCS arise basically out of these two facts—as explained below.

First, the simple rules of cost allocation based upon unit-level cost drivers like volume of production and direct labour hours hold good only when a firm's products and processes are highly homogenous so that indirect expenses vary in direct proportion to such drivers. But, when a firm produces multiple products with different designs and/or requiring different processes to produce and deliver to different customers, such simple unitized allocation rules will give highly distorted cost figures. This is because such a firm has to spend a sizeable amount of its indirect resources in activities such as setting up machines, scheduling production runs, moving materials, etc. (batch-level activities), or in designing, improving, branding, and promoting individual products (product-level activity)—which consume resources independent of the number of units produced. Thus, the TCS fails to capture the economics of production of firms with multiple products, complex processes, and diverse customers or channels.

The second limitation arises from the fact that the TCS allocates only production-centre costs to products. Period costs remain untraced to the products, services, channels, and customers that create the demand for or benefit from the related activities like sales promotion, advertising, and customer support.

Third, the TCS assigns and monitors costs on the basis of responsibility centres or departments whereas the business processes are cross-functional. Business processes like customer order fulfilment spans multiple departments and functions covering sales, production, purchase, delivery, billing, and invoicing. To be able to improve business performance through design, control, and improvement of business processes, firms need to have cost information for an integrated business process, rather than departmental costs. The TCS not only fails to supply such critical information but also encourages departmental level, rather than business level, optimization of results.

Thus, whenever there is product variety and/or process complexities, the TCS gives highly inaccurate and distorted cost estimates of products, services, and customers. Also, they cannot estimate the cost of a cross-functional business process. As mentioned earlier, none of these limitations hamper their ability to meet the external financial reporting requirements through balance sheets and income statements. Errors in costing of individual products get cancelled out in the process of aggregation for compilation of the reports. In summary, in today's competitive environment, the TCS is incapable of meeting the strategic and operational needs for cost information though it may still be fine for external financial reporting purpose.

The above discussion holds equally good for service and manufacturing firms. Unlike manufacturing companies, service firms have no statutory requirements to value their inventory or determine the cost of goods sold because they have no inventoriable products. Consequently, most service firms using the TCS do not suffer from distorted cost numbers, as they keep no such numbers at all! Service firms use the TCS largely for external financial reporting and departmental expenditure control only. With the limitations of the TCS analysed, let us now turn to an understanding of the ABC system and see how it proposes to remove the limitations of the TCS.

What is the ABC System?

The ABC system maps resource expenses first to activities and then to products, services, and customers (Figure 7.3). The best way to understand the architecture of an ABC system is to find answers to the four basic questions that it seeks to address. While answering these four questions, we describe four steps involved in building an ABC model for a firm.

Step 1. *Why is the organization spending money on indirect and support resources?*

Firms spend on resources to carry out activities that are directly or indirectly needed to develop, produce, and deliver goods and services to their customers. Expenses which can be directly (causally) traced to their beneficiaries (products, services, or customers) pose no analytical challenge. But every organization also spends resources on indirect support activities (like purchasing, planning, and quality assurance) and to provide infrastructural capabilities (like physical facilities, utilities, and information systems). The TCS either arbitrarily allocates such expenses to responsibility centres, or keeps them unanalysed by treating them as period costs. In contrast, the ABC system focuses on all these activities first by building up an activity dictionary that lists and defines all the major activities performed by the business unit. Activities are described by verb–object combinations: purchase materials, schedule production, inspect items, support customers, develop products, and so on. The size of the activity dictionary depends on the purpose of the ABC project (like product costing, or process improvement initiative) as well as on the size and complexity of the business unit.

Step 2. *How much does it cost to perform organizational activities and business processes?*

To know how much the firm is spending on its various activities, the ABC system drives resource expenses to the activities listed in the activity dictionary, by using resource cost drivers (Figure 7.3). This is a major innovation. It represents a 90° shift in thinking about expenses if you recall that the TCS allocates expenses only to departments and not cross-functional processes.

A firm's financial system categorizes resource expenses by a spending code—for example, salaries, electricity, travel, computing, communications and so on. To select the resource cost drivers the procedure followed is: (a) for personnel related indirect expenses employee surveys are carried out through a structured questionnaire to find out the percentage of time they spend on any activity on the list; (b) for non-personnel resources, the ABC project team either relies on direct measurement (for example, how much power, computer time, or telecommunication facilities), or estimates the percentage of the resource used by each activity in the dictionary.

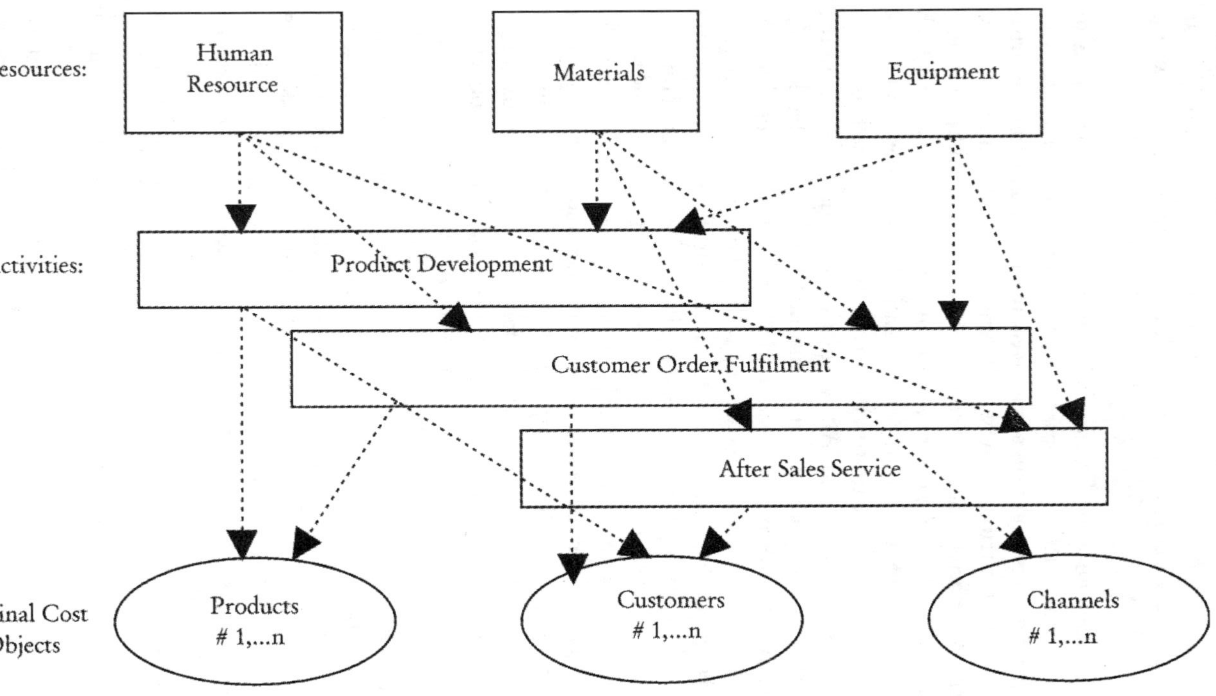

Fig. 7.3: ABC Traces Costs to Their Origins

As depicted in Figure 7.3, the fundamental purpose of the ABC system is to flow costs from resources to activities, and then to final cost objects like products, services, and customers. One does not need extensive time-and-motion studies to link resource spending to activities performed. The goal is to be approximately right (sufficient for strategic decision-making), than precisely wrong! TCS calculations of, say, product costs are invariably wrong because of the arbitrary allocation procedures followed.

Hierarchy of Activities: The second major innovation of the ABC system is its classification of a firm's activities based on their attributes. This activity classification is the key to building an accurate economic map of an enterprise. Activities with different attributes show different cost behaviours and need different cost drivers for driving activity cost to a final cost object like a product or customer. One of the most important activity attributes is the level at which cost arises: unit, batch, product, customer, and facility or business unit.

Unit-level activities are the activities that have to be performed for every unit of product or service produced. All production activities like machining and assembly, processing of a cheque or an insurance policy in a bank or an insurance company, etc. are unit-level activities. Indirect activities like 100 per cent inspection of any output and salary billing fall in this category.

Examples of batch-level activities are: scheduling a production run, setting up machines for a new batch production, sample inspection of a batch output, and processing a purchase indent or a customer order. The resources to be spent on a batch-level activity are independent of the number of units produced in the batch. For example, indirect labour and other resources required to set up machines will be independent of the number of units to be produced in a given production run. Product-sustaining or customer-sustaining activities relate to activities performed to support a particular product or customer. Expenses relating to design improvements or special tools and testing equipment required for the production of a product represent product-sustaining activity costs which are independent of both the number of units and batches of the product produced. These costs have to be incurred as long as the product is in production. Similarly, special facilities created or special customer support provided to a customer represent customer-sustaining activities. Related costs are independent of the volume and mix of the products or services ordered by the customer. Demand for these resources can cease only when we drop the customer concerned.

Activities like general administration and shared utilities are examples of facility-sustaining activities. The related expenses should not be burdened on to products. Instead they should be shown as such to help in the identification of their sources.

Similarly, one can think of brand-sustaining or channel-sustaining activities. Resources required for carrying out such activities (for example, advertising, trade shows, etc.) benefit a family of products. So, it would be incorrect to impose these costs arbitrarily on any individual product.

By classifying the activities of the firm into unit, batch, product or customer sustaining, and facility sustaining, managers get a clear picture of the costs driven by production or sales volume versus the costs arising due to variety and complexities of the products, services, and customers served. This knowledge alone can enable managers to proactively manage the related costs. The TCS which uses only unit level cost allocation drivers is not designed to provide such valuable cost information.

Depending upon the intended scope of activity accounting, firms may also use other types of activity attributes. For example, classifying activities on the basis of variability of activity costs with variations in demand over time (short, medium, long term) enable decisions on pricing, new product introduction, change of distribution channel or technology, and so on. Similarly, activities can be coded based on their criticality to the business of the firm, or efficiency of performance. This again may lead to a number of decisions on process improvement, redesign, or outsourcing.

As we will see later, these information (that is, the characteristics of a firm's activities and how much each activity costs) by themselves can be used for a range of process improvement actions and removal of redundancies.

Step 3. *Why does the organization need to perform activities and business processes?*

As already mentioned, firms perform activities to develop, produce, and deliver goods and services to their customers. At this stage the ABC project team identifies the firm's products, services, and customers—the ultimate beneficiaries of its activities. The firm spends its resources on them to generate its revenues. Then when we drive activity costs to these revenue generating entities it will be revealed whether they are earning their keep.

Step 4. *How much of each activity is required for the organization's products, services, and customers?*

In the fourth and the final stage of the ABC modelling, activity costs calculated in step 2 are driven to the final cost objects (products, services, and customers) identified in step 3, with the help of activity cost drivers (ACD). An ACD is a factor that causally affects the cost of an activity. Examples are given below.

Activity	Activity Cost Driver
Order processing	Number of orders
Customer service	Number of customers served, or hours spent with each customer
Product development	Number of products developed, or time-to-market a product
Bills payment	Number of bills processed
Set up machines	Number of set ups, or set up hours
Run machines	Number of machine hours

Selection of ACDs

There are three types of ACDs to choose from: transaction, duration, and intensity or direct charging. The choice of an ACD reflects a subjective trade-off between accuracy and the cost of measurement.

Transaction drivers (TD) count how often an activity is performed. Examples are: the number of orders processed, the number of machine set ups, and the number of customers served. They are the easiest to measure and, hence the least costly. But they will not be accurate when the amount of resources required to perform the activity varies significantly across products and customers. In such an instance, duration drivers (DD) are a better option. DDs represent the amount of time required to perform an activity. For example, production of a simple product may require only 15 minutes of set up time as against 3 hours for a complex product. The same may be the case in servicing the customers buying these products. Use of TDs would be inappropriate here because they will show the same cost per set up irrespective of whether a simple or a complex product is being produced. Thus, use of TDs will overcost simple products and undercost complex products. DDs would more accurately reflect the rate of resource consumption for setting up machines for the two products. However, this higher accuracy may have to be gained at a higher cost of collecting an additional piece of information, namely, the set up times for different products. Finally, there may be a need to directly charge for the resources used each time an activity is performed like, say, a particularly complex product requiring highly-skilled personnel and costly equipment for set up. Here, DDs cannot be used because they assume that all hours are equally costly—a condition not satisfied in the present case. This case would require the use of intensity drivers (IDs) which directly charges for the resources used, each time an activity is performed. IDs are the most accurate ACDs but they are the most expensive to implement too.

The choice among the three types of ACDs can occur for almost any activity. For example, for customer support activity, circumstance can justify: cost per customer (a TD),or cost per customer hour (a DD), or actual cost per customer (an ID)—depending upon how diverse is the resource consumption patterns among different customers served.

As already mentioned, classification of activities by their critical attributes and identification of the associated ACDs are the central innovations of the ABC system. But they are also their most costly aspects. End use of an ABC system should decide its design features. Product and customer costing do not normally require more than 30–50 different ACDs; while process improvement initiatives may call for more disaggregated information. With the installation of ERP systems in many organizations, most of such data become automatically available.

The Fundamental Equation of ABC

Firms procure resources like people, materials, equipment, and so on to create capacity for work. Costs arise from the acquisition and use of the resources by the firm. The fundamental equation is:

Cost of Resources Supplied (Cost of Capacity)	=	Cost of Resources Used	+	Cost of Unused Capacity

It is useful to recognize that firms use broadly two types of resources: committed and flexible. Committed resources are the ones that are acquired or contracted for in advance of the work to be accomplished with them. These resources are supplied ahead of actual demand. Examples are: building, equipment, and permanent employees. Expenses on committed resources (for example, depreciation or leasing charges, salary) are incurred irrespective of whether the resources are actually used or not during the period for which commitment exists. Examples of flexible resources are raw materials, electric power, and piece-work contract labour. These resources are always consumed commensurate with demand and, hence, their 'capacity' is always fully utilized. So, by definition, cost of unused capacity relates only to committed resources. Interestingly, most of the indirect or support resources the firms use are committed resources.

Let us clarify the concept of cost of resource capacity through a simple illustration. Consider a common support activity such as customer order handling. Suppose, after interview and survey procedures described in Step 2 of the ABC modelling, and using (historical) accounting data for the previous year, the ABC analysts estimate that an expenditure worth US$250,000 can be traced to this activity. Out of this, let us suppose, US$200,000 has been spent on equipment, office space, and personnel (committed resources), and the remaining US$50,000 on consumables like power, stationery, etc. (flexible resources). Let the number of customer orders handled in the previous year be 2500. So in the previous year the firm has spent: Committed resources = US$80 per order; Flexible resources = US$20 per order; and Total Expenses = US$100 per order. But the moot point is what do all the above figures do, or do not, tell us. More importantly, how do we use these data for managing the firm better in the following year.

First, the data do not tell us anything about the practical capacity of the committed resources: how many customer orders could be handled during the period by the committed resources supplied. Second, they also do not tell us anything about the efficiency of use of resources—both committed and flexible. The two issues, however, are interrelated. Any capacity calculation, particularly of the nature being discussed here, assumes a particular level of process efficiency. So we need more data for us to improve the following year's business results.

Suppose we undertake a survey and estimate that at the present level of staff efficiency and process technology, the department can process a maximum of 5000 customer orders per year. So 5000 orders per year is our practical capacity now. Let us suppose that judging the market situation, we expect to receive 4000 customer orders in the current year. If this be the situation, then what would be our budget for customer order handling expenses for the current year and how should we price our bids, or charge these expenses to the orders we actually receive. To answer these questions correctly, we need to keep the capacity-based view of resources in mind.

Since the committed resources like permanent staff, equipment, and office space are such that we cannot change their supply in the short run, the budgeted cost of committed resources would still be US$200,000. But while we price our bids or charge the order processing expenses to orders actually received, we cannot use either the budgeted or actual number of orders. That would be conceptually wrong. To obtain the correct cost driver rate for the committed resources, we have to divide the resource expense by the practical capacity. In this case this rate works out to US$40 per order. We received only 2500 orders in the previous year and so 50 per cent of our practical capacity remained unused. Our cost driver rate calculation of US$80 per order (US$200,000 ÷ 2500) for committed resources based on actual number of orders received last year had, in fact, two components:

Cost of Resources Supplied		Cost of Resources Used		Cost of Unused Capacity
US$200,000	=	US$100,000	+	US$100,000
(Practical Capacity)		(Capacity Used)		(Capacity Not Used)
5000 orders @ US$40		2500 orders received		2500 orders not received

With the budgeted number of 4000 orders expected to be received during the current year, the capacity equation would look as follows:

Cost of Resources Supplied		Cost of Resources Used		Cost of Unused Capacity
US$200,000	=	US$160,000	+	US$40,000
(Practical Capacity)		(Capacity Used)		(Capacity Not Used)
5000 orders @ US$40		4000 orders expected		1000 orders not received

It is clear from the above two equations that if we use actual or budgeted figures, we will commit the mistake of burdening the cost of orders we receive with the cost of orders we do not receive. There are at least two dangers of committing this error. First, the cost driver rate would give the wrong signal that the process is inefficient (US$80 per order as against US$40) when in fact the process has performed as per standard efficiency. Second, if we start using such higher rates, for example, to bid for new orders, then we are most likely to lose custom. In a price sensitive market, or when demand is depressed, use of such wrong cost driver rates may initiate a death spiral for the firm's business. As the firm receives less orders, its cost driver rates calculated based on actuals, would go up. The firm would then increase price which would then lead to further loss of custom.

As far as the flexible resources are concerned, the budgeted expense should be US$80,000 (4000 @ US$20 per order—as calculated earlier)—as we have assumed the process efficiency to remain unchanged. So the capacity-based view of resources suggests that the actual output should never be burdened by the cost of unused capacity. Rather, the cost of unused capacity serves as a constant reminder to the firm's managers that this cost should be managed out of the system. Cost of unused capacity can be managed out of the system only in two ways:

- by reducing the supply of the committed resources when their demand is less than their supply; or

- by increasing the quantity of activities (like, in the example discussed, getting more orders) to the level of the practical capacity.

Unless the managers are able to remove the cost of unused capacity out of the system in either of the two ways indicated above, the firm's bottom line results will not show any improvement because committed resource expenses would remain with the firm whether or not the related capacity is utilized.

As we shift our discussion from ABC to ABM, it will become apparent how managers can use ABC analysis to start new initiatives like process improvement, changing product–customer–channel mix, and reconfiguring customer and supplier relationships to enhance the practical capacity of a firm's resources and then manage those extra capacities for generating higher shareholder value.

What is Activity-based Management?

Activity-based Management (ABM) is the set of actions that managers can take on the basis of the ABC cost analysis to enable the firm to accomplish its desired business objectives with fewer demands on a firm's resources. That is, the firm incurs lower cost per unit of revenue earned. ABM initiatives can be classified into two types: operational and strategic ABM.

Operational ABM can be characterized as doing things well. Here actions are targeted at increasing the practical capacity of resources of every kind—people, machinery/equipment, material, or money—so that the output generated with given resource inputs is higher. It may involve actions like improving employee efficiency, reducing machine downtime, increasing inventory turnover, or decreasing accounts receivable, as well as radical steps like re-engineering processes to remove non-value adding activities and other forms of redundancies. Measurable outcomes of operational ABM are: reduced costs, enhanced asset utilization, and higher productivity. Broadly speaking, the goal is to increase the efficiency of operations by trying to find out how to produce the same level of output (products and services) with less resources.

Strategic ABM is what strategy is all about that is, doing the right things. The focus here is on first understanding the economics of the firm's operations through ABC analysis and then utilizing that knowledge to choose the most profitable mix of products, services, customers, and channels, and to design cost-effective processes to develop, produce, and deliver the goods and services desired by the firm's chosen customers. The idea, in essence, is to reduce the demand for resources required per unit of revenue earned through actions like redesigning products, reconfiguring customer/supplier relationship, shifting channel of delivery, and so on. That is, the focus is on the most profitable uses of a firm's resources so as to increase the profitability of the firm. Here efficiency of resource utilization, like employee productivity, is taken as given.

Obviously, a firm will maximize its business results when its tackles simultaneously the supply and the demand sides of its resources by reducing the rate of consumption of resources by its activities together with shifting its activities to more profitable processes, products, services, and customers. With this understanding of the differences between operational and strategic ABM, let us explore them in some more detail.

Operational ABM

Traditionally, a firm's cost and process efficiency improvement initiatives have been targeted at departments involved in direct operations, whether in manufacturing or service firms. But, in the present competitive scenario, such local optimizations cannot create competitive advantage for a firm. Moreover, in many cases, while a firm's products, services, and customer demands may have undergone fundamental changes, its business processes have remained unaltered and have become completely unsuited to the current needs. To be able to successfully compete in the market today, a firm needs to know the cost effectiveness and efficiency of its cross-functional business processes—not merely those of its manufacturing and service operations. Ironically, it is the cross-functional business processes, involving multiple departments and numerous hand-offs between these departments, that remained undermanaged because managers did not earlier have the necessary tools for analysing them. Traditional cost and performance measurement systems were not geared to meet these needs—as we have seen earlier.

By shifting the fundamental focus of organizational control from departments to activities, and driving the resource costs to the activities (instead of to the departments), the ABC makes visible the opportunities for cost reduction and improved efficiency of cross-functional business processes. At the end of Step 2 of the ABC modelling, organizations already have a dictionary of important activities and their costs. While preparing the activity dictionary and measuring the activity costs, the analysts can also gather information on activity attributes like criticality, efficiency, and value-addition, on a simple scale, say 1 to 5, that capture their rating of an activity on the attribute field. For example, analysts can grade activities on a 5 or 7 point scale starting from Highly Efficient (less than, say, 5 per cent apparent opportunity for improvement) to Highly Inefficient, and so on. These coded ABC information help managers to manage ABM projects as follows:

- develop the business case for a process improvement by showing its likely benefits,
- establish priorities among competing projects,
- provide financial justification for up-front project investment,
- track the actual benefits flowing from a project implementation against the plan, and
- identification of drivers of ongoing improvement of even transformed processes.

Setting priorities for improvement of business processes is best done using the framework of the BSC, in particular, by answering the internal business perspective question: which activity should we excel in? It identifies those processes that are most critical not only for their potential for cost reduction, but also for their ability to meet targeted competitive benchmarks and customer expectations.

As regards which methodology to be followed for process improvement, the managers have choices like total quality management (TQM), business process re-engineering, and competitive benchmarking. The choice may be driven by a number of factors, internal and external, like employee resistance to radical change and competitive position of the firm in its industry. Again, the BSC framework can inform the choice between continuous and radical improvement by revealing the strategic imperatives of the related processes.

Strategic ABM

Ultimately, demand for activities arises from products and services produced, and customers served. Different products, services, and customers may, however, demand different types and amounts of activities which will have different cost implications. Strategic ABM initiatives are about the most profitable deployment of a firm's resources. Broadly, they involve decisions on:

- product mix and pricing,
- customer relationships,
- supplier relationships, and
- product design and development

We briefly discuss each of these topics below.

Product Mix and Pricing

We have seen earlier how the TCS overcost high-volume standard products and undercost low-volume customized products. No wonder firms using distorted cost information provided by the TCS, overproliferate their product lines and overcustomize their offerings and enter into a vicious cycle of dwindling profits. They do this because the TCS cost data send them wrong signals that the existing standard products have declining margin while customized products are fetching higher profits. Cost of product variety and complexity manifest through higher spending in indirect and support resources is kept hidden from their view by the arbitrary cost allocation rules used by the TCS.

The moment the ABC system is used to estimate the product costs of a full-line producer, the cumulative product profitability graph typically looks like the back of a whale (Figure 7.4). A typical Whale Curve suggests that the most profitable 20 per cent products generate about 300 per cent of profits, next 40 per cent of the products just break even, and the remaining 40 per cent products erode 200 per cent of profits, leaving the business unit with its 100 per cent profit.

The ABC whale curve of product profitability forces the firm to take a hard look at the economic justification of its product and service variety. The

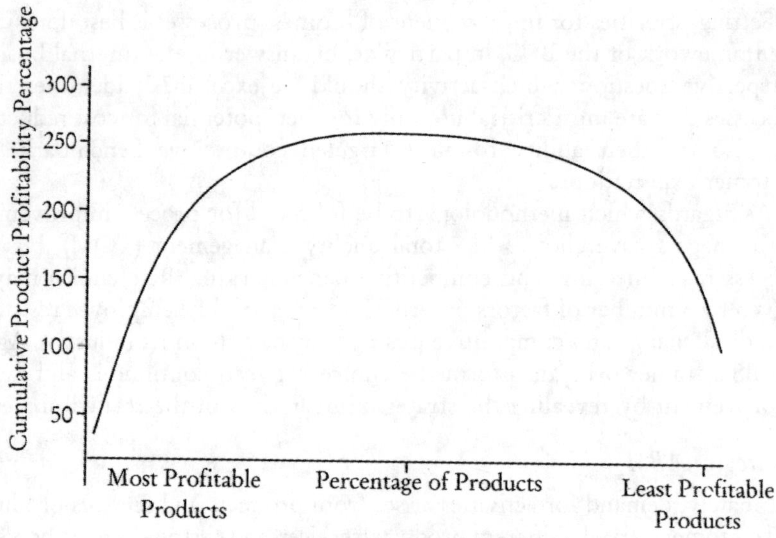

Fig. 7.4: Product Profitability Whale Curve

range of options that the managers typically have to increase the profitability of their product lines involves:

- reprice products,
- substitute products
- redesign products,
- improve production processes,
- change operating policies and strategy,
- invest in flexible technology, and
- eliminate products.

Newly introduced, customized, and more functional products can be repriced to earn a price premium over standard, mature commodity products. However, for such a differentiation policy to be sustainable, the price premium earned should be greater than the cost of differentiating. Scope for profitable product substitution always exists because customers make a trade-off between functionality, uniqueness, and price. So customers may themselves be willing to relax their specifications. The ABC system helps fact-based dialogue with customer so as to reduce diversity of customer demands. About 80 per cent of the product cost gets locked in at the design stage. The ABC system with its hierarchical cost drivers can provide valuable insights to the product designer to design for manufacturability and considerably reduce batch level and product-sustaining level costs by increasing the number of common components among product variants and reducing the number of parts to be used in a single product. The ABC map of product economics highlights why the products in the right-hand tail of the whale curve are not making profits. Again, the cost hierarchy of the ABC system directs attention to areas where processes need to be improved to reduce wasteful resource consumption. Technological improvement and upgradation of skills are the typical interventions necessary. Difference in the economics of production between high-volume standard products and small batch-size customized products (requiring high batch-level and product-sustaining activities) call for different strategies in their production; the former requiring high-speed special-purpose machines and semi-skilled labour as against the general-purpose machines and highly-skilled labour required by the latter. Differences in policies may also be required in other areas like inventory management, stocking, delivery, etc. Use of IT applications like computer-aided design, computer-aided software engineering, and computer-aided manufacturing are introducing a high degree of flexibility in designing, production, and delivery of products and services which is removing the classical trade-off between efficiency and flexibility. This has made low-cost, efficient production of small batches of customized products a reality. Shedding of unprofitable products should be done with caution. Managing variety and complexity requires sophisticated skills. Variety and complexity do not automatically lead to unprofitability. The ABC system provides a framework to ensure that the value customers receive from new and different products more than offsets the costs of offering them.

Customer Relationships

The versatility of the ABC system allows firms to explore the economics of customer relationship and their distribution and delivery channels. Traditionally, marketing, selling, and general administrative expenses have remained unanalysed and kept as a line item of period costs below the gross margin line in income statements. By analysing the related activities, the ABC system maps the consumption of resources made by individual customers and channels. The broad characteristics of customer behaviour that makes the cost of serving a customer high or low is indicated in Box 7.1

Box 7.1: Factors Determining High-cost- and Low-cost-to-serve Customers

High-cost-to-serve Customers	Low-cost-to-serve Customers
Order custom products	Order standard products
Small order quantities	Large order quantities
Unpredictable order arrivals	Predictable order arrivals
Customized delivery and packaging	Standard delivery and packaging
Frequent post-order changes	No post-order changes
Manual processing of orders	Electronic order processing
Large amounts of pre-sales support (marketing, technical, and sales)	Little to no pre-sales support (standard pricing and ordering)
Large amounts of post-sales support (installation, training, warranty, field service)	No post-sales support
Require the supplier to hold inventory	Immediate delivery
Pay slowly and long credit period (high accounts receivable)	Pay on time and short credit period

Interestingly, the individual customer profitability graphs of firms with diverse range of customers have the same whale-back shape as the product profitability graph shown in Figure 7.4. This means that such firms do not recover the costs to serve from more than 40 per cent of their customers. It is useful to categorize a firm's relationships with its customers as depicted in Figure 7.5 below. This simple classification can be of immense help in reconfiguring a firm's relationship with its customers and making it profitable.

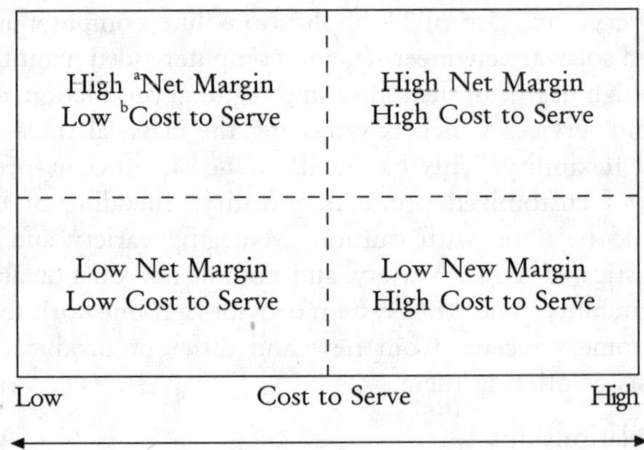

Fig. 7.5: Customer Profitability

Notes: [a]Net Margin = Net Price (Gross Price – All Sales Discounts) – Manufacturing Cost

[b]Cost to Serve = All order related costs + All customer-sustaining expenses

A firm can make its relationship with customers profitable in different ways. A price-sensitive customer, who will lie at the lower left quadrant, can be profitable if the customer behaviour conforms, or is made to conform, to low-cost-to-serve characteristics. Concurrently, the firm can make profits out of high-cost-to-serve customers (upper right corner), who are looking for unique functionality, features, and special support, if it can realize higher price, say by offering a menu-based price offer for the special services offered, to cover the extra costs of special offerings. Traditional mark-up based pricing hides the high cost to serve these customers making them hidden loss customers. However, the ABC system reveals the potential high cost to serve them. Customers at the upper left corner should be nurtured and keenly protected from competitive forays. These are hidden profit customers to whom a firm can always afford to offer discounts and incentives, or special services, if demanded. To meet the real challenge posed by the low margins and high-cost-to-serve customers at the lower right corner, firms have to rely on the ABC analysis to look for possible modification of the existing relationships to make them profitable. There may be several options: redesign internal processes, or negotiate with the customer sharing ABC data to modify its behaviour, or price out the special services rendered, so as to reduce the cost-to-serve. Sometimes such customers hold high future profitability through increasing volumes and profitable mix of business in subsequent years. Firms should handle such customers appropriately and plan for reaching for profitability in subsequent periods. There may be occasions when firms would like to retain some such customers who are high-profile for non-financial benefits like the prestige associated with dealing with them or the opportunity for learning state-of-the-art business practices. If none of these reasons or possibilities hold for some of these customers, then instead of firing them they should be encouraged to desert perhaps to a competitor by raising prices, cutting back services, or refusing customization.

ABM initiatives to redefine the customer relationship can dramatically improve a firm's profitability as well as its competitive position because the firm now knows which customers are profitable and which are not, and how to deepen the relationship with its profitable customers and also how to make the unprofitable ones profitable.

Supplier Relationships and Product Development

Since the ABC analysis covers all activities in a firm's value chain, ABM initiatives should cover correspondingly the back end of the value chain, namely, supplier relations, and product design and development.

Activities associated with ordering, receiving, inspecting, moving, storing, and paying for the purchases all consume resources. So purchasing, as an element of the supply chain, must be managed for cost, quality, reliability, and time. The latter three attributes can be ultimately denominated in terms of money and, hence, cost. The ABC analysis captures the total cost of such activities and helps managers to select the best vendors and structure the relationship with them in a manner that minimizes the total supply chain cost, as against selecting the lowest price suppliers. Moreover, once the economics of supplier relationship is deciphered, managers can work towards building win–win vendor relationships and convert the vendors into business partners. Thus, the ABM model can become the basis for creating competitive advantage for the firm by minimizing supply related costs and creating uniqueness in the inputs processed by the firm.

As mentioned earlier, 80 per cent of the product and service costs get locked in at the design stage. An ABC model provides the designers with a reliable and advance picture of the cost behaviour at the production phase, particularly those relating to batch-level and product-sustaining activities. This enables them to optimize the design without sacrificing functionality, or conform to target cost parameters set by competitive pricing.

But, how are the ABM initiatives linked to firm profitability—which is the ultimate objective? Let us move on to the next section for an answer.

Activity-based Budgeting

Operational ABM improves the efficiency of activities and strategic ABM reduces the demand for activities. Both, in effect, increases the practical capacity of organizational resources. A firm needs less resources for the same output, or it can produce more output with the same supply of resources. Neither of this by itself leads to lower spending and improved profit, unless managers are able to manage the cost of unused capacity out of the system—either by producing more, or by spending less by reducing the supply of resources. For this to happen, the supply and the demand of the resources during a period must match. This requires the cost of committed resources, which is traditionally treated as 'fixed', to be made variable, particularly, downward. But how do we do that? Again, the ABC system provides the answer.

Once the ABC model has been constructed, firms can use it to first determine, in advance, the demands for activities required to meet the forecasted volume and mix of products, services, and customers, and then budget the supply of resources to various responsibility centres based on that. This is termed as Activity-based Budgeting (ABB). It is simply ABC in reverse (Figure 7.6).

ABB demolishes the traditional classification of costs between the fixed and the variable. No cost is inherently fixed or variable. It is the managerial decisions or actions that make it so. ABC provides the necessary tool for such proactive decision-making which makes all costs variable.

ABB provides the vital link between the strategy and operations. Once the activity-based budget has been made, it can be used for authorizing supply of resources and control of spending, just like the traditional budgeting. Unlike traditional budgeting, however, ABB is based upon a reliable economic map of the enterprise. Budgeted activity cost driver rates can be used not only for the purpose of control (typical, budget-actual variance measurement) but also for purposes indicated in ABM discussions earlier, like continuous process improvement; making product- and customer-related decisions on pricing, minimum order size, and discounting; target costing; and new product design. Such decision-making can even involve alternative scenario analysis of the 'what if' nature about future products, services, customers, and operating processes.

ABB requires the firms to specify far more details about how production and sales demands will be met, about the underlying efficiency of all organizational activities, and about the spending and supply pattern of individual resources. If it is done successfully, however, managers will be able to adjust resource supply to match future resource demands and reduce the amount of unused capacity throughout the organization—both contributing to firm profitability.

One Integrated Cost System?

As mentioned in the beginning, firms need cost systems for three purposes:

- financial reporting to external stakeholders,
- estimating the costs of business processes, products services, and customers, and
- providing financial feedback on process efficiency for operational control.

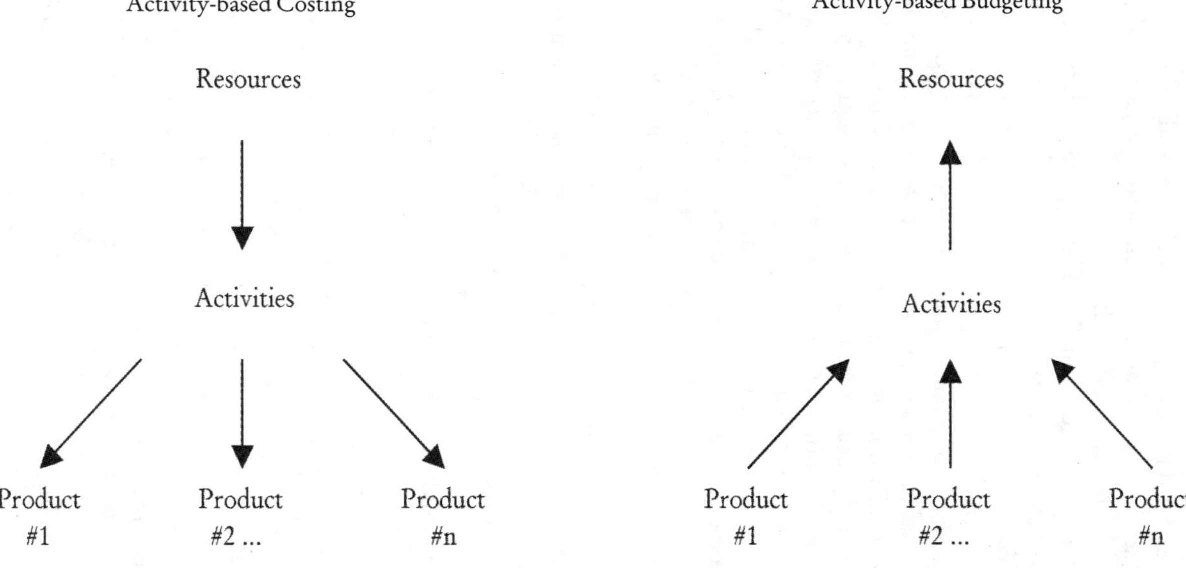

Fig. 7.6: Activity-based Budgeting—ABC in Reverse

ABC is a strategic cost system designed primarily to serve the second purpose. However, ABC can very well be used for meeting the two basic requirements of external financial reporting: valuation of inventory and measurement of the cost of goods sold. In order to conform to the statutory requirements of external reporting, the only change required is to separate out the expenses which are treated as non-inventoriable in accepted accounting principles. This can be easily effected.

The ABC system has a fundamentally different purpose from the operational control system (OCS) which serves the third purpose. The goal of the OCS is to provide accurate and timely feedback to employees on the efficiency, quality, and cycle times of operating processes. This fundamental difference in purpose requires it to define costs differently. The cost in an OCS represents the actual expenses of resources supplied to a responsibility centre as recorded in a firm's financial reporting system. So the OCS deals with efficiency of resource usage. In contrast, the ABC system adopts a capacity-based approach and classifies the cost of resource capacity supplied into two parts: utilized capacity and unused capacity. So the focus of the ABC system is on capacity usage. It uses standard cost driver rates calculated on the basis of the practical capacity and drives only the cost of capacity used to estimate product and process costs—assuming the process efficiency to be given. In comparison, the OCS uses actual expenses for analysing process efficiency—taking the process capacity as given.

A moment's reflection would suggest that while firms need to keep the ABC system and the OCS separate, making them 'talk' to each other would create valuable synergy. Capacity (created by supplied resources) and efficiency (usage of resources) are correlated concepts. The two systems can exchange vital information about efficiency, capacity usage, and sustained improvement in processes. This will help firms to have the greatest leverage on profitability by tackling the efficiency and capacity usage issues simultaneously. ABB links the ABC system to the OCS by establishing budgetary control norms which induces efficiency increases in operations. Complementarily, when significant and sustainable efficiency improvements do take place, feedback must flow from the OCS to the ABC system so that the ABC cost driver rates are revised in the light of these improvements. Thus, the two systems can positively impact one another through an iterative closed-loop linkage (Figure 7.7).

Finally, the ABC system and the OCS can be linked to the Financial Reporting System (FRS) realizing the vision of an Integrated Cost System (Figure 7.7) that support both internal and external reporting. In the integrated system, data, once captured, become available for use for all the three purposes. At that point, a cost system becomes a true management system that provides information for operational improvement and strategic learning, and accurate measurement of product and customer profitability. Increasing use of ERP systems by the firms is likely to make this vision a reality in the near future.

However, to realize the vision, managers have to conceptualize organizational costs differently from what has been done so far. They should

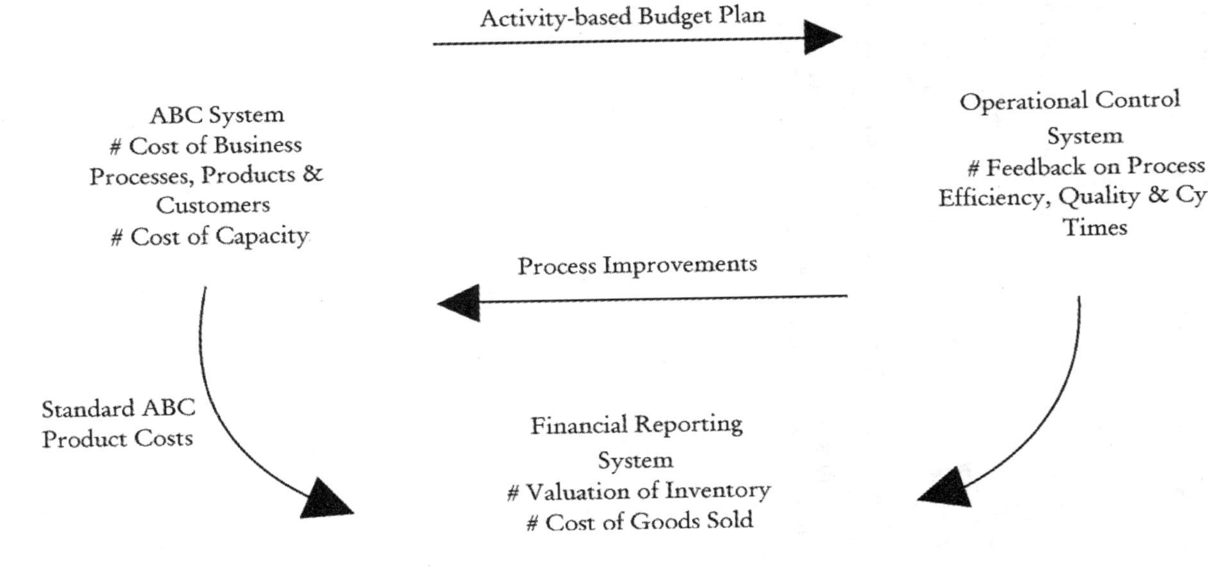

Fig. 7.7: Integrated Cost Systems

be able to view costs as effects of: what they choose to do, what they actually do, and what they are unable to do (like, find enough customers and use capacity in full, or run a process efficiently) with acquired resources. ABM provides the managers with this understanding about the fundamental origin of cost and the tools to manage costs and use cost-based information for gaining and sustaining competitive advantage for their firms.

References

Cokins, Gary (1996) *Activity-Based Management: Making It Work*, IRWIN Professional Publishing, London.

Cooper Robin and Robert S. Kaplan (1998) 'The Promise and Peril of Integrated Cost Systems', *Harvard Business Review*, July–August.

— (1991), 'Profit Priorities From Activity-based Costing', *Harvard Business Review*, May–June.

Kaplan, Robert S. (1988) 'One Cost System Isn't Enough', *Harvard Business Review*, January–February.

— and Robin Cooper (1998) *Cost & Effect: Using Integrated Cost Systems to Drive Profitability and Performance*, Harvard Business School Press, Boston, Mass.

8

Economic Value Added

Asish K. Bhattacharyya

The 'limited liability company' structure of business organizations is perhaps the most important innovation in business management. The unique feature of a limited liability company is the limited liability of its owners. In a partnership or sole proprietorship structure, creditors of the business have claim even on that part of the wealth of owners which is not invested in the business. This severely constrains the ability of owners to invest in business with high risk. The limited liability company structure has removed the constraint. Evolution of capital markets is another milestone in the growth of business. Theoretically, capital markets facilitate allocation of limited economic resources to most productive assets. However, in practice, this can happen only if companies listed in stock exchanges are transparent in financial reporting. There are many factors that limit the degree of transparency in corporate reporting. Even with this limitation, capital markets definitely provide listed public limited companies, popularly called publicly traded companies, access to savings by a very large number of investors. In the absence of capital markets we could not imagine the size of companies that we see today.

Theoretically, shareholders who provide risk capital to publicly traded companies are owners of the company. In practice, shareholders who do not control the management of the company behave like investors who expect growth in their investment. They do not participate in the management of the company. They expect return of capital and adequate return on capital. They exit the company if it underperforms and transfer their investment to companies that are expected to provide return equal to or higher than the expected return. This free mobility of capital from one company to another in the capital market compels the management of publicly traded companies to focus on shareholder value. Every action in a public traded company should be directed towards creating shareholder value. Companies endeavour to earn 'return on capital', which is higher than the cost of capital. Cost of capital is the return expected by investors. In this context, the concepts of 'Residual Income', christened as 'Economic Value Added' (EVA) by Stern Stewart & Co., a consulting firm in the USA, assumes importance. Another related concept is 'Market Value Added' (MVA), which is the capital market-based performance metric.

The Concept of EVA

Stern Stewart & Co., by popularizing the concept of EVA, has made managers reinvent the importance of residual income as a metric to measure overall business performance and the performance of a business segment. Use of the concept of residual income to measure business performance goes back to the year 1920 or earlier. Alfred Sloan's book, *My Years at General Motors*, describes how in the 1920s GM had a system where they set aside a 15 per cent rate of return on net assets (total assets – total outside liabilities) as the required rate of return in their business. 10 per cent of all operating profits after the 15 per cent of capital charge became the bonus pool to be shared by the management.

Residual income or EVA is calculated as follows:

EVA = (Rate of return – Cost of capital) × Capital
Rate of return = NOPAT/Capital

Net operating profit after tax (NOPAT) is calculated as follows:

NOPAT = Profit available to equity shareholders + Dividend on preference shares + Minority interest provision + Interest expenses, adjusted for income tax.

Minority interest provision shows the share of minority shareholders in the operating profit of a group company.

Capital is calculated as follows:

Capital = Equity capital + Preference shares + Minority interest + All debt excluding interest-free credits
Or
Capital = Total assets – interest-free credits

Equity capital includes share premium and retained profit.

Cost of capital is weighted average cost of capital (WACC).

WACC is calculated by taking after-tax cost of debt and equity. The proportion of the market value of equity to the value of the company is taken as the weight of equity. Similarly, the proportion of the market value of debt to the value of the company is taken as the weight of the debt value of the company and is the total of market value of equity and market value of debt. Minority interest is viewed as equity and preference share is viewed debt.

It may be noted that for every component of capital, there is a corresponding entry in the calculation of NOPAT. NOPAT is the sum of the returns attributable to all the providers of funds to the company. Thus, the NOPAT return is completely unaffected by the capital structure of the company. Assume that the NOPAT of a firm for the year 2003 was Rs 250,000. The capital was Rs 1,000,000 and the WACC was 15 per cent. The rate of return for the year 2003 was (250/ 1000) or 25 per cent. The EVA of the company for the year 2003 was: (25% – 15%) × Rs 1,000,000 = Rs 100,000.

The net profit in the profit and loss account is determined by deducting the cost of debt (interest) from NOPAT while EVA is determined by deducting the total cost of capital from the NOPAT. An asset that generates positive EVA generates surplus after meeting the total cost of capital used to finance that asset and thus creates value for shareholders. An asset that generates negative EVA destroys value. EVA is the internal measure of value creation.

A company's internal progress in creating value is measured by taking the change in EVA over the prior five- to ten-year periods. EVA increases if profits improve without tying up any more capital, if new capital is invested in projects that earn returns above the WACC, and if capital is withdrawn from uneconomic activities yielding less than the WACC. Changes in the capital structure and in the level of interest rates might influence EVA by altering the WACC.

The Concept of MVA

It is now well established that the management of a publicly traded company should focus on creating shareholder value. The capital market-based metric or the external metric for measuring performance is the MVA. MVA is essentially the difference between a company's current market value (market capitalization), as determined by its share price, and its 'economic book value'. A company's economic book value is the amount of capital that shareholders have committed to the firm throughout its existence, including profit that has been retained within the business. Although in the long term, the market capitalization of a company reflects the fundamental strengths or weaknesses of the company's performance, in the short term, market capitalization changes with changes in macroeconomic factors, market expectations, and market sentiments. MVA fails to fully capture the fundamental strengths or weaknesses of the company. Therefore, EVA is much more stable than MVA. It is free from the vagaries of capital market.

The creation or destruction of value is measured by calculating the change in MVA over the past five- to ten-year periods. MVA increases if value expands by more than the amount of new capital committed to the business, and vice versa. The rate of return, capital, and economic book value are calculated with reference to the figures in financial statements. Stern Stewart & Co. suggests a large number of adjustments to accounting figures to remove the accounting bias towards prudence and other accounting limitations. In theory, a company's MVA at a point in time is equal to the discounted present value of all the EVA it can be expected to generate in the future.

Adjustments to Accounting Figures

Capital being used in EVA calculation is not the book capital. It is defined as an approximation of the economic value of all funds invested in going-concern business activities. It is essentially a company's net assets (total assets less non-interest-bearing current liabilities), but with three adjustments:

(a) exclusion of marketable securities and construction in progress,

(b) addition of the present value of non-capitalized leases (operating leases) to net property, plant, and equipment, and
(c) addition of certain equity equivalent reserves to assets:
    i. Bad debt reserve is added to receivables.
    ii. Last in, first out (LIFO) reserve is added to inventories[1].
    iii. The cumulative amortization of goodwill is added back to goodwill.
    iv. R&D expense is capitalized as a long-term asset and smoothly depreciated over five years (a period chosen to approximate the economic life typical of an investment in R&D).
    v. Cumulative unusual losses (gains) after taxes are considered to be a long-term investment.

The above adjustments aim at removing the bias of Generally Accepted Accounting Principles (GAAP)[2] towards prudence. One of the fundamental principles of accounting is that capital contributed by owners should not be distributed because it might adversely affect the interest of creditors. GAAP endeavours to ensure that capital contributed by shareholders is not distributed. As a result many important assets are not recognized because of significant uncertainty about whether those assets will benefit the enterprise and also because of difficulties in measuring those assets reliably.

Stewart (1991) argues that distortions in GAAP-based accounting figures should be corrected to the extent that it is practical to do so, which means that adjustments should be made only if:

- the amounts are significant;
- managers can influence the outcome of the item being adjusted;
- the required information is readily available; and
- non-finance professionals can understand them.

Out of 160 odd adjustments suggested by Stewart, around 15 adjustments are considered crucial by diehard EVA proponents. In recent years this requirement has been scaled down significantly by many consultants to around five to six adjustments. These adjustments are aimed at:

- producing an EVA figure that is closer to cash flows and less subject to the distortions of accrual accounting;
- removing the arbitrary distinction between investments in tangible assets, which are capitalized, and intangible assets, which, in most situations, are written off as incurred;
- prevent the amortization, or write-off, of goodwill;
- eliminate the use of successful efforts accounting[3];

[1] LIFO reserve is required under the US GAAP. Indian Accounting Standards do not allow use of LIFO formula for valuation of inventories.

[2] GAAP refers to accounting principles and methods used in the preparation and presentation of financial statements. In India, Accounting Standards and Guidance Notes issued by the Institute of Chartered Accountants of India codify GAAP.

[3] The accounting method used by companies being engaged in oil exploration.

- bring off-balance sheet debt into the balance sheet; and
- correct biases caused by accounting depreciation (Young 1999).

Although many adjustments to GAAP-based accounting profit are possible, the following are the most commonly proposed:

- non-recurring gains and losses;
- research and development expenses;
- deferred taxes;
- provisions for warranties and bad debts;
- LIFO reserves;
- goodwill;
- depreciation; and
- operating leases.

Adjustments to capital should have corresponding adjustments in NOPAT. For example, if cumulative goodwill amortization is added to the capital, the goodwill amortized for the year is added back to the NOPAT for the year. Similarly, if cumulative R&D expenses are added to capital, the R&D expenditure for the year is added to the NOPAT for the year. Let us take an example.

Assume that a company spends Rs 100 million in R&D every year. Under the GAAP, including Indian GAAP, the company writes off the total R&D expenditure in the period in which the expenditure is incurred. It is suggested that for appropriate computation of EVA, R&D expenditure should be capitalized and should be amortized over a reasonable period, say, five years. The adjustment affects the NOPAT (ignoring income tax effect) and capital as follows:

(Rs in millions)

Year	R&D Expenditure for the Year	R&D Expenditure to be Amortized for the Year as Per Recommended Adjustment	Adjustments to the Capital as Recommended	Adjustments to the NOPAT as Recommended
1	100	20	+80	+80
2	100	40	+140	+60
3	100	60	+180	+40
4	100	80	+200	+20
5	100	100	+200	Nil

It may be observed that, if the company continues to spend Rs 100 million every year, from the fifth year onwards the adjusted NOPAT would equal NOPAT without adjustment, while capital would be higher by Rs 200 million from the reported capital. Thus, adjustments in NOPAT and capital would result in reporting lower EVA than EVA calculated without adjustments to capital and NOPAT reported in financial statements.

The GAAP in most countries requires amortization of goodwill. This is a reflection of the accounting bias towards prudence. Indian GAAP requires that goodwill should usually be amortized over a period not exceeding five years[4]. Similarly, International Financial Reporting Standard (IFRS)[5] requires that goodwill should usually be amortized over a period not exceeding 20 years[6]. The maximum amortization period specified in GAAP in various territories is arbitrary. The US GAAP does not require amortization of goodwill. It requires that goodwill should be tested yearly for impairment. However, till the recent amendment, in the year 2000, US GAAP required amortization of goodwill over a period of 40 years. Amortization of goodwill distorts the capital and the NOPAT, because it is inappropriate to amortize the goodwill and reduce its carrying amount in the balance sheet. Goodwill should be tested for impairment at each balance sheet date, because goodwill does not have a definite useful life. It might get impaired due to changes in the business environment.

Although arguments in favour of adjustments in accounting figures have strong logic, studies (for example, Young 1999) that endeavoured to find out the benefits of these adjustments concluded that they are largely irrelevant and result in only incremental addition to the information produced by EVA. The conclusion does not change even if adjustments are tailored to the nature of the business of the company. The main argument put forward is that even though the logic behind these adjustments is impeccable, whether these adjustments help in countering any dysfunctional or sub-optimal behaviour of the managerial staff is suspect. It is argued that these adjustments are more crucial for the external user. But for most firms, adjusted EVA offers few advantages over unadjusted EVA. Moreover, it carries the costs of increased complexity and other costs that arise when profit measures deviate from GAAP. In short, the residual income measure first proposed by Sloan 85 years ago is likely to offer the same advantages as today's highly advertised EVA.

As mentioned above, the veracity of EVA is dependent on various adjustments proposed to minimize the accounting biases, which in itself is a complicated process. Other than this, the increase in the number of adjustments increases the subjectivity involved in measuring EVA. It is very difficult to quantify all the value enhancement activities of a firm without involving a lot of subjective estimates. Therefore, with the various accounting adjustments proposed to remove the accounting biases in the estimation, EVA computation tends to increase the subjectivity in its estimate.

Although the idea of EVA is simple and theoretically elegant, its implementation is difficult and often takes away much of the potential benefits.

[4] IAS 14, Accounting for Amalgamation, Paragraph 38.

[5] International Accounting Standards Board (IASB), which has representation from more than 100 countries, issues the IFRS in an effort to harmonize accounting practices across the globe.

[6] IAS 22, Business Combinations, Paragraph 44.

Cost of Capital

Measuring WACC requires measurement of the cost of equity. Usually companies use Capital Asset Pricing Model (CAPM) to measure the cost of equity. Use of CAPM requires estimation of the 'risk-free rate of interest', market premium, and security 'Beta'[7]. None of these inputs can be measured precisely. Therefore, WACC cannot be measured precisely. Companies face problems in measuring WACC, particularly in measuring WACC for a business segment. However, most companies roughly estimate WACC, which they use in evaluating proposals for capital expenditure. Companies may use the same WACC for computing the EVA, unless the risk of a business segment is significantly different from the average risk of all assets of the company. Use of WACC which is not precisely correct does not take away from the major benefits of EVA.

Correlation between EVA and MVA

Capital market theories have established that the capital market values a company based on the amount of projected cash flow stream that it is expected to generate and the timing, and uncertainty of the cash flow stream. The present value (PV) of projected free cash flow is the value of the company. Analysts prefer to use cash flow based valuation models. It is highly improbable that a single number can capture all the inputs required by those models. Aggregation results in loss of information. Therefore, accounting standard setters and regulators, all over the globe, require firms to be transparent and disclose information that is relevant for projecting the future cash flow stream. Analysts use those information, along with information collected from other sources, to value companies. However, they often use a single figure, like ROI, as a signal for 'good or bad news'. EVA should be considered a superior substitute of ROI or similar measures only if it provides a better signal.

Independent researchers concluded that although EVA is correlated to stock returns, it is not much greater than the correlation between the accounting profit and stock return. Therefore, EVA might be incrementally better over other measures but it does not really provide any significant informational advantage. It is pertinent to note that this conclusion is drawn by empirical studies that used the database created and maintained by Stern Stewart & Co. (Dodd and Chen 1997, Biddle et al. 1999). Therefore, chances of bias in those studies due to incomplete data were almost eliminated. Empirical studies in other countries have also confirmed that EVA does not provide a better signal to the capital market. In India it is even more difficult to have a database for conducting such studies and, therefore, even if some studies show results different from the conclusions of global studies, the same should be viewed with utmost caution.

The appendix to this chapter presents a list of companies ranked by the popular business magazine, *Business Today*. The ranking of companies is based on MVA. It is difficult to find a correlation between incremental MVA and

[7] Beta measures the market risk of a security.

incremental EVA. One plausible reason for the lack of correlation is that in the short term MVA often fails to capture the company fundamentals. In the year 2002, MVA of seven out of 10 top companies was lower than their MVA in the year 2001. The drop might not be so much a reflection of the projected future performance of those companies as a reflection of the market condition.

EVA as a Corporate Philosophy

Although EVA may not have better informational value to capital markets, it can be very useful in improving the productivity of a firm, if adapted as a corporate philosophy. Productivity should be measured in terms of creation of wealth for shareholders. An appropriate corporate philosophy should result in goal congruence and should channelize all efforts of the management and employees towards a common goal and strategies for the firm. Over the years management experts and consultants have proposed many tools and techniques for improving productivity. Firms have tried these tools with varied degrees of success. Many of the success stories in relation to the implementation of these tools and techniques have attained a place in the annals of history. Some of the most notable of these are: Management Information Systems (MIS), Business Process Re-engineering (BPR), and ERP. Although all these tools have different perspectives, they aim at improving the productivity in physical terms and ignore the concept of value. They facilitate increase in the productivity and efficiency of the firm that ultimately contributes to an increased bottom line for the firm. But increased bottom line is no guarantee for increase in the shareholder value.

Almost all the tools and techniques are used to reorient the employees' perception towards managing 'value drivers' and that goes together with the empowerment of employees cutting across the hierarchical levels. All these tools aim at improving productivity by reducing redundancies in the 'value chain'—BPR by simplifying existing processes and eliminating non-value added activities, MIS by improving the quality and flow of information, and ERP by ensuring efficient allocation and utilization of enterprise resources.

The success of these tools reflects in reduced costs for delivering products or services to customers, although it may not always result in increasing shareholder value. Those tools fail to distinguish between activities that create value and those that destroy value because they do not measure 'economic surplus' being generated by different activities. Moreover, successful implementation of these tools and techniques involve extensive retraining of employees and constant monitoring of performance. In most cases the success or failure of these techniques depends on the effectiveness of communication of the philosophy and process of implementation to employees at all levels. The success of these tools to a great extent also depends on how well the firm is able to resolve the problem of resistance to change and the ability of the management to earn the commitment of employees to the implementation of these techniques. Given this scenario the implementation of these management tools across the firm is a long drawn process and the possibility of success is not very high.

In contrast, EVA is an easy to understand concept. If used, as a corporate philosophy, it will permeate every decision level in the organization. In fact, EVA should be adapted as a culture within the organization rather than as a project. EVA, when used as a corporate philosophy, does not require precise estimation. Therefore, hurdles in estimating EVA does not come in the way of building the EVA culture in an organization. There are more than 300 corporates, worldwide, that have adapted EVA as a corporate philosophy. Many of these organizations are successful MNCs like Coca-Cola, Bausch & Lomb, Briggs & Stratton, and Herman Miller. Some of the state-owned enterprises in the USA, including the US Postal Service which has the largest civilian labour force in the world, have adapted the EVA culture to improve efficiency in services and to motivate the employees.

The advantage of EVA over other similar tools is that it improves business literacy because of easy understandability and conceptual clarity. The one component that sets it apart over conventional measures is its consideration of the total cost of capital. This is the one component which should be understood by everyone involved in operations. Managers should not lose sight of the fact that the cost of equity is a very significant component of the cost of capital. Business literacy is the effort of management to convey to all the employees the fact that for any activity to be value enhancing, the return generated by it should be greater than the cost of capital employed for the activity. This small shift in the outlook of the employees immediately raises the threshold limit of the acceptable returns. Usually employees do not look at their actions from this perspective and, therefore, there is a need to continuously highlight the concept.

EVA as a Basis for Compensation

Building an EVA culture within an organization requires linking employee compensation with EVA. In the absence of reward for creating shareholder value employees would not be motivated towards improving the productivity of capital. As explained earlier, compensation methods based on EVA work better in achieving the objective of goal congruence and minimize the agency cost. Use of EVA improves 'internal corporate governance' in the sense that it motivates managers to get rid of value destructive activities and invest only in those projects that are expected to enhance shareholder value.

Ideally, a management control system should motivate managers for 'self' control rather than to be controlled. Linking compensation with EVA helps employees in conducting self-examination of every action taken by them to ensure that it enhances the EVA of the firm. Managers do have scope to enhance the EVA in the short run at the cost of long term value creation by rejecting good investment opportunities that have long gestation period, avoiding discretionary costs such as, advertising and training, or targeting a capital structure that might reduce the WACC in the short run while enhancing the financial risk in the long run. One way to counter these limitations is to defer payment of a part of the EVA based variable compensation. Variable compensation may be accumulated and released after a gap of, say, three years.

Empirical evidence supports the above observations. Empirical studies concluded that EVA, when used as an incentive compensation measure, tends to improve the value of the firm by inducing managers towards value creating activities (Biddle et al. 1999). Using EVA or residual income measures for incentive compensation leads to:

- the improvement in operating efficiency by increasing asset turnover;
- disposal of selected assets and reduction of new investments (the assumption is that these assets have failed in earning adequate returns when compared to the total cost of capital), and
- more shares repurchases (consistent with distributing under- performing capital to shareholders).

It may be concluded that although EVA fails to provide additional information to the capital market, it can be used to improve the internal governance of a firm. It is often argued that use of EVA provides a signal to the capital market that the company has focus on shareholder value.

EVA or residual income might be an age-old concept, but the Stern Stewart & Co. has done a good job in reinventing the importance of the metric. Many good companies across the globe have moved towards EVA. India is not lagging behind. Many companies (for example, Godrej & Boyce and TISCO) are using EVA for measuring divisional performance and for compensating employees. Many companies in India provide information on EVA in their annual report as voluntary disclosure. This definitely signals a transition of the Indian corporate sector from revenue/profit-oriented management to EVA-oriented management. This should lead to optimal allocation of economic resources. However, there is a real danger that too much focus on short-term EVA and shareholder value might result in undermining the interest of other stakeholders and the 'corporate social responsibility'. Therefore, it is of the utmost necessity that companies that are moving towards the EVA culture should have a strong corporate governance system to ensure that the management is not losing sight of long-term goals. A strong and balanced board of directors should effectively oversee executive management to ensure that rights of all stakeholders are protected, and that the company is behaving ethically. EVA, in short term, often fails to capture the benefits of good corporate governance.

References

Business Today (2003) 'BT MVA 500–BT-Stern Stewart Study' 13 April, pp. 45–98.

Bennett III, Stewart G. (1991) *The Quest for Value—a guide for senior managers*; Harper Collins Publishers Inc., USA.

Biddle G.K., R. Bowel, and S. Wallace (1999) 'Evidence on EVA'; *Journal of Applied Corporate Finance*; Vol. 12, No. 2.

Chen, Shimin, and James L. Dodd (1997) 'Economic value added: An empirical examination of a new corporate performance measure', *Journal of Managerial Issues*, Pittsburg.

Young, David S. (1999) 'Some reflections on accounting adjustments and Economic Value Added', *Journal of Financial Statement Analysis*, New York, pp. 7–19.

Annexe 8.1

MVA Rank 2003	MVA Rank 2002	Company	2003 MVA (Rs crore)	2002 MVA (Rs crore)	Delta MVA (Rs crore)	2002 EVA (Rs crore)
1	1	Hindustan Lever*	35,462	44,220	–8758	1003‡
2	2	Wipro	33,030	36,322	–3292	235
3	3	Infosys Technologies	27,503	25,856	1646	242
4	4	Reliance Industries	11,577	19,346	–7768	–318
5	5	ITC	11,501	13,013	1512	591
6	7	Ranbaxy Laboratories*	9711	6511	3200	–94‡
7	6	Satyam Computer Services	6057	6662	–606	33
8	8	Dr Reddy's Laboratories	5489	6411	–922	350
9	12	Nestle India*	4681	6319	363	100‡
10	9	Cipla	4133	6021	–1888	71
11	13	Hero Honda Motors	3950	4166	–216	311
12	10	HCL Technologies	2792	5847	–3055	–108
13	469	TELCO	2716	–795	3511	–507
14	N.A.	i-Flex Solution	2661	–348	3009	9
15	491	Hindustan Petroleum Corp.	2595	–1631	4226	–91
16	N.A.	Sun Pharmaceutical Inds.	2158	2367	–209	94
17	14	Castrol India*	2032	1833	200	44‡
18	462	National Aluminium Co.	1722	–357	2080	–246
19	21	Glaxo Smith Kline Pharmaceuticals*	1701	1428	273	–10‡
20	25	Digital Globalsoft	1660	1343	317	28
21	15	Colgate-Palmolive (India)	1595	1823	–328	20
22	26	Asian Paints (India)	1492	1210	281	32
23	20	Cadbury India*	1470	1453	17	17‡
24	24	Wockhardt*	1281	1359	–78	55‡
25	18	Associated Cement Cos	1277	1518	–241	–152
26	16	Bharat Petroleum Corpn	1253	1708	455	139
27	N.A.	Hindustan Copper	1172	1295	123	–194
28	500	Oil and Natural Gas Corpn	1167	–23,090	24,258	17
29	23	Britannia Industries	1067	1382	–315	46
30	49	Bajaj Auto	1066	324	742	–162
31	17	Dabour India	877	1570	–694	10
32	113	Bharat Heavy Eelctricals	847	64	783	–327
33	19	Gujrat Ambuja Cements<	829	1474	–645	–160
34	N.A.	Glaxo Smith Kline Consumer Health*	754	1395	–641	62‡
35	275	TVS Motor Co.	723	105	618	9
36	35	Gillette India	702	669	34	–59‡
37	43	Asea Brown Boveri*	695	463	233	8‡
38	29	Pfizer+	677	875	–199	21‡
39	28	Larsen & Toubro	671	961	–290	–412
40	44	Reckitt Benckiser (India)*	658	423	235	2‡
41	69	Mastek<	656	204	452	7
42	52	Siemens*	654	308	346	10‡
43	50	CMC	634	311	323	–15
44	361	Mangalore Refinery and Petrochem	629	–276	905	–911
45	39	Novartis India	627	542	85	15
46	86	Bharat Forge	608	127	481	–21
47	34	Procter and Gamble Hygiene&	600	728	–128	35
48	121	Aventis Crop Science India*	581	54	527	5‡
49	N.A.	Hinduja TMT	535	2	533	–41
50	32	Polaris Software Lab	525	747	–222	1

Rank	(Rs crore) 2001	Delta	ROCE (%)		WACC (%)		Capital Employed (Rs crore)		NOPAT (Rs crore)	
			2002	2001	2002	2001	2002	2001	2002	2001
1	765†	239	39.7‡	36.9†	13.7‡	15.3†	3868‡	3543†	1535‡	1370†
2	111	124	31.9	30.6	23.1	25.3	2680	2099	854	642
3	224	17	32.8	38.8	23.1	25.3	2483	1666	816	644
4	328	–646	10.8	14.5	11.4	13.1	47,536	23,305	5115	3381
5	420	171	25.0	22.0	13.7	13.0	5213	4637	1304	1020
6	–97†	2	9.4‡	11†	13.9‡	15.9†	2105‡	1994†	198‡	220†
7	160	–127	24.8	43.0	23.1	26.1	1939	941	481	405
8	36	315	34.1	19.1	13.9	15.5	1740	997	593	190
9	69†	30	29.0‡	24.5†	13.6‡	13.0†	649‡	605†	188‡	148†
10	43	29	19.7	20.6	13.9	16.0	1232	922	243	190
11	116	195	41.2	31.7	13.7	17.1	1133	795	466	252
12	–58	–50	18.2	23.0	23.1	26.2	2215	1776	404	408
13	–1149	642	1.7	–3.2	12.5	14.7	4710	6429	82	–204
14	N.A.	N.A.	24.9	32.2	23.1	N.A.	513	348	127	112
15	–52	–39	10.5	12.3	11.3	12.8	10,638	10,510	1113	1291
16	61	33	28.9	27.1	13.9	15.9	625	547	181	148
17	62†	–18	21.3‡	28.0†	12.7‡	14.9†	514	475†	109	133†
18	21	–267	8.5	14.9	13.0	14.5	5583	4690	477	701
19	–5†	–6	12.1	14.9†	13.9‡	16.0†	567‡	442†	69‡	66†
20	4	24	33.4	28.7	23.1	26.2	274	179	92	51
21	–4	24	19.5	14.7	13.7	15.7	345	423	67	62
22	5	27	17.5	15.6	13.2	15.0	744	776	130	121
23	16†	1	19.6‡	19.3†	13.7‡	13.1†	295‡	255†	58†	49†
24	16†	39	27.2‡	19.3†	13.9‡	15.6†	412‡	443†	112‡	85†
25	–285	134	8.0	5.5	13.1	15.3	2932	2935†	233	163†
26	–140	279	12.8	11.3	11.3	12.9	9170	8484	1178	955
27	–337^	143	–36.5	–15.1^	13.2	22.7^	390	891^	–142	–135^
28	–580	596	12.3	11.4	12.3	12.6	55,198	47,775	6817	5440
29	2	44	23.4	13.1	13.4	12.8	452	429	106	56
30	–310	148	9.8	7.1	13.2	14.8	4729	4050	464	289

(Contd.)

Rank	(Rs crore) 2001	Delta	ROCE (%)		WACC (%)		Capital Employed (Rs crore)		NOPAT (Rs crore)	
			2002	2001	2002	2001	2002	2001	2002	2001
31	6	3	15.0	16.4	13.5	15.3	644	593	97	97
32	-1127	800	5.5	-9.4	13.4	15.1	4159	4599	229	-433
33	-197	36	8.2	8.8	12.7	15.1	3488	3084	284	271
34	37†	25	25.2‡	25.7†	13.6‡	17.4†	530‡	441†	133‡	113‡
35	-19	28	14.4	12.4	12.9	15.3	609	640	88	79
36	-47†	-12	-0.2‡	5.8†	13.5‡	16.5†	430‡	444†	-1‡	26†
37	-15†	23	15.7‡	12.6†	14.0‡	16.1†	447‡	423†	70‡	53†
38	-14†	8	25.4‡	25.3†	13.9‡	16.0†	186‡	149†	47‡	38†
39	-588	177	7.7	6.6	12.9	13.6	7848	8400	603	555
40	-1†	3	14.9‡	14.8†	13.7‡	15.7†	146‡	136†	22‡	20†
41	-9	15	28.6	16.4	23.1	26.2	120	87	34	14
42	3†	7	16.6‡	16.8†	14.0‡	16.0†	386‡	416†	64‡	70†
43	-25	10	15.7	9.9	23.0	24.1	207	174	32	17
44	-936	26	-5.3	-1.9	11.3	13.7	5490	5998	-290	115
45	14	1	20.0	20.4	13.9	15.8	248	311	50	64
46	-20	-1	9.5	9.8	12.9	13.0	611	615	58	61
47	28	7	27.8	26.3	13.7	15.7	252	269	70	71
48	-24†	29	15.1‡	-0.5†	12.3‡	14.6†	198‡	156†	30‡	-1†
49	-66	25	11.7	7.5	23.1	26.0	362	356	42	27
50	7	-6	23.4	29.6	23.1	26.2	259	203	61	60

Notes:
+ Period ending 30 November.
* Period ending 31 December.
‡ For financial year (FY) 2001.
† For FY 2000.
^ For 9 months.
< Period ending 30 June.
N.A. Not available
EVA has been computed based on the ending capital of the respective financial years.
All figures are for 12 months ending 31 March, unless specified otherwise.
MVA has been computed using the average market capitalization for January 2003. Historical MVA has also been updated accordingly.
Source: *Business Today* (2003).

9

Options, Futures, and Derivatives

B.B. Chakrabarti

Most of the corporate organizations use debt to finance plant and machinery, buildings, raw materials, and other assets. Any increase in interest rates adversely affects the financial performance of the organization. We say that the organization is subject to financial risk. Similarly, an adverse change in currency exchange rates affects the financial performance of an organization importing raw materials from abroad. This also is an example of financial risk. An individual also faces financial risks by investing money in stock market. Any decrease in stock prices reduces his/her wealth. In fact, adverse changes in stock prices, interest rates, exchange rates, etc. can even threaten the survival of otherwise successful businesses. There are some instruments known as financial derivatives that can be used to reduce the extent of financial risks of organizations and individuals. We deal with such instruments in this chapter.

WHAT IS A DERIVATIVE CONTRACT?

Suppose an investor wants to buy immediately 100 equity shares of RIL. He places an order with a member of a stock exchange. The member buys the shares for him by matching the price of Rs 250 at which some other member, working for a seller of the shares, intends to sell the shares. The investor makes the payment of Rs 25,000 and receives the shares on the settlement date which may be three days later as per the prevailing regulations of the stock exchange. This buy/sell transaction is referred to as a transaction in the spot or cash or ready market. In this market, payment and delivery are effected immediately. Of course, 'immediately' does not always mean instantaneously. The definition of immediate settlement differs depending on the characteristics of financial markets. The settlement in Indian stock markets presently takes place after three days from the trading date (T + 3). In foreign currency market, settlements of transactions usually take place after two working days.

Now suppose the investor wants to buy 100 equity shares of RIL after 90 days. In this case, he has two alternatives. In the first case, he can buy the shares from the stock market after 90 days but he will have to buy at a price that will prevail in the market after 90 days. So, he then faces uncertainty about the price of RIL shares after the period of 90 days. The investor has another alternative if he uses the stock futures market. In this market he can buy 100. RIL equity shares today for delivery after 90 days at a price of, say, Rs 260 each. The price will be as per quotation in the futures market for RIL equity shares. By this process the investor is certain about the price at which he would be able to take delivery of 100. RIL equity shares after 90 days. This transaction of 'buy 100. RIL equity shares at Rs 260 each after 90 days' is referred to as a transaction in the derivative market. The buy/sell contract so defined is called a derivative contract. It is called a derivative contract because its price depends on the prevailing price in the spot market. The price of RIL equity shares in the spot market is Rs 250 each and so, the price for future delivery after 90 days is fixed at Rs 260 each. If the spot market price were different, then the derivative market price would also be different accordingly.

In summary, any buy/sell contract for delivery at a future point of time but whose price is fixed today, is a derivative contract. If the price is not fixed today, then the buyer will have to buy at a price that will prevail in the spot market after 90 days.

Financial and Commodity Derivatives

A derivative security's price is fixed today based on spot market price of the underlying security. As explained in the earlier section, the price of the derivative security on RIL shares to be delivered after 90 days is related to the spot market price of RIL shares today. We define a derivative security as an instrument whose value depends on the values of other, more basic underlying variables.

The underlying variables can be commodities or financial instruments. Accordingly, we have commodity and financial derivatives. Some of the commodities on which derivatives like futures are sold in exchanges are agricultural products like corn, soybean, wheat, etc., energy items like crude oil, heating oil, gasoline, etc., and metals like gold, silver, copper, zinc, lead, etc. Financial derivatives relate to financial instruments like stocks, stock indices, currencies, bonds, and other interest rate products. In this chapter our focus is on financial derivatives. The major types of derivatives are forward contracts, futures contracts, and options.

Forward Contracts

A forward contract is an agreement to buy or sell a specified asset at a specified future time for a specified price. For example, suppose a corporate organization has entered into a contract to buy US$ 1000 from a bank on the ninetieth day at the specified rate of Rs 48.75 per US$. This is an example of a currency forward contract. In this case, the corporate organization will pay Rs 48,750 (48.75 * 1000) to the bank on the ninetieth day to receive US$ 1000 from the bank. This payment, in most cases, would be different from the payment that the corporate organization would have paid to the bank on the ninetieth day, if no such forward contract existed and the corporate organization were to buy at the spot rate. A spot contract is an agreement to buy or sell an asset today.

In financial markets, buying is referred to as assuming a long position and selling as assuming a short position. So the buyer, in a forward contract, assumes a long position and the seller, a short position. The price of a forward contract is known as the delivery price.

Forward contracts are traded in the over-the-counter (OTC) market between two parties, that is, two financial institutions or a financial institution and its client. No third party is involved in such contracts. Forward contracts can be closed only by the process of buying and selling by the two concerned parties on the due date. If one of the parties does not buy or sell, then default takes place. The counter party then will have to proceed directly against the defaulting party to recover any financial claim.

Pay-off from a Forward Contract

Let us consider a currency forward contract where a trader intends to buy US$ 1000 from a bank after 90 days at the rate of Rs 48.75 per US$. Here the contracted delivery price on the ninetieth day is Rs 48.75 per US$ implying that the trader is committed to buying and the bank is committed to selling US$ 1000 on the ninetieth day at Rs 48.75 per US$. The trader and the bank assume the long and the short positions respectively.

Now, suppose the spot INR/US$ exchange rate on the ninetieth day, that is, on maturity of the contract, is Rs 49. We ignore the bid–ask spread (difference between selling or ask and buying or bid rates) on exchange rates. The trader (the long position holder) can then take delivery of US$ 1000 by paying Rs 48,750 (Rs 48.75 × 1000) and immediately sell US$ 1000 in the spot market at Rs 49,000 (49 × 1000), earning a profit of Rs 250. The bank (the short position holder) would have incurred a loss of Rs 250 if it had bought US$ 1000 in the spot market and then sold to the trader at the contracted forward delivery price. On the other hand, if the spot exchange rate were Rs 48.50 per US$, then the trader would have incurred a loss of Rs 250 and the bank would have earned a profit of Rs 250 for similar transactions. The profit earned or the loss incurred is the pay-off from the forward contract.

To generalize, the pay-off from a forward contract on maturity of the contract is as follows:

Pay-off $= S_T - K$ for long position and
$= K - S_T$ for short position

where T = maturity date
S_T = Asset spot price on the maturity date
K = Delivery price, that is, forward price fixed initially when the contract is undertaken.

The above pay-offs can be diagrammatically represented as shown below. The pay-off on maturity and the asset price are shown on the vertical and horizontal axes respectively.

Short Position

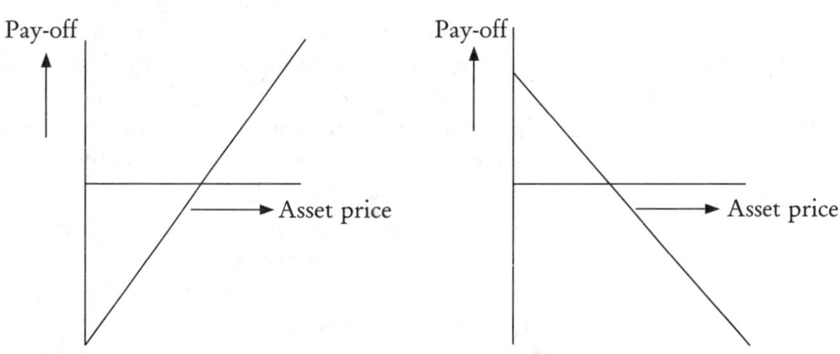

Regarding cash flows in a forward contract, the only cash exchange will be on maturity of the contract. The buyer need not pay any money to the seller at the time of writing the contract because both the buyer and the seller are equally hopeful of earning profit on maturity of the contract though, of course, for opposite reasons. The buyer hopes that the asset price on maturity will exceed the agreed delivery price and he/she will be able to earn profit. The seller hopes for the opposite movement of the asset price, which will provide an opportunity to earn profit. At maturity of the contract, however, one of the parties will earn profit and the other will lose. It is zero sum game for both the parties together on maturity.

Futures Contracts

Futures contracts, like forward contracts, are agreements to buy or sell an asset between two parties at a future time for a specified futures price but they tread through futures exchanges, unlike forward contracts, which are traded in OTC markets. The features of futures contracts are standardized to facilitate trading in exchanges. These features include contract size, quality of asset (wherever applicable), price quotes, limits on daily price movements, limits on the number of contracts to be held by a speculator, and delivery dates.

To take an example, it is possible to trade in futures on the stocks of RIL in National Stock Exchange (NSE) in India. The standardized features of futures contracts and trading on the stocks of RIL as specified by NSE, are as follows:

Contract Size—600 Shares

This is the number of shares under one contract. The contract size is specified by the exchange in such a way that it is neither too large nor too small. If it is too large, traders needing small exposures for hedging (that is, managing price risks in transactions in the spot market) or speculators wanting relatively small exposures will not be able to trade. Again, if the contract size is too small, trading may become expensive due to fixed transaction costs per contract.

Price Quotes

Base price of futures contracts on the first day of trading (that is, on introduction) would be the previous day's closing value of the underlying security. The base price of the contracts on subsequent trading days would be the daily settlement price of the futures contracts. The price step (tick size) is Re 0.05. This is the minimum price movement that can be quoted. Regarding price bands, NSE does not specify any day minimum/maximum price ranges for futures contracts. However, in order to prevent erroneous order entry by trading members, operating price ranges are kept at maximum +20 per cent over the last settlement price. With respect to orders which have come under price freeze due to price quotes above the allowed maximum price, members would be required to confirm to NSE that there is no inadvertent error in the order entry and that the order is genuine. On such confirmation NSE may approve such order.

Quantity Freeze

Orders which may come to the exchange as quantity freeze shall be the lesser of the following:

a) 1 per cent of the marketwide position limit stipulated for open positions on the futures.
b) Notional value of the contract of around Rs 50 million. NSE, however, at its discretion, may allow such orders on confirmation that the order is genuine. This is done to avoid market cornering or undesirable influencing of market prices by any trader.

Trading Cycle

Futures contracts have a maximum duration of a three month trading cycle—the near month (one), the next month (two), and the far month (three). New contracts are introduced on the trading day following the expiry of the near month contracts. The new contracts are introduced for three-month durations. NSE thus provides three contracts for trading for any security at any point of time.

Expiry Day of a Contract

The last Thursday of the expiry month is fixed as the expiry day of a contract. If that day is a trading holiday, then the contract expires on the previous trading day. Till date, futures contracts on individual stocks are cash settled in NSE but in global exchanges a trader can also claim delivery of stocks on maturity. Pay-off of a futures contract on maturity is similar to a forward contract.

Unlike a forward contract, a trader in a futures contract has to pay margin money to undertake a contract. This is because the futures exchange is the counter party to a trader for buy or sell transactions and guarantees completion of a transaction in case of default by the counter party trader. So the exchange needs margin money (initial as well as mark to market margin) from its members to allow any deal in the exchange. The members in turn require margin from traders for introducing any order.

Another feature of a futures contract is that a trader can get out of a contract by offsetting instead of taking or giving delivery of underlying assets on maturity because the futures contracts are exchange-traded. Offsetting or closing out a position means entering into the opposite type of trade from the original one. Suppose a trader is long on April 2003 futures contract for buying 600 stocks of RIL and in the month of March 2003 he decides to close out the position. He then goes short on April 2003 futures contract for selling 600 stocks of RIL. The trader is then out of market. In fact, a vast majority of futures contracts do not lead to delivery. They are offset before maturity.

Option Contracts

An option implies a right to perform an activity without any obligation to do that. There are two basic types of option contracts—call and put options. A call option gives the holder the right to buy the underlying asset at a certain price by or on a certain date but without any obligation to buy the asset. Similarly, a put option gives the holder the right to sell the underlying asset at a certain price by or on a certain date without any obligation to sell the asset. The price in the contract is known as exercise price or strike price and the date is known as expiration date or maturity. Options can also be classified as American and European Options. American Options can be exercised on any date up to the expiration date while European Options can be exercised only on the expiration date.

The purchaser of an option is said to have a long position (long call/long put) and the seller of an option (also known as a writer of an option) is said to have a short position (short call/short put). The purchaser of an option has to pay a price to the writer of the option to purchase the contract. This price is known as option price or premium. We now explain these by an example.

Suppose a trader A has purchased a European call option from another trader B to purchase 100 equity shares of RIL with a strike price of Rs 200 each after 90 days at a price of Rs 5 each. In this case A has a long call position and B has a short call position. Since the call option is European, A has the right to ask B to deliver the shares only on the ninetieth day at the price of Rs 200 each. At the time of getting into the contract A has to pay the premium of Rs 5 each for 100 shares to B, who is the writer of the option. A has no obligation to ask for delivery of the shares. If A asks for delivery of the shares then B has the obligation to deliver the shares to A against the payment of the strike price. If A does not ask for delivery of the shares, then the contract lapses.

Let us now work out the pay-offs or profits from European Option contracts. We will use the following notations:

X = Strike price
T = Maturity date
S_T = Spot price of the underlying asset on the maturity date.
c = Call option premium
p = put option premium

Long Call (European)

The holder pays an amount, c, to the option writer to enter into the contract to buy at the strike price of X. Obviously the holder will exercise his right to buy the underlying asset at the price of X, if the spot price of the underlying asset on maturity, S_T, is more than X. Then he can earn a profit or recover part of the premium paid earlier. If the spot price of the underlying asset is lower than the strike price of X, then he will not exercise his option to buy the asset since he will incur further loss by selling the purchased asset in the spot market.

The above pay-off position can be diagrammatically represented as follows. The pay-off on maturity and the strike price are shown on the vertical and horizontal axes respectively.

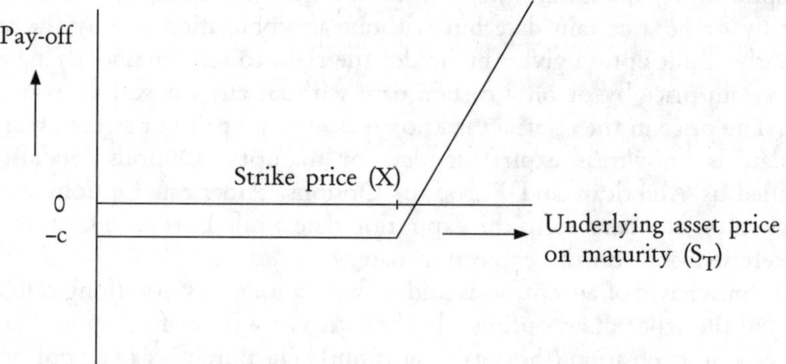

Algebraically, the pay-off on maturity of a European long call option can be represented as follows:

Pay-off = max (0, S_T – X) – c

Max (0, S_T – X) means that the pay-off would be S_T – X if S_T > X, when the option will get exercised. Otherwise, the holder does not exercise the option and loses the call option premium, c.

Short Call (European)

The holder of a short call option is the writer of the option and has agreed to sell the underlying asset to the holder of the long call option (purchaser) at the strike price, when the purchaser asks for delivery of the asset. In return he receives the premium money from the purchaser at the time of entering into the contract. Since the purchaser asks for delivery of the underlying asset only when the spot market price of the asset, S_T, is more than the strike price, X, the option writer loses money as he buys the asset from the spot market at a price higher than the delivery price, X. He has no right to refuse delivery even when he loses. He, however, earns a profit equal to the call option premium if the spot market price, S_T, is less than the strike price, X, since the purchaser will not exercise the option in that case.

The above pay-off position can be diagrammatically represented as follows. The pay-off on maturity and the strike price are shown on the vertical and horizontal axes respectively.

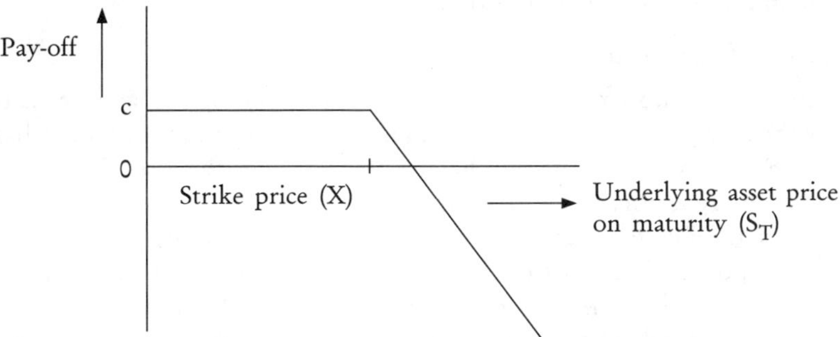

Algebraically, the pay-off on maturity of a European short call option can be represented as follows:

$$\begin{aligned} \text{Pay-off} &= -\max(0, S_T - X) + c \\ &= \min(0, X - S_T) + c \end{aligned}$$

Long Put (European)

The holder pays an amount, p, to the option writer to enter into the contract to sell at the strike price of X. Obviously the holder will exercise his right to sell the underlying asset at the price of X, if the spot price of the underlying asset on maturity, S_T, is less than X. Then he can earn a profit or recover part of the premium paid earlier. If the spot price of the underlying asset is higher than the strike price of X, then he will not exercise his option to sell the asset since he will incur further loss by buying the asset in the spot market to sell to the option writer.

The above pay-off position can be diagrammatically represented as follows. The pay-off on maturity and the strike price are shown on the vertical and horizontal axes respectively.

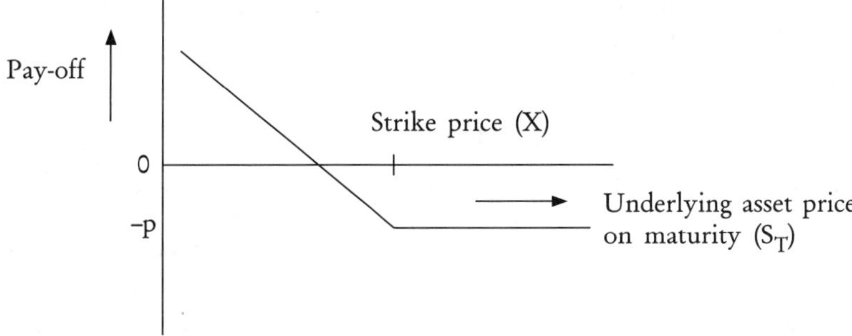

Algebraically, the pay-off on maturity of a European long put option can be represented as follows:

Pay-off = max (0, X – S_T) – p.

Max (0, X – S_T) means that the pay-off would be X – S_T if $S_T < X$, when the option will get exercised. Otherwise the holder does not exercise the option and loses the put option premium, p.

Short Put (European)

The holder of a short put option is the writer of the option and has agreed to buy the underlying asset from the holder of the long put option (purchaser) at the strike price, when the purchaser opts to deliver the asset. In return he receives the premium money from the purchaser at the time of entering into the contract. Since the purchaser wants to deliver the underlying asset only when the spot market price of the asset, S_T, is less than the strike price, X, the option writer loses money as he sells the asset in the spot market at a price lower than his purchase price, X. He has no right to refuse buying even when he loses. He, however, earns a profit equal to the put option premium if the spot market price, S_T, is more than the strike price, X, since the purchaser will not exercise the option in that case.

The above pay-off position can be diagrammatically represented as follows. The pay-off on maturity and the strike price are shown on the vertical and horizontal axes respectively.

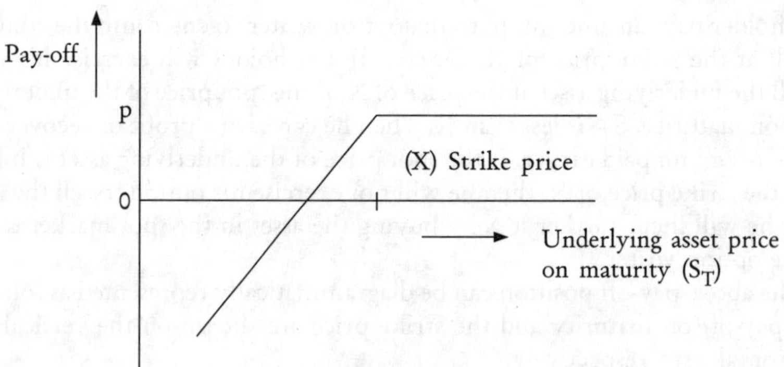

Algebraically, the pay-off on maturity of a European short call option can be represented as follows:

$$\begin{aligned} \text{Pay-off} &= -\max(0, X - S_T) + p \\ &= \min(0, S_T - X) + p \end{aligned}$$

It may be observed that option contracts, like other derivative contracts, are zero sum games. The profit of the holder of the long option is the loss of the holder of the short option and vice versa. Further, the holder of a short call or put option can only lose if the option is exercised. Then why should a writer write options? The answer lies in the divergent views of the holders of the long and short call or put option about the future spot market price. The holder of the long call or put thinks that the terminal asset price on maturity or exercise would be more than the strike price for call option or less than strike price for put option and he would be able to recover the premium paid and also earn additional profit. The holder of the short call or put option thinks the opposite and expects that he would not be asked to deliver the asset for call option or take delivery of the asset for put option. He would be able to retain the premium already received by him.

TYPES OF TRADERS IN DERIVATIVE MARKETS

Derivative markets attract a large number of traders—individuals, corporate organizations, mutual funds, and many others. Their purposes are also varied. They all can be grouped into three classes—hedgers, speculators, and arbitrageurs.

Hedgers use derivative markets to protect themselves against future price changes in an asset in which they have an interest and which is traded both in the spot and derivative markets. Let us take an example to explain the principle of hedging.

Suppose an investor holds 1000 equity shares of RIL bought at Rs 190 each earlier with the view that the market price of RIL shares may go down. He is worried that the value of his investment may significantly decline. He finds that three-month futures contracts are currently available at a price of Rs 195 each. This futures price of Rs 195 is the current market view of the price of RIL shares after three months. So if the investor sells (shorts) equivalent numbers of three-month futures contracts on RIL shares then he can ensure the value of his investment at Rs 195 per share over three months. We say that he has hedged the uncertainty about the value of his investment over a period of three months. Even if the spot market price of RIL shares falls after three months, the investor is assured of a value of Rs 195 each for his shares thus avoiding the price risk.

But there is also a downside to the use of the futures market. If the spot market price after three months is higher than Rs 195 each the investor would not get the advantage of higher spot price. He is committed to selling the shares at Rs 195 each, thus losing the opportunity to increase the value of his investment.

Speculators expect to earn profits by speculating about future price levels of an underlying asset of a derivative contract. Suppose, a speculator believes that the cash price of RIL shares after three months would be higher than the current price quote of three-month futures on RIL shares. Then, if his expectation comes true, he can buy (long) futures, take delivery, and sell the shares in the cash market to earn profit. But if he is proved wrong and cash price falls then he would lose money. Speculators play a very significant role in derivative markets. Most of the trades are speculative trades. Speculators ensure liquidity in the market and help in price discovery or understanding the movement of asset prices in future.

Arbitrage means locking in riskless profit by simultaneously buying and selling an underlying asset in two or more markets. Suppose it is found that one-month and two-month futures prices of RIL shares are Rs 200 and Rs 203 respectively and a trader can borrow money at the rate of 12 per cent per annum or 1 per cent per month for a mouth after one month. This gives rise to an arbitrage opportunity. A trader as an arbitrageur can buy one-month futures contract on RIL shares and sell two-month futures contract on the same security. He can borrow Rs 200 for each share, take delivery of the shares after one month by paying Rs 200 for each share, hold the shares and then deliver those against short futures contract to receive Rs 203 per share. His margin is Rs 3 per share out of which he pays Rs 2 (Rs 200 * 1 per cent) to the lender from whom he borrowed the money. The net result is a clear Re 1 per share arbitrage profit.

It may be observed that arbitrage opportunities do not last long. As traders try to take advantage of such opportunities, the forces of demand and supply force the prices to reach equilibrium levels thus wiping out further booking of profit by arbitrage.

Swaps

A swap is an agreement between two parties to exchange a sequence of cash flows over a period in the future. The parties are known as counter parties. The swap agreement defines the dates when the cash flows are to be exchanged and the method of calculation of the amounts to be exchanged. Two types of exchanges of cash flows are very common these days. One tied to the value of debt instruments known as interest rate swaps and the other tied to the value of foreign currencies known as currency swaps.

Suppose a company has borrowed Rs 100 million from an international lender with interest to be paid every six months at the rate of six months LIBOR + 2 per cent. Since the London Inter Bank Offered Rate (LIBOR) is a variable rate, the amounts of interest payments are uncertain. The company wants to avoid such uncertainty and intends to pay interest on the loan on a fixed rate basis. Interest rate swap is the solution. The company can approach a financial intermediary (say, a bank) who will pay to the company cash flows equal to interests at the floating rate on Rs 100 million (called notional principal) for the agreed period of time and on the agreed dates. The company in turn agrees to pay the financial intermediary cash flows equal to interests calculated at a predetermined fixed rate on the notional principal over the same period of time. In the process the company can utilize the floating rate interest payments received from the financial intermediary to pay the lender and continue to pay interests at the fixed rate thus removing the uncertainty about the amounts of interest payments. In interest rate swaps (IRS), since the currencies of the two sets of cash flows are the same, the notional principal amounts are not exchanged. The financial intermediaries often find out one or more other parties who have opposite cash flow requirements, thus entering into two offsetting swap transactions to avoid any financial exposure.

Another form of swap known as currency swap is also very popular for hedging currency risks. Suppose a corporation has borrowed, say, Japanese yen at a fixed rate and is unsure about future movements of the exchange rate between Japanese yen and its home currency. It is also of the view that the US dollar will remain more stable over a specified future time. In this case the corporation can approach a financial intermediary to receive its debt-service obligations in Japanese yen over a specified future time and in turn pay the intermediary in US dollars thus avoiding the uncertainty in the movement of Japanese yen exchange rate. The principal amounts are usually exchanged at the beginning and at the end of the life of a currency swap. The principal amounts are chosen such that they are equivalent at the exchange rate at the beginning of the swap.

Pricing of Forward/Futures Contract

Pricing of forward or futures contract means determination of the delivery price on the basis of the spot price of an underlying asset. The general formula for the forward/futures price is:

Forward/futures price = Spot price + Cost of carry

Cost of carry is defined as:

Cost of carry per unit = Financing costs per unit + Storage costs per unit
− Income earned per unit on the underlying asset

Cost of carry per unit is calculated for the period of the contract. The calculation of cost of carry depends on the type of asset. For financial assets like stocks, stock indices, currencies, bonds, etc. there is no storage cost but for commodities storage costs are incurred. The income earned on the asset also differs If a stock is not paying any dividend, then income is nil. But for dividend paying stocks and stock indices, dividend yield is taken as the income earned. For foreign currencies, risk-free rate of interest in the foreign country is taken as the income earned. The income earned on commodities like gold and silver is considered as nil since gold and silver are held for investment purposes by many investors though they may also have some industrial uses. Other commodities like crude oil, soybean, wheat, etc. are consumption assets since these are held primarily for consumption. The income earned on such consumption assets is the convenience yield.

The convenience yield on consumption commodities can be explained as follows. When there is a shortage of a physical consumption commodity, holders of the physical commodity are inclined to hold the commodity in the hope of higher gains in future, instead of supplying to the market to meet the shortage. We say that the commodity now has a convenience yield. This yield may not be directly measurable but gets reflected in the increase in prices providing an implicit return on the holder's ability to continue to supply to its known customers to preserve goodwill.

The financing cost is usually taken at the risk free rate of interest of the home country to avoid any arbitrage opportunity between spot market and forward/futures market. Let us take an example. Suppose we want to calculate the futures price of the shares of RIL after three months when the spot market price is Rs 200 each. Let us assume that the three-month risk-free rate of interest is 6 per cent and remains constant over time and no dividend is expected within the contract period of three months.

Then, financing cost = Rs 200 × $\frac{0.06}{4}$ = Rs 3
Storage cost = nil
Income earned during the contract period = nil
So, cost of carry = Rs 3
Hence, 3-month futures price = spot price + cost of carry
= Rs 200 + Rs 3
= Rs 203.

Finally, the forward and futures prices of a contract with the same delivery date are the same if the risk-free interest rate is constant and the same for all maturities or where it is a known function of time. When interest rates vary unpredictably as is usually the case in real life, the two prices would differ.

Pricing of Option Contracts

The price of an option contract is the premium that is paid by the buyer of the option to the writer or seller of the option. The premium is determined in the market place by the interaction of demand and supply of that option. It is, however, possible to relate various factors that determine demand and supply to calculate the fair value of the premium. The calculation of premium depends on whether the option is American or European type, a call or a put option and whether the underlying asset provides any income during the period of the contract.

There are broadly two approaches for the calculation of the premium-analytical approach and numerical method. The Black–Scholes–Merton Option Pricing Model is an analytical approach and provides a formula by which the option premium can be calculated. This model is better suited to pricing European options. There are a number of numerical methods—the Binomial model developed by Cox, Ross, and Rubinstein being one of them. This prices options by constructing a binomial tree and is well suited for both European and American options.

In this section, we briefly explain the Black–Scholes–Merton Option Pricing Model for pricing European call options on a non-dividend paying stock. Some restrictive assumptions are made in developing this model. These are:

(a) The stock price in the spot market follows a lognormal[1] distribution.
(b) All securities are perfectly divisible and continuously traded.

[1] This implies that the natural logarithm of the stock price is having a normal statistical distribution.

(c) There are no transaction costs or taxes.
(d) The short selling of securities is possible.
(e) There are no riskless arbitrage opportunities.
(f) The risk-free rate of interest is constant and the same for all maturities.
(g) The volatility[2] of stock price remains constant.

According to the model, the European call option price, c, on a non-dividend paying stock is given by the following formula:

$$c = S_o N(d_1) - Xe^{-rT} N(d_2)$$

$$\text{where } d_1 = \frac{\ln(So/X) + (r + \sigma^2/2)T}{\sigma\sqrt{T}}$$

$$\text{and } d_2 = d_1 - \sigma\sqrt{T}$$

and S_o = Current stock price
X = Strike price
T = Period of contract in years
σ = Volatility of stock price
r = Continuously compounded risk free rate of interest
$N(d_1)$ = Area under the standard normal curve N (0, 1) from $-\infty$ (infinity) to the point denoted by d_1
$N(d_2)$ = same up to the point denoted by d_2
e = 2.718282

To illustrate, suppose we want to calculate the European three-month call option price of RIL shares for a strike price of Rs 205 when the current stock price is Rs 200, the volatility of RIL stock price is 30 per cent per annum and the continuously compounded risk free rate of interest is 6.2 per cent per annum.

Here, S_o = Rs 200
X = Rs 205
T = 3 months = 0.25 year
σ = 0.30 per annum
r = 0.062 per annum

$$\text{So, } d_1 = \frac{\ln(200/205) + \{0.062 + (0.3)^2/2\} * 0.25}{0.3 * \sqrt{0.25}} = 0.013713$$

$$\text{and } d_2 = 0.013713 - 0.3 * \sqrt{0.25} = -0.136287$$

Using standard normal statistical table we get,

$$N(d_1) = N(0.013713) = 0.5055$$
$$N(d_2) = N(-0.136287) = 0.4458$$

[2] This is calculated as the standard deviation of the closing stock prices over a specified period.

Hence, 3-month European call option price

$$= S_oN(d_1) - Xe^{-rT}N(d_2)$$
$$= \text{Rs } 200 * 0.5055 - \text{Rs } 205 * e^{-0.062 * 0.25} * 0.4458$$
$$= \text{Rs } 11.12.$$

Further, the European put option price, p, on non-dividend paying stock can be found out by using the following formula:

$$P = Xe^{-rT} N(-d_2) - S_0N(-d_1)$$

Alternatively, the put–call parity formula for European options on non-dividend paying stocks can also be used to calculate the put option premium. The formula is given below.

$$p + S_0 = c + Xe^{-rT}$$

Derivative Markets in India

In India the trading of financial derivatives started in June 2000 through NSE and Bombay Stock Exchange. The market presently offers stock index futures and stock index options on two indices and stock futures on 31 stocks. Stock index futures were introduced first in June 2000 followed by stock index options in June 2001, options on individual stocks in July 2002 and futures on individual stocks in November 2001. Since inception the trading volumes have been growing steadily and trading data for the year 2001–2 in NSE is provided in Table 9.1.

Table 9.1: Trading Volumes of Derivatives in NSE in the Year 2001–2

Type of Derivative	Period	No. of Contracts Traded	Turnover (Rs crore)
Stock Index Futures	April 2001–March 2002	1,025,588	21,482
Stock Index Call Options	June 2001–March 2002	113,974	2466
Stock Index Put Options	June 2001–March 2002	63,926	1300
Individual Stock Call Options	July 2001–March 2002	768,159	18,780
Individual Stock Put Options	July 2001–March 2002	269,370	6383
Individual Stock Futures	November 2001–March 2002	1,957,856	51,516
Total		4,198,873	101,927

Source: *Indian Securities Market Review*, 2002, by SEBI.

Further, IRS and forward rate agreements (FRA) were introduced in June 1999 to enable banks, and other financial institutions hedge interest rate risks.

REFERENCES

Chance, D.M. (1998) *An Introduction to Derivatives,* fourth edition, Dryden Press, Orlando.

Duffie, D. (1989) *Futures Markets*, Prentice Hall, N.J.

Hull, John C. (2000) *Options, Futures and Other Derivatives,* fourth edition, Pearson Education, Delhi.

Jarrow, R.A. and S.M. Turnbull (2000) *Derivative Securities,* Second edition, South-Western Australia.

Kolb, R.W. (1997) *Futures, Options and Swaps,* Second edition, Blackwell, New York.

10

Relationship Marketing

Sudas Roy

Consider the following three scenarios.

Scenario1: The village grocer grins broadly and welcomes the customer, 'Good morning, Sir! What can I serve you today? Last time, that new brand of mustard oil that I recommended you should buy, how did you find it? Look at me, I am just talking shop. Please tell me how your son, Naren, has done in the Higher Secondary exam. When are we going to celebrate?'

Scenario 2: A polite letter reaches Mr Agarwal, a major owner of a fleet of trucks in Nagpur. The letter first thanks him for patronizing the brand of tyre 'X' for all his replacement requirements. Then the letter reminds him that the following tyres of brand 'X' which he bought from the dealer at Nagpur should now be ready for replacement based on the average estimated mileage covered since the date of purchase. Finally, the letter ends by inviting Agarwal to visit the dealer's showroom within a certain time period carrying this letter. The dealer would be very happy to offer him a 10 per cent rebate on his total purchase invoice.

Scenario 3: The busy executive checks into the 5-star hotel after a tiring and delayed flight. At the check-in counter, he is welcomed by name and asked whether he would prefer the corner room in the south wing as usual. After he has settled down in his preferred room, the room service bearer knocks and enters with a bowl of hot steaming chicken asparagus soup, which is his favourite.

What is the common thread connecting these three scenarios? From the rustic village grocer to the sophisticated 5-star hotel, all are practising what has come to be known as 'relationship marketing'. The underlying premise connecting all these cases is 'don't let go your valued customer. Try to keep her loyal to your products, services, or the store'. Customers are the most important assets for any organization and longer they stay loyal, more profitable and successful would be the supplier's business. Thus, the key concept to achieve this goal is to build 'relationships' with customers more and more on a one-to-one basis. Peter Drucker, the management guru, declared long back that the purpose of an organization is to create customers and retain them. This focus on customer retention is embodied in the paradigm of 'relationship marketing'.

THE GENESIS

Relationship marketing, like many other concepts in management, is not an original or a recent invention. It has been practised for many years without being called by this name. It took the confluence of many factors to lift this practice from its day-to-day informality to the pedestal of an academic concept that has influenced the marketing thought and practice in a significant way in recent times. In this sense it has been a case of 'reinventing the wheel' to meet the requirements of today's environment. In this section we shall examine the dynamics which have contributed to this process of rediscovery.

Visualize the village or the small town market as depicted in Scenario 1. Throughout the world, small village or town grocers, bakers, millers, or candlestickmakers used to develop a loyal clientele base by using social relationship building skills. In a small community each purveyor of goods and services knew most customers by name, understood their specific preferences, developed social bonding through familiarization, and provided add-on services like home delivery, credit, or courteous behaviour.

In the first decades of the twentieth century, industrial revolution matured into mass production, assembly line operation, and hierarchical organizations to deliver standard products in large batches. Economies of scale and learning curve benefits brought down the unit cost. Large city-based organizations gradually replaced the small and the cottage sector operations. In this new milieu, mass marketing and aggressive product selling pushed away the earlier orientation towards one-to-one marketing. Most of the product-markets were growing and new customers could be enticed by the new marvels of technology at an affordable cost. Newer tools of marketing like mass-media advertising and promotional techniques to induce trial by non-users gained primacy. Volume and transaction orientation replaced relationship orientation of the pre-industrial revolution days.

The first major jolt to this euphoria of mass production came in the 1930s with the western capitalist world getting caught in prolonged depression. Alfred P. Sloan, CEO of General Motors, was one of the first to recognize the need for segmenting the market to seek new demand potentials as well as to match the offerings more closely to the varying preferences of different segments. Segmentation, in its turn, gave rise to targeting specific segments with offerings positioned against such targets. Marketing started its journey back from mass marketing and hard selling. In the latter decades of the twentieth century, a number of factors came together to speed up the process of 'reinventing the wheel'. The most significant of these factors have been:

(a) The rapid maturity and saturation of many product-markets in the developed world.
(b) Closer academic and research attention being focused on the vast market place called B2B marketing.
(c) Emergence of the service sector as the major engine of growth in most countries.

(d) Rapid development of IT and the global connectivity of the worldwide web.
(e) Demand for more customization from a more demanding and affluent class of customers worldwide leading to increasing fragmentation of the market.
(f) Free market competition and globalization becoming the universal prescription for economic prosperity.

In this new environment, increasing cost and complexity of attracting new customers matched with the need for retaining a profitable customer. Technology started providing capabilities to identify individual customers and customizing the offerings to suit individual needs and requirements. In the B2B marketing, the markets are often small in terms of customer numbers but big in terms of per-customer value or quantity off-take. It is often observed that, say, 20 per cent of customers often account for 80 per cent of the revenue in a given industry or a category. Thus, retaining the 20 per cent big-cum-valuable customers has become imperative. The service industry is characterized by fragmented, specialized preferences involving large doses of value delivery through human interactions. IT and Internet-based global connectivity has created opportunities for global reach with individual based interactivity. A plethora of near-parity products and services has whetted the appetite of the customers to seek increasingly differentiated 'made-for-me' products and services. The coming together of these emerging trends has made the marketing wheel turn full circle again from transaction-based mass-marketing to relationship-based one-to-one marketing, at least in the sectors like institutional markets and service markets.

The Modern Paradigm of Relationship Marketing

In an increasingly competitive global marketplace, realization is dawning among the marketeers that traditional emphasis on transactions leading to a sale is no longer sufficient to ensure long-term success. Sales per se are no longer the ultimate goal of marketing, but continued profitable sales to a set of satisfied loyal customers, are. Classical marketing mix instruments have been too heavily weighed in favour of completing a sale transaction. In order to build a base of loyal customers, short-term transaction orientation must give way to a long-term relationship building with target customers. Thus, marketing would involve a set of relationship building steps encompassing before-, during-, and after-sales marketing activities. As the market becomes more competitive and customers become more demanding, cooperative and collaborative relations with customers become more crucial. In today's world, products are increasingly getting packaged in a whole set of services. The traditional dichotomous classification of products and services is getting blurred. Customers' need for more and varied services, even while buying and using a tangible product means that these service deliveries have to be managed properly and consistently. This need for marketing product service combinations brings into focus the importance of building customer-based relationships to design and deliver such a combination. It must also be understood that in an ultimate sense each product delivers an 'experience' to the customer. The more satisfactory such experiences are the more loyal the customers will be. Relationship marketing attempts to manage such a series of experiences, to the extent it is feasible, to create this loyal customer. When a firm shifts its perspective from immediate sales transaction to long-term customer retention orientation, it realizes the importance of investing resources in relationship building which would consistently deliver ideal product service combinations to enrich and enhance the 'experiential' benefits for its customers. Today's customers are 'spoiled' by a plethora of choices. Thanks to the rapid access to new technology, core products are becoming increasingly similar and inferior quality products have no hope of survival, at least in developed markets. In such a scenario, customers know that preference for a particular brand would ensure good quality and fair price. They, therefore, then start looking for other 'service' or 'experience' related values to augment their level of satisfaction. Customization, personalization, acquisition, and post-acquisition experiences reflect these values which relationship marketing seeks to track and satisfy.

It is evident in today's market that to build a mutually satisfying long-term relationship with the final customer, the marketeer has to build intermediate relations with a number of market-based players. Such entities can be the suppliers, the channel members, specialist service providers, and the like. Relationship marketing paradigm is an emerging field of conceptual development which is examining the nature, the process, and the outcome of these relations. Scholars like Jagdish Seth, Christian Gronroos, Adrian Payne, and Leonard Berry have notably contributed to this development. This chapter is heavily indebted to their pioneering work. The bibliography provided at the end of this chapter should help an interested reader to explore this topic in greater depth.

Relationship Marketing: Domain and Definition

Over the years, two broad approaches have dominated the debate on the domain and definition of relationship marketing. One school, consisting of mainly marketing practitioners, has viewed relationship marketing as an extension of direct marketing and an IT-enabled process to focus on one-on-one marketing with the goal of long-term customer retention. They have defined relationship marketing as 'an integrated effort to identify, maintain, and build up a network for the mutual benefit of both sides, through interactive, individualized, and value-added contacts over a long period of time' (Shani and Chalasani 1992).

The other school, drawn mainly from the Nordic countries, assigned a far more strategic role to relationship marketing and gave it primacy as the core paradigm in marketing. According to their definition, 'Marketing is to establish, maintain and enhance relationships with customers and other partners, at a profit, so that the objectives of the parties involved are met. This is achieved by a mutual exchange and fulfilment of promises' (Gronroos 1990). Thus, customer relationships are the key drivers for an organization and the role of marketing is to build, maintain, and enhance such relationships. This is a leap towards broadening the scope of the concept so much so that relationship becomes the 'core' and marketing becomes a process in the service of this 'core'.

This tendency towards broadening the scope of relationship marketing has sparked off a debate as to whether there should be a distinction between relationship marketing and marketing relationships. The two terms are not synonymous. Relationship marketing specifies the nature of the relationship—to be cooperative and collaborative. It implies interdependency and a long-term orientation. Such specificity is absent in the term 'marketing relationships'. Thus, scholars like Seth and Parvatiyar would prefer to treat relationship marketing as a sub-set of marketing and specifically focused on such marketing actions which foster long-term firm–customer relationships. Other types of relationships like supplier relations, competitor relations, or internal relations can only enter the domain of relationship marketing if such relations have a strong impact on the ultimate firm–customer relationships. Arising out of such a standpoint, Seth and Parvatiyar (2002) define relationship marketing 'as the ongoing process of engaging in cooperative and collaborative activities and programs with immediate and end-user customers to create or enhance mutual economic value at reduced cost'.

The preceding discussion on the domain and definition of relationship marketing has thrown up a few commonalities, which can be summed up as follows:

(a) the definitions are process-based,
(b) the nature of the relationship specified is collaborative and cooperative,
(c) interdependency for long-term mutual benefit is implicit,
(d) process outcomes need to be measured in terms of mutual exchange of enhanced value,
(e) customers include immediate customers like channel partners as well as end-use customers, and,
(f) besides the traditional customer market, some definitions include relations with other markets as well.

Relationship Marketing and the End-customer

Keeping the end-customer as the focus, we shall now examine a series of issues and concepts which arise when viewed from a relationship perspective. These issues fall within a large number of areas:

(i) the stage at which the customer is,
(ii) the tools and techniques for customer retention,
(iii) implication of the quality of relations with 'other markets' and its impact on end-customer market,

(iv) importance of process management on a cross-functional basis to manage customer relations,

(v) importance of interactivity to enrich relations,

(vi) the role of total quality management, including service quality, in relationship building, and

(vii) the incorporation of customer retention goals in an overall BSC strategy.

These are all relevant issues to be examined in this context. In the limited scope of this chapter, it may not be possible to touch upon all the myriad issues raised. However, attempt will be made to comment on the more critical ones.

In shifting the focus from transaction orientation to relationship orientation, the implied change that the marketeer seeks to bring about is how to keep the end-customer loyal in a universe of increasingly tempting alternatives. To put it dramatically, in a virtual market the options are only a click-of-the-mouse away! In such a milieu, the options for the marketeer are two-fold: (a) to raise the switching barrier and cost of switching by increasing the dependency of the customer on the marketeer through measures like heavy price discounts on bulk purchase, extended credit line, locking the customer through benefits of standardization based on the supplier's proprietary technology, material, or design or by creating preferences for the supplier's ingredients in the customer's products for the latter's buyers. The marketeer can also be aided in this by the high transaction cost involved in a market where search costs are high; that is, information on or availability of best options is not easy to obtain. (b) Alternatively, the marketeer can create such a high level of customer satisfaction through relationship marketing practices that the customer understands the win–win advantage of the present relationship and voluntarily foregoes market-based options. The basis of the relationship is founded on cooperation, trust, and commitment. Relationship marketing is, thus, the more proactive and positive approach to build up long-term customer loyalty through customer satisfaction but it is also the more complex, and often more expensive, process. We now examine the dynamics of this complex process and what it entails.

It is helpful to look at the end-customer and her relationship with the supplier as a process continuum which can be described as a loyalty ladder. Through relationship building tools the proactive marketeer attempts to help the end-customer climb the successive steps along this ladder. The steps can be summarized as prospect–customer–client–supporter–advocate–partner. Marketing's first task is to convert a prospect who has the need and the purchasing power, into a customer through the classical marketing-mix segmentation–targeting–positioning—strategies. In transaction-oriented marketing, as seen often in cases of marketing of FMCG, the marketeer keeps on emphasizing the first conversion step and hopes to retain customers essentially through brand-building exercises. However, under relationship marketing strategy, the major emphasis will shift to converting the initial customer to a loyal customer by making her climb the successive steps of this ladder. When a customer becomes a client, it is implied that a regular series of transactions mark the buyer–seller relationship. A client becomes a supporter when her distinct purchase preference gets routinized in favour of the seller's offerings. She actively supports the brand that she regularly buys. The next step is when she starts advocating the brand through positive word-of-mouth references to other prospects and assumes the role of an advocate. Finally, the collaborative, win–win relationship reaches a stage where willing partnerships replace traditional buyer–seller roles and involve joint planning and designing of the supplier's products for the buyer or integrating the supplier's supply chain with the buyer's inbound logistics to create just-in-time (JIT) efficiencies. The marketeer would seek to create appropriate economic, technical, structural, and social ties with the customer to facilitate this movement up the loyalty ladder.

End-customer—New vs Retained

One major plank on which the rationale for relationship marketing rests, is on switching the focus from continuous acquisition of new customers through transaction-oriented marketing to retaining existing customers through relationship building.

The factors in justification for such a shift lie in:

(a) the relatively high cost of customer acquisition as opposed to customer retention. Studies conducted across a wide variety of industries have shown that in a developed, matured market this cost differential could be as high as 5:1, that is, new customers cost the marketeer five times more to acquire compared to retaining an existing customer. Low growth of many markets, excessive cost of mass media, high initial promotion cost of inducing trials are some of the reasons explaining this. In a developing market like India this cost differential would be lower but would still remain significant.

(b) Even in developing-country markets where in many sectors the market growth rates can be pretty healthy, it makes sense to focus on customer retention as it provides insurance against business fluctuations by providing a steady, loyal group of customers.

(c) It is quite evident that retained customers are significantly more profitable than new customers for the company. High acquisition cost is incurred at the beginning of the relationship and the longer the customer stays this cost is amortized over a longer revenue stream. Conversely, if the customer is lost to competition, say, within a year, the acquisition cost may never be recovered leaving the organization to incur losses on such customers.

(d) Retained satisfied customers are a strong source of favourable word-of-mouth publicity about the company and its brands, which help to bring referral customers with little or no acquisition cost to the company.

Such publicity, being highly credible, helps to enhance the company's reputation and its brand equity as well.

(e) Long-term loyal customers can be more easily persuaded to buy other products as well as newly developed products from the same supplier. Such cross selling makes such customers even more profitable to the company.

(f) Studies have shown that retained customers are often less resistant to higher prices than new customers, since they have developed confidence in the supplier's sincerity and ability to offer higher value products and services while charging higher prices.

(g) Some cutting-edge loyal customers can be very important sources for new product development ideas. In an ideal situation, the customer might actually collaborate with the supplier to develop such products which would be essential for the customer's own new product development programmes.

In this way, retained customers often help the supplier to learn to absorb new technologies, new skills, and new processes.

Retained Customers—Measurement Issues

The above discussion brings into focus the need for developing measuring tools to properly leverage this crucial asset base called the 'retained customers'. As the saying goes, 'if you want to manage, you must measure'. Hence, in implementing relationship marketing programmes, the supplier must develop certain tools to measure a few parameters which will be of help in this context. Some of these tools are:

(a) *Tracking of Accretion and Defection to and from the Customer Base*: In any given time period, a certain number of people/institutions become first time buyers of the supplier's products/service. During the same period, some of the existing customers switch their patronage and buy from elsewhere. It is critical for the company's well being that the accretion rate should exceed the defection rate. Companies must gain new customers at a faster rate than that at which they lose existing customers. Tracking tools must be devised to measure these two rates with calibrated cut-off levels which, once reached, would automatically trigger early warning alarms for corrective actions. When the acquisition of new customers becomes difficult, it becomes critical to minimize the defection rate. In order to formulate a strategy for doing this, such measurement tools are essential to generate a decision-oriented information base. In case of high volume categories which are bought by large segments of customers, tracking the accretion/defection rate is extremely difficult. The only recourse could be using the consumer panel data over time and checking the defection rates on a sample basis and then projecting it on the overall market. However, in case of B2B marketing or service marketing this can be quite feasible not only to accurately estimate the respective rates but also to identify the actual first time or defecting customer. Such customers can then be further probed to ascertain the reasons for buying first time or for defecting. These interviews would provide rich data to formulate appropriate policies. Developing a measuring tool like this one poses another complication, which is, how would one define defection? A customer who has completely stopped buying or even a customer who has reduced his off-take by, say, a percentage like 60 per cent or so of the usual level. In either case, the period of defection must also be predefined.

(b) *Customer Market Share*: In relationship marketing successful retention of a customer should be measured by the progressive percentage share increase of the supplier's products in the total category basket bought by the customer from all suppliers.

(c) *Lifetime Value of a Customer*: Relationship marketing focuses on building long-term mutually profitable relationships. This presupposes an ability to identify which customers are worth building relationships with. One measuring tool that helps the supplier to make such a choice is the measure of 'lifetime value of a customer'. Assuming a certain length of period of continued patronage by a customer to represent a lifetime, accounting and financial tools would be used to project the stream of cash inflows and cash outflows over the lifetime period of a specific customer account based on forecasted purchase volume trends against estimated future price escalation trends. This would provide an estimate of projected cash inflows. Then the net present value of a lifetime customer can be computed based on the risk discounting factor. Such calculations enable customers to be ranked in terms of their potential lifetime value. Such a ranking list can then guide the decision as to which customers to target for relationship building.

(d) *Other Measuring Tools*: As a corollary to lifetime customer value, other measuring tools need to be developed to determine the long-term profitability of a customer. Costs of servicing a customer account which are unique and relevant for that account alone, have to be isolated and computed using tools like activity-based costing and segment accounting.

It is evident from the preceding discussion that such measuring tools are likely to be developed more easily in case of B2B and service marketing contexts. In case of large volume, frequently purchased business to consumer (B2C) FMCG categories, capturing of accurate and on-going point-of-sale data with the help of IT-enabled technologies would be the major option. In such a context, bar coded unit packages, using universal product codes would be tracked through scanner-readable systems for continuous recording and storing in the retail point computers when a transaction is completed. Such data combined with the ability to generate customer lists through mechanisms like the credit card-based purchase tracking or online purchases or through invoice analysis and supplemented by in-store research, consumer panel data analysis, analysis of suggestion and feedback forms filled by customers, can help link point-of-sale data with matching customer related data. This would result in a massive database, which would profile the actual purchase pattern of individual customers over time. Data warehousing and data mining software can then help retrieve a unique demand/purchase history of an identifiable individual customer. This can then form the basis for estimating the lifetime value of a customer and can also be leveraged for relationship building strategies on a one-to-one basis. Such an approach presupposes large scale retailing format and the presence of appropriate data capturing technologies right through the supply chain.

(e) *Mapping and Costing of Cross-functional Processes*: One of the significant lessons learned from relationship marketing is the importance of cross-functional processes in delivering customer satisfaction. It becomes increasingly clear that, to create a large base of loyal and retained customers, customer satisfaction has to be achieved through delivery of high quality, zero defect process-related values which are created through cross-functional participation and performance. Thus, measuring tools are needed to map these cross-functional processes to help improve the efficiency of such processes though process re-engineering. Similarly, costs of such processes have to be mapped accurately as well.

Apart from the measurement angle, these cross-functional processes have a deeper implication. It is implied that irrespective of the functional affiliation, organizational personnel must understand that their roles are ultimately linked to delivering values and satisfaction to the end-customer. These values are not created departmentally but through process-related participation and performance. In this sense every member of an organization is a part-time marketeer. When an organization can create such a universal mindset cutting across narrow departmental compartments, a truly customer—driven organization gets created. Such an organization is best positioned to practise relationship marketing.

Relationship with Multiple Markets

One of the major premises of relationship marketing is that successful practice of the concept with the end-customer market is only possible if the supplier is successful in building effective relations with a number of other markets. These relations are specific in nature in the sense that they have to be collaborative and mutually beneficial and the relationship building tools would broadly fall within the basket of marketing instruments.

Payne has identified six major markets with which a firm has to build such relations. These are: (i) customer markets; (ii) supplier alliance markets; (iii) referral markets; (iv) influence markets; (v) recruitment markets; and (vi) internal markets.

We have already discussed relationship implications with the end-customer market. Now let us examine the implications in dealing with the other markets.

Supplier Alliance Markets: How far the finished products of the firm would meet the customer satisfaction standards depends crucially on the quality, price, and other related parameters of the bought-out items and services. Thus 'ingredient marketing' (like the 'Intel inside' campaign) has been a strategic issue for the material suppliers. Companies in the auto industry, who would typically use bought-out materials to the extent of, say, 60 per cent of the total value of the assembled car, realize the importance of developing long-term collaborative relations with a select group of preferred suppliers. Customers in these relationships demand a whole host of services from the suppliers to strengthen their own competitive advantage. Such services would include zero-defect quality of materials supplied, long-term negotiated price contracts, JIT supplies to eliminate inventories, etc. Customers in such industries go about proactively to build structural, technical, economic, and social ties with a preferred group of suppliers. Planning tools like materials requirement planning, IT enabled processes like SAP, collaborative R&D with suppliers, are all used to realize the full potential of such relationships. Mutual gain through higher efficiency and sharing of such gains by both the parties provide the cementing element to such alliances.

Referral Markets: A firm has to build relations with intermediaries like the stockist, agents, brokers, specialized service providers, consultants, multipliers, etc. who help bring in referral business.

Influence Markets: Firms need to build strong relations with the society's opinion-makers, opinion moulders, legislators, bureaucrats, media, and other such agencies who wield strong influence on the behaviour of the end-customers and sometimes even regulate the firm's access to the end-customer market. Such relations become critical at the time of first entry into a new country-market or a new product-market. In an operational context, such relations can yield favourable policy environment for the firm to operate in. In specific marketing context, like pharmaceuticals marketing or project marketing, influences like the doctors and consultants play a critical role.

Recruitment Market: In the new millennium, industry is becoming increasingly knowledge-based. Knowledge management and knowledge workers are key value creators. In such a milieu, a firm must be assured of a steady supply of talented, skilled, trained, and knowledgeable workforce. Failure to ensure this would seriously erode the competitive position of such a firm. Hence, a firm must build strong relations with the supply sources and the potential talent pool on a long-term basis. The firm's ability to capture a significant talent-market share would be dependent on such relationship building.

Internal Markets: Relationships with the external markets would be only feasible if there is a strong relationship bonding within the firm between the management and the employees. People in the organization must have a shared vision about the mission and goals of the organization. Individual goals must remain in alignment with the organization's goals. Through an internal marketing programme, the corporate management must be able to imbue the employees with a sense of purpose to deliver satisfaction to the external customers. Internal marketing would involve motivation, training, multi-skilling, incentives, empowerment, and process improvement through flattening of hierarchies. Internal marketing would also imply bringing the market inside the organization where every member/department views itself as either a supplier or a customer of some other person or department. This would bring in market-induced discipline and efficiencies within the organization to make it better prepared to succeed in external marketing.

Paine's six-market model brings into focus the importance of network building and network management. In today's complex world no single organization, however big or resourceful, can exploit all relevant opportunities or service all target segments, particularly in a multi-country multi-product context, without the support infrastructure of an efficient network. Ultimately, competition ceases to be horizontal, that is, between firms at the same level, and becomes vertical with a firm and its network competing with another firm and its network. Network-related value additions created by strong relationship marketing can spell the difference between long term success and failure in the marketplace. Such networks also enable the firm to concentrate on its core competencies and outsource most other functions to external specialists. Such networks need to be connected through a strong IT backbone for real- time monitoring and control. Besides, contract-design skills are called upon to delineate the relationships with the network members for effective functioning.

Relationship Marketing—Operational Issues

We have noted from the various definitions discussed earlier that relationship marketing is sought to be practised through development of economic, technical, structural, and social ties between the two parties for mutual gain. In this section we shall examine, both in the context of end-customers as well as in the case of intermediate customers and including both B2C and B2B marketing contexts, how the elements of relationship marketing are made operational.

Seth and Parvatiyar have identified three types of relationship marketing programmes which can be aimed at all the three target customer types, namely, individuals, distributor-customers, and institutional buyers. These are briefly described below.

Continuity Marketing Programmes: The primary goal of such programmes is to increase loyalty and retention of the target customers. In case of individual customers, membership and loyalty card programmes are the most typical.

Customer membership and loyalty behaviour is rewarded through a range of services like price discounts, free offerings, upgrades, price-off on cross-sold products, additional services like bonus mileage for frequent flying, etc. For distributor-customers such programmes take the shape of frequent replenishment programmes, automatic reordering, JIT-based supplies, efficient customer response programmes, etc. In B2B marketing, continuity programmes would involve JIT supplies and/or special sourcing arrangements. Continuity programmes encourage long-term loyalty through special services which have economic, technical, and structural dimensions, which reduce uncertainty of doing business on the part of the customer, and are accompanied by reward incentives.

One-to-One Marketing: This concept is based on account-oriented marketing and seeks to satisfy the customer through uniquely configured marketing programmes customized to meet the unique needs of an individual customer. By using IT-enabled processes and online channels, the mass-marketeer can now develop individual-based frequency marketing, interactive marketing, and after-marketing programmes to develop long-term relationships with high profit yielding customers. In case of distributor-customers, such programmes take the shape of customer business development programmes. By bringing the domain-specific expertise from across many markets, the supplier helps the customer to improve his business efficiency and overall profitability. Such programmes are premised on mutual enhancement of value sharing. In the B2B context key account management programmes, where the marketeer forms account management teams to husband his resources for delivering customized benefits, are examples of one-to-one marketing.

Partnering Programmes: In these programmes, the marketeer and the customer join hands as partners to serve end-user needs. In the mass-markets, co-branding and affinity marketing programmes are the most common examples. In distributor–customer markets, joint logistics programmes or cooperative advertising programmes are instances of partnering. In the B2B context, partnering would often involve co-designing, joint product development, or co-marketing.

Brand Building

A successful brand is a strong relationship builder. This is true for mass-marketed goods as well as for industrial product or service category goods. In the case of FMCG goods, this is often the most potent instrument for relationship building. Over a period of time, brands arouse feelings which are partly rational and partly emotional. Customers develop a sense of nearness to them. In a complex world of mind-boggling choices, brands stand as beacons of stability and security. They encompass all the preferred values consistently offered to the chosen target markets. This paves the way for an enduring long-term relationship between the consumer and the brand marked by strong brand loyalty. Brand building is an ongoing process involving both transactional as well as relationship building instruments.

Relationship Marketing and the Issue of Interactivity

One major precondition for bringing continuous improvements in the relationship quality is to create opportunities for initiating dialogues with the relationship partner. The spread of the Internet has not only brought the world to one's door but has also given one the opportunity to initiate interactive communication. Company portals, call centres, help lines, toll-free numbers, etc. are examples of the ever-expanding interactive space between the supplier and the customer. With the rapid growth in cellular technology mobile phones provide a viable option for anytime-anywhere access. Embedded technology will soon produce smart products which can communicate with other machines. A 'malfunctioning' refrigerator will communicate the nature of the problem directly to the service centre computer. Technology is creating never-seen-before opportunities for interaction and multiplicity of 'touch points' between the supplier and the buyer–user. Along with such advances, the traditional system of being alert to the customer's voice would continue to exist. In nurturing relationships, this exchange of information and communication would be crucial. On a continuous basis, conditions must be created for recording the customer's voice. This would involve understanding her needs and requirements, as well as her grievances and complaints. Creating feedback opportunities, having a single-window access for the customer and a prompt complaint-redress mechanism would go a long way in proper relationship nurture. However, it must be underscored at this stage that even the best infrastructure for interactivity will not deliver results if the attitude and the mindset of the marketeer are not sincere and genuine. The success of relationship marketing will ultimately be expressed through the genuine customer concern and customer care that an employee displays in a 'moment of truth' encounter or in day-to-day dealings with the customer. It would also manifest in the ability to 'recover brilliantly second time' after a failure in service delivery.

Relationship Marketing and Customer Relationship Management

Over the last decade, enhancing customer value, delivering a superior level of service, strengthening the brand, have all been recognized as crucial to strengthening customer relationship which plays the critical role in a company's ability to grow profitably and consistently outpace competition. As a result, the relationship marketing concepts described in this chapter, have been operationalized through Customer Relationship Management (CRM) programmes by a large number of companies all over the world. To be specific, CRM capabilities have been created to support the crucial interactions between customers, channels, and brands. The success record of CRM initiatives has been mixed. Due to the absence of a unifying vision about end-goals or of a strategic road map or due to the inability to manage interplay between the customers, channels, and brands, CRM has often failed to meet the desired goals. What follows here is a brief illustration of how a service organization implemented the concepts of relationship management by putting in place an effective CRM programme. The example is adapted from *The Ultimate CRM Handbook* by Freeland (2002).

An international hotel operator in North America had a shared service organization brought about by its role as a franchiser of several well-known hotel brands. Shared services included a central reservation centre, e-commerce support, brand marketing, and a frequent-guest loyalty programme. Perception was growing that these shared services were lacking coordination and there were many stand-alone CRM investment requests lacking integration. As a result, the effectiveness of customer interaction was getting reduced. With the help of an international consultancy firm, the organization first developed an enterprisewide CRM strategy. This effort resulted in a 'touch point' analysis to identify the key points of customer interactions of the company's operations which resulted in maximum impact on customers. Touch points were grouped in four broad areas: establishing relationships, pre-trip experience, on-property experience, and nurturing the relationship. The specific CRM capabilities that related to each of these touch points were also identified. Based on this, analysis of the exiting CRM capabilities was conducted. It was found that enhancements were needed in direct-marketing implementations, call centre effectiveness, and sales. Such improvements could lead to a financial impact to the tune of US$65 million in net profit over five years by focusing on 15–20 key capabilities. These capabilities were then grouped under four distinct initiatives. These were:

(a) direct marketing effectiveness which would lead to better campaign management effort and provide offers more closely tailored to individual customers;
(b) call centre optimization which involved building more robust capabilities for effectively handling incoming calls and better access for the call centre representative to customer records;
(c) sales effectiveness which involved greater sales force automation and an integrated channel sales approach; and
(d) IT infrastructure enhancements which focused on creating more robust customer data models and enhanced guest profiles.

Thus, by using a diagnostic, strategic road map approach the company could put an integrated CRM framework in place for future sales and profit growth.

Relationship marketing is an emerging paradigm of marketing which encompasses in its ambit a whole set of concepts ranging from customer retention and loyalty to multi-market relation building and network-based competition. It focuses on internal processes, many of which are cross-functional in nature so as to deliver customer value. Relationship marketing leverages IT-enabled processes to customize its offerings and communications for segments of one. Drawing its sustenance from B2B marketing and services marketing, it has spread its wings to mass-market customers. The success of this approach is based on certain basic premises. These are:

(a) Customers often feel better off with fewer choices. Free market, with its plethora of choices, confuses the customer and she often seeks recourse to the comfort of familiar, proven, and trusted options. Life-simplification can be a basic goal even for a commercial entity.

(b) Trust, collaboration and commitment are crucial relationship building blocks which work well even in commercial contexts.

(c) Properly managed relations can, on one hand, raise the switching cost too high and, on the other hand, raise the transaction cost of market based solutions.

(d) Relationship marketing makes a fundamental paradigm shift by changing the relationship between exchanging parties from adversarial or competitive to collaborative and partnering.

(e) Customers, even in a successful long-term relationship can develop a 'seven-year itch' and start looking elsewhere. In today's world it is very easy to do so. Therefore, successful customer relationship would entail avoiding complacency and proactively seeking out ways to improve the quality of the present relationship through a process of continuous improvements.

References

Freeland John J. (2002) *The Ultimate CRM Handbook—Strategies & Concepts for Building Enduring Customer Loyalty & Profitability*, McGraw-Hill, New York.

Gronroos, Christian (1990), *Service Management and Marketing: Managing the Moments of Truth in Service Competition*, Lexington Press, MA.

Seth, Jagdish N. and A. Parvatiyar (2002) (eds) *Handbook of Relationship Marketing*, Response Books, Sage Publications Inc., New Delhi.

Shani, D. and S. Chalasani, (1992) 'Exploiting niches using relationship marketing', *Journal of Consumer Marketing*, Vol. 9, No. 3, pp. 33–42.

11

Supply Chain Management

Balram Avittathur

Supply Chain Management (SCM) is one of the very popular corporate buzzwords of the twenty-first century. A few trend-setting firms have shown the business world the immense potential for cost reduction and revenue maximization as a result of adopting SCM. Today more and more firms are discovering this potential and its capability to be a sustainable competitive advantage.

SCM refers to superior coordination of material, information, and financial flows between the various business entities in a supply chain, namely, suppliers, manufacturers, distributors, and consumers, to ensure that high quality product as desired by the customer is available at the lowest price at the right time in the right quantity. The SCM philosophy is centred on the concepts of integration, flow, and perfect matching of demand and supply.

To understand the reasons for SCM's growing popularity one has to look at how manufacturing has evolved over the last few decades. The first six decades of modern manufacturing, commencing with assembly line production of Ford automobiles in the early twentieth century, witnessed rapid urbanization and increase in demand for industrial goods in western economies. Most western economies were closed and protective during that period. Many industries were in the rapid growing phase, with capacity usually lagging behind demand. The competition in these industries in those years was less compared to the latter years, when these industries started maturing. There is sufficient business literature that describes those years as the era of the sellers' market. In a sellers' market, the competition was primarily on cost. Lesser costs meant higher profits, which implied higher surplus for expansion. There was room for sellers of poor quality products that hardly fit the customer requirements. For a long time the ruling concept was what is popularly known as mass production—producing few types of products in very large volumes.

However, things started to change after the oil shocks in the 1970s, which increased manufacturing costs in many industries. Moreover, many industries were reaching the maturity phase in the western economies. By the 1980s, low-cost and high-quality Japanese goods had started flooding the western markets. Supplies were gradually catching up with demand. Product variety too started increasing. The customer was finally being heard. Strategies for boosting profits could no more ignore the customer. It was clear that the path to sustainable profitability was through offering the product the customer wanted, cutting costs, improving quality, and providing good service. Realization broke that the Japanese firms were benefiting immensely from superior manufacturing practices like JIT manufacturing, total quality management (TQM), and total productive maintenance (TPM). These practices gave very high importance to customer needs. However, these were essentially firm level initiatives. Many firms that were successful in implementing JIT, TQM, or TPM in their manufacturing facilities were not successful in convincing their suppliers or customers to adopt these efficiency and quality boosting practices. This also limited the potential of these practices in achieving sustainable profitability. Nevertheless, the foundations for SCM were laid.

The 1990s witnessed a dramatic increase in product variety in many industries. Associated with the increase in product variety were the twin managerial challenges of shorter product life cycles and quicker obsolescence of products. Firms started discovering that demand forecasting techniques, though quite reliable for predicting overall or aggregate demand, were hardly reliable at the individual stock keeping unit (SKU) level. In the days of low product variety, inventory carrying cost was the only cost implication of stocking goods. However, in the new regime, where products are getting outmoded quickly, the additional cost implication is the markdown cost. This cost is the loss incurred by the producer when forced to sell his product at discounted price owing to the product getting obsolete. Another manifestation of increased product variety is the economic loss to a firm as a result of not having the product that the customer wanted. Increase in product variety is accompanied by increase in distortions in order processing from customer to manufacturing and further upstream to the suppliers. Increasingly, firms started realizing that the Japanese manufacturing practices alone were not going to be enough to ensure the survival of manufacturing firms. Superior management of demand and supplies, with minimal mismatches, soon became the need of the day. Thus, firms started embracing the SCM concept as a means of building competitive advantage. Implementation of SCM has enabled firms like Dell Computers, Hewlett Packard, and Wal-Mart to establish dominance in their industries (Chopra and Meindl 2004). In India, Asian Paints, HLL, and ITC are some examples of firms that have achieved industry dominance through SCM.

The following sections of this chapter describe the important issues related to SCM. They include impact of uncertainties, strategic lead-time management, SCM network design, product and process design for SCM, IT, order processing and inventory control, transportation, and organizational and environmental issues.

Impact of Uncertainties

Uncertainty is an all-pervading feature of businesses. They are of many different types but can broadly be categorized on the basis of where they originate from—supply-side uncertainties or demand-side uncertainties. The supply-side uncertainties are factors contributing to actual supplies varying from planned ones. Typical examples include loss owing to defective production, shortage of materials or plant resources, and delayed receipts of inputs. The demand-side uncertainties refer to variance in consumption owing to fluctuations in market growth, seasonality, business cycle swings, stage of product life cycle, introduction of a new competing product, etc. With increased competition, globalization, and product variety, the demand-side uncertainties have grown drastically in recent times.

Uncertainty, whether it originates from supply-side or demand-side, contributes to mismatch between supply and demand. Mismatch between supply and demand manifests as capacity, inventory, lost sales, or markdown costs. It is common knowledge that as capacity utilization approaches full utilization level, the ability of capacity to match uncertain demand reduces drastically. Thus, many firms invest in extra capacity so that their inventory or lost sales costs are not too high. If a budgeting exercise considers only 'average' figures and ignores the effects of uncertainties, the actual profit would turn out to be much less than the budget figures. In fact, many firms look at costs owing to uncertainties as costs that are managerially 'uncontrollable'. Under pressure to cut costs, such firms attack costs that are more tangible. Very often such moves result in further increase in costs owing to uncertainties. For instance, a firm trying to reduce material costs, which is an example of a tangible cost, may switch over from a supplier located next door to a supplier located hundreds of miles away. The move may result in reduction of material cost but the uncertainty of the supply increases owing to the greater distance between the new supplier and the firm. To counter this uncertainty the firm would be forced to either increase capacity or hold more raw material inventory, both resulting in higher cost due to uncertainty.

Box 11.1: Inventory, Markdown, and Lost Sales Costs

To understand inventory carrying cost and markdown cost, imagine a firm that forecasts demand for one of its products in a certain time period at a certain region as 100 units. However, actual demand may turn out to be 80 units. The firm is then left with 20 unsold units. It will either carry forward these 20 units to the next period (and incur inventory carrying cost) or dispose them at a discounted price if the product has no demand in future (and incur markdown cost).

The firm incurs lost sales cost when actual demand is greater than forecasted demand. Let actual demand turn out to be 120 units instead of 80 units. The firm is then short by 20 units. In many industries demand not met in a certain time period may turn out to be demand lost permanently. A typical example is that of music audio demand. In a competitive situation, characterized by low brand equity, demand not met will turn out to be sales lost to competitors. The firm is losing profit on the 20 units, which is referred to as lost sales cost.

As mentioned earlier, product variety is higher today than at any time in the past in many industries, which also implies shorter product life cycles and quicker obsolescence of products in these industries. Increase of product variety also means drastic increase in demand uncertainty at individual SKU level. For instance, if the aggregate demand for passenger cars of a particular manufacturer is more or less stable between 95 and 105 units per period, with an average demand of 100 units per period, it implies an uncertainty of ± 5 per cent. In the short-term horizon of a few months to a year, variation in aggregate demand is mostly accounted for by macroeconomic factors. It is possible to forecast aggregate demand quite accurately using modern forecasting techniques. However, the same does not hold true for individual SKU demand. If the above mentioned car manufacturer offers five models, each with an average demand per period of 20 units (hence, average aggregate demand of 100 units per period), one can conclude that uncertainty in aggregate demand and individual demands are similar if the individual demands vary in a narrow range of 19 to 21 units per period. It is very difficult to imagine such a scenario. A more reasonable scenario is one where the individual demands vary in the range of 17 to 23 units per period, which implies an uncertainty of ± 15 per cent. In other words, demand uncertainty as a proportion of mean demand increases with demand disaggregation. This is explained by the fact that substitution between commodities say, between passenger car and jeep in this case is much less than substitution between products belonging to a commodity category (different passenger car models). Uncertainty in demand contributes substantially to forecasting error, which is the deviation of actual demand from forecasted demand. As production and product supply is based on forecasted figures, forecasting error manifests as inventory, lost sales, or markdown costs.

Another significant effect of product variety is on the coordination of material and information flows within a firm and between firms in a supply chain. Higher product variety implies higher component and product proliferation throughout the system with more frequent production and assembly set-up changes, which implies higher volumes of information flows. Thus, it can be said that difficulty in coordinating material and information flows increases as product variety increases. Poor coordination of material and information flows manifest as mismatch between demand and supply, which results in inventory, lost sales, or markdown costs.

Controlling supply-side uncertainties is a striking feature of Japanese manufacturing concepts like JIT, TQM, and TPM. In a competitive environment, it is almost impossible for firms to control the demand-side uncertainties, which are influenced heavily by competition, macroeconomic factors, and consumer behaviour. Hence, the question is how well a firm can make its supply adapt to demand-side uncertainties.

In other words, SCM is about controlling supply-side uncertainties through techniques like JIT, TQM and TPM, and responding smartly to demand side uncertainties. The former has received plenty of corporate attention in the past two decades. Today it is quite difficult to come across a firm surviving in a competitive environment without following the principles of JIT, TQM, and TPM. However, 'responding smartly to demand side uncertainties' has not received much attention and is the area where plenty of SCM opportunities exist today. In the following portions of this chapter, the focus is on how firms can respond well to demand-side uncertainties.

Strategic Lead-time Management

Effective lead-time management is a fundamental requirement for firms to respond smartly to demand-side uncertainties. A typical supply chain comprises of innumerable stages passing through many firms, which results in frequent changeover of material and information ownership.

Let us try to understand a simple supply chain using the example of gasoline used by automobiles. The first stage of the gasoline supply chain is extraction of crude at the oil well. The next stage is transportation of the crude oil from oil well to petroleum refinery. Gasoline is one of the outputs at the refinery. It is shipped to the retail outlet through the firm's distribution network. The automobile user purchases gasoline at the retail outlet, which is the terminating point of this supply chain. There is a lead-time involved with every stage of the supply chain. The lead-time of a stage is the sum of processing time and waiting time at that stage. The waiting time at a stage is a function of the batch size at that stage as well as that of the various uncertainties associated with that stage. For instance, let average processing time of one barrel of crude be one minute. If batch size of transporting crude from oil well is 1200 barrels, a shipment will take place every 1200 minutes or 20 hours. Hence, the average waiting time of material at this stage owing to batch size is 10 hours. Let uncertainty involved at this stage be such that the well output in a 20-hour period varies in the range of 960 barrels to 1440 barrels, with an average value of 1200 barrels. In this situation the firm has to maintain safety stock inventory to ensure that it does not run short of material. Safety stock inventory, as the term suggests, is the excess stock that is maintained to ensure product availability is high when there are uncertainties in demand or supply. To ensure a batch size of 1200 barrels in all shipments, it becomes necessary to keep a safety stock of 240 barrels. This is equivalent to 240 minutes or four hours of production. If there are no other uncertainties it could be said that average waiting time at this stage is equal to 14 hours. The average lead-time for the entire chain is the sum of the average processing and waiting times of all stages. The activities associated with processing are value adding (extraction of crude) and activities associated with waiting are non-value adding (crude waiting for shipment). In many supply chains, characterized by high uncertainties and product variety, the ratio of time spent on value adding activities to the total supply chain lead time could be as low as 0.001, with the remaining time being spent on non-value adding activities. How does this impact SCM performance?

It is well known that forecasting horizon depends on the lead time. Suppose a firm makes a product whose lead time is six months. While planning its production in January of a certain year the firm would like to know the demand for the product in July of that year. Thus, its forecasting horizon is six months. However, if lead time were only one month, it has to know the demand for the product in February of that year. It is obvious that when demand exhibits uncertainty, forecasting demand for a particular month in the near future is more accurate than forecasting demand for a particular month in the distant future. Forecasting error increases exponentially as the forecasting horizon increases. In other words, in January, the demand forecast of February would be more accurate than the demand forecast of July. As explained earlier, forecasting error results in mismatch between demand and supply, which in turn manifests as inventory, markdown, or lost sales costs. Similarly, a longer lead time makes supply chain coordination of material and information flows more difficult and contributes to mismatch between demand and supply. Thus, lead-time reduction is imperative for minimizing inventory, markdown, or lost sales costs. This explains the origins of the concept of strategic lead-time management.

In a competitive situation, maximizing profit implies maximizing revenue by offering the right product at the right time in the right quantity and quality, and minimizing total cost, which includes the uncertainty costs. Strategic lead-time management refers to determining the optimal total supply chain lead time that ensures maximum supply chain profit and provides sustainable competitive advantage.

Strategic lead-time management effectiveness and, thus, supply chain performance is affected by SCM network design, product and process designs, IT, order processing, inventory control, and transportation issues. The following sections describe the impacts of these in the context of SCM and how they can be employed as strategic tools.

SCM Network Design

SCM network design is a concept that is synonymous with strategic lead-time management. The supply chain of a product can be considered as a network of suppliers, manufacturers, distributors, and customers who are the different business entities in the chain. The progress of a product, from raw material to finished good, is through a series of manufacturing facilities (including the suppliers' facilities), transportation equipments, and warehouses. SCM network design refers to determining the right locations of manufacturing facilities and warehouses, right technology, and best mode of transportation that fully satisfies the strategic lead-time management objective. When supply chains traverse provincial boundaries within nations or international boundaries, the SCM network design gets more complex as tariff issues too have to be factored in while determining ideal locations of manufacturing facilities and warehouses. SCM network design is a topic that is receiving immense research attention in recent times. Operations research and other quantitative techniques are widely used in the optimization of SCM networks modelled in literature. More and more firms are using these techniques to get the best out of their supply chains.

Product and Process Design for SCM

As mentioned earlier, lead time of an SCM stage is the sum of the processing time and the waiting time at that stage. The product and process designs critically influence the processing and waiting times of different stages.

Product Design for SCM

Consider the example of a firm producing passenger cars. A passenger car comprises of various components like piston, connecting rod, crankshaft, gears, valves, tyres, etc. If the firm's approach to product design is such that there is considerable differentiation among models at the components level itself (for example, different tyres for two similar models), it will be saddled with a huge bill of materials that will result in cumbersome materials management and production planning. For instance, if this firm is producing six models and each model has 8000 components of which 1000 are common to all the models, its bill of materials will have 43,000 components. Instead, if 3000 components are common, the bill of materials reduces to 33,000 components. It is a small proportion of critical items in the total components list that provides the distinctive identity to the model, in terms of its functional and other quality requirements. While developing a new model, the components design can be restricted to just these critical items. For most of the other items, like bolts and fasteners, the firm would be better off using standard components. This parts rationalization approach reduces the design effort and improves spare parts management. It also allows better utilization of production resources. For the car firm in question, if the engine connecting rod is different for each model, a fair amount of connecting rod production capacity will be spent in set-ups for changing over from one type of connecting rod to another if production facility is common. Separate facilities for each connecting rod may imply higher production cost. High set-up time and cost will result in large production lot sizes, which in turn will increase production lead time. Instead, if the connecting rod were the same for all models, the set-up time and cost is drastically reduced and high capacity utilization is possible. This also enables reduction of production lot-size, which in turn will reduce the production lead time. High part proliferation also results in mix ups at the assembly stages, which leads to quality problems.

In addition to using standard components, firms can improve their supply chain performance by employing modular designs for products. Modular designs enable firms to increase product variety without a corresponding increase in parts. As per modular design, the end product will be the assembly of many generic modules. The modules will in turn be assemblies of many generic sub-modules and standard components. In the design stage itself it is ensured that variants of a particular module type can match with the variants of another module. For instance, the automobile example of modular design is any gearbox matching with any engine. If a product comprises of four modules with three variants each, it is theoretically possible to get 3^4 or 81 different variations of the product. The number of parts required is only 12 to get these 81 variations. If parts were designed specifically for each product variation, 324 parts are required to get the 81 product variations. Modular design also ensures easier product assembly, better materials management, production planning, inventory control, spare parts management and product maintenance, and lesser production lead time.

Box 11.2: Lead Time vs Lot Size

Consider a component whose production process has two operations, the first at machine 1 and the second at machine 2. The processing time per component at machine 1 is 1 time unit and moving a processed lot from machine 1 to machine 2 takes 9 time units. The time taken per lot at the first operation, which is the sum of the processing time and the time taken to move the processed lot to machine 2, increases as the lot size increases and is shown by the figure below.

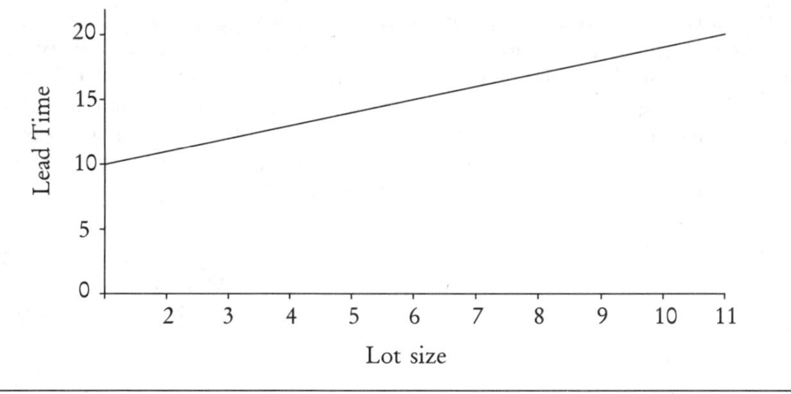

Process Design for SCM

Processes are generally designed keeping only the engineering and in-house logistics aspects in mind. However, this approach may not be sensible in the times of high product variety. Consider the example of the process for manufacturing TV sets. For a particular model, product variety is defined by the colour of the TV panel. Engineering and in-house logistics considerations may prompt the TV manufacturer to assemble TV sets with panel colour identity at the factory itself. In other words, the product differentiation happens at the factory itself. If the manufacturer comes up with five models, each in five panel colours, he has to forecast demand, plan production, and arrange packaging and distribution for 25 product variants. As discussed earlier, higher product variety results in higher forecasting errors and mismatches between supply and demand. This in turn implies higher stock-outs and unsold goods.

Instead of the above process, if the manufacturer were to re-design the process such that he supplies his retailers TV sets in one standard panel colour and the retailer provides a panel casing in the appropriate colour as demanded by the customer, the product differentiation occurs at the retailer point. As far as the manufacturer is concerned, his demand forecasting, production planning, and logistics planning for the TV sets is now only for five products. At the retailer end, stocks are kept for five standard TV models and different types of panel casings instead of the 25 product variants earlier. The reduced forecasting errors will result in lesser stock-outs and unsold goods. It will also reduce supply chain lead time as inventory levels across the chain reduce. The benefits are described by a simple example in Box 11.3.

Box 11.3: Delayed Product Differentiation

Imagine a firm selling two products that have many parts common to each other. Let the parts commonality in value terms be 80 per cent. The demand per day for each of these products at one of the firm's retailers varies between 20 units and 30 units, with an average demand of 25 units per day. Also, combined demand per day for the products varies between 44 units and 56 units, with an average demand of 50 units per day. To prevent any stock-out, the retailer has to start every day with a stock of 30 units of each product, which corresponds to a safety stock of five units each. Assuming an inventory carrying cost of US$1 per unit per day for both the products, the retailer incurs inventory carrying cost of US$10 per day. The retailer has an alternative of stocking material as parts and assembling the product on order from the customer. Let value of the parts that go into a product as percentage of final product value be 90 per cent. The inventory carrying cost for this alternative is as shown in the table below.

Item Description	Value Share	Safety Stock in Equivalent Units of Product	Inventory Carrying Cost Per Day
Common Parts	0.8	6	$= 0.9 \times 0.8 \times 6$ = US$4.32
Parts required only by 1st product	0.2	5	$= 0.9 \times 0.2 \times 5$ = US$0.90
Parts required only by 2nd product	0.2	5	$= 0.9 \times 0.2 \times 5$ = US$0.90
Total			= US$6.12

It is seen from the above table that by delaying the activity at which product differentiation occurs, the inventory carrying cost can be reduced by US$3.88 per day. There are two reasons for the reduction of inventory carrying cost. The first is the saving owing to demand pooling of common parts that has resulted in reduction of demand uncertainty, which in turn has resulted in the reduction of safety stock requirement (6 units instead of 10 units). The second reason is that value addition is also postponed, which has resulted in reduction of the value of goods stocked by the retailer. It may be kept in mind that this concept is easy to implement for goods like paint, bicycles, personal computers, etc. For these goods, the activity at which product differentiation occurs has short lead-time (customer would not mind the waiting), low capital investment (low economies of scale), and does not have serious quality implications.

Delayed product differentiation by appropriate process re-design is probably the most important strategy employed by firms in recent times to respond smartly to demand uncertainty. It is also known as postponement strategy.

Most paint manufacturers have employed this strategy. Among computer printer manufacturers, Hewlett Packard is famous for achieving cost reduction and delivery improvement (better product availability) using the postponement strategy (Chopra and Meindl 2004).

In many industries, the product differentiation could be happening at more than one activity in the manufacturing process. If there are inventory points between these activities, it is important that the activities be arranged in the increasing order of product differentiation. The famous garment manufacturer, Benetton, originally employed a process that started with thread dyeing, which was followed by knitting and assembly. The variety addition in the former is much higher than in the latter. Moreover, demand uncertainty on colour is much more volatile than demand uncertainty on style and size, which is defined by knitting and assembly activity. The dyeing activity is also shorter than the knitting and assembly activity. Benetton re-designed its process such that knitting and assembly of un-dyed thread became the first activity and garment dyeing followed it. In fact, dyeing activity for a huge proportion of total season volume is initiated only after understanding the initial market trends. This process re-design enabled Benetton to significantly reduce its inventories, production lead time, and stock-outs (Chopra and Meindl 2004).

INFORMATION TECHNOLOGY

The success of SCM hinges heavily on coordination of information and material flows among suppliers, producers, distributors, and customers. The increase in product variety that has been described in previous sections has resulted in drastic increase of information flow across the supply chain. Globalization of economies has resulted in firms expanding their markets geographically. Information technology enables firms to overcome the disadvantages of distance and physical separation. A large and significant proportion of total supply chain lead time in most industries is accounted for by the time spent in non-value adding activities. These wasteful activities distort information flow and impede material flow. Hence, it is pertinent to minimize the time spent in non-value adding activities in any supply chain. Information technology enables firms to automate and marginalize many routine and repetitive non-value adding activities. Automation using IT ensures that calculations necessitated by routine production planning exercises can be done quicker, cheaper, and more reliably than when they are done manually. It may be noted at this point that incorrect planning owing to wrong inputs and calculations contributes significantly to demand–supply mismatches. Automation also ensures that many non-value adding activities that were earlier done manually during firm working hours can now be done on a 24 hours a day, seven days a week basis. This means many decisions can now be taken on a real-time basis.

It is quite easy to understand that without IT it is close to impossible to achieve the objectives of SCM. Today, IT is enabling intra- and inter-firm integration, which is making SCM more realistic and attainable. The integration of various business entities in a supply chain through IT is referred to as virtual integration (Magretta 1998). The Dell Computers supply chain is a classic example of virtual integration. For a truly virtually integrated supply chain, there are no organizational boundaries for communication flow. Information within and between firms flow in real time, without any duplication of data entry activities. In many traditional supply chains, order placed by a downstream firm is entered manually in the database of the upstream supplier firm. However, using the latest networking technology it is possible for this order to be automatically recorded in the database of the upstream firm. Michael Dell, CEO of Dell Computers, describes virtual integration as the way of capturing the advantages of vertical integration without actually vertically integrating. In other words, benefits of inter-firm integration are achieved, though ownership of the firms in the supply chain could be different.

The greatest benefit of virtual integration is with respect to coordination of information and material flows in the supply chain. Better communication technology improves coordination helping producers to gauge the market on real-time basis. An order received by Dell Computers is today transmitted immediately to its components supplier and logistics provider. Technology permits tracking of individual components and products in the various stages of the supply chain and sharing of this information with all the relevant entities of the chain. Supply chain visibility contributes significantly to reduction of safety stocks in the system. Transactions on real-time basis or very short intervals have considerably reduced order lead time, which in turn has contributed to significant reduction of total supply chain lead time. Firms like Dell Computers have order lead times as low as five to six days, which provides them the liberty of producing to actual orders instead of producing according to firm generated forecasts. In the computer industry, where components get obsolete quickly accompanied by falling prices, short lead time enables Dell Computers to assemble computers with components which it purchases at a price lower than that which its competitors have to pay. All this has contributed significantly to cutting down the inventory, lost sales, and obsolescence costs and have provided a sustainable competitive advantage for Dell Computers.

The additional benefit of IT, owing to the rapid progress it has made in recent times, is the drastic increase in computing power and sharp reduction of computer memory cost. As a result, decision support software packages are available today that deliver near optimal supply chain decisions quickly and efficiently. The rapid growth of *i2* Technologies, a leading SCM software developer, in the late 1990s can be attributed to the growing popularity of these business software packages.

Order Processing and Inventory Control

During the days of mass production, characterized by high volumes and low variety, inventory was a source of capacity and a means to match demand and supply. However, as product variety increased, the utility of inventory, as a source of capacity, declined. This was essentially because demand forecasting at SKU level became more difficult as demand uncertainty increased. In the past, firms would be stuck with unsold goods that had to be disposed of at discounted prices. Firms started realizing that inventories had to be brought down to very low levels—if possible, zero—to cut cost and improve supply chain performance. In this context, two issues that receive immense attention are order processing and inventory control. Both are very critical from the viewpoint of efficient and effective management of the supply chain. Both directly contribute to the inventory carrying cost. At this stage it is important to understand the terms 'cycle inventory' and 'safety stock inventory', which are the principal components of inventory in a system.

Discussion of cycle inventory automatically takes one to the classic economic order quantity (EOQ) model, which tries to determine the optimal order size that minimizes the sum of ordering and inventory carrying costs. The ordering cost is fixed with respect to each order and does not depend on the order size. This prompts a firm to go for as big an order size as possible. However, increase in order size results in increase of inventory carrying cost. For instance, let annual demand, ordering cost, and inventory carrying cost for a particular item be 1200 units, US$25 per order, and US$6 per unit per year respectively. If an order is placed for one unit at a time, the sum of ordering and inventory carrying costs would be US$30,000 per year (only ordering cost). If only one order is placed for the whole year, the sum of ordering and inventory carrying costs would be US$3625 per year, of which US$3600 is the inventory carrying cost as a result of an average inventory of 600 units for the year (starting with 1200 units and ending with zero units). As the ordering quantity increases from unity, the sum of ordering and inventory carrying costs first decreases till a particular order quantity and increases from there on. This order quantity is referred to as EOQ. In this example, the EOQ is 100 units and the total cost for this order quantity is US$600 per year.

Obviously, the EOQ would have been one unit had the ordering cost been zero or negligible. There are several factors contributing to the ordering cost, which in turn prompts firms to exploit the associated economies of scale. The commonly known drivers of ordering cost are set-up time and cost in the production context, transportation fixed cost in the logistics context, and communications cost in the ordering context. Firms in a supply chain should jointly focus on identifying the ordering cost drivers at various stages of the supply chain and marginalizing their impacts so that material movement at all stages will be in small lots. Smaller lot or order size ensures better material flow and lesser time spent in non-value adding activities. An order size of one at all stages of the supply chain ensures that material flows continuously through the chain and lead time is least. This makes matching of demand and supplies an easier task. Producing in small lots is one of the principal elements of JIT philosophy. Lot sizes have already fallen drastically in the manufacturing domains of many industries with implementation of JIT.

Today, advances in IT are enabling firms to drastically cut down communication costs and implement concepts like joint ordering (different product types are ordered jointly). This is directly contributing to the reduction of cycle inventory in many industries. High ordering costs still continue to force many firms to plan procurement, production, and distribution on fortnightly or monthly basis. However, the percentage of firms planning these activities on a daily, hourly, or real-time basis is increasing gradually, thanks to their success in bringing down ordering costs.

Safety stock inventory has already been defined while discussing strategic lead-time management. The growing increase in product variety and consequent increase in demand uncertainty has resulted in drastic increase in safety stock requirements. It is owing to a desire to reduce safety stock that firms are increasingly looking at strategies like delayed product differentiation. Firms are also actively cutting down delivery lead time and increasing ordering frequency so that the safety stock requirements are brought down. For instance, if delivery lead time is 10 days and maximum demand for this period is 150 units with an average demand of 100 units, the average safety stock to be maintained to avoid stock-out is 50 units. However, if lead time is only four days with maximum and average demands of 70 units and 40 units respectively, the average safety stock to be maintained to avoid stock-out reduces to 30 units. The same logic applies to ordering frequency too. This is another reason for the increasing trend of daily, hourly, or real-time planning of production and distribution activities.

More and more firms are focusing their energies in transiting from the traditional Make-to-stock to the Build-to-order. In the computer industry, Dell Computers is the leading pioneer in producing products to order. Virtual integration of the computer supply chain has enabled the firm in this transition (Magretta 1998).

Transportation and Third Party Logistics

Transportation is the core sector of most economies. It is a major SCM issue in any geographically spread out supply chain, which is a common feature of the globalization era. With globalization the need for more and better transportation has increased as firms the world over seek new markets and cheap sources of materials. Transportation decisions can critically impact supply chain lead time. It is an activity that is characterized by high fixed costs, which prompts users to exploit economies of scale by transporting in large lot sizes. This explains the popularity of Full Truck Load (FTL) transportation when firms manage their outbound logistics themselves. Large transportation lot size, like large production lot size, implies lesser number of transportations and higher inventory cost. However, good supply chain flow requires material to be transported in small lots at very frequent intervals. It also requires material movement to be fast and reliable. These compulsions are making the concept of Third Party Logistics (TPL) popular in recent times.

TPL service providers combine the material transactions of many producers enabling the latter to transport economically without employing FTL. If the FTL for a particular truck type is 10 tonnes and the average daily demand at a retailer is one tonne, a shipment has to be made every 10 days if the supplier is employing his own means of transportation. However, engaging a TPL service provider may allow high flexibility in transportation lot size at unit transportation costs that are just slightly higher than unit transportation cost had the producer shipped using his own means. Thus, for slightly higher unit transportation cost, the supplier can ship material on a much more frequent basis. This enables the retailer to drastically reduce his inventory cost. Frequent orders also reduce the effective time taken for material to move from production facility to customer hands. Successful TPL service providers employ superior technology with modern tracking facilities. The higher scale of activities enables them to exploit various efficient transportation concepts and techniques like hub and spoke transportation, merge-in-transit, cross docking, and travelling salesman problem. They are more competent in managing various legal and regulatory requirements of inter-state or international material transactions. Today, the TPL firms are competent not only in basic transportation services but also in allied logistics activities like warehouse management and order processing. The rapid growth of TPL service providers like Federal Express and UPS is testimony to the growing popularity of TPL service and the potential it has for achieving high logistics efficiency.

Organizational and Environmental Issues

Organizational and environmental issues are very critical to supply chain performance. Organizational issues refer to aspects like organization structure and performance measures. It is quite obvious that performance measures for managers are dictated by the organization structure followed by the firm. A functional management organization structure is traditionally based on the principle of allocating duties on the basis of functional specialization. The performance measures that are developed as a result need not be aligned with the goals of SCM. For instance, the performance of the manager responsible for material procurement would be assessed on the basis of the cost of material procurement, while primary responsibility of keeping raw material inventory cost low would be that of the finance manager. This scenario would imply material procurement in huge quantities to exploit quantity discounts. However, this will also mean high raw material inventory cost, resulting in a conflict between interests of materials manager and finance manager. As has been discussed earlier, SCM is about controlling supply-side uncertainties and responding smartly to demand-side uncertainties. It is imperative that the organization has a structure that facilitates this objective rather than one that contributes to compounding supply-side uncertainties and creating rigidities in the firm's response to demand-side uncertainties.

The tariff and various government policy matters are chief amongst the environmental issues that impact supply chain performance. We had earlier discussed SCM network design as determining the ideal locations of manufacturing facilities and warehouses, the right manufacturing technology, and the best mode of transportation that fully satisfies the strategic lead-time management objective. However, location and sourcing decisions are also influenced strongly by trade related issues, the incentives provided by the government in the form of tax exemptions or input price subsidies, the local work culture, the economic and political stability of the particular area, the infrastructure support, and the quality of manpower resource available. While trying to exploit the environmental factors, a firm should evaluate whether the decisions taken are in line with SCM objectives.

Indian Context

The potential for improving supply chain performance is very high for firms based in India. The average finished goods inventory in manufacturing—a good indicator of supply chain performance—is about 45–50 days in India (Shah and Avittathur 1999). The corresponding figure for the USA is about 14 days (Rajagopalan and Malhotra 2001), though India is a much smaller country in terms of area. The present sales tax regime in India contributes heavily to many supply chain inefficiencies. In many instances, location of manufacturing plants and warehouses are decided with the singular objective of reducing sales tax. Being a state subject, sales tax is used by competing states to attract capital investments. However, in many firms the advantage gained from reduction in sales tax is more than compensated by high stock-outs, huge inventory costs, long supply chain lead time, and poor product availability. Urgent replacement of the existing sales tax regime by a simple value added tax (VAT) is one of the means to reduce the supply chain costs.

Though the manufacturing sector has seen considerable progress in terms of efficiency and productivity improvements, thanks to the induction of modern technology, the same is not true with respect to logistics activities. The poor transport infrastructure combined with various existing tariffs, which are anything but simple to follow, have contributed significantly to the logistics inefficiencies in the country. A population that is too spread out geographically, with almost 70 per cent residing in villages, limits the scope for improving efficiencies in retailing. However, it may be hoped that the entry of TPL service providers and large-scale retailers in recent years will contribute significantly to improving supply chain performance.

REFERENCES

Chopra, S. and P. Meindl (2004) *Supply Chain Management*, Pearson Education, Singapore.

Fisher, M.L. (1997) 'What is the Right Supply Chain for Your Product?' *Harvard Business Review*, Vol. 75, pp. 105–116.

Kopczak, L.R. and M.E. Johnson (2003) 'The Supply-chain Management Effect', *MIT Sloan Management Review*, Vol. 44, pp. 27–34.

Lee, H.L. (2002), 'Aligning Supply Chain Strategies with Product Uncertainties', *California Management Review*, Vol. 44, pp. 105–119.

Magretta, J. (1998) 'The Power of Virtual Integration: An Interview with Dell Computer's Michael Dell, *Harvard Business Review*, Vol. 76, No. 2, pp. 73–84.

Rajagopalan, S. and A. Malhotra (2001) 'Have U.S. Manufacturing Inventories Really Decreased? An Empirical Study' *Manufacturing and Service Operations Management*, Vol. 3, No. 1, pp. 14–24.

Shah, J. and B. Avittathur (1999) 'Improving Supply Chain Performance through Postponement Strategy' *IIMB Management Review*; Vol. 11, No. 2, pp. 5–13.

12

Negotiating a New Psychological Contract

Leena Chatterjee

The advent of the New Economy has led to considerable tumult and uncertainty in the business arena, with the rise in global competition, technological innovations, and breakthroughs in information management practices, bringing about tremendous changes in job opportunities, organizational forms, and employer–employee relationships. These changes have forced organizations to question traditional practices and policies and to develop new mechanisms for survival. The strategies for survival are taking the form of organizational upheavals such as restructuring, outsourcing, downsizing, and re-engineering which, in turn, have led to widespread and long-term consequences for both organizations and employees. An important casualty of these changes has been the concept of 'lifetime employment' that organizations had earlier offered to employees in return for their loyalty and services.

Traditionally, employees were accustomed to an employment relationship where employees could expect job security in return for commitment and loyalty to the organization. Employers and employees entered the relationship with the expectation that the employee would stay and grow with the same organization through his career. Today, flexibility and job insecurity are seen as the most striking features of the new work environment. A number of factors have contributed to this situation. First, with a large number of organizations engaging in downsizing and delayering exercises, large numbers of employees are being rendered redundant and many jobs are becoming obsolete. Moreover, with the innovations in IT, distances and boundaries are shrinking and, therefore, both employers and, employees have a much larger set of options available in the global labour market in terms of alternate employment. Again, the changing labour market conditions and global competition has forced businesses to keep their core workforces at a minimum. Full-time permanent employment is no longer the accepted practice. In order to reduce overheads, maintain workforce flexibility, and minimize liability for any potential violation of an employee's rights, many organizations have gone in for outsourcing work or part-time or short-term contractual appointments. This has led to a new breed of temporary employees who are referred to as 'a contingent workforce' or the flexible workforce.

Flexibility and insecurity at the workplace have led to a number of organizational fall-outs such as reduced trust, loyalty, motivation, and commitment, besides anger, depression, and lowered morale among employees. Employees are under increasing pressure to contribute, often feeling that their jobs could be on the line. The impact of this perceived insecurity on performance at work can affect the organization in two contradictory ways. On the one hand, it may reduce the complacency or passivity that can develop in employees who believe that they have a 'job for life', but, on the other hand, it may erode commitment and lower employee morale. Accordingly, both academicians and human resource (HR) management practitioners have been concerned about re-examining and redefining the relationship or contract between the employer and the employee, in order to manage some of the negative consequences of organizational restructuring.

A number of studies have reported that changes in the employer–employee relationship have led to a perceived violation of the psychological contract among employees which, in turn, has resulted in lowering of morale, perceptions of inequity and injustice, and reduced loyalty and commitment to the organization. Psychological contracts, in general, can be defined as an exchange where an implicit understanding exists between employers and individual employees concerning their mutual obligations and expectations and the assumptions they make about each other (Robinson and Rousseau 1994). For example, an employee may perceive that he/she has been promised fair pay, attractive benefits, opportunities for growth and advancement, a supportive work environment, sufficient resources, training, challenging work, and in return has promised to give the organization his/her energy, time, technical and analytical skills, loyalty, and commitment. The contract is usually articulated in terms of the fairness of the exchange and the willingness to trust the other and is considered important because it influences employment relations, organizational commitment, job satisfaction, turnover, absenteeism, and employee morale (Guest 1998).

The new or changing employer–employee relationships have been the focus of tremendous research interest of late, as they are believed to have implications for how companies can attract, motivate, and retain employees in the current scenario (Roehling et al. 2000). In examining the 'new deal' that employers are offering to employees, researchers have identified a number of features that characterize this changed relationship. Today, employees are at best entitled to interesting work and 'employability', but little else. They are expected to be 'free agents' and are often viewed as expendable. Again, more and more jobs are contract or project based and thus the relationship between the employer and employee is shifting from that of a long-term association or partnership to a more expedient and transient transaction.

It is widely accepted that intellectual and human capital is the basis of competitive advantage in the New Economy. Thus the struggle to attract and retain talent is currently seen as a key corporate challenge in a world where technological development and global competition are driving widespread changes in patterns of employment. Accordingly, organizations will have to manage and renegotiate their psychological contract with employees in order to regain the trust and commitment of existing employees. An additional challenge before organizations in the next decade or so will be to forge a new psychological contract with younger, more mobile, and less loyal employees. There are fewer ties binding the current employee's career to the employment organization than at any time in the past. With increasing job insecurity on the one hand, and the seemingly infinite range of options to earn a living in the new work environment on the other, the coming generation will need to have stronger—and more positive—reasons to commit its energy, creativity, and future to one organization alone. Employees need to perceive more meaningful returns on their investments if they are to resist the lure of lucrative alternative employment. All of this is occurring at a time of tremendous pressures on senior executives to produce more, with fewer human resources. This translates into placing greater demands on the same employees who are less committed to the company.

In this chapter we will examine issues relating to this changing employer–employee relationship and will focus on specific mechanisms and strategies that need to be considered in both negotiating and managing a new psychological contract with employees in the current scenario.

Understanding the Psychological Contract

The psychological contract is a subjective feeling that influences an employee's beliefs and behaviour in the workplace. It has been conceptualized as an inherently unique and subjective perception that each individual possesses based upon his/her own understanding of the reciprocal obligations in the employment relationship between the individual and the organization. Through the life cycle of an individual in the organization, the psychological contract plays an important role in influencing the attitudes, perceptions, and satisfaction of the employee. Contemporary literature has seen a number of attempts to define this construct.

Definition of the Psychological Contract

The term 'psychological contract' was first coined by Argyris (1960). He defined it as 'the perception of both parties to the employment relationship, organization and individual, of the obligations implied in that relationship'. This contract was seen as a set of unwritten or implicit reciprocal expectations that specified what each member in the relationship expected to give and receive from the other (Kotter 1973, Schein 1978).

Later authors have defined the psychological contract as an individual's perception of what he/she owes the employer and the inducements the individual believes that he/she is owed in return (Rousseau 1989). The psychological contract was visualized as being conceptually different from a formal contract in that it considered and focused on an individual's beliefs about the terms and conditions of an agreement between the individual and his/her employer. Thus unlike formal employee–employer contracts, the psychological contract is inherently perceptual and idiosyncratic and, therefore, subject to self-serving cognitive distortions. In other words, one party's interpretation of the terms and conditions of the obligations within the contract may be biased and may not be shared by the other (Rousseau 1995).

It has been further noted that, to a great extent, the psychological contract is oriented towards the future. Without the promise of future exchange neither party has incentive to contribute, and thus the relationship may not endure. In fact, the psychological contract has been frequently described as a belief wherein some form of promise has been made and which assumes that all involved parties accept the terms/conditions of the exchange. Moreover, since the psychological contract is an unwritten set of expectations between the employee and the employer, it is subjective and is often unarticulated and undefined.

Again, the psychological contract may change or be revised through an employee's tenure in an organization. It is believed that the longer a relationship continues between an employer and an employee, the greater will be the involvement between the two parties, and this will also foster feelings of trust, loyalty, and mutual support. This was brought out in a study that examined how psychological contracts changed over time. It highlighted that during the first two years of employment employees felt that they owed less to the organization while their employer, in turn, owed them more (Robinson et al. 1994).

It has also been suggested that psychological contracts lie along a continuum ranging from the transactional to the relational. Short time frames and specific obligations characterize transactional contracts. Such contracts are based on self-interest where financial resources are the primary medium of exchange. Relational contracts are long-term relationships with diffuse obligations, wherein the exchange includes not only financial resources, but also affective resources such as loyalty and affiliation. At this end of the continuum, the participants implicitly acknowledge the value of the relationship itself, and the individual may be willing to put the needs of the other party ahead of his/her own. Thus in relational contracts, obligations are unclear and constantly evolving.

Factors in the Formation of the Psychological Contract

While the formal written employment contract does outline some of the mutual obligations of employers and employees, it cannot address all aspects of the employment relationship. The psychological contract assumes importance because it fills in the gaps in the relationship and helps in reducing employee insecurity. From the point of view of the organization, the psychological contract facilitates the socialization process by shaping employee behaviour (Anderson and Schalk 1998). Research indicates that psychological contracts help to define the terms of the social exchange relationship that exists between employees and their organizations. In contrast to relationships based purely on economic exchange, social exchange relationships involve obligations that cannot be specified in advance, and require that the parties involved trust one another. Although the obligations making up these types of relationships are not always clearly articulated, an expectation of reciprocation provides impetus for their development. Thus, given that the norm of reciprocity is a part of any exchange agreement between an individual and his/her organization (Rousseau 1989), an employee often expects, seeks out, and creates a psychological contract, as a means of understanding and representing the employment relationship (Shore and Tetrick 1994). Again, from an equity theory perspective, individuals try to find an equitable balance between their own contributions and what they receive from the organization. Thus, a psychological contract assumes that the employment relationship is based on a 'fair exchange' wherein employees take steps to fulfil their part of the contract and look to the organization to fulfil its obligations within the terms of the contract.

The psychological contract is influenced not only by the experiences, assumptions, and expectations of the employer and the employee but also by the organizational culture and dynamics, the HR management policies and practices and the prevalent practices in other organizations and wider societal norms (Sparrow 1998). Researchers have indicated that employees develop the expectations that comprise their psychological contracts from three main sources: the specific promises made to them by organizational representatives, their perceptions of the organization's culture and common practices, and their unique (and often idealized) expectations of how the organization functions. To elaborate, while psychological contracts exist between individuals and organizations, the organizations perspective may be represented by a number of different agents, such as recruiters, supervisors, top management, and HR professionals who may make the promises that form the psychological contract. For example, a recruiter may tell a new employee that certain benefits (such as compensation or advancement) may accrue if the employee performs well during his or her first year on the job. Moreover, expectations may also be influenced by written recruiting material or from feedback about the company in the business community. Thus, not all the perceptions of the expected contributions from the organization come from one source, and not all sources are equally weighted or seen as equally credible in the formation of the employees' psychological contract.

Moreover, employees' perceptions of the organization's culture and practices are also likely to shape the beliefs that characterize the psychological contract. These beliefs are influenced by early socialization experiences that help the employee in making sense of the organization, and in determining how they will be treated by the organization and what they can reasonably expect to receive. Culture is transmitted through the prevalent norms and attitudes and behaviour of significant individuals within the system. For example, the energy and enthusiasm of new employees may be curbed over a period of time by a culture of cynicism or resistance to change and passivity among their superiors. Again, if coming late to work is not penalized, and is an accepted norm in the organization, then new employees will soon assume that coming to work on time is not a part of their obligations towards the organization. In addition, employees learn about the culture of an organization from the past experiences and history of the organization as embodied in the incidents, stories, rituals, and practices that are talked about or highlighted within the system. Stories relating to the effectiveness of the organization's appraisal systems and how past managers have got their promotion, or a plum appointment, abound, and these stories become sources of the beliefs and expectations that employees develop about the organization. Although these expectations arising from employees' perceptions of their organization's culture may never be explicitly discussed, they are likely to contribute substantially to the psychological contract.

Finally, the psychological contract is also shaped by mechanisms through which an employee processes information and by his/her values, attitudes, and idealized notions of how organizations do, and should, operate. In this context it should be emphasized that self-serving biases can impact individual perceptions, that is, it is possible that individuals will interpret the terms of the psychological contract in ways that tend to benefit themselves.

Psychological Contract Violations

Breach of the psychological contract occurs when employees perceive a discrepancy between what they were promised and what they actually receive. It has been suggested that there could be three main causes of psychological contract discrepancies. First, discrepancies may occur because the employee and the employer have a difference of opinion regarding what the organization is obligated to provide. In such instances, while employees may feel that they are not getting all that they were promised, they are able to recognize that those acting on behalf of the organization honestly believe that the organization is living up to its end of the agreement. Second, discrepancies may arise when, due to certain unforeseeable reasons, an organization is unable to live up to the commitments it had made. This may occur if the organization is undergoing a crisis such as financial hardship. In such cases it may be difficult, if not impossible, for the employer to actually fulfil all his/her promises to the employees. Finally, discrepancies may also arise when an organization is simply unwilling to live up to the commitments it had made to its employees. For example, even when the organization is doing well, it may decide to engage in layoffs or may limit raises.

Any of the above-mentioned circumstances can give rise to an employee's perception that the psychological contract has been violated. However, research suggests that some circumstances are more likely to result in perceived psychological contract violations than others. Typically, when individuals perceive a discrepancy between what they have received and what they were promised, they look for explanations. Employees are likely to be more resentful in those cases where they perceive that the organization's action is insufficiently justified.

Social exchange theory provides a general approach for understanding how employees are likely to respond when they perceive that their psychological contracts have not been fulfilled. When breaches or violations occur within an employee's psychological contract, they may be experienced as a kind of distributive injustice, where an employee may feel that promises have not been met and, therefore, he/she is deprived of the desired outcomes and benefits (Robinson and Morrison 1995, Robinson and Rousseau 1994). From the employees' perspective such discrepancies create inequality in the employment relationship. As long as employees perceive that they have adequately met their obligations to their employer they are likely to feel short-changed by the organization's failure to live up to its obligations and will be inclined to take actions to bring back the balance (or equity) in the employment relationship. One way that employees can do this is by reducing the extent of their contributions to the organization. In sum, violation may be seen as a cognitive process that is based on a calculation of the equity between what has been contributed and what has been received, in the context of what was perceived to have been promised. Studies have indicated that violation also involves a strong affective or emotional component where employees experience 'feelings of betrayal and deeper psychological distress', resulting in anger, resentment, hostility, a sense of injustice, and a feeling of wrongful harm (Rousseau 1989).

Research findings have consistently indicated that psychological contract violations can have a negative impact on employees' attitudes and behaviours. A longitudinal study (Robinson et al. 1994) reported that psychological contract violations negatively influenced employee perceptions of how much they owe their organizations. It was also found that employees' perceptions that their psychological contracts had been violated were related to undesirable employee behaviours such as increased employee turnover, reduced work performance, reduced organizational commitment and reduced willingness to engage in organizational citizenship behaviours. In addition, psychological contract violations resulted in reduced job satisfaction, reduced performance on both in-role and extra-role behaviours, and an increased intent to leave the organization. By and large, psychological contracts became more transactional and less relational following violations.

However, it has been pointed out that psychological contract violations do not always lead to adverse reactions among employees. Several researchers have recently examined situational moderators that impact the strength of the relationships between psychological contract violations and negative employee attitudes and behaviours. For example, one study reported that encouraging two-way communication moderated the relationship between psychological contract violations and subsequent trust in the organization (Robinson and Rousseau 1994). Similarly, it was found that employees responded less strongly to psychological contract violations when they perceived that the organization had been transparent and fair in managing changes in job security, compensation, and promotion policies (Turnley and Feldman 1998).

It has also been pointed out that the extent of psychological contract violations may depend on the nature of the violation (Neihoff and Paul 2001). Based on the type of perceived discrepancy, violations can be categorized as either a case of reneging of the contract or as a case of incongruence. Reneging occurs when either party to a psychological contract knowingly breaks a promise to the other. It may occur because one party is unable to fulfil its promise (that is, inability) or because one party does not want to fulfil the terms of the agreement (that is, unwillingness). Inability to keep promises may reflect on the reneging party (for example, they have many other obligations, or are incompetent), or the situation (for example, unexpected circumstances arose that made fulfilling the contract impossible). Unwillingness, on the other hand, reflects a lack of motivation to keep promises, or even manipulation on the part of the violating party. Thus, it is likely that there will be a greater magnitude of perceived violation along with a corresponding decrease in trust when unwillingness, rather than inability, is believed to be the source of the broken promise.

Incongruence occurs when there is a difference of opinion between the parties concerned about their obligations to each other. These different understandings may occur because the terms and conditions of psychological contracts are often perceptual and implied. Incongruence can result when the contract is formed, or it may develop over time as perceptions of the promises made change or get modified. Basic factors that may contribute to incongruence include difference in cognitive frameworks, complexity, or ambiguity in the relationship, and communication problems.

Either reneging or incongruence may result in perceptions of psychological contract violation. This perception is influenced by a comparison by members in the employment relationship of how well each party has upheld his/her respective promises. A perceived breach of the psychological contract will occur when one party perceives that his/her promised contributions have been made, but that reciprocation has not occurred.

The increased interest of late in the psychological contract between employers and employees is related to the belief that this framework is central to our understanding of attitudes and behaviour in the context of the changing relationships at work. Research has focused on two questions in particular. First, there has been considerable work conducted on the changing nature of the psychological contract and the decline of mutual loyalty between employees and employers. Second, a great deal of attention has been focused on the negative consequences of psychological contract violations on employees' job attitudes, work behaviours, and turnover. A review of the changes in the employer–employee relationship and the emergence of a new psychological contract will be presented in the next section.

The Changing Psychological Contract

In the past, employees had the assurance that performance, loyalty, and commitment to the organization would ensure lifetime employment. In the traditional model, there was an identifiable employee–employer relationship and employers and employees entered a relationship with the hope and expectation that the employee would stay and grow with the same organization through his/her career. The psychological contract was rooted in an assumption of permanence, predictability, and stability. Organizations usually offered lifetime employment and job security to their employees, and expected loyalty, commitment, satisfactory performance, and compliance in return. Companies took an interest in an employee's career prospects, and invested in their training and development, as a reward for their performance, loyalty, and commitment. Career planning and growth of individual employees was seen to be an organizational responsibility and was usually managed by the HR department (Anderson and Schalk 1998). In consequence, organizations were, by and large, perceived to be dependable, responsible, caring, and trustworthy.

Conditions Influencing Changes in the Psychological Contract

A rapidly changing economic and competitive environment, however, has changed the employment relationship such that performance and loyalty can no longer guarantee job security. It has been claimed that the 1990s marked the beginning of a new era, referred to as the 'new economy', with globalization and computerization providing the impetus for reshaping modern economy in a way that is fundamentally different from the earlier industrial age. Innovations in information and telecommunications technology have created a single electronic market that has changed the traditional boundaries of space and time. This is an economy where ideas and creativity are the new form of currency. Agility, innovation, and vitality are being seen as valuable qualities that will facilitate growth and survival. Specifically, organizations must increase innovation and new value creation, leverage the Internet and other new technologies, develop new business models to compete in multiple markets, establish collaborative relationships with other companies, create and distribute knowledge, and attract, develop, and retain talented people.

With technological innovations, changing labour market conditions, and global competition compelling businesses to keep their core workforces at a minimum, the two principal casualties today are the concepts of long-term and full-time employment. The recent trend of downsizing, real-sizing, delayering, restructuring and re-engineering in organizations as a means to improve efficiency, increase flexibility, and reduce costs, have contributed to these changing patterns of employment.

It should be emphasized here that the flexible workforce is not a homogeneous group. The experiences or problems of part-time, temporary, and contractual employment cannot be equated. However, the key point that links all these forms of employment is the lack of full-time, permanent employment. Thus, contingent work can be referred to as any work that does not carry the expectation by the employer or employee of regular, full-time employment. The number of such part-time or contractual employees in the workforce is on the rise and has doubled in the past decade. In fact, while predicting the future many experts feel that most organizations will have only a small core of full-time, permanent employees, working from a conventional office. Other non-core skills would be accessed on a contractual basis when required.

Moreover, over the years, in order to deal with the needs of an increasingly diverse workforce, organizations have introduced alternative work schedule options such as flexitime, job sharing, and telecommuting. Such flexible schedules were introduced to attract and retain employees who found it difficult or were unwilling to adjust to commuting to work five days a week. Now, new technologies make it possible to reach employees wherever they are and whenever they find it convenient, instead of bringing them, expensively and inconveniently, to a central location away from home.

It can, therefore, be surmised that while full-time employees have had to grapple with one kind of problem in managing organizational change and, consequently, changes in the psychological contract with the employer, the contingent workforce is confronted with somewhat different issues in negotiating their psychological contracts with the organization. Issues confronting the contingent employees will be addressed in the next section.

An added paradox that organizations have to deal with currently is that in the knowledge economy employees have become critical capital assets as they are responsible for acquiring, synthesizing, and transferring knowledge through the company. The success or failure of a knowledge organization thus depends on the ability of the organization to encourage loyalty and to motivate its employees. Without loyalty, knowledge may be easily lost. Without motivation, there is no incentive to acquire knowledge or to pass it on. Thus, loyalty needs to be valued and encouraged. However, employees today have to operate in a climate of doubt and insecurity, and this is unlikely to encourage openness and sharing. In the new employer–employee relationship there are no guarantees and the emphasis is on opportunism rather than on loyalty to the company.

In summary, the trends towards outsourcing, flatter organization structures, restructuring, and globalization have contributed to the changes in the psychological contract. A larger set of resources available worldwide has increased competition for jobs and allowed both employers and employees to have greater choice in employment opportunities. For the organization, this could mean that as there are many skilled potential employees available at competitive market rates, long-serving employees need not be promised jobs after restructures or relocations, nor will they necessarily be candidates for upward or lateral moves. From the point of view of the employee this has implied less reliance on the organization and greater loyalty to oneself and to one's profession.

The New Psychological Contract

Changes brought about in the psychological contract between the individual and the organization have led to considerable turbulence in the employer–employee relationship. In the past, when a job was for life and employees, by and large, formed strong loyalties to their organization, the relationship was almost like a family tie and the psychological contract was largely relational. However, today, contracts are more like transactions with few or no emotional ties. As opposed to their previous solicitous role, organizations have reneged on some of their earlier obligations, and left employees to manage the transition on their own. This sudden withdrawal of supports has led to a number of organizational fall-outs such as reduced loyalty, motivation, and commitment, besides lowered morale among employees. Accordingly, both academicians and HR management practitioners have been concerned about re-examining and redefining the relationship or contract between the employer and the employee, in order to manage some of the negative consequences of such organizational upheavals.

In this context, a question that many organizations have to grapple with today is whether employees can cope with permanent insecurity, without the safety and security of organizational structures, relationships, and systems which in the past provided training, development, and career growth. And, moreover, whether such organizations can still hope to get the best out of such employees. In order to ensure the employees' continuing commitment, both the contracting parties need to reinvest in a new, mutually beneficial relationship which would be in accordance with these changed sets of mutual expectations. Against such a scenario, the context of the existing psychological contract needs to be looked into afresh. Table 12.1 highlights and summarizes some of the changes in the past and present forms of the psychological contract.

Table 12.1: Psychological Contract: Past and Present Forms

Characteristic	Traditional	Current
Focus	Security, loyalty, continuity	Exchange, contextual
Underlying assumptions	Fairness, justice	Value-addition, employability
Employer–employee relationship	Permanent, stable	Temporary, uncertain
Attitude of employer	Paternalistic, benevolent	Indifferent
Employer's responsibilities	Job security, training and development, career management	Equitable reward for added value
Employee's responsibilities	Loyalty, commitment, compliance	Entrepreneurship, innovation, good performance
Assumption about career development	Organization's responsibility	Individual's responsibility

Source: Adapted from Anderson and Schalk (1998).

The introduction of flexible work schedules and a contingent workforce into organizations is also bringing about significant changes in management–employee relationships and thus would necessitate new designs in HR management. An organization that wishes to take advantage of workforce flexibility must have managers who are willing to learn how to plan for decentralized communications and supervision. Also, it has been reported that while organizations are embracing and advocating the use of flexible work opportunities, employees are still grappling with the reduction of job security and are trying to understand and manage the implications of this new contract with the employer. Again, trying to maximize commitment, loyalty, and competence among contingent employees is a challenge that most organizations have to deal with. Research on contingent employees has highlighted that the lack of structure, boundaries, feedback, and effective performance measurement mechanisms makes it more difficult for contingent employees to manage their relationship with the organization. In a climate of insecurity, if employment contracts are renewed based on social networks rather than on competence then contingent employees will focus more on building relationships than on work quality. Thus, it has been emphasized that it is critical for organizations to review their existing HR management policies to develop a better and more reciprocal relationship between such employees and the organization.

In contrast to the old contract, the new and emerging psychological contract focuses largely on temporary relationships. Accordingly, it appears to be more situational in nature, and is concerned with the here and now, rather than with the future. This impermanence makes it necessary for the contract to be more unstructured and flexible, adaptable enough to change with the needs of the situation existing at a particular point of time. This implies that contrary to the almost inflexible nature of the old contract, the new contract needs to be open for re-negotiation, in keeping with the changing demands of the situation. A key theme around which this re-negotiation would revolve is expected to be the concept of an individual's demand in the job market, explained through the construct of 'employability'.

The Concept of Employability

The concept of 'employability security' was developed in the late 1980s as a means of handling the loss of job security (Kanter 1989). Kanter noted that 'if security no longer comes from being employed, then it must come from being employable'. Also, 'employability security comes from the knowledge that today's work will enhance the value of the person in terms of future opportunities'. Other authors have advanced the concept of employability in different ways but most share the premise that it is the individual who is currently responsible for his or her own job security. The reality today is that layoffs and outsourcing will continue to be a means of reducing organizational costs, and employees will, therefore, need to adequately protect themselves. The old forms of security have been removed without any replacements and this increases the level of anxiety in a workforce accustomed to safety nets. Employability offers some security and is within an individual's control. For the individual, this translates into developing one's skills, keeping those skills current, and ensuring that one is marketable. With the reduction in job security, the employee mindset has changed and employees today are less tolerant and more market- aware. By and large, employability refers to a focus on sharpening and developing the skills that are highly valued in the marketplace. This implies that an employee has to engage in a continuous upgradation of his/her skills in keeping with current and future market demands. Employability thus involves personal mastery, continuous learning, and the careful building of a reputation, as a means of enhancing personal security in these uncertain times.

Organizations too are trying to come to grips with what it means to attract and retain employees. They are actively searching for a replacement of the old employment promise, and at the same time are trying to engender a new type of loyalty on the part of the organization and the employee. The proponents of employability believe that enlightened employers who are no longer able to guarantee job security need to offer a new deal to employees. If employees perceive that they are learning and developing new expertise, the opportunities provided by the organization for personal advancement and growth would be a source of motivation. Loyalty may then develop as a consequence of this motivation. Employers who facilitate this self-development and are seen to be supportive of employee development recognize that continuous learning is essential to the company's long-term future. Thus, the new psychological contract has, with employer assistance, encouraged employees to develop, primarily as a way of adding value to their organizations but also as a hedge against possible unemployment. Some companies are now imparting employability through the medium of training and development. Training programmes provide the opportunity to improve existing skills and/or acquire new ones. Under the new contract it should be the employer's responsibility to make such opportunities available; while it would be the employee's responsibility to take advantage of them. In the new employment relationship the real issue is not to focus on jobs that are obsolete but on those which will make people employable for life.

In this context, it has been pointed out that while employability is a useful concept, the type of employability could pose problems in terms of implementation (Roehling et al. 2000). In other words, while employers might favour internal employability (improvement of an employee's firm-specific skills), the employee himself/herself may be more keen on external (general) employability which would increase his/her opportunities in the job market outside the firm. This is because maintaining personal employability in a competitive job market and commanding the highest market rate for knowledge and experience would be a greater source of security for employees in the current environment, rather than focusing on organizational learning and loyalty. An absence of job security and guaranteed employment necessitates that employees keep themselves 'market current' (Capelli 1999). This focus on developing skills that are desired externally would also increase the likelihood of an employee moving on to the highest bidder.

This creates a serious problem of turnover for the employer. Important knowledge and skills are lost, and the organization will face increasing costs in recruitment, induction and on-the-job training. Given such a scenario, it is possible that since organizations can no longer guarantee job security to their employees they might be less willing to invest in training employees, only to have to release them or lose them to competitors in the future. Reports indicate that while many organizations believe that training of employees is a priority, it is also felt that training encourages skilled employees to find employment elsewhere. Again, some employers believe that training programmes are a waste of time, money, and effort and that it is difficult to assess the usefulness of such interventions. Furthermore, restructuring efforts often result in flatter organizations where employers may have to manage with fewer employees and, therefore, have less time to spare for employee development and may not be motivated to invest in the long-term career development of employees. This attitude is even more prevalent with respect to contingent employees. Organizations expect to benefit from the resources and competencies that a contractual employee brings in to the system, but are unwilling to contribute to his development. Few organizations are willing to sponsor the training and development of non-core employees.

It has also been argued that the content of the new contract is not the same for all individuals or organizations. Effective employment relationships should not be viewed as being driven solely by an organization's strategies and environment but may change with respect to what different employees require and value in an employment contract. Psychological contracts are significantly influenced by individual predispositions, values, and expectations, which are in turn shaped by the values, assumptions and, beliefs of one's society and national culture. Hence, the assumptions underlying the psychological contract and reactions to its perceived violations could be markedly different for an employee belonging to a predominantly individualistic society like the USA, as compared to that of an employee belonging to a more collectivistic and fatalistic culture like India (Hofstede 1980). It has also been pointed out that although the new generation of first-time employees will not be encumbered by expectations of the employer–employee contract as in the past, it will, nevertheless, have expectations of some implicit psychological contract being in place.

Implications of the Changing Psychological Contract

What then are the broad salient components of the new psychological contract and how does it affect employees and the organization as a whole? Insecurity, transience, and change have become the established norms (Capelli 1999, Sparrow 2000), and this has had a significant impact on the attitudes of employees, as well as on the strategies of the organization. There have been both positive and negative consequences of the changes in the employer–employee relationship and it is necessary to summarize the implications for both employees and organizations before one can examine strategies to manage the new psychological contract.

Over time, as new people have entered the workforce, the 'new deal' has become more standard and expected. Many employees have viewed these changes as a chance to change jobs and take advantage of new opportunities. Employees are being offered greater flexibility in terms of work arrangements and there is an emphasis on continuous learning, skill development, and career self-management. Many organizations are focusing on job content and opportunities for growth as a means of attracting and retaining talent. The downside, however, is that there is increased job insecurity and uncertainty, fewer long-term benefits, fear of obsolescence, and increased pressure to upgrade skills.

From the point of view of the organization there is greater flexibility, lower fixed labour cost, reduced responsibility, and a better-trained workforce. Organizations, however, have also to grapple with the risk of losing valuable employees, managing a more opportunistic and less loyal workforce, and coping with the negative consequences on organizational learning and employee commitment and contribution.

In summary, employees today are more likely to take the initiative in managing their own career development and do not expect the organization to take responsibility for their career advancement. Additionally, it can be expected that employees will exhibit reduced loyalty and commitment to the organization and that the relationship with the employer would be more opportunistic and transactional rather than relational. Organizations too have to cope with the increasing pressures of change and competition and the formidable task of managing and motivating a less committed workforce. Thus, while organizations are now asking their employees to work even harder and to be even more flexible, many employees are less willing to be good organizational citizens and focus on organizational interests. It is advocated that organizations would benefit by remembering that the employer–employee relationship is a reciprocal one where the organization and the employee are dependent on one another and can mutually benefit from each other. A willingness to invest in the employee may encourage the employee to reciprocate with loyalty and commitment. In effect, both the employer and the employee need to take the initiative and joint responsibility in negotiating a new psychological contract based on openness and cooperation.

In the next section an attempt is made to outline strategies that may be used to renegotiate an effective psychological contract and to manage the negative consequences of the changes that are taking place in the employer–employee relationship.

Managing the New Psychological Contract

Organizations today are more inclined to building temporary and flexible contracts with employees. Such a flexible arrangement will help companies to remain lean and adaptable in a rapidly changing environment without gathering expertise which may become obsolete or which they may need to shed in the future. Having dealt with the feelings of betrayal and anger among employees who were downsized, organizations are playing safe and are avoiding making promises or entering into relationships that they may have to break at a later date. Looked at in this way it would seem that organizations are trying to win back the trust of employees by being open and transparent about what they can realistically offer employees in the present times. But this is not enough. The implementation and communication of an effective HR strategy that manages the anxieties and expectations of the workforce and develops employee potential will go a long way in fostering and rebuilding trust and fairness in the organization. Specifically, employers need to take the lead in establishing an acceptable psychological contract with employees.

Effective psychological contracts are not just a matter of keeping promises, but also involve the management of needs and expectations. There are strategies that can facilitate the formation of appropriate expectations, while other strategies may help in maintaining the contract during the course of the employment relationship. By and large these involve establishing effective communication systems within the organization, and encouraging openness, trust, and reciprocity in the employer–employee relationship.

As discussed earlier, employee perceptions of contract obligations may begin even prior to the hiring process. Organizational presentations, publications, and literature create an initial impression of the values espoused by the employer and clarify how employees are treated. To prevent the creation of false impressions, employers should review company communication to ensure that the image reflects the reality. Interviewers and other representatives of the organization need to be trained on how to present company information so that the meaning drawn by recruits is accurate. Once an offer is made to a job candidate, the negotiation process presents an opportunity to further clarify the specific parameters of the job, expectations, and obligations of each party. It is imperative that the employer ensures that all promised obligations are being met. Performance norms should be clearly communicated to employees and enacted in an equitable and consistent fashion when violations occur. The psychological contract is also tested in times of resource allocation and organizational change. Transparency and a willingness to share rationale or discuss issues provide employees with the sense that the organization is trustworthy. Effective feedback mechanisms allow employees an opportunity to clarify and share their expectations.

The maintenance of effective psychological contracts is closely linked to commitment and integrity towards the employee. A trusting relationship between employers and employees creates an environment that allows for disagreements and conflicts to be dealt with in a constructive manner. The commitment to integrity must be accompanied by an equitable compensation and benefit package. Employers would be wise to study their own compensation and benefit programmes relative to the market. Including employees in this process can contribute to their understanding of pay issues, increase the accuracy of communications surrounding the studies, and help establish realistic pay expectations.

Moreover, involving employees in any change management exercise undertaken by the organization, from sharing of the rationale for change, to the search for alternative solutions, to designing possible solutions and implementation, provides employees with the feeling that they have been taken into confidence and have participated in the whole exercise. The benefits of establishing trusting relationships between employees and employers are immeasurable. Employees feel respected by the organization and perceive that the company is involving them rather than using them. Employers are able to maintain a secure workforce, minimize turnover, and build a strong base of organizational citizens. By making a sincere effort in establishing clear and transparent psychological contracts and by continually communicating with employees, employers can minimize misunderstanding within the system.

An interesting and innovative approach to bringing in transparency in the psychological contract is illustrated by interventions initiated in Kodak (Grant 1997). Kodak has formalized the development of a 'social contract' with each employee, where the employee pledges to understand the business and the customers, as well as give his/her utmost to the job. The organization on its part pledges to provide extensive training, career development opportunities, and the appraisal of managerial performance. Here, the organization has tried to transform subjective expectations into a concrete social contract by putting both parties' obligations in writing.

Again, reciprocity is an important ingredient in facilitating a new psychological contract between employers and employees. When the employee accepts responsibility for his/her own career and own self-development, the employer must also accept responsibility for providing opportunities for the employee's self-development. Reciprocity can be established when the employee stays committed to the organization and shares his/her skills openly, but this will happen only if the employer offers the employee a chance to further develop that skill and expertise for the good of both the individual and the company.

Managing the New Psychological Contract in India

A preliminary investigation of how Indian organizations are managing the psychological contract post downsizing reveals that few HR managers are familiar with the term 'psychological contract'. The managers who are aware of the impact of the psychological contract violations on the system are uncertain about the measures that can be taken to cope with the consequences of the changing employer–employee relationship. There seems to be an assumption that it is up to the employee to accept and cope with the 'new deal'. Such an approach is, at best, short term and simplistic and may have far reaching consequences on behaviour in, and commitment to, the organization. For the present, organizations have continued to remain passive observers, content to let their employees fend for themselves in terms of ensuring their own employability.

Given that in the past the employment relationship was largely based on a paternalistic attitude on the part of the employer and a need for dependency on that of the employee, there may be a greater expectation on the part of employees that the organization should take the initiative in redefining the relationship. If today, employees are to take on a responsibility that they had been unused to before, it would be up to the organizations to facilitate a change in their mindset and encourage employees to be more self-reliant. This would involve helping and training employees to become more self-dependent in planning and managing their own careers.

The new contract should be based on an assumption of an equitable and mutual relationship, with both sides willing to share the consequences and gains of their expectations and obligations. On the part of the employee this would imply taking more personal responsibility for ensuring one's employability, rather than expecting the organization to do it for them. Though employees might not, in light of the changing contract, be looking for job security from their employers, what they would continue to expect, is fair and equitable treatment. It is, therefore, imperative that the Indian organizations negotiate a new contract which would equip both the employer and the employee to sufficiently cope with the changing times. This would require the management to play a more proactive role in helping employees to become aware of the skills that are required currently both within and outside the company and those that are likely to be important in the new workplace of tomorrow.

This chapter has brought out the importance of the psychological contract and the impact of its violation and change on the dynamics of the employment relationship. The psychological contract is an important factor in the relationship between employers and employees and can be a strong determinant of behaviour and attitudes. Such contracts are subject to change and development throughout the duration of the employment relationship. Due to their subjective nature such contracts are frequently unarticulated and are also prone to perceptions of violation by both employers and employees. It is important, therefore, that organizations take cognizance of the psychological contract and its consequences, and work towards effectively managing the employer–employee relationship.

REFERENCES

Anderson, N. and R. Schalk (1998) 'The Psychological Contract in Retrospect and Prospect', *Journal of Organizational Behavior*, Vol. 19, pp. 637–47.

Argyris, C. (1960) *Understanding Organizational Behavior*, London, Tavistock.

Capelli, P. (1999) *The New Deal at Work: Managing the Market-driven Workforce*, Harvard Business School Press, Boston, Mass.

Grant, L. (1997) 'Can Fisher Focus Kodak?', *Fortune*, 13 January, pp. 76–9.

Guest, D. E. (1998) 'Is the Psychological Contract Worth Taking Seriously?', *Journal of Organizational Behavior*, Vol. 19, pp. 649–64.

Hofstede, G. (1980) *Culture's consequences: International differences in work related values*, Sage, London.

Kanter, Rosabeth Moss (1989) *When Giants Learn To Dance*, Simon & Schuster Inc., New York, p. 321.

Kotter, J. (1973) 'The Psychological Contract: Managing the Joining-up Process', *California Management Review*, Vol. 15, No. 3, pp. 91–9.

Niehoff, B.P. and R.J. Paul (2001) 'The Just Workplace: Developing and Maintaining Effective Psychological Contracts', *Review of Business*, Jamaica, Spring.

Robinson, S., M. Kraatz, and D. Rousseau, (1994) 'Changing Obligations and the Psychological Contract: A Longitudinal Study', *Academy of Management Journal*, Vol. 37, pp. 137–152.

Robinson. S.L. and E.W. Morrison, (1995) 'Psychological Contracts and OCB: The Effect of Unfulfilled Obligations on Civic Virtue Behavior', *Journal of Organizational Behavior*, Vol. 16, pp. 289–98.

Robinson., S.L. and D M Rousseau (1994) 'Violating the Psychological Contract: Not the Exception but the Norm', *Journal of Organizational Behavior*, Vol. 15, pp. 245–9.

Roehling, M. V., M.A. Cavanaugh, L.M. Moynihan, L. M and W.R. Boswell, (2000) 'The Nature of the New Employment Relationships: A Content Analysis of the Practitioner and Academic Literatures', *Human Resource Management*, Vol. 39, No. 4, pp. 305–20.

Rousseau, D. (1995) *Psychological Contracts in Organizations: Understanding Written and Unwritten Agreements*, Sage Publications, Thousand Oaks, CA.

— (1989) 'Psychological and Implied Contracts in Organizations', *Employee Responsibilities and Rights Journal*, Vol. 2, pp. 121–139.

Schein, E. A. (1978) *Career Dynamics: Matching the Individual and the Organizational Needs*, MAS: Addison-Wesley, Reading.

Shore, Lynn M. and Lois E. Tetrick (1994) 'The Psychological Contract as an Explanatory framework in the Employment Relationship', *Journal of Organizational Behavior*, Vol.1, pp. 91–109.

Sparrow, P.R. (2000) 'New Employee Behaviours, Work Designs and Forms of Work Organization: What is in Store for the Future of Work?', *Journal of Managerial Psychology*, Vol. 15, No. 3, pp. 202–18.

Sparrow, P. (1998), 'Reappraising Psychological Contracting', *International Studies of Management and Organization*, Vol. 28, No. 1, pp. 30–63.

Turnley, W.H. and D.C. Feldman (1998) 'Psychological Contract Violations During Corporate Restructuring', *Human Resource Management*, Vol. 37, 1, pp. 71–83.

13

Knowledge Management: An Overview

Haritha Saranga • Vidyanand Jha

The acquisition of knowledge has concerned mankind from time immemorial. So why is there so much noise and hype about knowledge management in recent times? Perhaps one could attribute it to the explosion of IT, or to the disappearing national and international business boundaries, or to the ever changing business environment that is keeping the modern firms on their toes. Whatever the reason may be, today's industry is feeling the heat and the need to effectively capitalize on all their resources, especially the knowledge or intellectual capital, to survive and grow in this volatile business environment. Interestingly, even though the knowledge-intensive firms like IT, pharmaceuticals, and consulting companies contend that knowledge management is meant for them, and even if it might seem fair enough, one needs to be careful not to confuse information management with knowledge management. There are major debates going on between the *pundits* of knowledge management and the IT experts as to how knowledge management is not just about creating a network between various departments of a firm, storing a lot of information in data warehouses, and giving access to it, but also about managing the intellectual capital of the employees of the firm and leveraging on it for a better performance of the organization as a whole. In this chapter we will try to shed some light on these debates and the various perspectives of knowledge management and their implications.

Knowledge Acquisition—A Continuing Obsession

Although the word 'knowledge' is very commonly used in day-to-day life, it is very difficult to give a unique definition of knowledge. There is a branch of western philosophy called 'Epistemology', which is entirely dedicated to the study of knowledge. Since the classical Greek era there have been numerous debates on various aspects of knowledge, including the definition, between eminent scholars in various fields. Two of the most prominent epistemological positions in the literature are empiricism, which considers knowledge as the product of sensory perception that primarily uses inductive logic, and rationalism, which treats it as a product of rational reflection and primarily uses deductive logic.

However, in the present context, we are only interested in knowledge from an organizational point of view, and try to provide a suitable definition. Organizational knowledge is embedded in the organization's culture and identity, processes, experiences of employees, policies, systems, and documents. It is not easy to imitate and, hence, provides the organization with a sustainable competitive advantage (Grant 1996a, 1996b). However, it is crucial to know what the relevant knowledge is in the organizational context and one should be able to differentiate useful knowledge from the hoards of data and information that is accumulated in organizations over the years. There has always been confusion between the definitions of data, information, and knowledge, and they are aften used interchangeably. Data is raw numbers and facts, information is processed data, and knowledge is authenticated information (Dretske 1981). Therefore, knowledge may be defined as 'personalized information' as it is processed in the minds of individuals. On the other hand, knowledge must exist first which, when articulated, verbalized, and structured, becomes information which, when assigned a fixed representation and standard interpretation, becomes data (Tuomi 1999). Thus, one may say that knowledge, information, and data form a never-ending spiral, each one giving rise to the next.

Huber (1991) and Nonaka (1994) define knowledge as 'justified belief that increases an entity's capacity for effective action'. The authors of this chapter define organizational knowledge as 'a system of justified beliefs about cause and effect relationships'.

KNOWLEDGE MANAGEMENT—PRESENT *AVATAAR*

The learning-centric view defines knowledge management as a function that accelerates learning and the information-centric view defines it as a discipline that promotes an integrated approach to identifying, managing, and sharing all of an enterprise's information assets, including databases, documents, and procedures, as well as unarticulated expertise and experience resident in individual workers. Knowledge management is also defined as the process through which organizations generate value from their intellectual and knowledge-based assets (Santosus and Surmacz 2001). Most often, generating value from such assets involves sharing them with one's employees, departments, and even with other companies in an effort to devise best practices.

For example, consider a restaurant. Imagine that the waiter, while offering the menu card, gives a simple description of the special items of the day. With the exchange of simple pleasantries he can not only create a home-like environment for you, but also find out what kind of food you prefer—spicy or non-spicy, oily, sweet, salty, etc. He can then advise the cook about the necessary modifications, so that a meal may be prepared to suit the expectations of each customer. This will enhance the experience of the customers and will make them want to go back to the same restaurant whenever they want to enjoy a nice relaxed meal. The waiters can always share their knowledge of a particular customer with each other so that they can improve their performance uniformly and give a good service to all the customers, irrespective of which waiter is serving them. This will not only increase the profits for the owner, but also improve the goodwill and create a brand name, which may benefit other businesses. In order to encourage the staff to share their knowledge with each other and increase the performance levels, the owner needs to reward them either through a proper incentive system, or recognition, or both. If the owner is running a chain of restaurants at various locations he can take the best suggestions or practices from each place and print them so that they can be easily circulated around all the restaurants and be preserved for future references.

This was a simple case of how the experience and the knowledge obtained in a work environment by each employee can be leveraged to create value for the organization as a whole. In complex environments like consulting firms or pharmaceutical companies, where vast amounts of knowledge are created on a daily basis, IT resources like intranets, extranets, databases and warehouses are used to enable knowledge sharing and storage.

Motivations for Knowledge Management

For centuries intellectual capital has been considered to be the most important asset of civilizations. But never was there a more appropriate time for assigning it such a critical role than today, with its ever changing economy. Past and present experiences show that companies like 3M and Sony, that emphasized innovation and capitalized on their intellectual assets, have always thrived in the market. When products become obsolete overnight and a new competitor enters the market every other day, successful companies are those that can sense the market nerve and innovate new products before the competitor does. Here the question is, how do these companies manage their knowledge and leverage it to achieve organizational goals, and what is stopping others from following them?

The exponential growth in IT in the last two decades has brought about major changes in the way business is carried out all over the world. One of the most obvious results of this is globalization. As access and communication became ever so easy, firms all over the world started exploring new frontiers, resulting in greater competition, demanding customers, and an erratic market environment. In an era where local players have to compete with MNCs and vice versa, it is very crucial for any organization to utilize all the available resources to their fullest extent possible. Although technological advances facilitate an effective use of tangible resources like monetary investments and manpower, a different perspective based on knowledge started emerging in more recent times. The knowledge-based perspective postulates that the services rendered by the tangible assets depend on how they are combined and applied, which in turn depends on an organization's know-how, that is, knowledge (Alavi et al. 2001). Whether it is a simple day-to-day routine or a critical business solution obtained after many endeavours, it is not cost effective for an organization to repeat the same processes over and over again to reach the same solution. Especially in the era of MNCs, where each branch is situated in a different city or a country, and work progresses in different time horizons, maintaining temporal and spatial continuity is the secret of success. Therefore, it is essential for the management to identify the best practices, benchmark the existing knowledge within the organization, facilitate the transfer of this knowledge amongst relevant groups of employees, and leverage it to manage the tangible resources more effectively.

Historical Development

Even though it was not formally given a name, knowledge management has been around since the emergence of mankind. However, in those days, it was much easier to manage knowledge as it was not astronomical in size like it is today. For example, in the village, from time immemorial, the elder, the traditional healer, and the midwife have been the living repositories of distilled experience in the life of the community. 'In ancient Greece, the philosopher, Plato, in his dialogues, captured and elaborated the thinking of his mentor, Socrates, and so succeeding generations have been able to discover and share that thinking and, in turn, reinterpret those thoughts and to be stimulated to achieve fresh insights and creativity' (Denning 2000).

However, in the modern business environment it has been recognized that, if organized and leveraged efficiently, knowledge-based assets can bring that competitive edge which is essential for the survival and growth of an organization. By knowledge-based assets we mean the employees of the organization, the data warehouses, manuals, reports, procedures and organizational policies, etc., Although organizing makes sense in the latter cases, by definition, knowledge is the processed information in the minds of individuals. Thus, enabling the employees to expand their personal knowledge to apply it to the organizational needs should be given first priority. The extent and nature of this expansion depends on the existing knowledge base and the working environment of the organization.

Even though it is not really clear who invented the term 'knowledge management', a number of management theorists have contributed to the evolution of knowledge management. Among them are such notables as Peter Drucker, Paul Strassmann, Carl Erick Sveiby, and Peter Senge of the USA. While Senge focused on the 'learning organization', a cultural dimension of managing knowledge, Drucker and Strassmann stressed the growing importance of information and explicit knowledge as organizational resources. Chris Argyris, Christoper Bartlett, and Dorothy Leonard-Barton of Harvard Business School have examined various facets of managing knowledge. In fact, Leonard-Barton's well-known case study of Chaparral Steel, a company which has had an effective knowledge management strategy in place since the mid-1970s, inspired greatly the research in knowledge management (Barclay and Murray 1997).

During the 1980s systems for managing knowledge that relied on work done in artificial intelligence and expert systems were developed, and gave rise to concepts like knowledge acquisition, knowledge engineering, knowledge-base systems, and computer-based ontologies. By 1990, a number of management consulting firms had begun in-house knowledge management programmes, and several well-known US, European, and Japanese firms began focused knowledge management programmes. However, the most influential work on knowledge management by Nonaka and Takeuchi came out in 1995, providing the well-known theory of the possible conversion between explicit and tacit knowledge with a spiral process. In the same year Sveiby, working at the Swedish insurance company, Skandia, published the so-called 'Navigator', attempting to measure the intellectual capital of the firm (Barclay and Murray 1997).

Nonaka and Takeuchi

Nonaka and Takeuchi (1995) discuss the human perspective of knowledge management where the communication and interaction between the employees of an organization is given much emphasis. Their work has been the most influential so far in the field of knowledge management, since they consider the employee of the organization and the knowledge embedded in his mind as the fundamental source of knowledge. Drawing from the work of Polanyi (1962, 1967), Nonaka divided organizational knowledge into tacit knowledge and explicit knowledge.

Tacit Knowledge

Tacit Knowledge consists of cognitive dimension, comprising mental models, beliefs, and paradigms and the technical components like concrete know-how, crafts, and skills of human beings, with reference to a context. The cognitive dimension is ingrained in the personality and profoundly shapes the perception of the world around us. The technical know-how is the knowledge one attains with experience, after mastering a particular task for a number of years, the knowledge that differentiates a maestro from a novice. It may not always be possible to explicate tacit knowledge in entirety, although a part of it can be acquired by imitation, observation, and practice. This is how teaching was done in ancient Indian *gurukulas*, the residential educational institutions where students mastered various arts by watching and following their *gurus*.

Explicit Knowledge

This consists of articulated, codified knowledge that is in the form of rules, maps, manuals, etc. and are readily accessible. Anyone with sufficient knowledge of the context can understand and make use of this knowledge with a little effort.

The interaction between tacit and explicit knowledge gives rise to new knowledge in social institutions where individuals are continuously engaged in an active pursuit of knowledge. When an individual articulates his ideas and beliefs, whether it is during a new product design or a strategy development, he is basically sharing his experience and expertise along with his world vision and wisdom. The receivers of this explicated tacit knowledge, in turn, enhance their knowledge base and worldview. Thus, when the employees reinvent new knowledge, they are also reinventing themselves, the company and even the world. In group meetings and discussions the opportunity to debate and hear other points of view on issues that are close to one's heart opens up new vistas of knowledge creation and personal enrichment. Thus knowledge creation is very personal and always begins at an individual level. But this individual knowledge will result in an improved organizational performance only when it is made available to others and is expanded further from the knowledge of others, whether tacit or explicit.

Organizations contain both tacit and explicit knowledge and, in order to create new knowledge, they need to create a space (called 'Ba')—a platform where the interaction between tacit and explicit knowledge can take place. Nonaka proposed a model for organizational knowledge creation, called 'SECI', standing for Socialization, Externalization, Combination, and Internalization (Nonaka and Konno 1998).

	Tacit	Explicit
Tacit	Socialization	Externalization
Explicit	Internalization	Combination

Fig. 13.1: Organizational Knowledge Creation through SECI Model
Source: Nonaka and Konno 1998

Socialization: Socialization involves sharing of tacit knowledge between individuals, through joint activities like spending time together, living in the same environment, etc. rather than through written and verbal instructions (tacit to tacit). Examples of socialization process are training or long years of apprenticeship under an expert craftsman that can help one to master the nuances of the craft, which are otherwise difficult to acquire. Another aspect of socialization involves disseminating one's tacit knowledge to colleagues or subordinates through direct transfer of ideas and mental images. Socialization is a very effective way of exchanging knowledge. Studies show that 80 per cent of the tacit knowledge can be transferred in this process (Lee 2001). However, since an individual can be in direct contact with only a limited number of persons, the creation of total organizational tacit knowledge is limited in this process. Also, neither the seeker's knowledge nor the provider's knowledge becomes explicit and, thus, cannot be leveraged by the organization as a whole.

Externalization—Express the Inexpressible: Externalization requires expression of tacit knowledge and its translation into comprehensible forms that can be understood by others (tacit to explicit). There are two aspects to it. The first one involves an individual explicating his ideas and images to the group with the help of figurative language such as metaphors, analogies, or narratives. The second aspect involves translation of highly personal or highly professional knowledge of customers or specialists into explicit forms that are easy to understand. This is the most important process in organizational knowledge creation as it can be easily stored, transferred, and leveraged by the organization.

Combination: Combination involves the conversion of explicit knowledge into more complex sets of explicit knowledge by capturing and integration (explicit to explicit). This requires collection, diffusion and systemization processes. For example, public data may be collected, to be presented in group meetings and then documented in terms of plans or reports by processing or editing. In this way the data becomes more usable to the organization. Information technology plays a significant role in this phase of knowledge creation through the use of online networks, group-ware, documentation, knowledge discovery from databases, etc.

Internalization: This involves conversion of relevant, new explicit knowledge into an individual's tacit knowledge (explicit to tacit). The employees use the new explicit knowledge of the organization to broaden, extend, and reframe their own tacit knowledge. The internalization process actualizes organizational concepts or methods about strategy, tactics, innovation, or improvement for the individual employee. For example, through training programmes and crash courses the larger organizations help the trainees to understand the organizational goals and objectives and make the employee feel one with the organization. Another way to internalize knowledge is by using simulations or experiments to trigger learning by doing processes.

In summary, the SECI model describes a dynamic spiral of knowledge creation in which tacit knowledge is converted into explicit, which is then reconverted into tacit knowledge. It is important to note that knowledge creation requires a high degree of personal commitment from the employees, as can be seen from externalization and internalization processes. The management should understand this fact and create an organizational atmosphere that will foster feelings of freedom and trust, which are essential to the carrying forward of the organizational vision.

One interesting insight into the combination process is that explicit to explicit without the help of tacit knowledge is not possible as no knowledge creation occurs without the interaction of tacit knowledge. The collection, diffusion, and systemization processes that are used in combination definitely use some amount of tacit knowledge from the processor in order to be carried out. For example, the individual who collects and presents the public data in a group meeting uses some amount of his tacit knowledge while analysing it to make it presentable. Again, the rest of the group members use their prior tacit knowledge to internalize the presentation and, as a result of which, each individual member's understanding differs slightly from the other. Also, while documenting this diffused knowledge for further usage, the process of editing is influenced by the tacit knowledge of the processor. Thus combination is, in fact, a combination of internalization and externalization processes.

Other Prominent Authors in the Field

Sveiby is the founding father of the very early 'Swedish Movement' in knowledge management and intellectual capital. In 1986, he published his first book in which he explored how to manage the rapidly growing field of knowledge companies—organizations that have no traditional production, only the knowledge and creativity of their employees. Sveiby was the first to recognize the need to measure human capital, and he pioneered accounting practices for these intangible assets, testing them in his own company. In 1989 he published the results of the Konrad working group in the book, *The Invisible Balance Sheet*, proposing a theory for measuring knowledge capital by dividing it into three categories—customer capital, individual capital, and structural capital. The approach was adopted by a large number of Swedish-listed companies and, in 1993, the Swedish Council of Service Industries adopted it as their standard recommendation for annual reports—the first ever standard in this field.

Brown and Duguid (1998) talk about 'Know-How', which is the product of experience and insights that are born from practice. They emphasize the importance of collective knowledge that is shared and created by work groups like communities of practice and hybrid groups of overlapping and interdependent communities.

Patricia et al. (2001) came up with a strategic framework to capitalize on intellectual assets of the organization. In a similar line with Svieby, they divide the intellectual capital of a firm into three elements: *human capital* which is the tacit knowledge of the employees of the firm; *structural capital*, which is the explicit knowledge embedded in the work processes and documentation of the firm; and social capital, which was not explicitly considered as part of intellectual capital in the earlier literature, but was implicitly present. Social capital is that element of intellectual capital, which reflects the ability of groups to collaborate and work together and is a function of trust. The authors emphasize the criticality of *social capital* in the creation and use of knowledge. They also discuss interdependency of different types of knowledge and ways of investing on them to achieve organizational goals.

Knowledge Management Systems

As we saw in the previous section there are umpteen numbers of models, with various representations and terminology developed by various prominent authors in the field of knowledge management. However, just as it is said that all religions are different routes leading to one single god, so also one can safely conclude from the discussion so far that knowledge management is all about identifying the existing knowledge and using it to create new knowledge that can be leveraged to achieve organizational objectives. In order to carry out this process, a few inherent sub-processes like storage, retrieval, and discovery of knowledge from data and information are required. This is where Knowledge Management Systems (KMS), which constitute knowledge management tools and techniques like knowledge discovery in databases, data mining, etc. come into the picture. KMS refers to a class of information systems used for managing organizational knowledge. The main objectives of KMS are to support and facilitate the knowledge management processes, namely, creation, transfer, storage and retrieval, and application of knowledge in organizations. In the following sections we will describe some of the tools and techniques of KMS that are associated with these processes. Unfortunately, KMS and data mining have become so popular that many novices of knowledge management mistake KMS and data mining for knowledge management. One has to be extra cautious in this respect, as it is very easy to get caught up in the techniques and procedures and forget the original objective of the process. Most of the failures in knowledge management initiatives may be attributed to this. While the IT aspect of knowledge, which is mainly focused on organizing and discovering patterns in data and information by coding, storing, and transmitting it through intranets, extranets, browsers, data warehouses, etc., is crucial to give access of knowledge to employees, it is equally important to create and motivate the entire organization into a learning organization. It is no use having access to hoards of information if the real objective of the knowledge management initiative is lost in the process.

Storage and Retrieval

Various empirical studies have shown that it is only too common for organizations to forget or lose track of the acquired knowledge as time goes by (Argote et al. 1990). The accessibility and inexpensive availability of computer hardware and software has enabled organizations, irrespective of size or nature of work (whether private or public) to accumulate enormous amounts of data about their daily transactions. This data is collected, coded, and stored in databases, data warehouses, and repositories and is retrieved as and when required. The amount of data collected is immense and, today, the largest corporate databases are measured in terabytes. For example, the package-level database at UPS, a company that ships packages, contains as much data as all the books in the Library of Congress—which were more than 17 million at the last count. Thus the task in front of organizations is not just storing these huge piles of data, but storing them in such a way that they are readily retrievable and accessible for decision support systems and other applications.

To manage these huge piles of data, which is potential knowledge, KMS came up with data storage tools like databases, data warehouses, repositories, etc. While traditional databases hold operational-type data (most often of the transactional-type), a data warehouse contains summarized information, which is extensively used for knowledge management purposes like knowledge creation. A data warehouse is generally modelled as a multi-dimensional data cube where each dimension represents a particular characteristic of the data, for example, a three-dimensional data cube representing sex, profession, and age of the customer. Each dimension in a data cube can, in turn, be subdivided, and these dimensions are basically the perspectives or entities with respect to which an organization keeps its records. The techniques of warehousing deal with collecting summarized information from disparate sources and storing it in such a way that this disparity can be reconciled and different applications can make use of the same information.

The next question is how does one manage such huge and complex databases, and most of all, are they of any use? Before the 1990s the answer to this question was 'not much'. But since the early 1990s, a lot of work is being done in this area and many new software have been developed. Advanced computer storage technology and sophisticated retrieval techniques such as query languages, multimedia databases, and database management systems are found to be effective tools in enhancing organizational memory (Alavi and Leidner 2001). These tools increase the speed at which the data can be accessed, which, in turn, can be combined to respond to customer problems and product information effectively. For example, tools like OLAP (On-Line Analytical Processing) are very effective in accessing and analysing complex sets of data.

Knowledge Creation—Through KMS

As has already been discussed, most of the knowledge management pundits agree that knowledge creation occurs when tacit knowledge interacts with explicit knowledge. However, there are debates regarding whether an IT-enabled system can actually create knowledge without human intervention. In this section we try to give an account of KMS techniques that are actively used to generate information from data, and knowledge about unknown patterns from information. We leave it to the reader to decide whether the structures, patterns, and rules extracted from the data warehouses and repositories should be called knowledge or not.

The availability of stored data has the potential to infer future market trends depending on the present and past buying patterns. This idea of whether some valuable information can be gathered from these archives and be used to improve the business efficiency gave rise to the advent of knowledge discovery from databases. For example, the information collected by retailers, telecom service providers, and credit card companies on their customers can be of great value, if some kind of buying and calling patterns of customers, which were previously unknown, can be inferred from this information.

Knowledge Discovery in Databases

This is the process of identifying a valid, potentially useful and ultimately understandable structure in data. This process involves selecting or sampling data from a warehouse, cleaning or processing it, transforming or reducing it (if needed), applying a data mining component to produce a structure and then evaluating the derived structure (Pujari 2001).

Data Mining

This is concerned with identifying valid, novel, potentially useful patterns in data. It exploits the data assets from the data warehouse to gain deeper insights into the key aspects of business environment. According to Pujari (2001), data mining takes the evolutionary process from beyond retrospective data access and navigation to prospective and proactive information delivery. He defines data mining as follows: 'The data mining system self-learns from the previous history of the investigated system, formulating and testing hypothesis about rules which the system obeys. When concise and valuable knowledge about the system of interest is discovered, it can be interpreted into some decision support system which helps a manager to make wise and informed business decision'.

To get a better understanding of how data mining works, let us consider an example of, say, the shopping habits of customers in a bookstore. Suppose the majority of customers who are buying book A are also buying book B and book C. Then it makes sense for the marketing manager to club them together or inform the customer about the other two books whenever he/she is planning to buy one of them. He can go one step further and offer a bulk discount if all three are bought together so as to encourage the readers who want to buy book A but may also have a slight inclination towards books B and C. However, when we are talking about huge shopping malls or retail chains the buying patterns of the customers may not be very obvious and this is where the data mining techniques come into the picture.

According to Berry and Linoff (2000), there are two styles of data mining: (a) directed data mining, which uses activities like classification, estimation, and prediction to build a model that describes one particular variable of interest in terms of the rest of the available data. This is a top-down approach, used when we know what we are looking for; and (b) undirected data mining, which tries to establish a relationship between all the variables of data with the help of tasks like clustering, description, visualization, etc. This one is a bottom-up approach that lets the data speak for itself.

A lot of research is being done on data mining techniques and new algorithms are being invented every day to discover new emerging patterns from the databases. Traditional clustering methods, more recent Neural Networks and Genetic Algorithms, and techniques for Sequence Mining, Web Mining, Text Mining, Spatial Data Mining and so on are a few examples.

Thus, while KMS techniques like data mining help organizations create knowledge from the vast amount of data, the next question is how to transmit this knowledge to relevant individuals, groups, and departments in the organization to create a common platform for knowledge.

Knowledge Transfer

Before we proceed to the discussion of whether KMS facilitates knowledge transfer in an organization, and how it does so, it would be a good idea to reflect upon how knowledge transfer occurs in reality between any two entities in an organization. Let us consider (a) individuals and (b) groups as entities; and tacit and explicit as the types of knowledge to be transferred. Then we have (i) individual to individual, (ii) individual to group, (iii) group to individual, and (iv) group to group as the possible knowledge transfer processes involving tacit and explicit knowledge. The foremost observation would be that the transfer occurs through verbal and face-to-face communication between individuals and groups involving socialization, externalization, internalization, and combination of Nonaka's SECI model. The IT-enabled knowledge transfer technologies help the organizations to expedite these processes by enabling the individuals and groups to efficiently exchange large amounts of data, information, and knowledge through group ware, intranets, extranets, etc. But the problem which may arise here is that of information overload, which may put off the individuals from exploring for relevant pieces of information for decision-making. To deal with this problem, KMS have come up with pull and push technologies. While pull is used by the knowledge seeker by typing in a specific query into a web browser or a search engine to get the required information, push is used by the provider to automatically send the relevant information to the individuals and groups that are thought to be requiring the specific information. Bukowitz and Williams (1999) thought that balancing the pull and push technologies is the key to efficient knowledge transfer within an organization. In more recent years, Kluge et al. (2001) argue that 'push is easy, so work on pull'. The optimum solution to this problem is to build a system that would continuously learn the usage and communication patterns of both knowledge seekers and providers in order to predict current and future interests which, in turn, can be used to balance the knowledge flow.

However, the main question here is whether the face-to-face interactions can be replaced by electronic means such as email and online discussion forums and, if so, whether it would it be an effective way of knowledge transfer. According to Walsham (2001) the answer to this question really depends on individual circumstances, but it is likely that a mixture of modes would be better than either extreme.

Knowledge Application

Finally, we arrive at the ultimate goal of leveraging knowledge to achieve organizational objectives. If one gets caught up in the web of knowledge creation, storage/retrieval, and transfer and does not reach this ultimate step of leveraging the knowledge for the benefit of the organization, then the sole purpose of these processes is defeated. Ironically, this is exactly what happens to most knowledge management initiatives. According to Pfeffer and Sutton (2000) organizations have gaps between what they know and what they do. Organizational members access and assimilate knowledge but do not apply it as they may distrust the source of the knowledge, lack time or opportunity to apply the knowledge, or display risk aversion (Davenport and Prusak 1998).

One may loosely attribute the lack of knowledge application in organizations to the following reasons.

1. Very little research is done in the area of knowledge application.
2. Explicit knowledge obtained through the above mentioned means (for example, knowledge discovery in databases and data mining techniques) may be new and not validated by experience.
3. People inherently are wary of applying new knowledge.
4. The organizational atmosphere may not be conducive to failures.

In order to overcome these barriers and carry out the most crucial step of knowledge application, organizations need to focus on creating an atmosphere that is conducive to knowledge application. One can start by encouraging knowledge application to innovative ideas, whether they finally yield any results or not. This not only gives the employees the freedom to try out new ideas, but also validates the existing knowledge. In the long run, this practice will enable the organization as a whole to absorb the knowledge created in a continuum. By nature, knowledge application is an integral part of the knowledge management process, as each step in creation, storage/retrieval, and transfer requires the updating and application of knowledge generated in the process. Organizations must understand this dynamic nature of knowledge and involve as many members as possible in the knowledge spiral. Being part of the process will give them an insight into the process and will generate the required trust for application, enabling them, in turn, to share their experiences and induce trust in the rest of the organization.

The second step in this direction is to disperse and facilitate the access and application of available knowledge to all corners of the organization so that employees can carry out the knowledge application with ease. This is where the ubiquitous KMS tools can be of great help, although the extent of knowledge used will depend on the system quality, information quality, and usefulness (Delone and McLean 1992). System quality is influenced by attributes such as ease of use, characteristics of human–computer interface, and flexibility and effectiveness of search mechanisms (Alavi and Leidner 2001). A great deal of research focusing on KMS use process, and development of intuitive search, retrieval, and display is needed to enhance KMS quality. Also KMS usefulness can be examined by testing the ratios of knowledge accessed to knowledge available and knowledge used to knowledge accessed. However, it is ultimately human initiative which is required to apply the available knowledge for organizational tasks like problem solving and decision-making.

STRATEGIC FRAMEWORK FOR KNOWLEDGE MANAGEMENT INITIATIVE

One of the major questions regarding knowledge management that organizations face in the twenty-first century is whether a knowledge management initiative is required in their organizations or not. The next question would be that, if it is required, what should be the most effective way of implementing it. Finally, how is one to measure the effectiveness. While addressing the first question, there is no single straightforward solution. Some knowledge management consultants have come up with a few thumb rules depending on the type of the organization and the nature of the management.

However, experience has proved that an outside consultant is not very suitable in judging whether a company is in need of a knowledge management programme. It is the job of the experienced middle managers or various department heads who have a good understanding of the system and who are in a position to influence the top management. The first step in this direction would be to integrate all the theoretical models or different perspectives of knowledge management in the literature. Based on an extensive literature survey, Reinhardt (2001) identified four analytical core perspectives on organizational learning and knowledge management: learning levels, learning modes, learning types, and the learning process with its different phases. Figure 13.2 describes the distinct characteristics of this model.

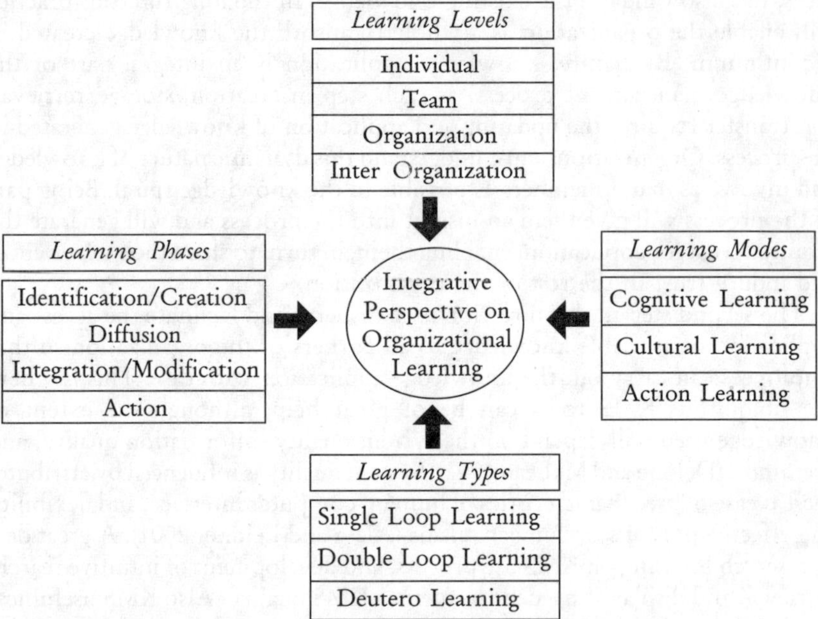

Fig. 13.2: Integrative Perspective on Organizational Learning Concepts

Source: Reinhardt 2001

Learning Levels: These are divided into individual, team, organizational, and inter-organizational, out of which, team-learning processes have been found to be the most crucial for organizational learning (Duncan and Weiss 1979, Senge 1994). Inter-organizational learning takes place in the context of mergers and acquisitions.

Learning Modes: They deal with cognitive, cultural, and action learning. While cognitive perspective is based on organizational decision-making and concepts of bounded rationality[1], cultural perspective is based on interpretative human

[1] Concept propounded by the nobel laureate, late Herbert Simon. Simon advocated that there was no absolute rationality in human affairs. Organizations and their

behaviour concepts. On the other hand, action learning is rooted in experimental learning concepts and socio-technical approach (Revans 1982).

Learning Types: They were first identified by Argyris and Schon (1978) as single loop, double loop, and deutero-learning. Single loop learning is only concerned with conformity to the standard levels of performance, whereas double loop learning analyses and questions the rules and assumptions behind the actual theory in use. Finally, duetero-learning includes the learning from the reflection of learning processes and is essential for a sustainable change of norms, values, and assumptions.

Learning Process: This has already been discussed in the previous section. In this context, knowledge is created/identified and diffused between several learning systems, which is then integrated and modified depending on the adopting system. Finally, this knowledge is transformed into action and applied in organizational routines for a better performance.

The integrative perspective outlined in Figure 13.2 describes the complexity of organizational learning and knowledge management processes that occur in an organization. One should identify the various learning levels, types, and modes of learning that take place in his/her organization and whether the quality of learning processes needs an improvement, and if so, how. For example, if we consider an educational institution, with students as the customers, there may be three learning levels. The individual faculty, various groups or departments, and the institution as a whole. If it were a chain of institutions, then the fourth level would be intra-institutional. Here, the aforementioned types of learning take place at four levels. For example, from the teacher to the student, that is, at the individual level; from the teacher to the whole class, from a group of teachers to an individual student, or from a group of teachers to the whole class of students, that is, at the group level; the learning of the institute from the insights of the faculty and groups, that is, at the institute level; from one institute to the others, that is, at the intra-institutional level.

The type of learning may be single loop, if it is just the discussion of the theoretical concepts in the classroom. It becomes double loop if it involves the application of the theory to practice or is a research-oriented learning for both the teacher and the student. The long-term understanding the teacher gets about the subject and the pedagogy after teaching for several years, forms the deutero-learning.

All the insights of the individual faculty and the groups regarding the interconnections between the personal, market, and environmental demands and the subjects taught, the pedagogy used, and how they influence the student's present and future needs like employment, personal growth, and self-fulfilment, are very crucial for the institutional objectives. If the institute's objective is to be one of the best in the world, in terms of teaching or research or in the all-round development of the student, then this can only be achieved through an effective utilization of all institutional resources, including faculty

members had a limited rationality defined by their access to limited amount of information and their limited capacity for processing information.

expertise and experience. Thus the success of the institute depends on whether there is sufficient sharing of knowledge between the individual faculty and group, amongst the groups, and between the groups and the management, and how well the knowledge thus evolved is being leveraged for the betterment of organizational performance.

This analogy can be applied to any type of organization, whether a consulting firm, a pharma company, a public sector unit, or an FMCG organization. After fitting the concerned organization into the above model, one should be able to identify if there is a need for learning processes at the various levels and, if so, whether the organizational culture is conducive to knowledge creation, sharing, and dispersion. Once the requirement for a knowledge management initiative is identified it is important to get an insight into the various issues that need to be tackled during the implementation process. Before initiating a knowledge management programme, it is essential for the management to chalk out the exact business objectives of the programme and develop a suitable strategic framework to achieve these objectives. Any initiative without clear-cut objectives and motivation will fail to win the wholehearted attention of the employees and, hence, will not survive long enough to bear fruitful results. Also, learning's for learning sake, or just to imitate other firms, or to build on historical practices and strengths is never effective. It is important to align knowledge management initiative with the current business strategy and requirements to ensure that the knowledge generated supports the present and future needs of the firm. Based on the experiences of worldwide practical implementations of knowledge management initiatives, the following ground rules have been evolved:

1. Shape the organizational culture into a learning and sharing mode.
2. Involve and commit top management to a knowledge management initiative.
3. Align the knowledge management objectives with the organizational objectives.
4. Put structured as well as unstructured framework for a knowledge management initiative in place.
5. Adopt a measurement system that can measure the employee participation and the organizational performance due to knowledge management implementation.
6. Design a well defined incentive system.
7. Create short-term and long-term goals with visible results.
8. Involve all levels of employees in the knowledge management initiative.
9. Publicize and emphasize the importance of knowledge management for the progress and sustainability of the organization

The most difficult of all is establishing the organizational culture that is conducive to knowledge creation and sharing. This needs a genuine and persistent effort from the top management and the knowledge management team. Also, a great deal of commitment and involvement from the top management is required to reap the fruits from a knowledge management initiative, otherwise it can very easily get abandoned in midway. There are a lot more issues involved, which will be discussed in the next section. Once the above ground rules have been established, one can go to work on the implementation process.

Assuming that the learning culture of the organization fosters socialization, the next step of the strategic framework focuses on mobilizing the relevant tacit knowledge, in other words, the human capital in terms of groups or teams of individuals to create and conceptualize organizational knowledge. This involves selecting and grouping various personnel across divisions, with experience and expertise required for the particular project or objective, and creating a space or 'Ba'[2] as Nonaka (1994) calls it, where the embedded knowledge in the minds of these individuals can flow freely through discussions, presentations, debates, etc. Of course, initially, this requires an amount of trust, or social capital, between the individuals which, in turn, gets generated through meetings and interactions and reinforces itself.

The purpose of this grouping is to transfer the tacit and embedded knowledge of individuals into the explicit and permeating knowledge of groups. Through dialogue, the individual's mental models and skills are converted into common terms and concepts. Two processes operate in concert—individuals share the mental models of others, but also reflect and analyse their own (Nonaka 1994). Here, both double loop and deutero-learning take place, where the individual's tacit knowledge is integrated through the team into organizational and inter-organizational knowledge base. Although this may initially require some investment of time, the explicit knowledge generated through this process accelerates the entire progress of the project, by reducing repetition of work and making effective use of resources.

The third step is to capture the knowledge created—not just the end results, but also the knowledge generated in the process which should be encoded for future use with the help of KMS. For example, when the group takes a business decision, various possibilities are considered, a lot of debates and arguments occur and, finally, under certain constraints, and keeping the business objectives in mind, one particular path is chosen and implemented. However, it is always a good practice to record the remaining choices for future reference. One reason being that, if something goes wrong, it will be easy to trace back to this junction and change the path, instead of starting all over again. Also, all the time spent on arriving at a decision can be saved if a similar problem comes up in the future. One of the strategic objectives of knowledge management initiative should be to pursue these remaining possibilities, at least theoretically, parallel with the original choice that is implemented to see how good or bad the decision was.

[2] 'Ba' can be thought of as a shared space for emerging relationships. This space can be physical (office, dispersed business space, a coffee vending machine where informal interactions take place), mental (shared experiences, ideas, ideals), virtual (email, teleconferences), or any combination of these.

The KMS tools and techniques facilitate the storage, retrieval, transfer, and dispersion of knowledge thus captured throughout the organization. However, unless the employees are motivated to use this knowledge for their day-to-day operations and stop reinventing the wheel, all the effort becomes futile. Thus it is important to publicize and emphasize the usefulness of the knowledge and information that is available with the data warehouses and repositories and facilitate an easy access to this knowledge. Employees should be encouraged to share their experiences through Intranets and bulletin boards. Documenting his/her experiences and making it available for future reference can capture and leverage tacit knowledge acquired by a particular employee during an ongoing project or a decision-making process. Organizations with knowledge management programmes have established award systems that select and award best articles in order to recognize and encourage knowledge sharing. This not only gives the employees visibility but also helps them in their performance appraisals.

The next step of the framework answers the question of effectiveness and involves measuring the knowledge management performance and demonstrating a cause and effect relationship between the knowledge management initiative and superior business results. For knowledge management to endure for a long term in this ever-changing business world, it is essential to be able to measure and demonstrate the role of knowledge management best practices in achieving organizational objectives. There is a lot of pressure on the knowledge management team to capture the results and highlight the link between knowledge management programme and net profits, which may not be very obvious. As someone once said, success always has many fathers. Thus it is important to design short-term as well as long term goals in the framework. The results and visibility of short-term goals will help sustain the momentum of the knowledge management process to reach the long-term objectives.

Case Studies on Knowledge Management

Knowledge Management at Tata Steel

One of the very first organizations in India, outside the IT sector, to have implemented knowledge management is Tata Steel. With 48,000 employees, an asset base of US$2.3 billion, and annual turnover of US$1.5 billion, this steel manufacturer sells long and flat steel products to over 5000 customers around the world. The company aggressively embraced IT-enabled processes in the late 1990s, and by 1999 had installed a corporate Intranet, an SAP ERP system, an employee portal and established special interest groups focusing on various operational and manufacturing issues.

However, there was no systematic way of aligning the employee portals for solving business problems and the knowledge of the experts was not being captured into intellectual assets. An eye-opener in this regard occurred in 1999 and prompted Tata Steel into knowledge management. A foreign technical consultant was summoned to the Indian steel giant to solve a problem which had already been solved by the same person the year before. Realizing the importance of 'to know what they know' and stop 'reinventing the wheel' Tata Steel embarked on the knowledge management programme in May 1999. To begin with they wanted to capture the available abundant knowledge assets in the form of tacit (experience, thumb rules, etc.) and explicit (literature, reports, failure analysis, etc.) knowledge, organize and transform the captured knowledge, and facilitate its usage at the right place and at the right time.

A core team of five members (experts in various fields with good experience) was formed, which studied best practices, devised knowledge taxonomies, created knowledge repositories, formed knowledge communities, and drilled employees on knowledge management behaviours. HR interventions have been made in performance management and also to recognize employees who perform well in the knowledge management related activities.

However, as always, issues like poor connectivity, irrelevant and superfluous contributions coming into the knowledge repositories, and cultural problems like technology phobia and attitude of some employees who felt that this was another method to downsize and were reluctant to share their knowledge, were hampering knowledge sharing (website of Tata Steel 2003).

To deal with these problems a new, refined strategy was adopted and put into place in May 2000, which included a seminar on knowledge management, consultation on Communities of Practice (CoP) by an external firm (McKinsey), and identification as well as recognition of successful knowledge management efforts. CoPs aligned with business processes and strategy were formally launched in 21 areas, including iron-making, steel-making, rolling, maintenance, mining, waste management, cost engineering, energy management, HR, IT, and knowledge management. Care was taken to ensure that each CoP had a champion, convener, and senior manager. One of the very crucial steps in the direction of institutionalizing knowledge management was to incorporate knowledge management activities in performance evaluation. A directory of experts and skills was devised, a formal rewards and recognition system was put in place, and seminars on knowledge management were conducted.

There were still unanswered issues like inadequately planned budgetary outlays for knowledge management community support, and problems in summarizing knowledge contributions and identifying which contributions were similar or redundant in nature. And there were major questions like 'was KM approach really encouraging innovation' and 'how to involve the grassroots levels as well' (website of Tata Steel 2003).

To tackle the problem of innovation, in February 2002, the company began to formally focus on the promotion of innovation by encouraging more active experimentation, and rewarding intelligent failures as well. These efforts really paid off. It was learnt that the number of knowledge management users had grown from about 1000 in early 2001 to over 3000 by late 2002. In the same period, page views of the body of knowledge grew from barely 200 to almost 2000 per day. The number of new products manufactured significantly increased, downtime decreased, and costs came down. In monetary terms, according to Ravi Arora, head of Knowledge Management, savings of about US$ 725,000 were realized from the KMS. At a cultural level also employee attitudes started changing for the better. Previous notions like 'I am an expert, I do not need new knowledge' gave way to a continuous quest for knowledge. Employees started off by asking for help and gradually started to offer help. The extent of organizational knowledge changed from narrow and shallow silos to wider and more permeable silos. (website of Tata Steel 2003).

Funds have now been allocated to enhance knowledge activities, and Tata Steel has not only started providing knowledge management guidance to sister companies of the vast Tata group in India but also started sharing its experiences with other Indian organizations. Future plans for knowledge management at Tata Steel include linking e-learning with the knowledge management repository and knowledge management communities, devising an intellectual capital index, networking with retired employees, employee skill development for better externalization of knowledge, and integration with customer's knowledge.

Knowledge Management at Infosys

Infosys was the first Indian company which made it to the finals of the 2001 MAKE (Most Admired Knowledge Enterprises) awards. The company operates on a global scale with eight development centres in India, five in North America, and one in the UK, and has 10,500 employees on its rolls.

The primary driver for Infosys' knowledge management strategy was that, as a company climbs the value curve, it increasingly needs effective mechanisms for speedy and efficient consolidation of expertise. The mission of Infosys' knowledge management effort is to ensure that all organizational learning is leveraged in delivering business advantage to the customer. The objectives are to minimize the effort dissipated in re-learning that which has already taken place elsewhere, and ensuring that Infoscions (as the employees of Infosys are called), in contact with the customer, have the collective knowledge of the organization behind them. The company thus aims to move towards a 'Learn Once, Use Anywhere' paradigm (Kochikar 2000).

A number of initiatives related to knowledge dissemination, sharing, and reuse have been happening in a decentralized way even before knowledge management programme was launched formally at Infosys. An organization-wide easy-to-interface system called Body of Knowledge (BoK) which enshrines experiential learning gained by past projects, a knowledge directory with pointers to expertise available within the organization, and the company-wide Intranet, Sparsh, a central information portal and emailing system that supports bulletin boards, queries, etc. were already in place. To create more transparency and expose its intangible assets to its global investors, Infosys adopted Sveiby's (1997) 'Intangible Assets Monitor' in its annual financial reports from the year 1998. A web-based virtual classroom was developed and deployed that allows access to various courses that are developed internally and to several online tutorials that have been purchased. Practices that have worked are also propagated through regular seminars and best practice sessions.

While all these knowledge management-related activities were being carried out in various organizational pockets like the quality department, the information systems (IS) group, the marketing group, education, and research (E&R), etc., the need to focus and prioritize knowledge management efforts and raise the level of knowledge management maturity (KMM) prompted Infosys to launch a comprehensive knowledge management programme in late 1999. Infosys's knowledge management strategy revolves around the key constituents of people, content, process, and technology, conceptually underpinned by Infosys's proprietary KMM Model. The KMM model is based on the realization that the path to achieving knowledge management success involves significant change—in terms of culture, process, and systems—within an organization.

Following the KMM model, a 'Content Architecture' was defined for both internal and external knowledge assets, which are accessed through a central knowledge management portal under Technology Architecture. Under People Architecture, a central knowledge management group was formed, which develops, deploys, and maintains Technology Architecture and anchors all stages of content management process. However, creation of internal content happens in practice and is facilitated by the knowledge management group.

In order to promote and publicize the knowledge management initiative, Infosys decided to establish a strong, visible correlation between attaining a high profile in the organization and contribution to knowledge management. Thus a combination of hard, performance correlated incentives and soft, peer recognition-based measures were introduced. For example, introduction of Knowledge Currency Units (KCUs), which people can earn for contribution towards knowledge sharing, accumulate and 'encash' for various rewards, is a hard measure and a KCU scoreboard on the central knowledge management portal, which gives high visibility to strong contributors and Quarterly Knowledge summits where knowledge sharing is highlighted and contributors felicitated, are soft measures.

A great concern for Infosys, which is primarily an IT firm, was not to get caught up by and overspend on technology solutions for the knowledge management implementation. However, they managed to follow successfully the popular yardstick that 'not more than a third of the effort and investment of implementing knowledge management should go into technology'. The commitment from the top management through a steering committee for knowledge management, which has a representation from the board of directors and other members of the senior management representing various key functions of knowledge management, has given the push that is required for a knowledge management initiative in any organization, and has greatly contributed to the success story of knowledge management at Infosys (Kochikar 2000).

ISSUES IN KNOWLEDGE MANAGEMENT

Though there have been large scale developments in the methods of storage and retrieval of information and knowledge due to the advances in IT, at this point some important issues remain which will determine how successful the attempts at managing knowledge are going to be.

Sharing Issues

One of the most important issues is the gap between the normative stance that everybody should share their knowledge with everybody else in the interest of the organization and the empirical reality where people actually do not always do so. This reluctance to share one's tacit knowledge with others can stem from many factors. If the individual employee does not feel confident about his own self-esteem then he may not feel comfortable sharing his knowledge with others. Similarly, if the employee does not feel very confident about the veracity of the knowledge itself, he may again feel very diffident in sharing such knowledge. Another reason for not sharing knowledge comes from the dictum 'knowledge is power'. But this dictum is used with a twist—'hoarded knowledge is power'. So some employees who have knowledge about a specific domain may feel that due to the possession of that knowledge they become unique and powerful. Through dispensing that knowledge selectively to persons of their choice and on the occasions of their choice they make themselves indispensable. In such a scenario, they may fear that if they share their knowledge freely with others in the organization they may lose their importance within the organization. In many cases they may even fear job loss.

This brings us to another important factor in the sharing of knowledge—organizational culture. If an organization's culture promotes interpersonal trust and cooperation as its guiding values, then we see much more of knowledge sharing. On the other hand, if competition becomes the guiding norm, then employees may not like to share their knowledge. In organizations where rewards are given through competitive procedures for the best knowledge generator, individuals and groups would like to hoard their knowledge. This brings us to a more fundamental issue about the kind of appraisal and reward system which an organization adopts. If the organization judges and rewards people on the basis of individual performance then, to hope that people will naturally share knowledge with others, would not be a reasonable assumption. So in some ways, to encourage knowledge sharing, the organization also needs to look at its appraisal and reward systems.

Another related aspect concerns the hierarchical orientation of the organization. What is considered as valid knowledge? Can valid knowledge come from any source in the organization or are some sources more equal than others? In many cases, if the organization has a highly hierarchical orientation, there may be a reluctance to accept and imbibe the experiences of the people from the lower rungs in the hierarchy as valid knowledge by others in the organization. This would lead to an overall lower level of performance. Over time it would also lead to a dual structure of the organization—that of the thinkers on the *Brahmins* and the doers or the *Sudras*. Thus the large majority of organizational members would be discouraged from contributing their knowledge for the betterment of the organization.

Complexity Issues

The assumption behind most knowledge management attempts right now is 'the more, the merrier'. Is it true that more knowledge leads to better decisions? Intuitively, we may argue that this may not be the case. If we plot the amount of information against the quality of decisions, the resultant curve may not be of an upward going straight line. We can see that after some time it may actually start going down. This would be because of information or knowledge overload. Based on the work of people such as Herbert Simon and his other colleagues, we can see that managers do not look for all the relevant information in their decision-making due to two reasons. First, the information gathering has time and cost implications. Second, human mind has a limited capability for information processing. With the advent of knowledge management tools it can be argued that both information gathering and processing and, to some extent, the ability of the human mind to handle large information has improved. Tools such as decision support systems play a very important role in this process. The assumption about the nature of the reality made by many of the knowledge management enthusiasts is that of a neatly ordered unidirectional reality. But this may not be the case. As the information and knowledge in an organization's knowledge repositories increase, beyond a point, this knowledge may add to the complexity of the situation rather than simplify them. Thus the hope that individual managers would be able to make better decisions would perhaps be merely a fond hope. In fact, what may happen is that, faced with such a complex situation which resembles reality itself, individuals may feel comfortable taking recourse to personal contacts or short cut oblique heuristics rather than formal searches as envisaged by KMS designers.

Therefore, a related aspect of knowledge management is also to look at the size of knowledge repositories so that they are manageable in terms of an individual's ability to make sense out of them. Thus not only more information gathering and processing but the periodic removal of information from this repository also becomes an important task of the KMS.

Dangers of Determinism

Once an organization builds and starts using a comprehensive KMS, after some time it runs the danger of dogmatically believing in the comprehensiveness of its KMS. Then, even if the environmental situations change, the organization may not like to look at fresh information with the respect such information may deserve. It can also be argued that a managed system may lead to narrowing down of the range of ideas and, hence, may not lead to continuous innovations. Therefore, one of the greatest challenges before a KMS is how to keep continuous learning alive.

Thus we see that knowledge and its proper management can act like invaluable resources for an organization and can give it a sustainable competitive advantage. Development of IT has acted as a catalyst in the storage, organization, analysis, and retrieval of information and, consequently, knowledge within organizations. However, this is just a necessary infrastructure which alone cannot ensure effective use of knowledge resources within an organization. For effectively using its knowledge resources an organization needs to undergo a change to usher in a culture which encourages cooperation and sharing of knowledge. Formal organizational processes like appraisal and rewards need to be aligned with the requirements of a sharing culture. Similarly, the organizational structure and the communication systems also need to be aligned with such a culture. If an organization can achieve such an alignment and can use proper IT tools it can effectively harness its knowledge resources for sustainable competitive advantage. However, it must be recognized that knowledge management itself is a tool in the service of larger organizational objectives. Hence, even if an organization starts by looking at implementing knowledge management as an act of imitation, in the long run, to achieve any meaningful results, it should align its knowledge management programmes to broader strategic initiatives of the organization.

References

Alavi, M. and D.E. Leidner (2001) 'Knowledge Management and Knowledge Management Systems: Conceptual Foundations and Research Issues', *MIS Quarterly*, Vol. 25, No. 1, pp. 107–134, March.

Argote, L., S. Beckman, and D. Epple, (1990) 'The Persistence and Transfer of Learning in Industrial Settings', *Management Science*, Vol. 36, pp. 1750–63.

Argyris, C. and D.A. Schön (1978) *Organizational Learning*, Reading.

Barclay, R.O. and P.C. Murray (1997) What 'is Knowledge Management?' http://*www.media-access.com/whatis.html* (last accessed on 31 July, 2003).

Berry, M.J.A. and G.S. Linoff, (2000) *Mastering Data Mining: The Art and Science of Customer Relationship Management*, John Wiley & Sons, New York, pp. 39–64.

Brown, J. and P. Duguid, (1998) 'Organizing Knowledge', *California Management Review*, Vol. 40, No. 3, pp. 90–111.

Bukowitz, W. and R.L. Williams (1999) *The Knowledge Management Fieldbook*, Pearson Education Ltd, Harlow, UK. pp. 50–4.

Davenport, T.H. and L. Prusak (1998) *Working Knowledge*, Harvard Business School Press, Boston.

Delone, W. and E. McLean, (1992) 'Information Systems Success: The Quest for the Dependent Variable', *Information Systems Research*, Vol. 3, No. 1, pp. 60–95, March.

Denning, S. (2000) *History of Knowledge Management*, *http://www.stevedenning.com/history_knowledge_management.html* (last accessed on 31 July 2003).

Dretske, F. (1981) *Knowledge and the Flow of Information*, MIT Press, Cambridge, Mass.

Duncan, R. and A. Weiss (1979) 'Organizational Learning: Implications for Organizational Design', in Barry M. Staw and LL. Cummings *Research in Organizational Behavior*, Jai Press, Greenwich.

Grant, R.M. (1996a) 'Prospering in Dynamically Competitive Environments: Organizational Capability as Knowledge Creation', *Organization Science*, Vol. 7 No. 4, pp. 375–87, July–August.

— (1996b) 'Toward a Knowledge-based Theory of the Firm', *Strategic Management Journal*, Vol. 17, pp. 109–122, Winter Special Issue.

Huber, G. (1991) 'Organizational Learning: The Contributing Processes and Literatures, Organization Science, Vol. 2, No. 1, pp. 88–115.

Inmon, W.H. (1996) *Building the Data Warehouse*, second edition, John Wiley and Sons, New York.

Kluge, J., W. Stein, and T. Licht, (2001) *Knowledge Unplugged*, Palgrave, pp. 25–56.

Kochikar, V. P. (2000) *Knowledge—The Currency of the New Millennium*, *http://www.infosys.com/knowledge_capital/knowledge/knowledge4.asp* (last accessed on 28 June 2003).

Leonard-Barton, D. (1992) 'The Factory as a Learning Laboratory', *Sloan Management Review*, Vol. 34, No. 1, pp. 23–38.

Machlup, F. (1980) *Knowledge: Its Creation, Distribution and Economic Significance*, Vol. 1, Princeton University Press, Princeton, NJ.

Nonaka, I. (1994) 'A Dynamic Theory of Organizational Knowledge Creation', *Organization Science*, Vol. 5, No. 1, pp. 14–37, February.

— and H Takeuchi (1995) *The Knowledge Creating Company: How Japanese Companies Create the Dynamics of Innovation*, Oxford University Press, New York.

— and N. Konno, (1998) 'The Concept of Ba: Building a Foundation for Knowledge Creation', *California Management Review*, Vol. 40, No. 3, pp. 40–54.

Patricia, S., D.L. David, S. Susan, and G. Edwa (2001) 'Building Intangible Assets: A Strategic Framework for Investing in Intellectual Capital,' in M. Daryl et al. (eds) *Knowledge Management: Classic and Contemporary Works*, The MIT Press, USA.

Pfeffer, J. and R.I. Sutton (2000) *The Knowledge-Doing Gap: How Smart Companies Turn Knowledge into Action*, Harvard Business School Press, Boston, Mass.

Polanyi, M. (1967) *The Tacit Dimension*, Routledge and Keoan Paul, London.

— (1962) *Personal Knowledge: Towards a Post Critical Philosophy*, Haper Torchbooks, New York.

Pujari, A.K. (2001) *Data Mining Techniques*, Universities Press, Hyderabad.

Reinhardt, R. (2001) 'Knowledge Management: Linking Theory with Practice', in M. Daryl et al. *Knowledge Management: Classic and Contemporary works*, The MIT Press, USA.

Revans, R.W. (1982) *The Origins and Growth of Action Learning: The enterprise as a Learning System.*

Rüdiger, R. (2001), 'Knowledge Management: Linking Theory with Practice', in M. Daryl et al. (eds) *Knowledge Management: Classic and Contemporary works*, The MIT Press, USA.

Santosus, M. and J. Surmacz, (2003) *The ABCs of Knowledge Management*, http://*www.cio.com/research/knowledge/edit/kmabcs.html* (last accessed on 31 July, 2003).

Seemann, P., D.D. Long, S. Stucky, and E. Guthrie, (2001) 'Building Intangible Assets: A Strategic Framework for Investing in Intellectual Capital.', in M. Daryl et al. (eds) *Knowledge Management: Classic and Contemporary Works*, Universities Press, pp. 85–98.

Senge, P.M. et al., (1994) *The Fifth Discipline Fieldbook*, San Francisco.

Sveiby, K.E. (1997) 'The Intangible Assets Monitor', *Journal of Human Resource Costing and Accounting*, Vol. 2, No.1.

— (1889) 'The Invisible Balance Sheet'.

Tuomi, I. (1999) *Data is More Than Knowledge: Implications of the Reversed Hierarchy for Knowledge Management and Organizational Memory*, proceedings of 32nd Hawaii International Conference on Systems Sciences, IEEE Computer Society Press.

Walsham, G. (2001) 'Knowledge Management: The Benefits and Limitations of Computer Systems, *European Management Journal*, Vol. 19, No. 6, pp. 599–608, December.

Journey of KM in Tata Steel (2003) *http://www.tatasteel.com/tatanet/km/journey.htm* (last accessed on 31 July, 2003).

14

System Dynamics

Amitava Dutta • Rahul Roy

> The world we have made as a result of the level of thinking we have done thus far creates problems that we cannot solve at the same level (of consciousness) at which we have created them.... We shall require a substantially new manner of thinking if humankind is to survive.
>
> —Albert Einstein

Etoys, an online toy retailer, was in desperate need of a blockbuster holiday season. For a company that at one point had become synonymous with online retailing, initially symbolizing the concept's potential, sales in the previous year was nothing short of spectacular. Site visits in the month of November itself had reached 4.9 million, and third quarter sales touched US$107 million. The bumper sales stretched the retailer's supply chain, which was clearly not ready to handle the volume, to extremes. The consequence was obvious—4 per cent late deliveries, bad publicity, and lost reputation. This year, however, the company did not want to take a chance. Expecting a repetition of the previous year's sales, it built an automated warehouse to bring packing and shipping in-house. But customers did not show up in the required numbers and sales was less than half of what had been expected. The cash reserve situation, depleted significantly by the heavy investment in the warehouse, did not improve quickly enough and the company experienced financial difficulties. A Wall Street analyst commented, 'it's a classic case of them overbuilding relative to what consumers actually wanted.'

In 1987, Analog Devices Inc., a leading manufacturer of integrated circuits, initiated a Total Quality Management (TQM) programme that was broad based covering all major aspects of the business. The innovative programme drew on established principles of TQM and spared no effort to make the programme successful. Two notable aspects of the programme were, the Half-life System for setting realistic targets for improvement and a BSC to monitor results achieved. The resulting improvements were, in some aspects, dramatic. For example, by 1990, product defects had fallen by a factor of 10, manufacturing cycle time had been reduced by half, and semiconductor yield had almost doubled. Surprisingly, however, not all results were as rosy. By 1990, Analog's share value fell to one-fourth of its value in 1986 and return on equity dropped from 7 per cent to 4 per cent. One plausible explanation of the poor performance might have been the slowdown facing the semiconductor industry in general at that time. But the performance of Analog, known to be a leading player, was worse than average. It was unlikely, therefore, that the slowdown could have been the sole or even the major cause. Faced with unfavourable financial results, in 1990, Analog was forced to lay people off for the first time in its history. The workforce had to be reduced by 12 per cent. The fact that the dramatic achievements of the TQM programme in terms of internal production efficiencies had translated itself into this kind of unfavourable side effects on the financial front was paradoxical.

Some time in the mid-1990s, America Online (AOL) switched from usage-based to fixed all-you-can-use pricing for Internet services. The intent was to maintain or increase customer base in the face of fixed-price plans introduced by smaller competitors. But the immediate consequence was a lot of disgruntled AOL customers facing constant busy signals, unable to log on using their dial-up modems. This had major financial consequences for AOL and also led to customer retention problems. The marketing move did not appear to be coordinated with network operations (there were not enough dial-up modems in place to handle the increased load), resulting in wholly unintended business consequences.

The cases of Etoys, Analog Devices, and AOL illustrate complexities of management intervention in contemporary organizations. As competitive pressures force organizations to operate 'faster, better, cheaper', their value chains are becoming increasingly more integrated. Additionally, there is tighter coupling among different components of the environment. In an increasingly integrated environment, the mental models on which management decisions are based need to be more holistic than ever before in order to foresee the chain of consequences resulting from an intervention. However, the cognitive ability of the human mind to sift through a multitude of interdependent variables and deduce the likely consequences, is known to be quite limited. As an illustration of the claim, try to predict how the supply chain described below would respond when it is exposed to a demand shift.

In this simplified supply chain dealing in a consumer product (say, beverage), there are only four agents—retailer, wholesaler, distributor, and factory—all of whom operate fairly independently (collaborative forecasting, planning, etc. are yet to become the norm) The retailer sells out of stock to his customers. At the end of the day the inventory position is reviewed and replenishment order is placed with the wholesaler. Every Monday, a truckload of shipment comes from the wholesaler. The wholesaler, in turn, places orders on a weekly basis with the distributor and receives shipment every 15 days. The wholesaler also bases his ordering decision on the inventory on hand. The distributor is careful not to end up in a stock-out situation. With that goal in mind he maintains close liaison with the factory. The factory is also keen that the distributor gets what he wants. Occasional requests for extra shipments are, therefore, accommodated in spite of the fact that production planning is done once a month. Accommodating such ad hoc requests puts extra pressure on production. For some time the supply chain has been in a steady state—shipments have been matching the orders placed, inventory levels at all points have remained steady at the desired level, and no stock-outs have been observed. The factory is about to embark on an aggressive promotion scheme targeted at the consumers. As the retail stores manager, can you guess how retailer inventory would behave in response to a 20 per cent increase in consumer demand?

It would be normal to guess that initially, for a few days, the inventory would drop due to the increased demand. But it is really difficult to visualize that inventory levels all across the supply chain will start to oscillate in response to this one step increase in consumer demand. Incredible as it may sound that is what is going to happen here. Why is it so difficult to come up with a reasonable guess about the behaviour of even such a simple system? Experiments carried out with subjects drawn from diverse backgrounds (MBA students, doctoral students, executives) have conclusively proved (Sterman 1989) that the fault lies primarily with the following three shortcomings of our mental model:

(a) It has a lot of details about our immediate surrounding but not a great deal about what lies beyond. The retailer understands how his sales and shipments affect his inventory but does not understand how his orders affect the wholesaler's inventory.
(b) The thinking mostly proceeds in a linear fashion (increase the order—shipments will increase). Worse still, feedback relationships are mostly absent.
(c) The learning processes that hone the mental models are imperfect.

Managers, therefore, need rigorous tools with which to express their mental models, share it among decision-makers across the organization, question assumptions, test hypothesis, and assess the consequences of different management actions. Without such holistic understanding, policies can have unanticipated side effects in today's integrated business environment, or their intended effects can be diluted or defeated by the reaction of the environment itself to policy actions. 'Systems thinking' has, therefore, become one of the critical skills of the twenty-first century manager.

The late Barry Richmond, founder-president of HPS Inc., the company that created ithink and Stella, had defined systems thinking as the art and science of linking structure to performance, and performance to structure—often for purposes of changing structure (relationships) so as to improve performance'. Richmond also articulated that 'doing good systems thinking means operating on at least seven thinking tracks simultaneously. These tracks are: dynamic thinking, closed-loop thinking, generic thinking, structural thinking, operational thinking, continuum thinking, and scientific thinking' (Richmond 1993).

Broadly, systems thinking encompasses a large and fairly amorphous body of methods, tools, and principles, all oriented to looking at the interrelatedness of forces, and seeing them as part of a common process. The field includes cybernetics and chaos theory, gestalt theory, the works of Gregory Bateson, Russell Ackoff, Eric Trist, Ludwig von Bertallanfy, and the Santa Fe Institute, and the dozen or so practical techniques for 'process mapping' flows of activity at work. All of these diverse approaches have one guiding idea in common—that the behaviour of all systems follows certain common principles, the nature of which are being discovered and articulated over time. Among the various methods and techniques available, one form of systems thinking, known as system dynamics, has gained substantial following because of its ability to support systems thinking in a rigorous and intuitive manner.

System dynamics provides a set of tools and techniques to develop shared mental models of organizational systems, represent them rigorously, test their validity through simulation, and gauge the impact of policy alternatives via sensitivity and what-if types of analyses. System dynamics can help to gain insights into underlying mechanics that determine the behavioural dynamics of organizational systems. This can help improve decision-making in today's integrated value chain.

The first article on system dynamics (Forrester 1959) appeared in the *Harvard Business Review*. In that article, Forrester utilized principles of information-feedback control, found in servomechanisms, to explain how aggressive advertising by a company could create workload fluctuation on the shop floor. At the time, this approach to modelling management processes was quite novel but, more than that, it introduced the notion that the dynamics of an industrial system arises as a result of its underlying structure. The basic structural element is the feedback loop and the underlying structure refers to the collection of interacting feedback loops comprising the system. This linkage between structure and behaviour remains the guiding principle for practitioners of system dynamics. In 1961, Forrester wrote the seminal book, *Industrial Dynamics*, in which he described the methodology of modelling industrial systems with physical flows (personnel, money, material, and machinery), their respective accumulations, and information-based decision-making mechanisms that control the flows to achieve the desired accumulation levels. The central theme was that all decisions get made in the information-feedback structure. A study of the feedback structure could, therefore, provide a good understanding of the system's dynamics. The concept was founded on theories of control systems but there were augmentations to handle non-linearity and intangibles that characterize industrial systems. Modelling elements to represent lags, information attenuation, and forecasting–processes commonly found in industrial systems—were also presented to round out the methodology.

Since it provides a generic framework to model the structure of any part of an organization, and its interlinkages with other parts, system dynamics is well suited for visualizing the organization from a holistic perspective. In the period following the publication of the book, the methodology found application in different problems varying widely in scope (single organization to national and economies), business processes (supply chain management, project management, service delivery, IT infrastructure, and strategic planning), and business types (manufacturing, service, R&D, health care, insurance, military, and government). Roberts (1978) and Sterman (2000) report several interesting applications made by corporate organizations over the years using system dynamics. Over the same time, the field has been enriched with methodological enhancements in modelling and analysis (Sastry and Sterman 1993). In 1990, Peter Senge's book, *The Fifth Discipline—The Art and Practice of Learning Organizations*, highlighted the connection between system dynamics and systems thinking, and gave fresh impetus to the practice of the field and increased its visibility in the practising management community.

Systems thinking, or the idea of viewing an organization as a whole, was already well known due to the earlier works of Ludwig Von Bertalanffy, Norbert Wiener, Russel L. Ackhoff, and others in the area of cybernetics. The idea was considered important but its application in management was limited and convenient tools for practising systems thinking were not readily available. Senge's book established system dynamics as a tool for systems thinking. It also introduced the concept of 'System Archetypes', which are generic structures observable in business systems demonstrating qualitatively similar behaviour. Availability of visual modelling and simulation software also contributed significantly in making the methodology popular. In the early days of system dynamics, the only software available were DYNAMO and DYSMAP, which were compilers that could create object code from model equations. In spite of the power that these compilers provided, the requirement to learn a programming language limited its use among managers. Today there are at least three visual modelling and simulation software (ithink, Vensim, and Powersim) packages available commercially to develop and test systems dynamics models. They are comparable in terms of their ability to create a system dynamics model graphically, simulate the same, and perform sensitivity analysis.

A Brief Overview of System Dynamics

The philosophy of system dynamics modelling is founded on three principles:

(a) Structure determines behaviour. Structure refers to the complex interlinkages among different parts of an organization and includes human decision-making process. An example of this is a supply chain which involves complex interaction of the components (customer, retailer, wholesaler, distributor, factory, and raw material supplier) through order and material flows and decisions made about these flows. The structure of organizational systems often involves 'soft' variables—for example, perceptions of quality, user satisfaction, morale, etc. A supply chain structure includes how each agent forms perceptions about the future behaviour of its customer. The mental models of people play a crucial role in determining the dynamic behaviour of organizational systems.

(b) Significant leverage can be obtained from understanding the mental model and changing it.

Modelling in system dynamics starts with problem definition wherein symptoms of the problem are expressed by means of 'reference mode behaviours'—time dependent behaviour of one or two important variables of the system, which the model would try to explain. The term 'important' connotes the significance of the variable in describing the state of the system. For example, for modelling the supply chain it is usual to take cost of inventory and/or the cycle time as the variable whose dynamic behaviour is used as the reference mode.

In the next step, the causal loop diagram, a pictorial representation of the underlying structure that is thought to explain the reference mode behaviour, is drawn. Typically, modellers and subject matter experts will be involved in the process of arriving at a causal loop diagram. In doing so, they have to resolve differences in their individual mental maps and arrive at a shared understanding of the underlying causes of the reference mode behaviour. As has been explained earlier, structure is made up of stocks and flows that make up important business processes and how these flows are controlled. For example, in a manufacturing firm, business processes centre around the flow of orders, material, skilled labour, machinery, and money. For a health care firm, flow of doctors, health care workers, patients, and medical equipment are important. Accumulations of these flows depict the state of the firm. Stock of materials determines the level of inventory held by a firm, stock of orders determines the backlog of orders pending with the firm, etc. By controlling the flows, the management tries to achieve a favourable level of accumulation. Thus the production manager tries to maintain a low level of order backlog so that customers do not experience large delivery delays. The materials manager makes sure that an appropriate level of raw material is maintained on the shop floor so that neither does the production suffer from shortages nor is there a huge inventory build up. So while flow determines the state, the state also guides the action to change the flow.

The causal loop diagram of Figure 14.1 shows the circular relationship between flow and accumulation in the following manner. In the diagram, each arrow represents a cause and effect relationship. The polarity of the link

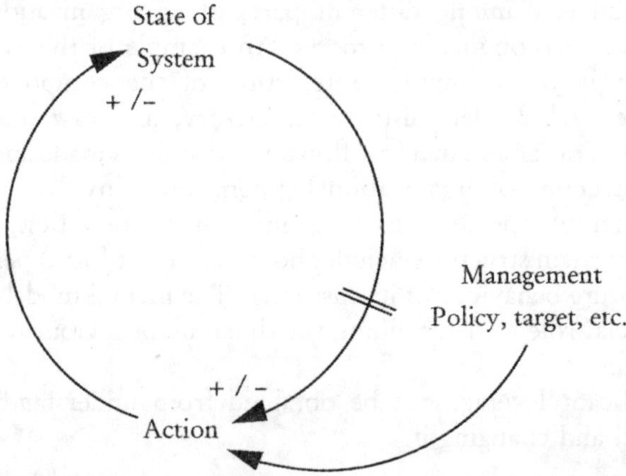

Fig. 14.1: Information-feedback View of Management Intervention

(+/–) indicates the direction of change in the effect resulting from a change in the cause. A positive sign indicates change in the same direction (increase/decrease in cause induces increase/decrease in effect) while a negative sign indicates change in the opposite direction (increase/decrease in cause induces decrease/increase in effect). The pair of parallel lines across a link indicates time delay between cause and effect. It is easy to see that this structure models situations where management decision controls a flow, thereby changing the level of accumulation and so on, giving rise to a sequence of decisions over time that determine the dynamic behaviour of the system.

Depending on the polarities of causal links present, a feedback loop can generate one of two types of effects. The first of these, called a snowball effect is one in which a change in state generates action that causes a bigger change in the state. In that case, the loop is called a positive feedback or reinforcing loop. The causal loop given below has a reinforcing loop that generates the snowball effect.

This one shows the dynamics of growing cash balance in an interest earning account. Let us assume that initially the system is in a steady state whereby the cash balance is zero and so the question of earning interest does not arise. Then at some point in time a rupee gets deposited into the account. The change of state of the account starts a snowballing motion. The increased cash balance causes accrual of some 'interest' that is dependent on the current value of cash balance and the interest rate. The accrued interest increases the cash balance further and the cycle continues. This causal structure and its behaviour are shown in Figures 14.2 and 14.3.

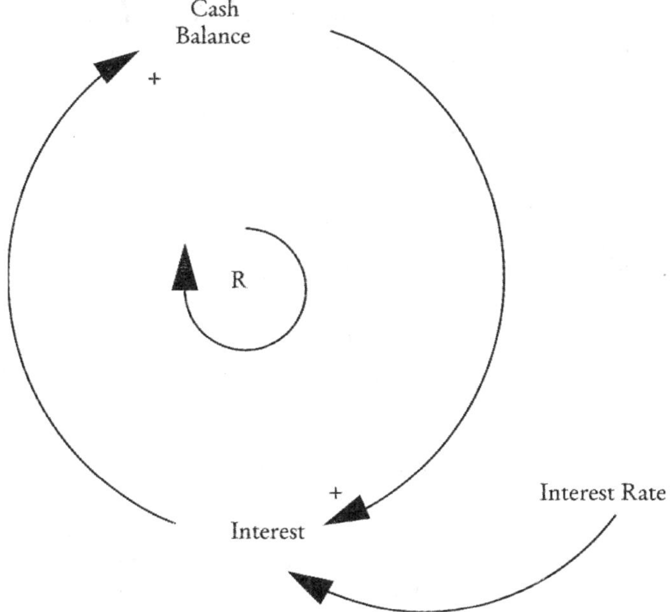

Fig. 14.2: A Reinforcing Loop

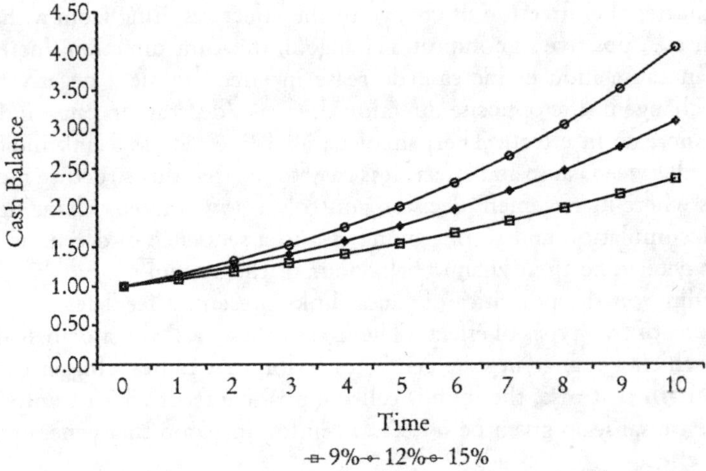

Fig. 14.3: Behaviour of Reinforcing Loop

The plot of Figure 14.3 shows how the cash balance starting from an initial value of one grows over time, moving away from the initial value at a higher rate over time. Note that higher values of interest rate causes higher rate of growth. It is easy to see that while a reinforcing loop causes an exponential growth, it is also capable of inducing a exponential decay. Imagine how the system would have behaved if, instead of depositing a rupee into the account, we had borrowed a rupee from the account. The cash balance would have gone one below zero. Assuming that no part of the debt was ever paid up, the interest accrued on the balance would have increased the negative balance and cash balance would have become more and more negative moving away from the initial value at an increasing rate. It is easy to see that the simple structure of a reinforcing loop can model a wide variety of situations that show symptoms of growth (or decay) in the manner explained here.

The second type, called balancing effect, is one where a change in state generates action to counteract the change. In the parlance of system dynamics this is termed a balancing loop. Figures 14.4 and 14.5 show a simple production–inventory system that illustrates this effect. Here consumption is made out of the inventory held.

The level of inventory is required to be maintained at the target inventory level and that is achieved by adjusting production. To understand the dynamics once again we assume that the system is initially in a steady state wherein consumption and production are both set a value of zero and the available inventory is equal to the target inventory. At this point consumption takes away a few units from inventory. To make up the drop in inventory, an appropriate level of production is carried out and that brings back the level of the inventory to that of the target inventory. The adjustment takes place continuously, moving away from its initial value at an increasingly slower rate and, eventually, reaching the target state. The structure thus balances deviation from the target state and, hence, is termed as such. In reality, a

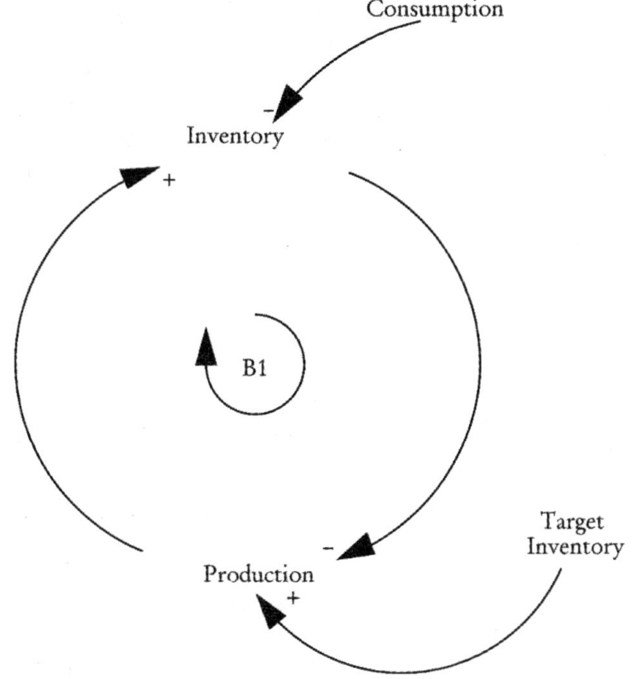

Fig. 14.4: A Balancing Loop

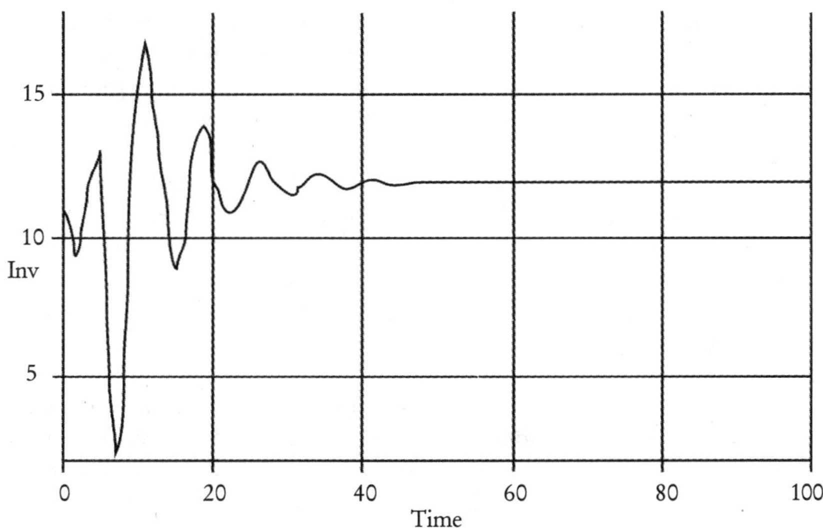

Fig. 14.5: Possible Behaviour of Balancing Loop

balancing structure often includes delay in observing the current state (level of inventory) that causes information attenuation (underestimation or overestimation), and variables that denote organizational 2policy on how to adjust the gap between current state and target state. Due to the presence of these variables, balancing loops in some situations cause over or under adjustment around the desired state and, as shown in the plot above, even cyclical behaviour under certain conditions.

In a typical system, the presence of a number of such feedback loops of both types generates the complex dynamics of the system. For illustration, Figure 14.6 shows the causal loop diagram depicting the well-known Bass model of innovation diffusion (Bass 1969).

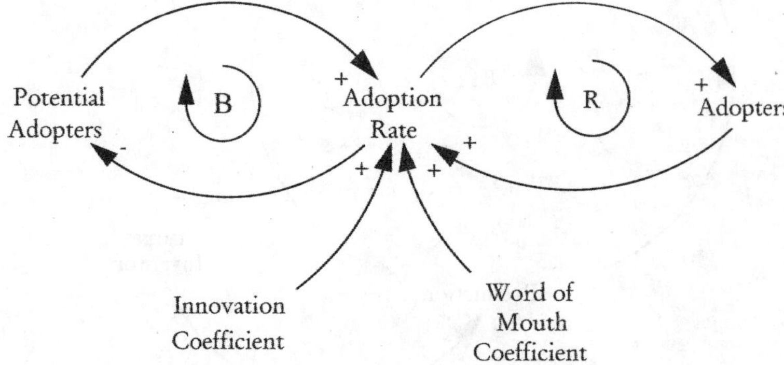

Fig. 14.6: System Dynamics Model of Innovation Diffusion

In this structure, potential adopters represent the pool of people among whom the innovation is yet to diffuse while the variable adopters represent those who have already adopted. The variable adoption rate represents the time dependent rate at which potential adopters convert to adopters. The linkages are drawn to indicate that adoption rate depends on potential adopters, adopters and two constants, namely, innovation coefficient and word of mouth coefficient. Adoption rate, in turn, affects potential adopters and adopters, decreasing the former and increasing the latter. The diagram also tells us that increase in values of the constants causes increase in the adoption rate and vice versa. When a new innovation is launched both the loops are set in motion. Initially, as the number of adopters grows, it causes more potential adopters to convert and become adopters. The adoption rate also increases.

With growing adoption, the pool of potential users shrinks at an increasing rate and the number of adopters grows exponentially. Beyond a point, however, the shrinking size of potential users starts having more effect on the adoption rate and the latter's value reduces with time, finally reaching zero. Progressive reduction in the adoption rate increases adopters at an increasingly slower rate. When adoption rate becomes zero, the value of the adopters saturates to a steady state value.

To summarize, we say that a reinforcing loop generates exponential growth behaviour, while a balancing loop stabilizes the system around a target state. In some cases, depending on loop conditions, a balancing loop can generate oscillations around the target state. In a typical system where a number of feedback loops are present the behaviour evolves as system conditions change and loops become stronger and dominate the system behaviour. Understanding how the dominance shifts among different feedback loops is an important aspect of model analysis.

During the course of model building, analysts first select the variables considered important for describing the problem. The principle of 'small is beautiful' is followed and in the beginning only the smallest set of variables is chosen. Additional variables are added only when it is felt that the selected set has not adequately captured the problem boundary. Next, causal links are drawn among the chosen variables. When drawing links greater stress is laid on the identification of a meaningful causal relationship rather than mere correlational relationship. Of course, presence of correlational relationship only strengthens the validity of the model. Along the way, one constantly attempts to check that the causal structure will be capable of reproducing the pattern of the reference mode behaviours.

In the next step of model building the stock and flow structure of the system is drawn, based on the causal loop diagram. The stock and flow structure helps simulate the dynamic behaviour of the system. (There are technical limitations of determining system behaviour from causal loop diagrams, which are ignored in this overview.) The stock and flow structure shows stocks, flow controllers, and decision structures within the system. Conserved physical flows connect stocks in the diagram. Information flows drive different physical flows. For example, the causal loop structure of the innovation diffusion model gets mapped to the stock and flow diagram shown in Figure 14.7.

The thick arrows with regulating valves indicate physical flows. Rectangles (adopters, potential adopters) indicate accumulations or stocks. The valves (adoption rate) on the physical flows control flows in and out of the stock. In system dynamics parlance they are termed as flow variables. Circles

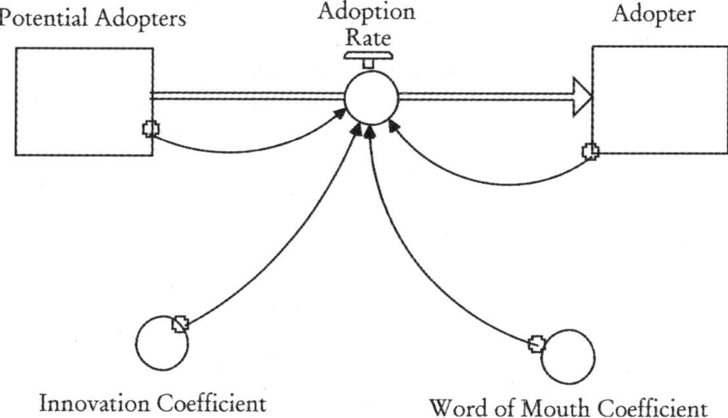

Fig. 14.7: Stock and Flow Model of the Diffusion Process

(innovation coefficient, word of mouth coefficient) indicate converters that are used to capture decision rules or perform intermediate computation. Thin arrows represent information flows connecting converters with stocks. The stock and flow structure of the system is simply a graphical shorthand for an underlying system of difference equations which can then be simulated. The result of simulating Figure 14.7 is shown in Figure 14.8.

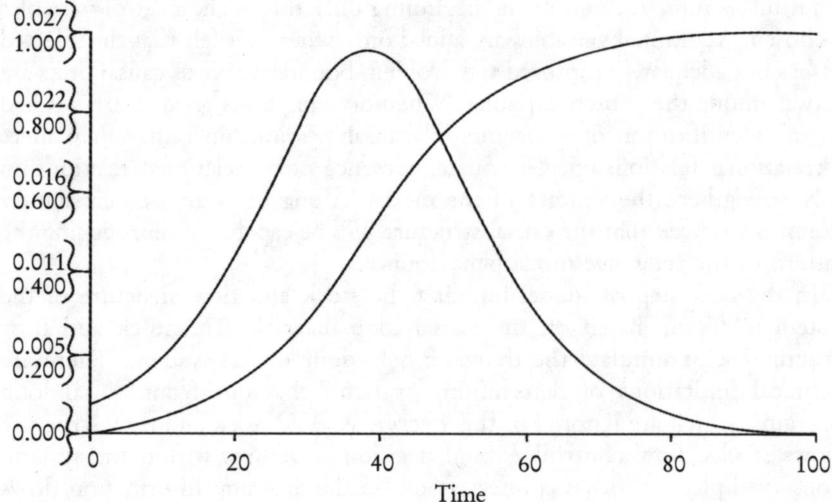

Fig. 14.8: Simulated Behaviour of Diffusion Process

Validating a system dynamics model requires, at the least, verifying that its structural components correspond to what is known about characteristics of the real problem domain and that the model, when simulated, is able to replicate observed behaviour. In other words, the micro structure of the model and its macro behaviour must mimic reality. Once validated, the model offers a synthetic version of reality, which can then be used for performing different kinds of analysis like sensitivity analysis and 'what-if' analysis to support decision-making about the future course of action. One important analysis involves experimental identification of feedback loops that dominate the dynamics at different points of time. Termed as loop dominance analysis, this provides further insight into the structure of the system and leads to design of policy structures that result in favourable dynamics.

Software Support for System Dynamics Modelling

The main objective of system dynamics modelling is to capture mental models of the structure underlying the behaviour of organizational systems. The modelling software available on the market today contribute greatly towards achieving that objective by allowing model builders to concentrate on conceptualizing the system rather than on the technicalities of model building. As of now, we can report the availability of three popular commercial software packages—Powersim[1], ithink[2], and Vensim[3]. All three provide the following basic capabilities:

(a) Drawing the model using a graphics user interface,
(b) Writing the underlying system equations in a user-friendly manner,
(c) Simulating the same with different values of simulation intervals,
(d) Publishing the results both as table and graph, and
(e) Performing sensitivity analysis and publishing comparison of run results.

Figure 14.9 shows the user interface for ithink version 7.0. The interfaces of other packages look similar with minor differences. Modelling elements from the tool bar are dragged and dropped on the white area to create the structure. For stocks, initial values need to be specified. Decision rules for the flow variables and converters are written by getting into the dialogue box. A rich set of built-in functions allows the representing of most real-life situations. The packages also allow writing the relationship in the form of a graphical function linking the cause and effect variables. The graph can be drawn by clicking on the appropriate point on the plot area. The equations for the variables get written automatically.

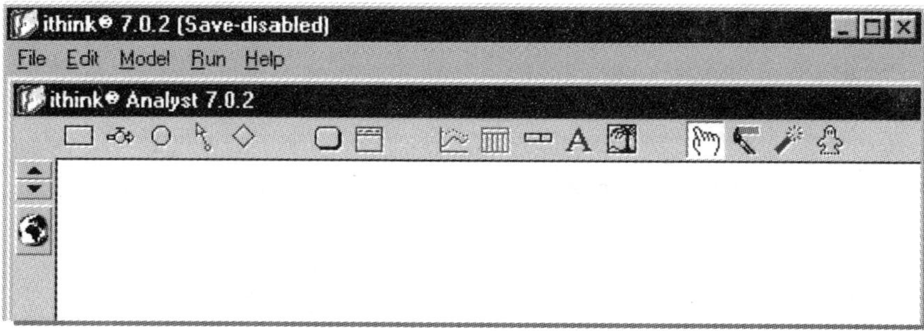

Fig. 14.9: ithink Interface

Beyond these basics, each package also provides additional features. ithink, for example, provides a multi-level modelling interface that allows for separating out the user interface, the stock and flow model, and the equations into three different levels. The interface level can be used to show an overview of the system, the causal loop diagram, and model outputs. The model tracing facility provides an easy way to navigate through the feedback loops and learn about the reasons behind the dynamics. In recent times, ithink has been building multimedia games meant to give managers an experimental

[1] Product of Powersim Corp, Bergen, Norway, *http://www.powersim.com*

[2] Product of High Performance Systems Inc., Hanover, NH 03755, *http://www.hps-inc.com*

[3] Product of Ventana Systems Inc., Harvard, MA 01451, *http://www.vensim.com*

set up for experiential learning. Vensim enforces strict rigour in writing model equations. It provides features for tracing feedback loops. In addition, the 'Causes Tree' and 'Uses Tree' features help in debugging the model. Powersim comes with the powerful feature of adding user written functions. This can be useful in a modelling situation where new concepts (for example, fuzzy logic) need to be incorporated. The latest version of Powersim can also build reusable model components that can be plugged in without much

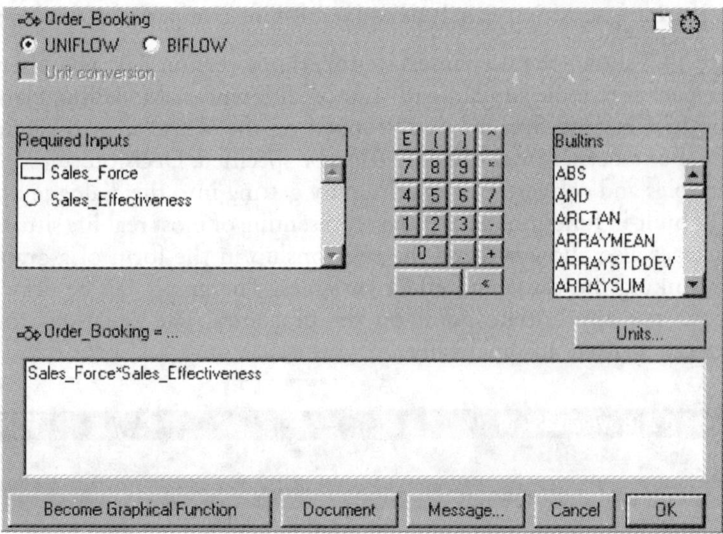

Fig. 14.10: Flow/Converter Input Dialogue Box

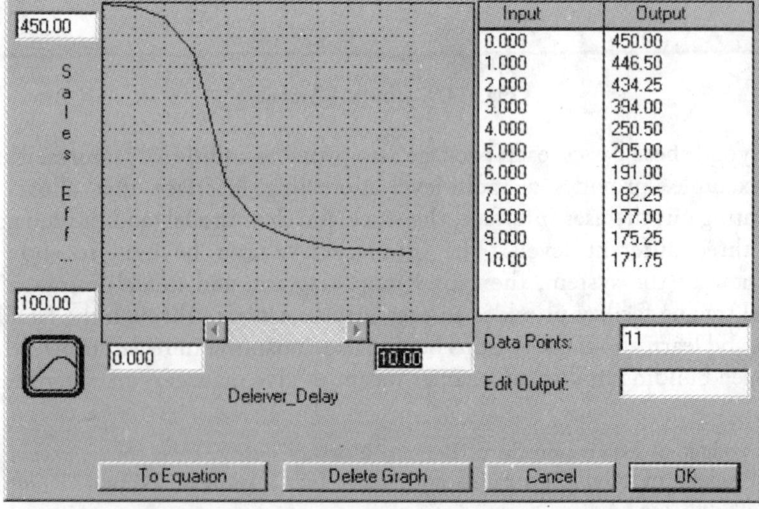

Fig. 14.11: Graphical Function Input Dialogue Box

difficulty. In summary, while the basic capabilities are present in all three packages, the additional features provided make each one suitable for one particular modelling situation.

System Archetypes—Drawing Commonality across System Structures

Although management problems seem to vary widely at first glance, a deeper look brings out generic and common underlying structures. Consider the following example concerning the growth of a company in a market that differentiates product (or service) mainly on delivery (service) delay. This situation exists in a number of different industries such as restaurants and Internet service provisioning. Let us assume that a new entrant to the market uses its sales force to aggressively market its product and get orders. As sales persons get orders, the company recruits more sales persons with the hope of getting more orders. The relationship between orders booked and sales force constitute a reinforcing feedback (shown in Figure 14.12) and, as a result, orders booked increases exponentially. The delay mark on the link between orders booked and sales force occurs due to the time taken in recruitment of additional sales personnel.

However, the stream of orders booked increases order backlog and progressively pushes service capability to the limit and increasing delivery delay. The increased delivery delay experienced by the customer causes

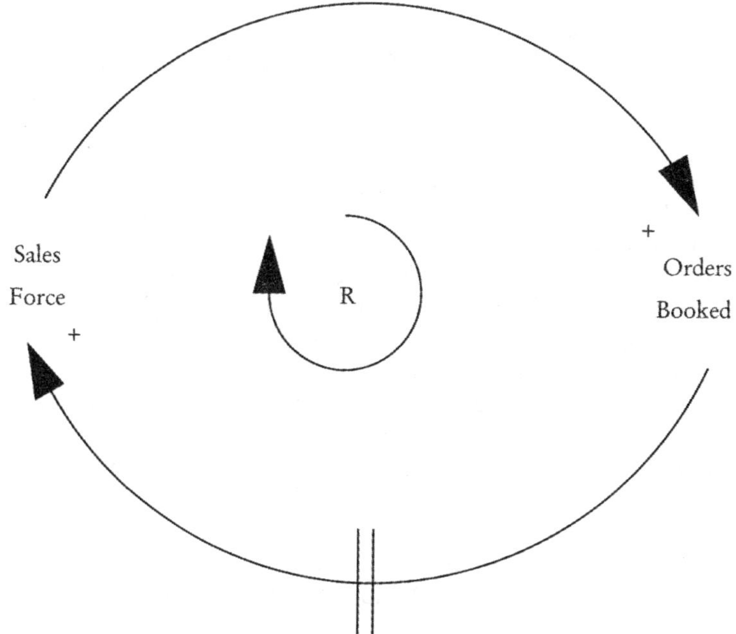

Fig. 14.12: Sales Force–Orders Booked Loop

deterioration in sales force effectiveness (they find it harder to sell) and reduced orders booked. So, in spite of an unlimited market, orders booked by the company saturates. This balancing loop (shown in Figure 14.13) limits the growth of the company. Note the delay on the link between delivery delay and sales effectiveness. It accounts for the reality that delivery delays experienced by each customer slowly changes the perception of the market regarding delivery delays that future orders can expect to experience.

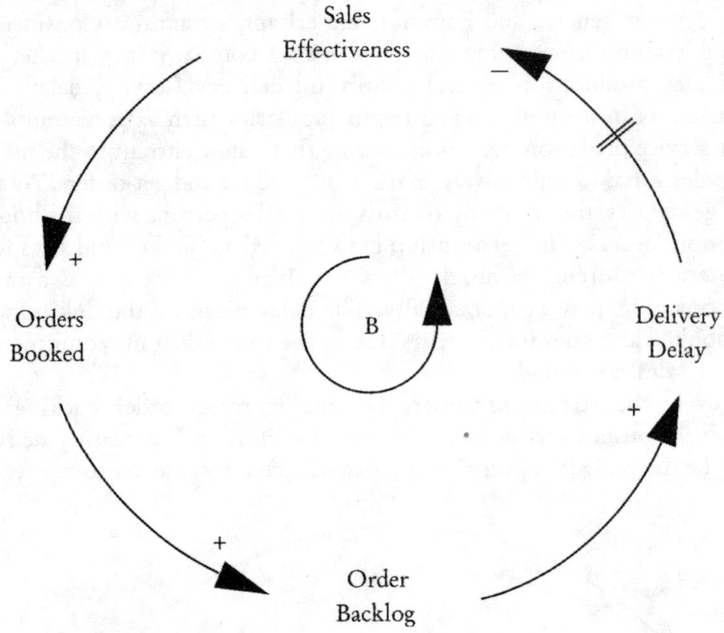

Fig. 14.13: The Order Backlog Loop

In Figure 14.14 we see that orders booked shows initial exponential growth terminated by saturation with oscillation around the terminal value. The oscillation occurs as a result of delays present in the system.

When we compare this model with that of innovation diffusion, a striking similarity emerges—both systems initially grow under the influence of a reinforcing loop, but then saturation ensues because the dominance shifts to a balancing loop. One of the interests of system dynamics practitioners is identifying such generic structures or systems, since it provides a way to suggest solutions that are known to work in similar situations. At present, system dynamicists have at their disposal a catalogue of eight system archetypes. For the purpose of illustration we present one such archetype—limits to growth—which can be seen to abstract from the models for innovation diffusion and the sales saturation. A more complete discussion can be found in Senge (1990).

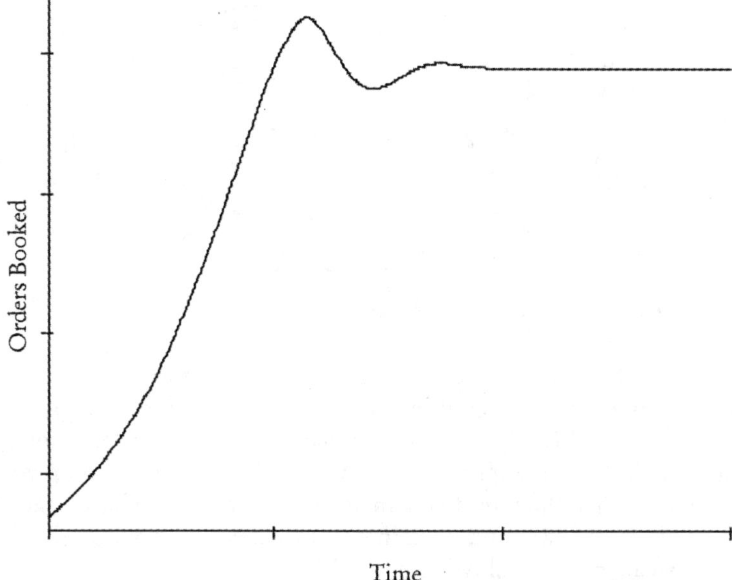

Fig. 14.14: Simulated Behaviour of Order Backlog

Limits to Growth Archetype

In this archetype, shown in Figure 14.15, the system structure is made up of a reinforcing loop and a balancing loop. Initially, the reinforcing loop causes the current state to increase. However, as the current state increases, the level of slowing action increases as well because of the balancing loop. The balancing loop gradually limits the growth of the current state.

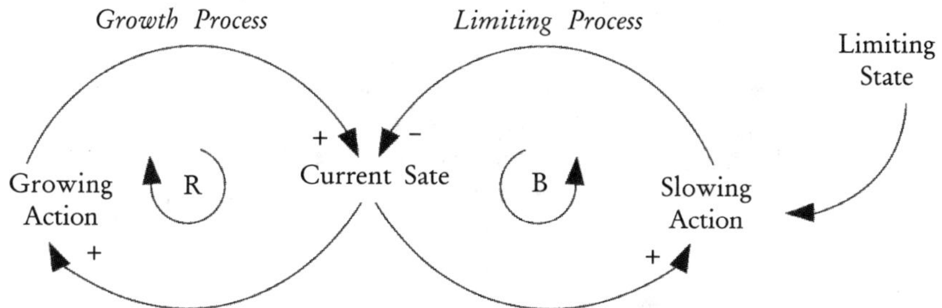

Fig. 14.15: Limits to Growth Archetype

In a system where limits to success archetype is present, a good way to defeat the slowdown would involve constantly pushing the limiting state based on the level of current state as shown in Figure 14.16.

In the case of innovation diffusion, for example, it would imply keeping tabs on the rate of adoption and acting whenever slowdown becomes imminent.

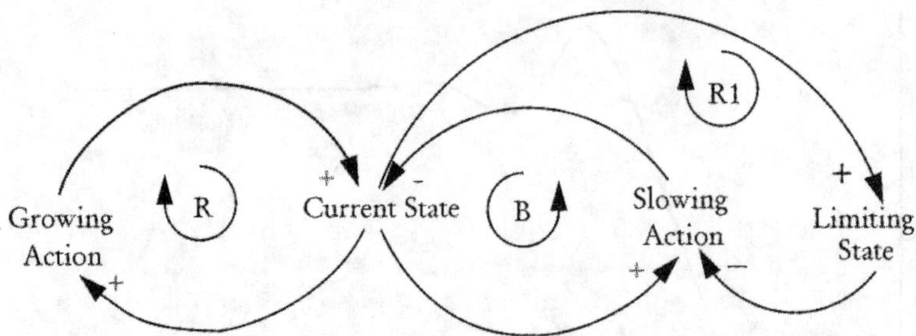

Fig. 14.16: Limits to Growth Archetype with Intervention Loop

Action may involve either identifying new markets for the same innovation or introducing the next version of innovation. The case of Intel Corporation is worth noting in this regard. The company depended on technological innovation for its growth, spending as much as 10 per cent of its revenues (more than US$2.3 billion in 1997) in its R&D activity. The causal loop diagram in Figure 14.17 could explain the mechanism by which Intel has successfully weakened the 'slowing action' loop.

In Figure 14.17, 'owners of obsolete version of microprocessor' represent the pool of potential customers for Intel—people who either do not own an Intel microprocessor or own older versions of the Intel microprocessor. 'Replacement rate' indicates the rate at which these people buy the new version and join the pool of 'owners of the new version of microprocessor'. 'Replacement rate' generates revenue for Intel—a part of which gets invested

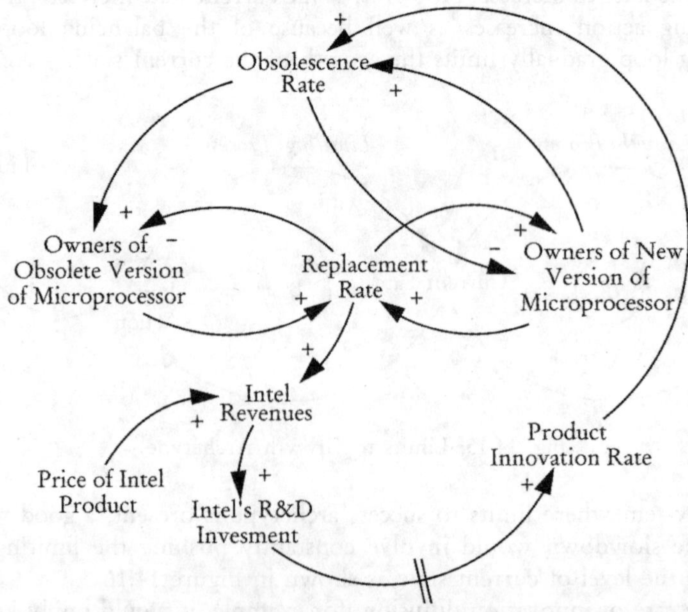

Fig. 14.17: A Model for Intel's Growth

in R&D which, in turn, results in product innovation. Innovation pushes older existing products into obsolescence.

In the 45 years since the appearance of the first article, the use of system dynamics has grown considerably. Every major management-consulting firm has a practice in this area. Sterman (2000) reports three interesting business applications of system dynamics undertaken at GM, Ingalls Shipbuilding of Pascagula, Mississippi, and Du Pont. At GM, the modelling exercise showed how new car leasing policies, intended to increase new car sales, were actually causing a large supply of late model used cars and cutting into the new car sales. The insight gained resulted in GM modifying its leasing schemes to eliminate short-term leases. Ingalls used a system dynamics model to establish the reasons for project delays and win a legal battle with the US Navy over project cost and time overrun. At Du Pont, system dynamics modelling was used in a learning workshop for changing people's perceptions about the effectiveness of proactive maintenance strategies. The attitudinal change helped Du Pont save significantly in direct maintenance cost. Among the topics that the authors have studied using system dynamics are Internet diffusion in developing countries (Dutta and Roy 2001) and network service planning (Dutta 2001).

In our view, the ability to conceptualize organizations holistically in systemic terms should be considered an essential skill for managers of the twenty-first century. For example, the AOL experience cited at the start can be seen to be a natural behaviour of that system's structure. If you switch from variable to fixed pricing, you may initially attract more customers. But in the absence of network capacity increases, service quality drops, leading to an exodus of existing customers. This negative feedback loop dominates system behaviour. Qualitative systems thinking is a first step in that direction, but system dynamics imparts more rigour into the process and overcomes human inability to reason about interacting forces. System dynamics, under different names, is taught at many management schools across the world, sometimes as a full course and sometimes as a part of related courses like business policy, business simulation, process re-engineering, etc. The System Dynamics Society (*http://www.systemdynamics.org/*), the official forum of system dynamics practitioners the world over, publishes the quarterly journal, *System Dynamics Review*, and holds annual meetings for exchange of ideas. In addition, application of the methodology regularly gets reported in major management journals. System dynamics is a mature discipline that has the necessary tools and techniques to analyse the causes of organizational performance (or lack thereof) and take appropriate management action.

References

Bass, F. (1969) 'A New Product Growth Model for Consumer Durables,' *Management Science*, Vol. 15, pp. 215–227.

Dutta, A. (2001) 'Business Planning for Network Services: A Systems Thinking Approach', *Information Systems Research*, Vol. 12, No. 3, pp. 260–85.

— and R. Roy (2001) 'Internet Diffusion in India: Lessons for Developing Countries,' Proc. ICIS2001, New Orleans.

Forrester, J. W. (1961) *Industrial Dynamics*, Cambridge, MIT Press, currently available from Pegasus Communications, Walthum, MA.

— (1959) 'Advertising: A Problem in Industrial Dynamics', *Harvard Business Review*, Vol. 37, No. 2.

Richmond, B. (1993) 'Systems thinking: critical thinking skills for the 1990s and beyond', *System Dynamics Review*, Vol. 9, No. 2, pp. 113–133.

Roberts, E. (1978) (ed.) *Managerial Applications of System Dynamics*, Pegasus Communications, Walthum, MA.

Sastry, A. and J. D. Sterman (1993) 'Desert Island Dynamics: An Annotated Survey of the Essential System Dynamics Literature', in E. Zepeda, and J. Machuca (eds), proceedings of the 1993 International System Dynamics Conference, Albany, NY, System Dynamics Society.

Senge, P. (1990) *The Fifth Discipline: The Art and Practice of the Learning Organization*, Doubleday, New York.

Sterman, J. D. (2000) *Business Dynamics: Systems Thinking and Modeling for a Complex World*, Irwin McGraw-Hill.

— (1989) 'Modeling Managerial Behavior: Misperceptions of Feedback in a Dynamic Decision Making Experiment', *Management Science*, Vol. 35, No. 3, pp. 321–39.

15

Corporate Reporting for Corporate Governance

Asish K. Bhattacharyya

Corporate governance is the governance system of publicly traded companies[1] that ensures return of and return on investment to providers of fund. This definition is narrow as compared to many other definitions of corporate governance available in the literature. However, this is the most appropriate definition in the context of corporate financial reporting. In most publicly traded companies equity shareholders[2], who provide a significant part of the risk capital, are dispersed and do not actively participate in the management of the company.[3] Shareholders have voting rights, which enable them to appoint the board of directors to manage the company in its best interest. However, in practice, individuals nominated by the incumbent management are usually elected as directors due to the apathy of shareholders with small holdings to attend general meetings and due to the absence of a system of 'proportional representation'.

Professional managers or promoter-managers control the management of the company. Controlling right of the executive management far exceeds its ownership right. Theoretically, a group of shareholders, by holding little

[1] Publicly traded companies are limited liability companies whose equity shares are being traded in one or more capital markets. Shares change hands in the capital market. Shareholders enter the company by purchasing shares and exit the company by selling shares. However, most transactions in the capital market are speculative. They are settled without physical delivery. Speculative transactions add volume and help to discover the correct share price.

[2] Equity shareholders supply risk capital to a limited liability company. Their claim on the profit earned by the company and its assets is residual in the sense that it is subordinate to claims of creditors and preference shareholders. Thus, equity shareholders take the business risk. However the liability of an equity shareholder is limited to the amount of capital he has committed to supply as per the terms of share offer. In case of fully paid shares, there is no further liability even in bankruptcy.

[3] This statement is more true for companies in the USA than companies in other territories. Indian Securities Market Report 2001, issued by the National Stock Exchange observes that public float (holding by foreign institutional investors, mutual funds, and the Indian public) is, at best, 27 per cent.

more than the 50 per cent of voting rights, obtains the right to control the total assets of the company. In practice, the promoter group controls the total assets of the company by holding much less than 50 per cent of ownership right (voting right). Thus, shareholders holding majority voting rights have no control over the company. The separation of 'control' and ownership results in the 'agency problem'[4]. Models of corporate governance focus on executive incentives, effectiveness of the board of directors in its supervisory function, and the transparency in the corporate financial reporting.

Transparency in corporate financial reports enhances discipline in management, facilitates correct valuation of the company, and reduces the opportunity for a few to benefit themselves by using sensitive information not available to the capital market. Appropriate valuation of companies in the capital market exposes under-performing companies to the risk of takeover. From the owners' perspective, the fear of losing control acts as a stimulus to perform at the optimum level. The quality of corporate financial reports is an essential determinant of the quality of corporate governance. Moreover, transparency in corporate financial reporting is essential to enforce accountability of the board of directors to shareholders. Therefore, regulators protect the right of the capital market to receive timely and complete information necessary to evaluate the performance and financial position of the company and to forecast its ability to generate adequate cash flows in the future.

This chapter discusses various issues concerning corporate financial reporting in the context of corporate governance.

Transparency and Accountability

Accountability refers to the need to justify actions and policies and accept responsibility for decisions and results. The board of directors of a limited liability company acts as an agent and is in fiduciary relationship with shareholders. It owes accountability to the providers of capital. It should provide complete information to investors to enable them to evaluate the board in its stewardship function.

Transparency in corporate financial reporting creates an environment where information on existing conditions, decisions, and actions are made accessible, visible, and understandable to investors and other market participants. Transparency is necessary to enforce accountability. According to Greuning and Koen (2000), 'Transparency and accountability are mutually

[4] Agency problem refers to the problem that agents often do not perform to achieve optimal results for the principal. This problem arises because the utility of an agent may not converge with the utility of the principal. Moreover, perfect monitoring and enforcement of contracts required to ensure that the agent takes due care of the principal's interest may be impossible. In most situations, it is impossible to write a complete contract because a contract cannot cover contingent situations. Business is surrounded by uncertainties and, therefore, writing of a complete contract is almost impossible for owners of the firm.

reinforcing. Transparency enhances accountability by facilitating monitoring, and accountability enhances transparency by providing an incentive for agents to ensure that the reasons for their actions are properly disseminated and understood together'. Together, transparency and accountability impose a discipline that improves the quality of decision-making. This, in turn, increases the economic performance of the company. Transparency in corporate financial reporting also enhances the quality of decision-making in the capital market and the quality of risk management by all market participants. It enhances the quality of resource allocation and, thereby, increases economic performance at the macro level.

However, there is a dichotomy between transparency and confidentiality. The release of proprietary information may give competitors an unfair advantage. This deters market participants from full disclosure. Similarly, companies are reluctant to pass on sensitive information to regulators. The current trend shows a transition from the regime of 'minimum disclosure' to 'full disclosure', although there is still a long way to go.

Accounting Policy

Within the constraints of transparency, cost, and time, companies provide relevant[5] and reliable[6] information to investors, potential investors, creditors, suppliers, and other market participants. However, the choice of accounting policy and the degree of disclosure are not left wholly to the companies. Decisions are taken at two levels. At the first level, regulators stipulate acceptable alternative accounting policies and the minimum disclosure in financial statements that are at the centre of the corporate financial report. At the second level, individual companies choose accounting policies from available alternatives. The task for setting accounting standards[7], which

[5] Information is relevant when it has the potential to influence the economic decisions of users by helping them evaluate past, present and future events or to confirm/correct their past evaluation. The relevance of information is affected by its nature and materiality (which is always the threshold for relevance). Information overload, on the other hand, can obfuscate information, making it hard to sift through the relevant nuggets and making interpretation difficult (Greuning and Koen 2000).

[6] Information is reliable if it is free from material errors and bias. The essential aspects of reliability are faithful representation, priority of substance over form, neutrality, prudence, and completeness. Greuning and Koen (2000). An information is reliable only if it is verifiable. Verifiability by itself does not improve the quality of information. It helps to identify material error or bias in the information. An information is verifiable if different experts arrive at the same result or results varying within a narrow range. For example, the value of brand equity is not verifiable because different experts arrive at different values of brand equity of the same company. Therefore, the measurement of brand equity is not reliable.

[7] In the USA, accounting standards are known as 'Generally Accepted Accounting Practices' (GAAP). Usually GAAP is a broader term as compared to accounting

stipulate acceptable accounting policies and minimum disclosure in financial statements[8], is assigned to a properly constituted standard setting body. In some countries, the standard setting body is in the private sector, while in others it is in the public sector. However, in almost all countries, the accounting standard setting body has representation from the accountancy profession, the industry, the academia, regulators, and others who have interest in corporate financial statements. In India publicly traded companies are required to comply with accounting standards issued by the Institute of Chartered Accountants of India (ICAI)[9].

Information provided by different companies should be comparable. It should be presented in a consistent manner over time and consistent between companies to enable users to make significant comparisons. In deciding allocation of fund, investors and potential investors evaluate the relative performance and financial position of companies, and assess relative returns on investment. Lack of comparability reduces the usefulness of the information. Regulation of the accounting policy of companies helps to achieve comparability. With globalization of stock markets and flow of capital across countries, efforts are on to harmonize accounting practices across the globe. In India and in many other countries, International Financial Reporting Standards (IFRS) issued by the International Accounting Standards Board (IASB)[10] are used as a benchmark in formulating accounting standards. Many territories, including the European Union, have decided to adopt IFRS after due modification. Many consider the US GAAP as the most robust accounting standard in the world. In a recent move the Financial Accounting Standard Board (FASB) and IASB have agreed to harmonize the IFRS and the US GAAP.

---

standards. GAAP includes accounting standards and other pronouncements by the standard setting body and bodies representing the accounting profession. For example, in India, GAAP includes 'Guidance Notes' issued by the ICAI. The main source of the US GAAP is pronouncements by the FASB.

[8] Corporate financial statements are at the centre of a corporate financial report. A corporate financial report includes corporate financial statements, auditor's report on corporate financial statements, report of the board of directors, performance analysis, forward looking information (management discussion and analysis) about the future performance of the company, and some other reports such as corporate governance report. Thus, corporate financial report is a wider term as compared to the term, 'corporate financial statements'. However, their objectives are the same.

[9] Section 211 of the Companies Act 1956 stipulates that where the profit and loss account and the balance sheet of the company do not comply with the accounting standards, such companies shall disclose the deviations from the accounting standards, the reason for such deviation, and the financial effect, if any, arising due to such deviation. Section 217 of the Act stipulates that the Board's report shall include a 'Directors' Responsibility Statement' which, among other things shall state that in the preparation of the annual accounts, the applicable accounting standards had been followed along with proper explanation relating to material departures.

[10] IASB is a part of the International Accounting Standard Committee (IASC). IASC was formed in 1973 by 16 professional accounting bodies from nine countries,

The Fundamental Principle

The fundamental principle of corporate financial reporting articulated in various documents issued by standard setters such as FASB, IASB, and ICAI is to provide reliable information that is relevant for decision-making in the capital market. Accounting principles and methods for valuation of assets and liabilities balance between relevance and reliability.

Another important objective of financial statements is to provide information on the performance of a company. Usually, a company can distribute dividend out of net profit reported in the income statement of the period, and net profits reported in previous periods and retained in the business. Compensation to the executive management under contractual arrangements is often based on the reported net profit of the company. Therefore, financial accounting has a bias towards prudence. Prudence is the accountant's approach towards uncertainty. The operating rule is 'do not recognize an unrealized profit, but recognize an estimated loss'. However, prudence does not permit understatement of assets or overstatement of liabilities. In practice, most accountants take the view that in a situation of uncertainty understatement of profit is preferable to overstatement. The contemporary literature is questioning this approach.

Application of the principle of prudence reduces the chances of distribution of capital. As a rule distribution of capital is prohibited because it impairs the ability of the company to generate cash flows in future, and adversely affects the interest of creditors.

Capital

The Concept of Capital

The concept of capital is the corner stone of financial statements. Capital is the contribution of the owner to the fund invested in the business. The owner's contribution at any point of time is the total of his original contribution and the profit earned and retained in the business. Withdrawal by the owner reduces the capital.

The difference between the capital at the end and the capital at the beginning of the period measures the operating result for the period. Increase in capital measures the profit and reduction in capital measures the loss. Capital is usually measured in terms of money. For example, if Rs 1,00,000 was the capital at the beginning of the period and Rs 1,20,000 was the capital

---

primarily from Europe and North America. The formation of IASC has been an important step forward towards the international harmonization of accounting standards. India joined IASC as an associate member and is now a full member of IASC. International Accounting Standard Board (IASB) issues International Financial Reporting Standards (IFRS). Earlier IFRS were known as International Accounting Standards (IAS).

at the end of the period, the profit earned by the company during the period is Rs 20,000. The capital at the beginning of the period is not adjusted for change in the purchasing power due to inflation or deflation. In other words, the capital is not measured in terms of the purchasing power. This is one of the limitations of the contemporary accounting models. A better way to measure capital is to measure it in physical terms. Let us take an example. A company, engaged in merchandizing business, had 1000 units of the merchandize at the beginning of the period. In order to measure the operating result for the period, the end capital should be measured in terms of the units of the merchandize. An increase represents profit and a decrease represents loss. In practice it is difficult to measure capital in terms of units of assets at the beginning and at the end of the period because firms hold a large number of different types of assets. Therefore, physical capital is measured in terms of the replacement cost of assets. However, in the absence of markets for used assets even measurement of replacement cost is difficult. Therefore, the concept of physical capital is not used in accounting models.

The fundamental principle stated above is often presented in the form of the following equation, termed as the accounting equation:

Capital = assets – liabilities

The terms capital, net worth, and equity are used interchangeably. In the context of limited liability companies, the capital is the aggregate of the share capital[11] (nominal value[12]), the share premium,[13] and the retained profit

[11] A company issues two types of shares, that is, the equity shares and preference shares. Preference share holders have preferential right over equity share holders in distribution of profit and assets of the company. Preference share holders are eligible for a pre-determined dividend. Thus, a holder of 12 per cent preference shares is entitled for 12 per cent of the face value as dividend, provided the company earns profit. Usually, companies issue cumulative preference shares. Undistributed dividends on cumulative preference shares are accumulated and the same is distributed in the year in which the company earns profit. Under the Companies Act, 1956, a company is required to redeem preference shares within 20 years from the date of issue. Company may issue equity shares with differential rights. Equity share holders take the business risks, and in that sense are owners of the company. Therefore, the capital is determined with reference to equity shares.

[12] Nominal value or face value of shares is determined by dividing the authorized capital by the number of shares the company intends to issue. For example, if the authorized capital is Rs 10,00,000, and the company intends to issue 1,00,000 shares, the face value is Rs 10 per share. If the company intends to issue 10,00,000 shares, the face value is Rs 1 per share. The company has discretion to decide the number of shares it will issue against the authorized capital. The 'memorandum of association' describes the name of the company, objectives of the company, the address of its registered office, and the authorized capital. Authorized capital is important for determining the registration fees. Nominal value has no economic significance.

[13] Share premium is the difference between the price at which a share is issued by the company and its face value. For example, if the face value of the share is Rs 10 and the company issues the shares at Rs 120, the share premium per share is Rs

(reserve and surplus). Accumulated loss is deducted to determine the amount of capital in the balance sheet. Understatement or overstatement of assets or liabilities results in under or over statement of the operating result.

Recognition and Measurement

Appropriate recognition of measurement of capital is important for measuring the operating result. Therefore, accounting standards focus on recognition and measurement of assets and liabilities. Recognition implies recognition of assets and liabilities in the balance sheet for measuring capital. In other words, principles of recognition are applied to identify assets and liabilities to be considered for measuring the capital. For example, contemporary accounting principles do not permit recognition of brand equity and human resource. This implies that brand equity and human resource are not counted for measuring the capital.

Use of appropriate attributes in measuring assets and liabilities is important to determine the capital correctly. Let us take an example. Inventory is valued at the lower of cost or net realizable value (NRV). Assume the cost is Rs 5,00,000 and the NRV is Rs 4,50,000. Thus, the inventory is measured in the balance sheet at Rs 4,50,000. On the other hand, if the inventory is measured at cost, the capital would have been higher by Rs 50,000, and consequently the profit (loss) would be higher (lower) by Rs 50,000. Thus, the principle applied in measuring assets and liabilities has a direct bearing on the measurement of the capital and the operating result. Measurement in accounting is more a convention than a science. The accounting convention changes with economic development and developments in allied disciplines like economics and finance. For example, fair value[14], which until recently was not used in measuring assets and liabilities, is now considered the most appropriate basis for measuring financial assets and liabilities.

RECOGNITION OF ASSETS AND LIABILITIES

Assets are resources embedded with economic benefits. For the purpose of financial statements, a resource is an asset only if the firm has control over the resource and it is probable that economic benefits will flow to the firm

110. The market price at which shares are traded in the secondary capital market is not reflected in the balance sheet and it does not determine the share premium.

[14] Fair value is the value in an arm's length transaction between knowledgeable and willing parties. The US GAAP defines fair value as the amount at which the asset (or liability) could be bought (or incurred) or sold (or settled) in a current transaction between willing parties, that is, other than a forced or liquidation sale. Usually, observable prices in active markets are best measures of the fair value. In the absence of an observable price, observable prices of similar assets or liabilities are used as a benchmark to determine the fair value. In the absence of observable prices of similar assets or liabilities, present value of future cash flows determined with market perspective and assumptions is used to measure the fair value.

in the future. Control implies the right to enjoy the benefits of the resource to the exclusion of others. Let us take an example. Although both the railway-siding within the premises of the firm and the road outside the premises provides economic benefits to the firm, the railway-siding is an asset of the firm while the road is not. The firm enjoys the sole benefits of the railway-siding, while it has no right to exclude others from the benefits of the road. Let us take another example. HR, which is an important asset of any firm, is not an asset for the purpose of financial statements because the firm has inadequate control over the asset. Usually, if the firm has control over a resource, it is probable that economic benefits will flow to the enterprise. However, there are situations in which it is probable that economic benefits will not flow to the firm that has legal control over the asset. Let us take an example. A firm has a property in a country which has imposed a ban on remittance of money outside the country. The firm should not recognize the property as an asset in the balance sheet.

Liability is a present obligation[15] and it is probable that economic benefits will flow out of the firm in settling the obligation. Usually, obligations arise out of a contract or by operation of a law. For example, the liability for product warranty arises from a contract, while income tax liability arises from the operation of law. An obligation may arise neither from a contract nor from the operation of law. For example, if it is the practice of the industry to repair a damage identified in the product even after the warranty period, an obligation arises because of the industry practice, although there is no legal or contractual obligation. Such obligations are termed as 'constructive obligation'. The concept should be applied carefully. A wide interpretation might result in recognition of obligations, which are not present at the balance sheet date. A narrow interpretation might result in non-recognition of obligations, which are present at the balance sheet date. Indian accounting practices do not recognize a constructive obligation. The general principle is that an obligation should be recognized as a liability only if the firm has no discretion to avoid the obligation.

The definitions of assets and liabilities are used as the first screen in recognizing assets and liabilities in the balance sheet. The second screen is the ability of the firm to measure the cost or value of the assets or liabilities reliably. An asset or a liability is not recognized if the firm is unable to estimate the cost or value reliably. Let us take an example. Brand equity is not recognized in financial statements because of two reasons. The first reason

[15] A distinction is being made between the present obligation and the possible obligation. A possible obligation is one that might crystallize at a future date on the outcome of a future event, on which the firm has little control. The 'possible obligations' are termed as 'contingent liabilities'. Contingent liabilities are not recognized in the balance sheet, and thus are not counted for measuring the capital. They are disclosed by way of a note. Examples of contingent liabilities are: guarantees given on behalf of third parties, claims by third parties not admitted by the firm, bills discounted with bank, and disputed claims under arbitration.

is that, in most situations, control over brand equity is inadequate because it depends on market factors over which the firm has little or inadequate control. The second reason is that the value of the brand equity cannot be measured reliably.

THE ACCOUNTING APPROACH

There are two accounting approaches. One focuses on the income statement (profit and loss account) and the other focuses on the balance sheet. The income statement approach emphasizes on measuring the operating result for the period is a fair manner. It focuses on matching income and expenses. This approach requires allocation of expenditure over periods that are expected to benefit from the expenditure, although the expenditure does not pass through screens for the recognition of assets.

The balance sheet approach emphasizes recognition and measurement of assets and liabilities fairly. Let us take an example. Advertisement expenditure on launching a new product cannot be recognized as an asset as it fails to pass through the first screen, the definition of asset. The income approach requires allocation of the advertisement expenditure over the periods, which are likely to benefit from the expenditure. However, the balance sheet approach requires recognition of the advertisement expenditure as an expense in the income statement for the period in which the expenditure is incurred.

Globally, the balance sheet approach is considered superior to the income statement approach. The balance sheet approach captures the fundamental principle that 'capital should not be distributed'. Let us take an example. In the year 2000, a firm incurs an advertisement expenditure of Rs 5,00,000 to launch a product. Under the income statement approach the firm should allocate Rs 5,00,000 over the accounting periods which are expected to benefit from the expenditure. Assuming that the firm decides to allocate the expenditure over a period of five years, we can say that it recognizes only Rs 1,00,000 as expenses for the year 2000. It results in reporting the net profit for the year 2000 as higher by Rs 4,00,000 than the net profit that would be reported under the balance sheet approach. Assume that the firm distributes the total net profit for the year 2000 as dividend. In the year 2001, the firm could not sell the product due to significant changes in market perception about the safety of the product. The firm does not expect to sell the product in the future. The unamortized advertisement expenditure of Rs 4,00,000 should be recognized as an expense for the year 2001 because future periods will not benefit from the expenditure. Assuming that there is no other income or expense for the year 2001, thus, the firm would report a loss of Rs 4,00,000. This would result in the reduction of capital at the beginning of the year 2001 by Rs 4,00,000. The capital at the beginning of the year 2001 was the same as the capital at the beginning of the year 2000 because the firm had distributed the net profit reported in the year 2000. This implies that the firm distributed capital in the year 2000. The balance sheet approach avoids this situation. Under this approach the firm would have recognized the total advertisement expenditure of Rs 5,00,000 as expense for the year 2000. Thus, it would have distributed an amount that was lower by Rs 4,00,000 than the amount it had distributed in the year 2000.

The US GAAP was the first to adopt the balance sheet approach. India has committed to this approach in the year 2000. At present India is in transition from the income statement approach to the balance sheet approach.

In the balance sheet approach expenses recognized in the income statement are of the following three types:

(a) Expenditure which has a direct cause and effect relationship with the income recognized in the income statement. For example, the cost of goods sold recognized in the income statement has a direct cause and effect relationship with sales for the period.
(b) Expenditure which does not have a direct cause and effect relationship with the income but has contributed to earn the income. An example of such expenses is depreciation, which is allocation of the depreciable amount of depreciable assets[16].
(c) Expenditure which cannot be recognized in the balance sheet as an asset, although it has no relationship with the income recognized in the income statement. An example of such expenses is the research expenditure incurred during the period.

Measurement of Assets and Liabilities

Classification of Assets

Fixed Assets: These are assets that are held by the firm for use in production or administration. Usually fixed assets provide the infrastructure and benefit the firm over more than one period. Examples of fixed assets are goodwill, land, railway-siding, plant and equipment, building, furniture and fixtures, vehicles, and patents and copyrights.

Current Assets: These are assets that the firm intends to convert into cash in the course of an operating cycle. In case the operating cycle is shorter than 12 months, the 12-month period is considered to classify an asset as a current asset. Examples of current assets are cash and cash equivalents[17], receivables

[16] Depreciable assets are fixed assets having limited useful life. Usually, land is not a depreciable asset. Depreciable amount is the difference between the cost of acquisition of the asset and the estimated realizable value the firm expects to realize at the end of the useful life of the asset. The useful life is the period over which the firm intends to use the asset. Thus, useful life is more a matter of policy than a technical estimate.

[17] Cash equivalents are short term, highly liquid investments that are readily convertible into known amounts of cash and which are subject to an insignificant risk of changes in value. In practice, investments in government securities or deposits with maturity of not more than three months from the date of purchase are considered cash equivalents.

from customers, deposits with statutory authorities, inventories, advances to suppliers, and loans and advances to employees.

Investment: These are assets that are not used by the firm in its business. A firm holds those assets for a regular return such as rent, interest, and dividend, or to gain from capital appreciation or for some trade advantages. Examples of investments are shares and debentures issued by another firm, gold, and investment property. Firms usually hold shares in subsidiaries and associates to have trade advantages.

Classification of Liabilities

Current Liabilities: These are liabilities that are payable within a year from the balance sheet date or which are to be settled in the course of an operating cycle. Examples of current liabilities are loans payable on demand or within a year from the balance sheet date, trade creditors, provisions, and advances from customers.

Non-current Liabilities: These are liabilities that cannot be classified as current liabilities.

Secured Liabilities: These are liabilities for which the firm has provided collaterals as security. Examples of secured liabilities are debentures, cash credit from bank, and loan from bank or financial institution.

Unsecured Liabilities: These are liabilities for which the firm has not provided any security other than the personal guarantee. An example is public deposit.

Measurement of Assets

The measurement principles that firms generally use to measure assets and liabilities are applicable only if the firm is a 'going concern'. A firm is viewed as a going concern if it has neither the intention nor the necessity of liquidation or of curtailing materially the scale of operation in the near future. Usually, a 12-month period is considered in evaluating whether a firm is a going concern or not. In the absence of any disclosure to the contrary, users of financial statements assume that the reporting firm is a going concern. In case a firm is not a going concern, assets and liabilities are measured by applying principles that are different from the principles which are used for measuring assets and liabilities of a going concern.

Fixed assets are measured at the cost of acquisition, reduced by accumulated depreciation and accumulated impairment loss[18], if any. Cost of acquisition

[18] As a general principle, an asset is not carried in the balance sheet at an amount higher than its recoverable amount or fair value. If at the balance sheet date the recoverable amount or the fair value falls below the carrying amount of the asset, it should be written down to the recoverable amount/fair value. The difference between the carrying amount and the recoverable amount/fair value is recognized as impairment loss in the income statement. The recoverable amount is the higher of the present value of the net cash inflows that the asset is expected to generate over its useful life,

includes costs incurred to bring the asset to the location and condition for intended use. Cost incurred before the management commits to the acquisition of the asset should not be included in the cost of an asset. Similarly, cost incurred after the asset is ready for use should not be included in the cost of the asset. Let us take an example. The travelling expenses of directors for their visit to a foreign country to identify the appropriate equipment and its source should not be capitalized because during the visit the management was not committed to the acquisition of a particular equipment. Similarly, cost incurred on the security and maintenance of a multiplex which is yet to receive clearance from the government for commercial use, should not be capitalized.

Current assets are carried at the lower of the cost or realizable value. For example, inventory is carried at the lower of the cost or the NRV. Similarly, receivables from customers (debtors) are written down to the realizable value.

Investments are classified as current investment and permanent investment. Investment which the firm intends to sell within a year from the date of purchase is classified as current investment. Other investments are classified as permanent investment. Investment property is always classified as permanent investment. Current investments are measured at the lower of the cost or the market value. Permanent investments are carried at cost. However, they are written down to recognize diminution in value, which is not temporary. Let us take an example. A firm purchases IDBI shares at Rs 130 per share. The market price of IDBI shares continues to be significantly lower than the purchase price of Rs 130 per share. The firm should write down the carrying amount of investments in IDBI shares. The compliance of this principle is difficult, particularly for investments in shares of closely held companies. Valuation of investments in closely held companies and assessment of the nature of the diminution in value involves judgement.

Internationally accepted accounting principles of accounting for investments are different from Indian accounting practices. Internationally, investments are classified into the following categories:

(a) Investments that the firm holds for trading purposes. Derivatives, unless used for hedging purposes, are always classified as held for trading securities;
(b) Investments that are available for sale, but in which the firm does not intend to trade, or even sell, in response to a change in the interest rate;
(c) Debt instruments which the firm intends to hold till maturity;
(d) Loans and receivables originated by the enterprise, usually by banks and financial institutions.

---

and the net selling price of the asset. In practice, individual assets generate cash flows together with other assets. Therefore, the recoverable amount/fair value is determined by grouping the assets at the lowest level of the firm, which generates cash flows independently from cash flows being generated by other assets. The term 'cash generating unit' is used to identify a group of assets.

Investments that are classified as held for trading or available for sale are carried at the fair value. Other investments are carried at cost and discount (premium) received (paid) on acquisition is amortized over the balance maturity period. In case of trading securities, that difference in the fair value at the beginning and at the end of the period is recognized as income or expense in the income statement. In case of available for sale investment, the firm has a choice either to recognize the difference in the fair value in the income statement or to recognize the difference in the equity (capital) directly in the balance sheet. If the firm chooses to recognize the difference in the equity, the accumulated difference is recycled to the income statement and recognized as gain or loss for the period in which the investment is sold.

Measurement of Liabilities

Liabilities are recognized at the undiscounted amount of estimated cash outflows. Liabilities include provisions. Provisions are estimated liabilities of uncertain timing or amount. Provisions are carried at the best estimate of the management. Examples of provisions are those for income tax, product warranty, and for environment remediation costs.

INTANGIBLE ASSETS

Intangible assets are fixed assets without any physical presence. Examples of intangible assets are patent, copyright, brand, masthead, and customer list. Goodwill is the most common unidentifiable intangible asset. Goodwill encompasses all intangible assets that a firm creates in the course of business. Recognition and disclosure of identifiable intangible assets separately from goodwill provide useful information to users of financial statements. However, uncertainties surrounding intangible assets are much higher than uncertainties surrounding tangible fixed assets. Therefore, as a matter of prudence, internally generated intangible assets, including goodwill, are not recognized in the balance sheet. In most situations, a firm's control over intangible assets is inadequate. It is also difficult to measure the cost or value of intangible assets reliably. Therefore, it is prudent not to measure internally generated intangible assets as capital.

Intangible assets acquired separately are recognized in the balance sheet at cost. For example, a brand, copyright, or customers' list purchased from another firm is recognized in the balance sheet and is measured at cost. Intangible assets acquired as a part of acquisition of a business or amalgamation of two firms are recognized in the balance sheet at fair value.

Goodwill arises when a firm buys another business, and the purchase consideration exceeds the fair value of identifiable net assets (assets–liabilities) acquired in the transaction. For example, if the purchase consideration is Rs 5,00,000 and the fair value of identifiable net asset is Rs 4,00,000, the goodwill is measured at Rs 1,00,000.

In India, firms do not recognize an asset from the research expenditure. They recognize an asset from the development expenditure, subject to fulfilment of certain conditions stipulated in the relevant accounting standard[19]. Under the US GAAP, no asset is recognized from the R&D expenditure. Although the principles of accounting for R&D expenditure appear to be harsh, they are based on the principle of prudence. In practice, the outcome of research projects is uncertain and recognition of an asset from research expenditure might result in counting an asset that does not exist for measuring capital. Consequently, it might result in distribution of capital. Moreover, it is difficult to identify projects that will provide economic benefits to the firm. Therefore, it is difficult to identify the expenditure that should be recognized as an asset in the balance sheet. The principles of recognition and measurement of assets and liabilities do not take into account the intention of the management in incurring the expenditure. They are based on the level of uncertainties surrounding the expenditure. The underlying principle is 'capital should not be distributed'.

It is difficult to estimate the useful life of intangible assets. In India, there is a rebuttable presumption that the useful life of an intangible asset cannot exceed 10 years from the date when it is available for use. The goodwill recognized in an amalgamation should be amortized over a period not exceeding five years. The international accounting standard (IASB 2000) stipulates that there is a rebuttable presumption that the useful life of an intangible asset should not exceed 20 years from the date when it is available for use. The US GAAP does not provide any arbitrary ceiling on the useful life of intangible assets. Under the US GAAP intangible assets should be amortized only if the management is able to estimate the useful life of the asset. Intangible assets with indefinite useful lives should not be amortized. They should be tested for impairment at each balance sheet date. Similarly, the US GAAP does not stipulate amortization of goodwill. It should be tested for impairment at each balance sheet date or more frequently, if required.

Capital and Revenue Expenditure

The distinction between the capital and revenue expenditure is important for the preparation and presentation of financial statements. The capital expenditure generally refers to expenditure incurred to acquire or produce a fixed asset or expenditure that is added to the cost of an existing fixed asset. Capital expenditure is allocated to periods that are expected to benefit from it. The revenue expenditure is the expenditure that is accounted for as expense for the period in which it is incurred. Under the balance sheet approach, the term 'revenue expenditure' is a misnomer. The term connotes expenditure incurred to earn revenue, but under the balance sheet approach

[19] Accounting Standard (AS) 26, Intangible Assets, stipulate the principles for accounting of R&D expenditure. It stipulates that a firm may recognize an asset from the development expenditure, if it demonstrates its intention and ability to complete the project and to use the new method or product, and the commercial viability of the new method or product.

expenses charged to the income statement may or may not have a cause and effect relationship with the revenue. Usually, judgement is involved in deciding:

(a) the point in time when accumulation of expenditure against a particular fixed asset should commence and when the accumulation should cease;
(b) whether the expenditure incurred on a existing asset will increase its 'service potential', and
(c) whether the expenditure qualifies for recognition as an asset.

The principles for accumulation of expenditure against a particular fixed asset are well established and, therefore, firms do not face much problem in determining the acquisition cost of fixed assets. However, firms may bend rules in favour of earnings management. There is a temptation to capitalize expenditure to present better performance. The problem arises in accounting for subsequent expenditure on existing fixed assets. Subsequent expenditure on intangible fixed assets are usually accounted for as revenue expenditure because it is difficult to attribute an expenditure to a specific intangible asset and to establish that the expenditure has enhanced the service potential of the asset. In case of tangible fixed assets, expenditure is capitalized if it can be established that the expenditure has enhanced the service potential of the asset. Usually, the service potential of an asset is measured in terms of its utility, useful life, and capacity. For example, expenditure to convert a temporary building into a permanent building is a capital expenditure. Similarly, expenditure to convert a machine into numerically controlled (n/c) machine is a capital expenditure. Increase in safety or decrease in the level of waste emission is also considered as increase in the service potential of the asset. In situations where it is difficult to form a judgement on whether the expenditure should be accounted for as capital expenditure or revenue expenditure, it is prudent to treat the expenditure as revenue expenditure.

Revenue Recognition

Revenue is the gross inflow of cash, receivables, or other consideration arising from core activity of the business. It arises from the sale of goods or from rendering of services. Income from other activities is classified as other income. For example, income from ROIs is other income for a non-finance company. Inter company transfer of products or services is not for sale. Therefore, transfer prices are not revenue. Principles for revenue recognition are straightforward, but have potential for earnings management. In most cases of restatement of profits, companies overstate revenue in previous years.

Amount received on another's behalf is not revenue. Therefore, a travel agent should recognize the commission earned on tickets sold as revenue but should not recognize the cost of tickets as revenue. Recognition of the cost of tickets as revenue and corresponding recognition of the same as expense does not change the bottom line. However, it distorts the analysis of financial statements, and sometimes the valuation of companies. For example, until recently, analysts valued Internet companies based on revenue, and inappropriate application of the principles of revenue recognition resulted in over valuation of those companies. Sometimes unscrupulous companies bend the rule of revenue recognition to present a better picture. Let us take an example. A travel agent purchases tickets on its own account and then sells those tickets to its clients. It correctly recognizes the gross value of tickets as revenue, because it bears the risk of having unsold tickets. If it has an arrangement to return unsold tickets, it does not bear the risk and, therefore, it should not recognize gross value of tickets as revenue. Sometimes disclosure in financial statements is inadequate to understand the revenue earning process of the enterprise.

The general principle of revenue recognition is that revenue should be recognized only when the earnings process is complete, no significant uncertainty exists regarding the amount of consideration, and it is reasonable to expect its ultimate collection. The completion of the earning process depends on the arrangement with the customer. As a thumb rule, the earning process in sale of goods is complete when the significant risks and rewards of ownership passes on to the buyer. For example, the earning process is complete when the goods are delivered to the agent of the buyer. In sale of services, the earning process is complete when the activity of providing service is complete as per the terms and conditions of the contract.

In case of service contracts, if a number of activities are to be performed in sequence, the earning process is complete when the significant activity which is the last in the sequence has been performed. Let us take an example. A software company enters into a contract to develop software for a bank. Under the contract, the software company will train the employees of the client company. The training forms the significant last event in the sequence of events in the revenue earning process. The software company should not recognize revenue until the training is complete. Often service companies, such as Internet companies, receive one-time fees like membership fees or commitment fees. Fees so received should be allocated to the different accounting periods over which the company will be rendering free services to subscribers. It is inappropriate to recognize the total amount as revenue for the year in which the fee is received. Determining the allocation rules involves judgement. For example, allocation of fees received depends on the churning rate of customers and the average period over which an average customer remains with the firm.

In case of a long-term contract that covers more than one accounting period, the contractor recognizes proportionate revenue for each period, based on the proportionate completion of the contract. However, it provides for estimated loss, if any, on completion of the contract.

In case of transactions involving exchange of similar assets, no revenue is recognized because the transaction does not culminate into earning of revenue. Let us take an example. There is an arrangement between two media companies under which one company publishes the other's advertisements in its publications. This arrangement does not result in recognition of revenue. Neither of the companies should recognize either revenue or expense. Let us take another example. Two milk suppliers swap inventories of milk in various locations in order to fulfil demand on a timely basis in a particular location. This swap transaction does not result in recognition of revenue.

Transactions involving exchange of dissimilar assets result in revenue recognition. Revenue is recognized at the fair value of the consideration received. Let us take an example. A media company swaps advertisement space with products of an FMCG company. The media company distributes the products free of charge to subscribers of its magazine to improve circulation. The FMCG company gets free advertisement space while disposing its slow moving stock of consumer goods. Both the companies should recognize revenue at the fair value of the consideration received. The FMCG company should recognize the revenue at the fair value of the advertisement space and the media company should recognize revenue at the fair value of the products received. Both the companies should correspondingly recognize expenses in their respective income statement. Estimation of the fair value involves judgement.

Interest is recognized as income on accrual basis. Let us take an example. J Limited has invested Rs 1,20,000 in 10 per cent debentures in another company on 1 January 2002. The interest is payable twice in a year—on 30 June and 30 December. J Limited closes its accounts on 31 March. It should recognize in the income statement for the year 2001–2, Rs 3000 towards interest received, being the interest accrued from 1 January 2002 to 31 March, 2002. Dividend should be recognized when it becomes legally due, that is, when the company declares the dividend.

Revenue and income should be recognized only when it is reasonable to expect collection. In situations of significant uncertainty about the collection, the revenue recognition should be deferred until the uncertainty is resolved. Let us take an example. S Limited executed certain contracts in a foreign country. The government of the country suddenly imposes restriction on the remittance of any amount out of the country. S Limited should not recognize the revenue until the restriction is withdrawn. Let us take another example. Y Limited generates electricity and sells the same to different state electricity boards. Electricity boards perennially fail to clear overdue payments to Y Limited. Y Limited has raised invoices for penal interest as per the agreement. The company should not recognize penal interest as revenue, because it is unreasonable to expect collection from customers who perennially fail to clear payments due for the supply of electricity.

Borrowing Costs

Borrowing costs attributable to a particular asset which takes a significantly long period for production or construction should be included in its cost of production or construction. Usually, a 12-month period is considered significantly long.

Borrowing can be attributed to a particular production or construction activity provided the borrowing might have been avoided had the enterprise not taken up those activities. It is not necessary that the amount be borrowed specifically for those activities. Borrowing costs for the period from the commencement of the production or construction activity until substantial completion of the activity should only be included in the cost of the asset. Borrowing cost for the period when the activity was suspended should not be included in the cost of the asset, unless the suspension of the activity was normal. For example, suspension of the construction of a bridge on a river during monsoon might be normal and, therefore, borrowing cost for the period for which the construction activity was suspended should be included in the cost of the bridge.

Usually, borrowing costs are not included in the cost of the inventory. However, in certain situations, cost of inventory includes borrowing costs. For example, cost of wine or seasoned wood should include borrowing cost for the period it is kept for seasoning because seasoning is the production process which takes a significantly longer period for completion. Borrowing costs for the holding period should not be included in the cost of inventory.

Accounting Estimates

Estimate is central to the preparation and presentation of financial statements. Estimation involves judgement. Therefore, it has the potential for earnings management. Estimation should be supported by convincing evidence. Usually, higher weightage should be given to external evidence. Events which occur after the balance sheet date[20] should be considered to estimate the carrying amount of assets and liabilities.

Given below are examples of accounting estimates which involve judgement. The list, however, is not exhaustive.

[20] Events occurring after the balance sheet date refers to events occurred between the balance sheet date and the date on which the appropriate authority has approved the issue of financial statements. Events occurring after the balance sheet date are classified into adjusting events and non-adjusting events. Adjusting events provide additional evidence on conditions that existed at the balance sheet date. Therefore, carrying amounts of assets and liabilities should be adjusted, based on additional evidence provided by those events. For example, insolvency of a customer usually provides additional evidence about the condition existing at the balance sheet date. Therefore, the carrying amount of receivables should be adjusted based on the information about insolvency of a customer. Non-adjusting events are events that provide evidence about new conditions that arose after the balance sheet date. Carrying amounts of assets and liabilities should not be adjusted based on evidence provided by non-adjusting events. However, if non-adjusting events provide evidence about conditions that might invalidate the going concern assumption, financial statement should not be prepared based on that assumption. Non-adjusting events are disclosed in the report of the board of directors. Examples of non-adjusting events are fire in the factory, plan to discontinue an operation, expropriation of major assets by the government, and commencement of a major restructuring process.

(a) Assessment of the point in time when the management has commenced the production or construction of the fixed asset and when the construction or production is substantially complete.
(b) Estimation of the useful life and the residual value of a fixed asset for charging depreciation.
(c) Assessment of whether an expenditure on an existing fixed asset will enhance its service potential.
(d) Assessment of the uncertainty surrounding the collection of the amount due from customers.
(e) Identification of significant activities in the earning process and assessment of the point in time when each activity is complete.
(f) Assessment of whether a liability should be recognized for an obligation which could otherwise be reported as contingent liability.
(g) Assessment of whether the conditions for recognition of assets from development expenditure are fulfilled and the date at which the conditions were fulfilled.
(h) Estimation of future cash flows and discounting rate for measuring recoverable amount to estimate the impairment loss.

Business models are now more complex than ever before and firms are exposed to a variety of risks. Firms are entering different types of complex arrangements and using a variety of composite financial instruments to manage risks. Accounting for complex transactions and financial instruments is more judgemental than accounting for conventional business transactions. Therefore, the reliability of information depends a lot on the effectiveness of the supervisory function of the board of directors, particularly of the audit committee, and the quality of audit. The audit committee and auditors should ensure that the accounting policies selected by the enterprise are appropriate and that estimates are supported by convincing evidence.

Independent directors and auditors are accountable to a larger section of the society than the executive management is. Therefore, there is a need to search for a system that protects their independence from the executive management. The current debate on the independence of independent directors and auditors is an endeavour to search for a system that is workable without unduly increasing the cost of governance.

Off-balance Sheet Items

Off-balance sheet items are also a concern to investors, regulators, and analysts. Therefore, standard setters aim at reducing the number of off-balance sheet items. For example, accounting principles and methods of accounting for finance lease[21] stipulated in the accounting standard on lease

[21] Accounting Standards on lease accounting makes a difference between operating lease and finance lease. Finance lease is principally a non-cancellable lease, in which the substantial risks and rewards associated with the ownership of the assets is passed on to the lessee. In operating lease risks and rewards remains with the lessor.

accounting requires accounting of the transaction as a financing transaction. Earlier lease was considered as a source of off-balance sheet financing. Similarly, new accounting standards require derivative instruments to be recognized as an asset or a liability, and to recognize the holding gain or loss in financial statements. The current debate on accounting for 'Employees Stock Options' (ESOP) reflects the concern of regulators, investors, and others about the tendency of firms to keep complex transactions off-financial statements. In most situations off-balance sheet items result in understatement of liability and expense.

It is common for enterprises to prefer to report obligations which will crystallize on the outcome of contingent future events as contingent liabilities, although experience of the firm and of others indicates the probability of outflow of economic benefits. This helps to keep the liability off-balance sheet. There is a thin difference between provision and contingent liabilities. An enterprise should recognize a liability if, according to its best estimate, it is probable that economic benefits will flow out of the enterprise and it is able to estimate the amount reliably. For example, guarantees given by an enterprise on behalf of third parties is usually disclosed as contingent liability. However, if the total amount of guarantees is significantly high, it adversely affects the financial position of the enterprise and increases the chance of outflow of economic benefits arising from enforcement of guarantees. Therefore, it is important that the company estimates the probability of economic benefits that might flow out of the enterprise due to the secondary obligation arising from issuance of guarantee. Similarly, an enterprise may file a frivolous appeal against the demand from the revenue authority to keep the liability off-balance sheet. Thus, contingent liability has the potential to camouflage 'present obligations' and keep them off-balance sheet. Therefore, the Naresh Chandra Committee (Government of India 2000) has recommended that the management should provide a clear description in plain language of each material contingent liability and its risks, accompanied by the auditors' clearly worded comments on the management's view.

De-recognition of liabilities is an important issue in the preparation and presentation of financial statements. The rules have now been made clear by accounting standards (FASB 2000), recently issued by FASB and IASB. A liability is de-recognized, only when the obligation of the enterprise has been extinguished. A liability is extinguished if the debtor is legally released from being the primary obligor under the liability, either judicially or by the creditor. In case of securitization,[22] the accounting standard has taken the

---

Therefore, accounting for finance lease requires recognition of the asset and corresponding liability in the books of the lessor,

[22] Securitiation is the process by which financial assets are transformed into securities. Usually, an enterprise transfers its financial assets to an SPE, usually a trust, which, in turn, issue securities to beneficiaries. Securitiation results in de-recognition of the asset, without recognition of any liability, if the securitiation is without recourse. In case the securitization is with recourse, the enterprise should estimate the liability and recognize the same in the balance sheet.

financial-components approach and requires recognition of a liability if transfer of the asset results in assumption of a new liability. For example, securitization with recourse might result in the recognition of a liability.

Special Purpose Entities

Enterprises use special purpose entities (SPE) for 'off the books' transactions. They have their origin in the rules for consolidation. Under the US GAAP, historically, consolidation is based on majority ownership of one enterprise by another. Thus, an enterprise is not required to consolidate an SPE in which it has less than 50 per cent ownership, although it might have significant economic influence and controlling right over the entity. The enterprise presents transactions with those SPEs in a manner that is appropriate for presenting arm's length transactions. In the absence of consolidation, it is difficult to understand the full substance of the operations of the group. In many situations, the enterprise exposes itself to unwarranted risks without disclosing the same. The most important reason for the bankruptcy of Enron Corporation was that it exposed itself to significantly high risk through SPEs without disclosing the same. Therefore, regulators are debating replacing ownership with the criteria of control. However, the project has been kept in the back burner due to difficulties of defining control.

In India, presentation of consolidated financial statements of the holding company with its subsidiaries is not required. Only recently has the Securities Exchange Board of India (SEBI) made it mandatory for listed companies to present consolidated financial statements. Absence of the requirement for presenting group accounts resulted in complex chain holdings among group companies. Requirement to present consolidated financial statements by listed companies is definitely a right step towards improving corporate governance. In India, most companies are managed by promoters and they use company resources to benefit themselves by investing in business managed by closely held companies. Presentation of consolidated financial statements will improve transparency and accountability and thus, will reduce diversion of funds for personal benefits.

Disclosures

Disclosures form an important part of corporate financial reports. Disclosures are required:

(a) to clarify and explain the accounting policy, assumptions in accounting estimates, nature of complex transactions, and additional information necessary for understanding financial statements;
(b) to disclose material events that occurred after the balance sheet date, which are relevant in decision-making;
(c) to disclose additional information relevant for decision-making; and

(d) to disclose the management's perception about past performance, future business environment, business risks and strategy, and factors that will influence business performance in the future.

Disclosures mentioned in (a) above form a part of financial statements. They are subject to audit. Thus, the reliability of these disclosures is higher than the reliability of disclosures elsewhere in the corporate financial report. The quantity and quality of disclosures has enhanced over the years. The companies now require disclosing segment information, information on discontinuing operations, and information on related party relationships and transactions. Disclosure of information on business and geographical segments provides insights into the risk and return profile of the firm. This also enforces the accountability of the board of directors in selecting strategies to achieve the corporate goal. Disclosure of information on discontinuing operation improves projection about the future performance of the firm. Related party information enhances accountability and helps to understand the benefits and risks to the enterprise from related party relationships.

Regulators stipulate the minimum information to be disclosed in the corporate financial report. For example, the Companies Act 1956 stipulates the information, at the minimum, to be disclosed in the board of directors' report. Similarly, SEBI stipulates the information, at the minimum, to be disclosed in the corporate governance report, and management discussion and analysis. regulators across the globe encourage voluntary disclosure, that is, disclosure in addition to minimum disclosures required by law or regulations. Voluntary disclosure is necessary to fill in the gap created between the information need and information provided by financial statements due to the limitations of financial accounting. Financial accounting is primarily transaction based and it presents only financial information ignoring the effect of inflation. Moreover, it has bias towards prudence. For example, employee turnover and satisfaction, which is an important information for knowledge-based companies, cannot be captured by financial accounting. Similarly, formulations in the pipeline, which is an important information for pharmaceutical and biotech companies cannot be captured by financial accounting. Therefore, enterprises provide non-finance information that is helpful in projecting the future performance. Similarly, enterprises provide information on intangible assets, such as brand equity and human resources. Many enterprises provide inflation adjusted financial statements as a part of voluntary disclosure.

Future of Financial Reporting

The face of the corporate financial report is changing. The financial reporting practice is evolving. The trend towards full disclosure is clearly visible. Good companies are improving voluntary disclosure to provide a signal to the capital market that they are committed to improving corporate governance and that they believe in transparency. For example, in India, Infosys Limited is the leader in voluntary disclosure. Infosys is a company promoted by professionals who are first-generation entrepreneurs. It mobilizes funds from capital markets, including capital markets in the USA. Therefore, it is motivated to be transparent in sharing information with the capital market. The trend established by Infosys should percolate down to family-managed companies. However, it will take time. Therefore, the transparency in corporate financial reporting will improve only if regulators can enforce compliance of rules, including corporate governance code, strictly.

Another issue, which is of wider interest, is the relevance of audited financial statements. The currently accepted model of financial reporting might be replaced by electronic information systems providing financial and other forms of information which would be widely available via the Internet. In such a scenario, decision-makers could decide on the types of information that are important and then arrange the information in the ways they see fit. However, as Baker and Wallage (2000) argue, even in the changed scenario, the audited financial statements will be considered an important component of corporate governance.

In future, the corporate financial report will address concerns of all stakeholders. Thus, it will provide additional information that is of interest to stakeholders other than shareholders. The Global Reporting Initiative (GRI), which is a long-term, multistakeholder international undertaking, has developed globally applicable sustainability reporting guidelines for voluntary use by organizations. The GRI sustainable reporting guideline encompasses the three linked elements of sustainability—the economic, the environmental, and the social. For example, the environmental component should report the impact of processes, produces, and services on a air, water, land, bio-diversity, and human health. Similarly, social component should include information on workplace health and safety, employee retention, labour rights, human rights, wages, and working conditions at outsourced operations.

References

Baker, C. Richard and Phillip Wallage (2000) 'The future of financial report in Europe: Its role in Corporate Governance', *The International Journal of Accounting*, Vol. 35, No. 2, pp. 173–187.

Financial Accounting Standards Board (2000) Statement of Financial Accounting Standards No. 140, Accounting for Transfers and Servicing of Financial Assets and Extinguishment of Liabilities, Connecticut.

Greuning, Hennie Van and Marius Koen (2000) *International Accounting Standards—a practical guide*, D.C. World Bank, Washington.

Government of India (2000) Naresh Chandra Committee on Corporate Governance, The Department of Company Affairs, Ministry of Finance and Company Affairs, New Delhi.

International Accounting Standards Board (2000) International Accounting Standard (IAS) 38, Intangible Assets, London.

Index